Adobe®

After Effects® CS3 Professional

Professional

STUDIO TECHNIQUES

Mark Christiansen

W9-CZL-792

Adobe

Adobe After Effects CS3 Studio Techniques

Mark Christiansen

Copyright © 2008 Mark Christiansen

This Adobe Press book is published by Peachpit. For information on Adobe Press books, contact:

Peachpit
1249 Eighth Street
Berkeley, CA 94710
(510) 524-2178
Fax: (510) 524-2221
www.adobepress.com

To report errors, please send a note to errata@peachpit.com

Peachpit is a division of Pearson Education

Development and Copy Editor: Linda Laflamme
Project Editor: Karen Reichstein
Production Editor: Myrna Vladic
Technical Editor: Alexandre Czetwertynski
Proofreader: Liz Welch
Compositor: Deborah Roberti, Espresso Graphics; Rick Gordon, Emerald Valley Graphics
Indexer: Karin Arrigoni
Cover design: Charlene Charles-Will
Cover illustration: Regina Cleveland

Notice of Rights

All rights reserved. No part of this book may be reproduced or transmitted in any form by any means, electronic, mechanical, photocopying, recording, or otherwise, without the prior written permission of the publisher. For information on getting permission for reprints and excerpts, contact permissions@ peachpit.com.

Strings images and footage courtesy of Crystal Us © 2008. Photographed by Joshua Hess. All rights reserved.

Notice of Liability

The information in this book is distributed on an "As Is" basis, without warranty. While every precaution has been taken in the preparation of the book, neither the author nor Peachpit shall have any liability to any person or entity with respect to any loss or damage caused or alleged to be caused directly or indirectly by the instructions contained in this book or by the computer software and hardware products described in it.

Trademarks

Photoshop, Premiere, Premiere Pro, Illustrator, Flash, Encore DVD, and After Effects are either trademarks or registered trademarks of Adobe Systems Incorporated in the United States and/or other countries. Many of the designations used by manufacturers and sellers to distinguish their products are claimed as trademarks. Where those designations appear in this book, and Peachpit was aware of a trademark claim, the designations appear as requested by the owner of the trademark. All other product names and services identified throughout this book are used in editorial fashion only and for the benefit of such companies with no intention of infringement of the trademark. No such use, or the use of any trade name, is intended to convey endorsement or other affiliation with this book.

ISBN 13: 978-0-321-49978-3
ISBN 10: 0-321-49978-6

9 8 7 6 5 4 3 2 1

Printed and bound in the United States of America

Contents at a Glance

Contents

About the Authors

Dedication:
To the artist seeking to do the best possible work.

Mark Christiansen is a freelance creative director, computer graphics artist and writer based in San Francisco and also located at http://flowseeker.com and http://christiansen.com. Mark has created visual effects and computer-generated animations for feature films, live events, television, computer games, and more. Feature effects credits at The Orphanage include *The Day After Tomorrow* and a pair of Robert Rodriguez films; more recently Mark composited shots on *Pirates of the Caribbean: At World's End* for Evil Eye Pictures. His independent directing and design work has been featured at the Los Angeles International Short Film Festival, and Mark has partnered with the good people at fxphd.com to create classes based on this book.

Previous writing by Mark includes *After Effects 5.5 Magic* (New Riders), and for a decade he was a Contributing Editor for *DV Magazine*. Mark has made guest speaking appearances at SIGGRAPH, NAB, DV Expo, and GDC, as well as for professional groups in the Bay Area. Mark was officially the "number one beta tester" of After Effects 6.0 and began using the software in the art department at LucasArts Entertainment, where his project *Behind the Magic* was honored with *Entertainment Weekly*'s pick of Number 1 of 1998. Mark is a graduate of Pomona College.

Stu Maschwitz is a cofounder and the CTO of The Orphanage, a San Francisco-based visual effects and film production company. Maschwitz spent four years as a visual effects artist at George Lucas's Industrial Light & Magic (ILM), working on such films as *Twister* and *Men in Black*, and went on to create the award-winning Magic Bullet software. At The Orphanage, Maschwitz has directed numerous commercials and supervised effects work on films including *Sin City* and *The Last Mimzy*. Maschwitz is a guerilla filmmaker at heart and combined this spirit and his effects knowledge into a book: *The DV Rebel's Guide: An All-Digital Approach to Making Killer Action Movies on the Cheap* (Peachpit Press).

Acknowledgments

Thanks to everyone who has taught me everything I know, in particular a couple of contributors to present or past editions of this book, Stu Maschwitz and Brendan Bolles, colleagues from The Orphanage, where I honed skills using After Effects in a visual effects context.

Thanks for footage and examples to Alex Lindsay and Pixel Corps, Julie Hill and Artbeats, and my good friends and colleagues at fxphd.com, John Montgomery and Mike Seymour, along with the vast worldwide network of artists associated with that site from whom I've learned as I taught.

Jeff Almasol (www.redefinery.com), now an Adobe employee, continues to be an invaluable source of After Effects scripts, including the two offered exclusively with this book.

Clients gave me the firsthand experience that went into this book, and some were willing to commit time (and even money) to secure elements or final shots for use in this book's figures despite no benefit to themselves: Christina Crowley, President of The Kenwood Group; Rama Dunayevich at The Orphanage; Coral Petretti at ABC Photography; David Donegan at Red Bull USA; Tim Fink of Tim Fink Events and Media; Gary Jaeger and Cameron Baxter at Core Studio; Jonathan Barson at The Foundry UK; Fred Lewis and Inhance Digital; Boeing and the Navy UCAV program; Patrick Campbell of Suburban Imageworks; and Matthew Ward of ImageMovers Digital.

Thanks also to the worldwide community of After Effects artists who offered imagery for this book, including Ross Webb at Mars Productions in Cape Town, South Africa; Luis Bustamente and 4charros in Mexico; and Jason Denzel of Argonaut Entertainment. I mined http://flickr.com/creativecommons/ for a few difficult-to-find source stills; a huge thank you to the gifted photographers who voluntarily chose to add the Creative Commons tag to their work: Micah Parker, Jorge L. Peschiera, Shuets Udono, Eric E. Yang, and Kevin Miller.

To the people at Adobe who've made After Effects what it is, in particular Dave Simons, Dan Wilk, Erica Schisler, and Steve Kilisky, and to some of the developers who've helped me understand it better over the years, including Michael Natkin and Chris Prosser. Thanks to Vladimir Potap'yev for patient responses to questions about color management, and to Peter Constable for kindly reading through passages on that same complex topic.

Thanks to the companies that contributed to the book's DVD: Peder Norrby, who *is* Trapcode, Russ Andersson of Andersson Technologies, Sean Safreed of Red Giant Software, Andrew Millin of ObviousFX LLC, Marco Paolini of SilhouetteFX, Pierre Jasmin of RevisionFX, and Timur "Taron" Baysal of Taronites. These were my choices for inclusion because they all provide something vital to effects compositing in After Effects.

Other people who were helpful e-mailing their feedback on various topics include Bruno Nicoletti at the Foundry UK, Dan Ebberts (www.motionscript.com), Scott Squires (www. effectscorner.com), Tim Dobbert at The Orphanage, Don Shay at *Cinefex Magazine*, and Matt Silverman at Phoenix Editorial. Major thanks this time around goes to Pete O'Connell of Bar X Seven (www.barxseven.com) who dropped me an e-mail describing major improvements he devised for rotoscoping in After Effects; these are featured in Chapter 7.

A huge thank you to Peachpit, who collectively show a strong commitment to producing the highest quality books, in particular Karen Reichstein, who takes great care with comments and correspondence, and Linda Laflamme, whom I trust to tell me when I'm not making sense. Alexandre Czetwertynski is a great technical editor because he cares enough about this work to pay attention to the details.

Thanks to all of the thoughtful folks who have dropped me a line at aestudiotechniques@gmail.com; you'd be surprised at the difference your comments make.

Foreword

I can't see the point in the theatre. All that sex and violence. I get enough of that at home. Apart from the sex, of course.

—Tony Robinson as Baldrick, *Blackadder*

Who Brings the Sex?

"Make it look real." That would seem to be the mandate of the visual effects artist. Spielberg called and he wants the world to believe, if only for 90 minutes, that dinosaurs are alive and breathing on an island off the coast of South America. Your job: make them look real. Right?

Wrong.

I am about to tell you, the visual effects artist, the most important thing you'll ever learn in this business: Making those Velociraptors (or vampires or alien robots or bursting dams) "look real" is absolutely *not* what you should be concerned with when creating a visual effects shot.

Movies are not reality. The reason we love them is that they present us with a heightened, idealized version of reality. Familiar ideas—say, a couple having an argument—but turned up to eleven: The argument takes place on the observation deck of the Empire State building, both he and she are perfectly backlit by the sun (even though they're facing each other), which is at the exact same just-about-to-set golden-hour position for the entire ten-minute conversation. The couple are really, really charming and impossibly good-looking—in fact, one of them is Meg Ryan. Before the surgery. Oh, and music is playing.

What's real about that? Nothing at all—and we love it.

Do you think director Alejandro Amenábar took Javier Aguirresarobe, cinematographer on *The Others*, aside and said, "Whatever you do, be sure to make Nicole Kidman look *real?*" Heck no. Directors say this kind of stuff to their DPs: "Make her look like a statue." "Make him look bullet-proof." "Make her look like she's sculpted out of ice."

Did It Feel Just Like It Should?

Let's roll back to *Jurassic Park*. Remember how terrific the T-Rex looked when she stepped out of the paddock? Man, she looked good.

She looked *good*.

The realism of that moment certainly did come in part from the hard work of Industrial Light and Magic's fledgling computer graphics department, who developed groundbreaking technologies to bring that T-Rex to life. But mostly, that T-Rex *felt real* because she *looked good*. She was wet. It was dark. She had a big old Dean Cundey blue rim light on her coming from nowhere. In truth, you could barely see her.

But you sure could hear her. Do you think a T-Rex approaching on muddy earth would really sound like the first notes of a new THX trailer? Do you think Spielberg ever sat with sound designer Gary Rydstrom and said, "Let's go out of our way to make sure the footstep sounds are authentic?" No, he said, "Make that mofo sound like the *Titanic* just rear-ended the Hollywood Bowl" (may or may not be a direct quote).

It's the sound designer's job to create a soundscape for a movie that's emotionally true. They make things feel right even if they skip over the facts in the process. Move a gun half an inch and it sounds like a shotgun being cocked. Get hung up on? Instant dial tone. Modern computer displaying something on the screen? Of course there should be the sound of an IBM dot-matrix printer from 1978.

Sound designers don't bring facts. They bring the sex. So do cinematographers, makeup artists, wardrobe stylists, composers, set designers, casting directors, and even the practical effects department.

And yet somehow, we in the visual effects industry are often forbidden from bringing the sex. Our clients pigeonhole us into the role of the prop maker: Build me a T-Rex, and it better look real. But when it comes time to put that T-Rex on screen, we are also the cinematographer (with our CG lights), the makeup artist (with our "wet look" shader), and the practical effects crew (with our rain). And although he may forget to speak with us in the same floury terms that he used with Dean on set, Steven wants us to make that T-Rex looks like a T-Rex should in a movie. Not just good—*impossibly* good. Unrealistically good. Sexy good.

Have you ever argued with a client over aspects of an effects shot that were immutable facts? For example, you may have a client that inexplicably requested a little less motion blur on a shot, or for an object for which you've calculated the exact rate of fall from a known height to fall "just a little slower?" Do you ever get frustrated with clients who try to art-direct reality in this way?

Well, stop it.

Your client is a director, and it's their *job* to art-direct reality. It's not their job to know (or suggest) the various ways that it may or may not be possible to selectively reduce motion blur, but it is their job to feel it in their gut that somehow this particular moment should feel "crisper" than normal film reality. And you know what else? It's your job to predict that they might want this and even propose it. In fact, you'd better have this conversation early, so you can shoot the plate with a 45-degree shutter, that both the actors and the T-Rex might have a quarter the normal motion blur.

Was It Good for You?

The sad reality is that we, the visual effects industry, pigeonhole *ourselves* by being overly preoccupied with reality. We have no one to blame but ourselves. No one else on the film set does this to themselves. If you keep coming back to your client with defenses such as "That's how it would really look" or "That's how fast it would really fall," then not only are you going to get in some arguments that you will lose, but you're actually setting back our entire industry by perpetuating the image of visual effects artists as blind to the importance of the sex.

On the set, after take one of the spent brass shell falling to the ground, the DP would turn to the director and say, "That felt a bit fast. Want me to do one at 48 frames?" And the director would say yes, and they'd shoot it, and then months later the editor would choose take three, which they shot at 72 frames per second "just in case." That's the filmmaking process, and when you take on the task of creating that same shot in CG, you need to represent, emulate, and embody that entire process. You're the DP, both lighting the shot and determining that it might look better overcranked. You're the editor, confirming that choice in the context of the cut. And until you show it to your client, you're the director, making sure this moment *feels* right in all of its glorious unreality.

The problem is that the damage is already done. The client has worked with enough effects people who have willingly resigned themselves to not bringing the sex, that they now view all of us as geeks with computers rather than fellow filmmakers. So when you attempt to break our self-imposed mold and bring the sex to your client, you will face an uphill battle. But I'm here to give you some advice to help ease the process: Do it without asking. I once had a client who would pick apart every little detail of a matte painting, laying down accusations of "This doesn't look real!"—until we color corrected the shot cool, steely blue with warm highlights. Then all the talk of realism went away, and the shot got oohs and ahs.

Your client reacts to your work *emotionally*, but they critique *technically*. When they see your shot, they react with their gut. It's great, it's getting better, but there's still something not right. What they *should* do is stop there and let you figure out what's not right, but instead, they somehow feel the need to analyze their gut reaction and turn it into action items: "That highlight is too hot" or "The shadows under that left foot look too dark." In fact it would be better if they focused on vocalizing their gut reactions: "The shot feels a bit lifeless," or "The animation feels too heavy somehow." Leave the technical details to the pros.

You may think that those are the worst kind of comments, but they are the best. I've seen crews whine on about "vague" client comments like "give the shot more oomf." But trust me, this is exactly the comment you want. Because clients are like customers at a restaurant, and you are the chef. The client probably wants to believe that "more oomf" translates into something really sophisticated, like volumetric renderings or level set fluid dynamics, in the same way that a patron at a restaurant would hope that a critique like "this dish needs more flavor" would send the chef into a tailspin of exotic ingredients and techniques. Your client would never admit (or suggest on their own) that "oomf" is usually some combination of "cheap tricks" such as camera shake, a lens flare or two, and possibly some "God rays"—just like the diner would rather not know that their request for "more flavor" will probably be addressed with butter, salt, and possibly MSG.

The MSG analogy is the best: Deep down, you want to go to a Chinese restaurant that uses a little MSG but doesn't admit it. You want the cheap tricks because they work, but you'd rather not think about it. Your client wants you to use camera shake and lens flares, but *without telling them*. They'd never admit that those cheap tricks "make" a shot, so let them off the hook and do those things without being asked. They'll silently thank you for it. Bringing the sex is all about cheap tricks.

Lights On or Off?

There are certain visual effects supervisors who pride themselves on being sticklers for detail. This is like being an architect whose specialty is nails. I have bad news for the "Pixel F*ckers," as this type are known: *Every* shot will *always* have *something* wrong with it. There will always be something more you could add, always some shortcoming that could be addressed. What makes a visual effects supervisor good at their job is knowing which of the infinitely possible tweaks are important. Anyone can nitpick. A good supe focuses the crew's efforts on the parts of the shot that impact the audience most. And this is always the sex. Audiences don't care about matte lines or mismatched black levels, soft elements or variations in grain. If they did, they wouldn't have been able to enjoy *Blade Runner* or *Back to the Future* or that one *Star Wars* movie—what was it called? Oh yeah: *Star Wars*. Audiences only care about the sex.

On a recent film I was struggling with a shot that was just kind of sitting there. It had been filmed as a pick-up, and it needed some help fitting into the sequence that had been shot months earlier. I added a layer of smoke to empirically match the surrounding shots. Still, the shot died on the screen. Finally, I asked my compositor to softly darken down the right half of the shot by a full stop, placing half the plate along with our CG element in a subtle shadow. Boom, the shot sang.

What I did was, strictly speaking, the job of the cinematographer, or perhaps the colorist. The colorist, the person who designs the color grading for a film, is the ultimate bringer of the sex. And color correction is the ultimate cheap trick. There's nothing fancy about what a Da Vinci 2K or an Autodesk Lustre does with color. But what a good colorist does with those basic controls is bring heaping, dripping loads of sex to the party. The problem is (and I mean *the* problem—the single biggest problem facing our industry today), the colorist only gets their hands on the shot *after it has already been approved.* In other words, the film industry is currently shooting itself in the foot (we, the visual effects artists, being that foot) by insisting that our work be approved in a sexless environment. This is about the stupidest thing ever, and until the industry works this out, you need to fight back by taking on some of the role of the colorist as you finalize your shots, just like we did when we made those matte paintings darker and bluer with warm highlights.

Filmmaking is a battleground between those who bring the sex and those who don't. The non-sex-bringing engineers at Panavision struggle to keep their lenses from flaring, while ever-sexy cinematographers fight over a limited stock of 30-year-old anamorphic lenses because they love the flares. I've seen DPs extol the unflinching sharpness of a priceless Panavision lens right before adding a smear of nose grease (yes, the stuff on your nose) to the rear element to soften up the image to taste. Right now this battle is being waged on every film in production between the visual effects department and the colorists of the world. I've heard effects artists lament that after all their hard work making something look real, a colorist then comes along and "wonks out the color." In truth, all that colorist did was bring the sex that the visual effects should have been starting to provide on their own. If what the colorist did to your shot surprised you, then you weren't thinking enough about what makes a movie a movie.

Bring It

One of the great matte painters of our day once told me that he spent only the first few years of his career struggling to make his work look *real*, but that he'll spend the rest of his life learning new ways of making his work look *good*. It's taken me years of effects supervising, commercial directing, photography, wandering the halls of museums, and waking up with hangovers after too much really good wine to fully comprehend the importance of what he'd said. I can tell you that it was only after this particular matte painter made this conscious choice to focus on making things look *good*, instead of simply real, that he skyrocketed from a new hire at ILM to one of their top talents. Personally, it's only after I learned to bring the sex that I graduated from visual effects supervising to become a professional director.

So who brings the sex? The answer is simple: The people who care about it do. Those who understand the glorious unreality of film and their place in the process of creating it. Be the effects artist who breaks the mold and thinks about the story more than the bit depth. Help turn the tide of self-inflicted prejudice that keeps us relegated to creating boring reality instead of glorious cinema. Secretly slip your client a cocktail of dirty tricks and fry it in more butter than they'd ever use at home.

Bring the sex.

Stu Maschwitz
San Francisco, October 2007

I

Introduction

If you aren't fired with enthusiasm, you will be fired with enthusiasm.

—Vince Lombardi

Why This Book?

*A*dobe After Effects CS3 Professional Studio Techniques is about creating realistic visual effects—the art and science of making disparate elements look like they were taken with a single camera (and moreover, look good). It goes deep into issues such as color correction and keying that are only touched on by books more focused on using After Effects for motion graphics, while leaving motion-graphics-only tools (Text, Shapes, and like) more or less alone.

This book does not shy away from strong opinions, even when they deviate from the official line. These opinions have been formed through actual work in production at some of the finest visual effects facilities in the world, and they're valid not only for "high-end" productions but for any composited shot.

The visual effects industry is traditionally quite protective of techniques, often reflexively treating all production information as proprietary and top secret. Work on a major project, however, and you will soon discover that even the most complex shot relies heavily on techniques and practices that are by definition commonplace; the art is in how these are applied, combined and customized, and what is added (or taken away).

Each shot is unique, and yet every shot relies on techniques that are tried and true. This book offers you as much of the latter as possible so that you can focus on the former. There's not much here in the way of step-by-step instructions; it's more important that you grasp how things work so that you can repurpose the technique for your individual shot.

Finally, this is not a book for beginners. Although the first section is designed to make sure you are making optimal use of the software, it's not an effective primer on After Effects in particular or digital video in general. If you're new to After Effects, first spend some time with its excellent documentation or check out one of the many books available to help beginners learn to use After Effects, such as *After Effects CS3 for Windows and Macintosh: Visual QuickPro Guide* (Anthony Bolante, Peachpit Press), *Adobe After Effects 7 Hands-On Training* (Chad Fahs and Lynda Weinman, Peachpit Press), or *Adobe After Effects CS3 Professional Classroom in a Book* (Adobe Press).

The Keys

There are a few overall keys to your success as a compositor, whether or not you work in After Effects:

- ▶ **Get reference.** You can't re-create what you can't clearly see. Study up.

- ▶ **Simplify.** This book is about helping you eliminate needless steps. To paraphrase Einstein, a good solution is as simple as possible, but no simpler.

- ▶ **Break it down.** As I said above, the most complicated shot consists of small, comprehensible steps—perhaps thousands of them—and each image consists of three or more channels each containing thousands of pixels.

- ▶ **It's never good enough, so go ahead and be restless and surround yourself with perfectionists.** My old colleague Paul Topolos (at this writing employed in the art department at Pixar) used to say that "recognizing flaws in your work doesn't mean you're a bad artist. It only means you have taste."

This is how it's done at the best companies, and so this is how you should do it, too.

Organization

Adobe After Effects CS3 Professional Studio Techniques is organized into three sections:

▶ Section I, "Working Foundations," is about the software. The goal is not to drag you through each menu and button and be a second manual, but instead to offer you tips and techniques that will help you into the coveted state of *flow* in After Effects, where you are focused entirely on the job at hand because you no longer have to think about the tools.

▶ Don't assume that you're too advanced to at least skim this section; I virtually guarantee there's something in there you don't already know.

▶ Section II, "Effects Compositing Essentials," focuses on the core techniques of effects compositing: color matching, keying, rotoscoping, motion tracking, and optics, as well as such advanced topics as expressions and HDR color. This is the heart of the book.

▶ Section III, "Creative Explorations," demonstrates actual shots you are likely to re-create, offering best practices for techniques every effects artist needs to know.

What you won't find in these sections are menu-by-menu descriptions of the interface or step-by-step tutorials that walk you through projects with little connection to real-world visual effects needs.

Workflow Comparison

There's nowhere else in the book as suitable, so at the outset here's a helpful overview of how the After Effects workflow is unique from every other compositing application out there. Each application is unique, and yet the main competitors to After Effects—Shake, Nuke, Flame, Fusion and Toxic, to name a few—are probably more similar to one another than any of them is to After Effects, which is often said to be a lot more like Photoshop.

Unique features in After Effects include:

▶ Render order is established in the Timeline and via nesting compositions, one inside the other. After Effects has Flowchart view but you don't create your composition there the way you would with a tree/node interface.

▶ Transforms, effects, and masks are embedded in a layer and render in a set order that you cannot easily change.

▶ After Effects has a persistent concept of any image having four channels: red, green, blue, and alpha. The alpha is always treated as if it is straight (not premultiplied) once an image has been imported and properly interpreted.

▶ After Effects projects are not scripts, actions are not recordable and there is no direct equivalent to Shake macros, although scripting and Animation Presets offer similar capabilities.

▶ Temporal and spatial settings tend to be absolute in After Effects because it is composition and timeline-based. This is a boon to projects that involve complex timing and animation, but it can snare users who aren't used to it and suddenly find pre-comps that end prematurely or are cropped. Best practices to avoid this are detailed in Chapter 4, "Optimize the Pipeline."

Of these differences, some are arbitrary, most are a mixed bag of advantages and drawbacks, and a couple of them are constantly used by the competition as a metaphorical stick with which to beat After Effects. The two that come up the most are the handling of precomposing and the lack of macros.

This book attempts to shed light on these and other areas of After Effects that are not explicitly dealt with in its user interface or documentation. The truth is that Shake, Nuke, and others require that you understand their own rules, such as the need to manage premultiplication in your pipeline, in order to master them. After Effects spares you details that as a casual user, you might never need to know about, but that as a professional user you should understand thoroughly. This book is here to help.

What's on the DVD

If you want to find out more about some of the plug-ins and software mentioned in this book, look no further than its DVD-ROM. For example, the disc includes demos of

NOTES

To install the lesson files, footage, and software demos included on the DVD, simply copy each chapter folder in its entirety to your hard drive. Note that all .aep files are located in the Projects subfolder of each chapter folder on the disc, while .ffx files can be found in the Animation Presets subfolders.

▶ Andersson Technologies' SynthEyes (3D tracking software)

▶ Red Giant Software's Instant HD, Primatte, Magic Bullet, Image Lounge, Knoll Light Factory, Key Correct Pro, Instant HD, Colorista, Film Fix, Trapcode Shine, Trapcode Starglow, Trapcode 3D Stroke, Trapcode Particular, and more.

▶ ReelSmart Motion Blur, PV Feather, and RE:Flex from Revision FX

▶ ZBornToy from Taronites

▶ Erodilation and CopyImage from ObviousFX

You'll also find HD footage from Artbeats, fxphd.com, and Pixel Corps with which you can experiment and practice your techniques; for more such footage, see www.artbeats.com and www.pixelcorps.com. Finally, there are dozens of example files to help you deconstruct the techniques described.

The Bottom Line

NOTES

If you have comments or questions you'd like to share with the author, please e-mail them to AEStudio-Techniques@gmail.com.

Just like the debates about which operating system is best, debates about which compositing software is tops are largely meaningless—especially when you consider that the majority of first-rate, big-budget, movie effects extravaganzas are created with a variety of software applications on a few different platforms. Rarely is it possible to say what software was used to composite a given shot just by looking at it, because it's about the artist, not the tools.

The goal is to understand the logic of the software so that you can use it to think through your artistic and technical goals. This book will help you do that.

SECTION I

Working Foundations

1

Compositing in After Effects

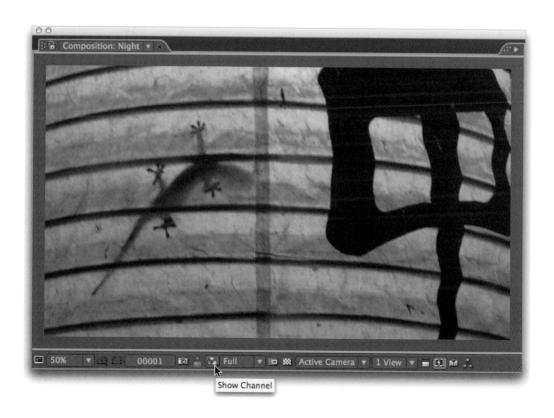

Good surfing is power, speed, and flow. The rest of it doesn't matter to me at all.

—Gary Elkerton, Australian surfer

Compositing in After Effects

This is a book about visual effects compositing in general, and about Adobe After Effects in particular. If you use After Effects, the goal is to help you composite believable shots from elements that were not shot together, and to do it with less effort. This first section of the book focuses on the "less effort" part, offering a jump-start (if you're new) or a refresher (if you're already an After Effects artist) on the After Effects workflow.

"Workflow" is essentially the methodology used to get things done. A successful compositor obviously needs to get a lot of stuff done, as even a simple A over B shot is comprised of many, many combinations of artistic and engineering decisions. The less effort expended on each individual decision, the freer you are to experiment and make changes, and that's what it's really all about. Iteration, maybe more than anything else, separates great effects shots from mediocre ones.

And so, this chapter and Section I focus on how to get things done in After Effects as effortlessly as possible. This first chapter assumes you already know your way around the basics of After Effects and are ready to learn to work smarter. So, even if you're an experienced compositor, keep reading. You may discover techniques and options you did not even know were available to you. I encourage you to look through this chapter and the rest of Section I carefully for new ideas about working with After Effects.

NOTES

If this book opens at too advanced a level for you, check out *Adobe After Effects CS3 Professional Classroom in a Book* (Adobe Press), a helpful beginner's resource.

Workspaces and Panels

Figure 1.1 shows the Standard workspace that appears when you first open After Effects CS3. The interface consists of one main *application window* containing *panel groups*, separated by *dividers*. Each group contains one or more *panels*. If a group contains multiple panels, the tab of each panel can be seen at the top, but only the contents of the forward tab can be seen; a tab moves forward when you select it. Some panels are *viewers*; these include a pull-down menu in the tab that lets you choose what is displayed.

TIP

Figure 1.1 uses darker user interface colors than are displayed in After Effects by default. The User Interface Brightness control resides in Preferences > User Interface Colors.

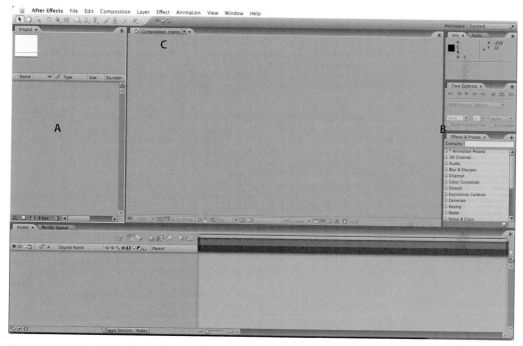

Figure 1.1 The Standard workspace layout is all contained in a single application window. The frame containing the Project panel (A) is currently active, as indicated by the yellow highlight around the panel's border. Dividers such as the long one (B) between the Composition panel and the smaller panels at the right separate the frames. The tab of the Composition viewer (C) includes a pull-down menu for choosing a particular composition, and a lock icon for keeping that composition forward regardless of what else is clicked (its usage is explored in Chapter 4, "Optimize the Pipeline").

The heart of After Effects can be found by choosing the Minimal workspace (**Figure 1.2**), either using the pulldown menu at the upper right of the Tools panel or via the Window > Workspace menu. This reveals two panels only:

▶ The Composition panel is a viewer, where you examine the shot.

▶ The Timeline panel is the true heart of After Effects, where elements are layered and timed for individual compositions (or shots). A project may have many of these open at any given time, and a whole composition can appear as a layer in another composition.

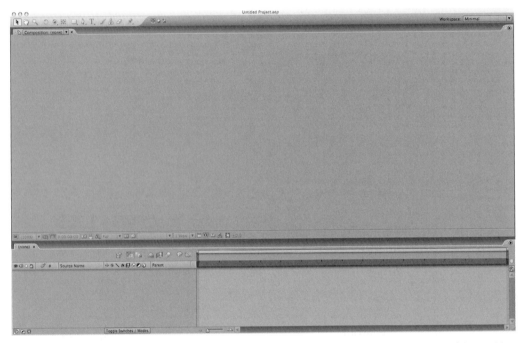

Figure 1.2 The Minimal view serves up the two most used panels in After Effects: Timeline and Composition.

All available panels in After Effects are listed under the Window menu; some even list preset keyboard shortcuts for rapid access.

Now choose Window > Project (**Cmd/Ctrl+0**) to add the Project panel. This is the equivalent of the Finder or Explorer of your system software. It contains the file resources used in your compositions (source footage, stills, solids that you create, audio, even the compositions themselves) and folders to contain them. A completed composition is typically placed in the Render Queue (**Cmd/Ctrl+Alt/Option+0**) for final output.

The fundamental workflow of After Effects, concisely summarized, is to create a new composition, typically containing items from the Project panel, which you add to the Timeline so that they appear in the Composition panel. Saving the project doesn't affect the items in the Project panel; the compositions made using these elements are rendered into new items that can in turn be imported or sent elsewhere (such as to a nonlinear editor or NLE).

Of course, there is much more to creating a shot than that, and that's why you have this book. It's quite typical to apply effects to individual layers; these can be selected in the Effects & Presets menu, and once applied, they appear in the Effect Controls panel when the given layer is selected. Other panels (found in other workspaces, or by selecting them under the Window menu) contain controls for specific tools such as paint (Paint and Brush Tips), or text (Character and Paragraph). Don't enable the All Panels workspace unless you're ready to feel a little overwhelmed—at first, anyhow.

The default workspaces to anticipate common usages of After Effects: Animation, Effects, Motion Tracking, Paint, and Text, but you'll find that you can (and should) customize these, and even create your own.

Customize the Workspace

By choosing the Minimal workspace and adding the Project panel above, you customized the workspace; switch to another workspace and back and you'll see that the Project panel remains, until you choose Reset "Minimal" under either Workspace menu. If instead you choose New Workspace, and save the layout, then reset will give you that.

When you added the Project panel it probably appeared at the lower left, next to the Timeline. You might choose to move it somewhere else, such as the upper left or right. To do so, click and drag its tab around the screen. As you move it over another panel, purple geometric shapes like those in **Figure 1.3** appear. These are the *drop zones*. The *docking zones* along the edges let you place a panel adjacent—for example, to the left of the Composition panel. The *grouping zones* in the center group panels together in one frame.

TIP

If you like the changes you've made to a workspace and want to keep them in your preferences, choosing New Workspace under the Workspace menu and entering the name of an existing workspace will overwrite that one.

Figure 1.3 Six possible drop areas are shown. Dropping on the center or along the top has the same result: grouping the dropped panel in the same frame as Info; dropping in any of the other four positions the dropped panel just to that side of Info.

Maximize the screen

When you tear off a panel and move it to a second monitor as a floating window, you may notice that it lacks the Zoom button along the top to send the window to full screen.

The shortcut **Ctrl+\ (Cmd+\)** can zoom the window instead. If the selected floating window is not occupying the full borders of the screen (or has been moved or offset), pressing the shortcut keys maximizes the window. If you press again, the shortcut toggles off the top menu bar, filling the entire screen with the window. This also works with the main UI window; if you don't like seeing the top of your monitor taken up by the After Effects menu bar, you can use **Ctrl+\ (Cmd+\)** to maximize the entire UI.

It is not uncommon these days to preview to a monitor that shares at least one dimension with your footage. For example, I often work with HD footage (1920×1080) on a set of 1920×1200 monitors. To see my Composition panel at 100% on one of those monitors, I make it a floating window and then use this shortcut.

As is noted later, you can always RAM Preview in full-screen mode by checking the Full Screen box in the Time Controls.

You can tear off any panel and make it float by holding down the **Ctrl/Cmd** key as you drag it away; my personal preference is to tear off the Render Queue, as in **Figure 1.5a**, because I only use it at specific times, and I can toggle it on and off via its shortcut (**Alt+Ctrl+0/Opt+Cmd+0**).

Drag a panel to one edge of the application window and aqua colored bands appear along the edge; the panel will occupy that entire side when dropped there (**Figure 1.4**).

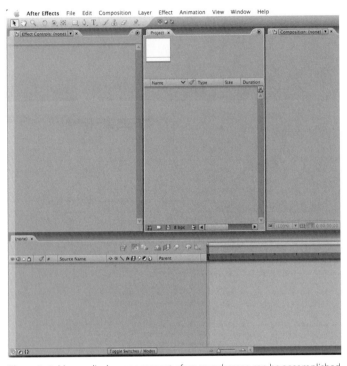

Figure 1.4 More radical rearrangement of your workspace can be accomplished by making a panel occupy one entire side of the workspace, as shown.

Special arrowed icons appear when you move the cursor between two or more panel groups, allowing you to resize adjacent panels. I don't habitually resize panels this way because of one of my favorite After Effects shortcuts, the Tilde key (~), which toggles the currently active panel (with a yellow borderline) to occupy the entire application window. This shortcut makes small and large monitors more usable when you want to focus on one big thing, typically lots of layers and keyframes in the Timeline or a zoomed-in shot in the Composition or Layer viewers.

Figures 1.5 a–c show a few workspaces that I like for various monitor configurations; these could even help you decide which is best for you for After Effects, one big monitor or multiple smaller ones. More methods for customizing views are explored in later chapters.

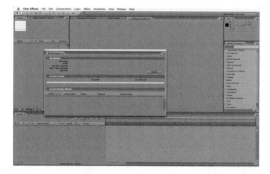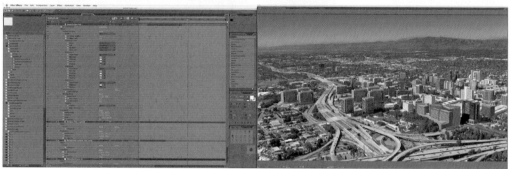

Figures 1.5a, b, and c Different monitors setups require different workspaces, whether for a laptop (a), 30-inch display (b), or two HD-resolution monitors side by side (c).

Make Use of the Interface

The ideal workflow is an effortless one, and so we now turn our attention to how best to perform steps repeated many, many times in a normal After Effects workday.

Organize your Source

Getting a source file from a disk or server into After Effects is no big deal. You can use File > Import > File. With several sources in various locations, File > Import > Multiple Files reopens this dialog until you cancel, a good option for image sequences. It doesn't matter which specific image in a sequence you select; they are all imported provided you select only one. However, by holding the **Shift** or **Ctrl (Cmd)** key as you select more than one frame, you can:

▶ specify a subset of frames to be imported in a sequence.

▶ select frames from more than one sequence in the same folder; a Multiple Sequences checkbox appears to make certain this is really what you want to do.

▶ specify sets of frames from multiple sequences (a combination of the above two modes).

TIP

The Force alphabetical order option which appears when a sequence is available adds placeholder files for any numbered stills missing from the sequence; this allows you to set up using a temporary render (say, a sequence containing only the first and last frame) before a full sequence is rendered.

A folder of still images will import as a sequence when dragged in, but if you actually wanted the folder and individual stills, hold the **Option/Alt** key while dragging.

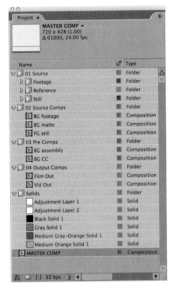

Figure 1.6 Even with a modest project it's pleasing to the eye and mind to keep things well organized.

On a Mac without a right mouse button, such as a MacBook Pro, you must hold the Control key while clicking in order to context-click.

Thus the Import dialog doesn't group multiple sequences together for you.

The most popular shortcut for importing is to drag footage directly into After Effects from a Finder or Explorer window, and dragging anywhere in the workspace will do it. To drag a sequence into After Effects, drag in the folder containing the sequence while holding the **Ctrl** (**Cmd**) key.

Want to get re-hired repeatedly as a freelancer, or be the most valued member in your organization? Organizing your projects well makes you a valued member of the team.

 An ordinary project uses some source footage, a main composition, a couple of pre-comps, some reference footage, and at least one solid layer. For this project, you could employ project organization along the lines of that shown in **Figure 1.6**; each type of item resides in its own folder. Only the main composition resides in the root area of the project, and its main components are organized according to how they are used. An artist unfamiliar with the project—including you yourself, several months or even years in the future—can investigate it in this hierarchical fashion.

Context-Clicks (and Keyboard Shortcuts)

Between keyboard shortcuts and context menus, an advanced user rarely visits the After Effects menu bar. The saved mouse movement and clicks may not seem like much at first, but once you learn to work this way, convenience is king.

Throughout the book are references to *context-clicking* on interface items. You could also call this "right-clicking" although certain devices, such as a Wacom tablet or one-button Mac mouse, don't have a right mouse button. Without detailing each individual context menu, **Figures 1.7a-c** contain a few of the most useful.

Context-click on a panel to see its panel menu (or use the little triangular icon on the upper right tab of each panel). These contain options also available via the top menus or on the panels themselves, but some of these are among the least discoverable features in After Effects, such as View Options for each viewer panel.

Redundancy, often considered a bad thing in logical design, is an often overlooked advantage of the After

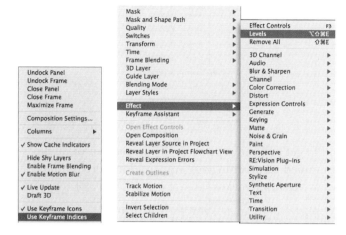

Figures 1.7a, b, and c Context menus are everywhere your cursor is, and for that reason, very effective. Context-click the tab of the Timeline panel (a), and you will see very different selections than if you context-click a layer in that panel (b), or the empty space below the layers (c). Depending on whether a layer is a camera, a solid, or footage, different options will appear.

Effects interface; because features are available in multiple ways you can find them more easily and develop your own preference for how you access them.

Missing Footage

After Effects links to source footage files that can be anywhere, so footage essential to your comps will become unlinked as things are moved around (**Figure 1.8**). Assuming you can still locate a given source file, re-link it as follows:

▶ Double-click the missing footage item in the Project panel

▶ Context-click the missing footage, choose Replace Footage, and then choose File

▶ Highlight the missing footage, and press **Ctrl+H/Cmd+H**

These all activate the Replace Footage File dialog, where you choose the missing footage item (or, alternatively, an alternate file of your choosing).

NOTES

On larger and more ambitious projects shared by several artists, it is typical to create a project template that anticipates a certain workflow, so that items are easy to find in predictable locations. Chapter 4 offers an example of such a template and demonstrates how to work with multiple compositions.

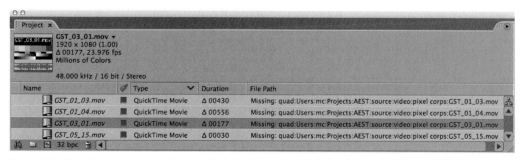

Figure 1.8 Missing footage appears with a small color bar icon. In the File Path column, After Effects also displays the path where the file was expected to be, which can help when searching on a drive or network for a missing, unlinked file.

TIP

After Effects will typically discover adjacent files in the same directory as the first missing file you replace and offer to re-link them, one more good reason to keep things well organized. For advice on organizing backups, see the next section, "Collect, Combine, Consolidate."

TIP

To simply reload footage instead of replacing it, context-click the item in question and choose Reload Footage (or use **Ctrl+Alt+L/Cmd+Option+L**).

CLOSE-UP

Edit and Replace Source

You notice a change needed to source material in your project created or edited in another application. **Ctrl+E/Cmd+E** opens a file from the Project in whatever application created it (according to its file type). When changes are made and saved in the other application, After Effects updates using the result, but only if you save over the same file (if instead you choose Save As, you must replace the source).

You may receive a warning upon opening a project that files are missing, but this warning does not indicate which files it has flagged. To identify missing source files in your project, click the binoculars icon beneath the Project panel and, leaving the text field blank, check Find Missing Footage and click OK. Repeat as needed (this feature lacks a shortcut).

If a file you attempt to re-link or import is gray and cannot be highlighted in the import dialogs, the file is somehow not recognized by After Effects. Typically, adding a missing three-character extension will solve this, although certain formats do not read equally well on Mac and Windows (for example, Mac-generated PICT); see the Source Formats section later in this chapter for the most useful and universal file types to use.

After Effects has no mechanism to manage media should several items from various directories become unlinked. Therefore, keep source items grouped together in as few places as is practical; for example, I typically place all locally stored project footage in a Source folder with Footage and Stills subfolders.

Collect, Combine, Consolidate

If you need to move a project along with all of its linked source, and the source isn't neatly contained in one location, or you're only using a sub-set of what's there, you can employ File > Collect Files. This command supports multi-machine Watch Folder rendering (see Chapter 4) but is also useful for backup, as it allows you to create a new folder that contains a copy of the project and all of its source files (**Figure 1.9**).

Figure 1.9 The Collect Files dialog includes several options. Select the master composition (if your shot has one) prior to Collect Files, then toggle Collect Source Files: For Selected Comps (as well as Reduce Project). Only the files you need are collected. A summary is shown in the lower-left corner, and you can add comments.

You can reduce the number of source files collected using the Collect Source Files menu; for example, select the master composition for a finished project and choose For Selected Comps; After Effects collects only the footage needed to create that comp.

To combine two After Effects projects before collecting files, import one into the other, or import both into a new project. The imported project appears in its own folder (**Figure 1.10**) with the complete organization of its Project palette intact. Therefore, if you've been organizing your projects as is encouraged here, you will have redundant folders to re-integrate manually.

NOTES

When you use Collect Files, source files are re-organized using the folder organization of the Project itself. Any image sequence will be placed into its own sub-folder.

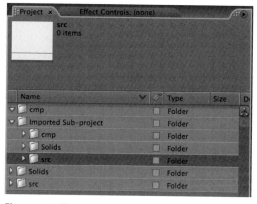

Figure 1.10 The imported project folder contains subdirectories that are redundant to those in the master composition. After Effects offers no built-in quick fix to reorganize these, but this book does; look for rd_MergeProjects.jsx on the book disc, by Adobe employee Jeff Almasol, which merges folders in the subfolder and folders of the same names in the master project.

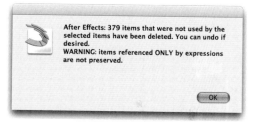

Figure 1.11 A warning, but no real cause for alarm. Reduce Project removes items from the project (not from the source disk). The admonition regarding expressions applies only if a property's expression links to a separate, otherwise unused composition (a somewhat rare case).

Select the main compositions in your project and choose File > Reduce Project; After Effects eliminates project items not used in the selected comps. You even get a warning dialog telling you how many items were removed (**Figure 1.11**).

File > Consolidate All Footage looks for two or more instances of a source file and combines them, choosing the first instance, top to bottom, in the Project. File > Remove Unused Footage rids a project of footage not included in any composition.

TIP

Consolidate All Footage always keeps the first instance of any redundant source in the project; therefore, to specify a particular folder to be eliminated, you can add the letter "z" before it's name to send it to the bottom of the Project list.

Advanced Save Options

Because After Effects projects are saved unique to the elements they contain, there are a few unique options for saving them that are worth knowing about.

File > Increment and Save attaches a version number to your saved project, or increments whatever number is already there, at the end of the file name before the .aep extension. It turns out that projects evolve in versions; sometimes a new version coincides with a new day's work, but in other cases you might want to try some risky, destructive edits in quick succession. After Effects projects are typically relatively small (unless they include a lot of paint strokes!) so there's little harm in saving a new version before trying something new.

After Effects has a well-earned reputation for stability, but beyond crashes, other bad things can kill a project file— power outages, accidental shut-downs, hardware failures— and even the most talented artist can forget to save when engrossed in a tricky shot.

Preferences > Auto-Save contains the toggle option to automatically save projects as you work on them. It saves the number of versions you specify (5 by default) using your specified interval (default is 20 minutes). A folder called After Effects Auto-Save is created in the same folder as the project file, and the maximum number of versions for the open project has been reached, the oldest (lowest-numbered) version is deleted. The interval clock only runs when you are actually working, should you forget and leave a project open during lunch hour.

Project, Footage, and Composition Settings

After Effects is optimized to anticipate the settings you need so that the defaults often work for the novice; however, the settings are there for good reason. Artists who don't know them well typically find themselves fighting unnecessary uphill battles, kludging compromise solutions.

Project Settings

The Project Settings dialog (**Ctrl+Alt+Shift+K/Cmd+Option+Shift+K**) opens a dialog (**Figure 1.12**) to control the following within your project:

▶ Display Style determines how time is displayed —the Timecode Base as well as a choice between Timecode or Frames

▶ Color Settings include the project-wide color depth (8, 16, or 32 bits per channel), as well as the Working Space and linear light handling (all explained in Chapter 11)

▶ Audio Settings allow you to lower the default 48 kHz sample rate, to lower the memory overhead if you are working at a lower sample rate. In previous versions of After Effects, this was a Preference setting (applied to all projects).

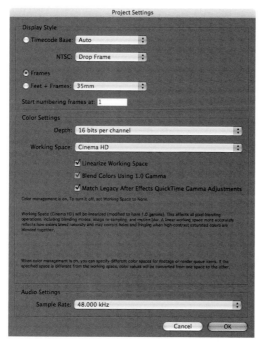

Figure 1.12 Time is displayed according to the Display Style section of File > Project Settings. Color Settings are covered in detail in Chapter 11, which explores how Depth and Working Space change the look of your footage, and how to use these settings.

TIP

Why set Timecode Base to anything but Auto? It can be useful to compare times or durations for items with differing frame rates, or in a case where you absolutely know that everything must conform to a particular rate.

TIP

To specify a particular frame, or even timecode, for a given composition, you can do so in the Start Frame field in Composition Settings (**Ctrl+K/Cmd+K**).

The Auto setting for Timecode Base is useful as it allows you to freely mix footage of varying frame rates without forcing you to choose one underlying frame rate to display for the entire project. Timecode Base only controls how timecode is displayed in the Timeline, it doesn't change the timing of footage—if the setting doesn't match the frame rate of the composition, values will round off to the nearest number, which is not generally what you want.

After Effects displays timecode by default, but particularly if you're working in film, you may want to choose Frames instead, as it's typical to refer to "frame 97" rather than "at 4:01." It's also typical to start numbering frames at 1, rather than the After Effects default of 0, but you can choose any number you want. The truly old-school option is to use Feet + Frames (which applies to actual reels of physical film, that format which is quickly becoming obsolete).

Even when the Frames option is active, the Timecode Base of an individual composition is displayed beside the frame counter in the Timeline (**Figure 1.13**).

Figure 1.13 The Timeline provides a constant reminder (in parentheses) of what frame rate is being used in the current project, regardless of how time is displayed (in this case, in frames, which tends to be standard for film work while timecode is more often used for video).

Interpret Footage

This book generally eschews the practice of walking through After Effects menus, but sometimes the UI perfectly encapsulates a given set of production challenges. The Interpret Footage dialog is one such case, a section-by-section checklist of all the decisions to be made about imported footage:

- ▶ Alpha interpretation
- ▶ Frame Rate
- ▶ Fields and Pulldown
- ▶ Pixel Aspect Ratio (under Other Options)
- ▶ Color Management (under More Options with certain file types and the new Color Management tab)

To bring up the Interpret Footage dialog for a given clip, select it in the Project panel and press **Ctrl+F/Cmd+F** or context-click and select Interpret Footage > Main.

Alpha

To be a good compositor, you must thoroughly understand alpha channels. **Figure 1.14** shows the most visible symptom of a misinterpreted alpha channel: fringing.

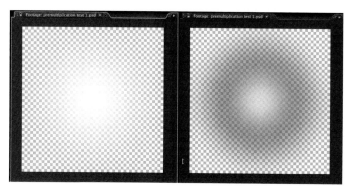

To try the Figure 1.14 example for yourself, import premultipliedAlpha.tif from the CH01 folder; try changing each from the correct Premultiplied setting to the incorrect (in this case) Straight setting.

Figure 1.14 It's easy to distinguish a properly interpreted (left) from an incorrect alpha channel (right) if you're looking carefully. The giveaway is fringing, caused in this case by the failure to remove the background color from the edge pixels by unmultiplying them (with black). The left image is premultiplied, the right is straight.

For those getting started, here are a couple pointers and reminders:

▶ If the alpha channel type is unclear, click Guess in the Interpretation dialog that shows up when importing footage with alpha. This often, but not always, yields a correct setting.

▶ Preferences > Import contains a default alpha channel preference. Beware of setting this to anything besides Ask User until you are certain you know what you are doing and that your project isn't likely to have unexpected variables.

For the rest of the information on alpha channels and how they operate in After Effects, see Chapter 3.

Frame Rate

Footage appears herky-jerky in a composition with the intended frame rate? After Effects may be misinterpreting the frame rate. Misinterpreted frame rate is typically an issue with image sequences only, because unlike QuickTime, the files themselves contain no embedded frame rate.

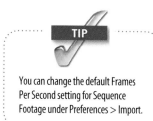

You can change the default Frames Per Second setting for Sequence Footage under Preferences > Import.

Why Sequences for Moving Footage?

While movie formats such as QuickTime (.mov) or Windows Media (.avi) are convenient, it is typical to render and import image sequences in a video effects production environment because

▶ A bad frame in a sequence can (typically) be replaced; a bad frame frame will (typically) make a movie unusable, perhaps costing hours of rendering or transfer time

▶ It's easy to replace a section of an image sequence precisely; simply over-write specific numbered frames

▶ Still image formats are more universal, particularly cross-platform (see Source Formats, below, for which ones are preferable and why)

▶ HD or film resolution movie files are huge and cumbersome to move or edit

Adobe's handling of image sequences isn't entirely ideal; neither the After Effects Import dialog nor Bridge groups them together automatically, so it's up to you to notice if a single folder contains multiple image sequences. There is also no mechanism to import part of a sequence; to work with a range of images from a sequence, especially long ones with thousands of images, it is often best to choose the range you need and copy it, or symbolic links to it, into a separate folder.

Therefore, when importing still image sequences to use as moving footage, remember

▶ Just because Project Settings contain the proper frame rate (e.g. 24 fps for a feature film project), image sequences may still import at 30 fps (the default).

▶ You can assign any frame rate to any moving footage, even overriding the rate specified in a QuickTime or Windows Media file.

Keep in mind that when a clip is selected in the Project panel, its current frame rate, duration, and other information is displayed at the top of the panel (**Figure 1.15**).

Figure 1.15 Useful information about any selected footage item can be found atop the Project panel. To see and select specific comps in which it is used, click the carat to the right of the file name. The selected file itself also shows size, type, and source location.

Fields, Pulldown, Pixel Aspect Ratio

One surprise for the digital video novice is that moving images are often not made up of whole frames containing square pixels like the still images we're all used to; instead, a video frame is often interlaced into two fields, and its pixels are stored non-square, all in order to enable faster and more efficient playback.

Fields combine two frames into one by interlacing them together, vertically alternating one horizontal line of pixels from the first with one from the second. The result is half the image detail but twice the motion detail. **Figure 1.16** details this principle in action.

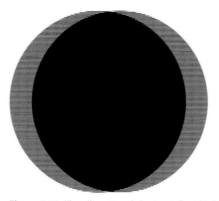

Figure 1.16 The ellipse travels horizontally at high speed, creating clear interlaced fields. This describes two frames' worth of motion via every other vertical pixel of a single frame.

Figure 1.17 The foreground pickup truck spells trouble if you're planning on doing much more than a simple color correction; fields were not removed for this clip. If you see a problem like this, check your Interpret Footage settings immediately.

Figure 1.17 shows how a frame of footage with heavy motion and interlacing looks with Separate Fields set to Off. It's okay to roll this way if you're not doing any compositing, transformation, paint/masking, or distortion (color correction is okay); otherwise, it's best to match the Separate Fields setting to that of the footage, causing After Effects to recognize the interlace frame as two separate frames of video.

Pulldown uses fields to run 24 fps film footage smoothly at 29.97 fps by repeating one field every five frames. This creates a pattern that After Effects can accurately guess if there is sufficient motion in the first few frames of the footage. If not, the backup option (which still works) is trial-and-error, trying each initial pattern listed under Remove Pulldown until the field artifacts disappear in a 23.976 fps comp. There are two basic types of pulldown (3:2 and 24Pa), each with five potential initial patterns.

Pixel Aspect Ratio (PAR) is another compromise intended to maximize image detail while minimizing frame size. The pixels in the image are displayed non-square on the broadcast monitor, with extra detail on one axis compensating for its lack on the other.

NOTES

Both legacies discussed here (interlacing and non-square pixels) carry over from standard definition (SD) formats (NTSC and PAL) into newer high definition (HD) formats because they enable higher throughput and smaller file sizes.

NOTES

3:2 pulldown is the traditional format designed to make footage that originated at 24 fps play smoothly at 29.97 fps; telecine conversions from film to television use this. 24P Advance Pulldown was introduced to allow the best possible recovery of the original 24 frames by grouping them together; the pattern allows the interlaced frame to be discarded because it is always bookended by two whole frames.

NOTES

To accustom yourself with non-square pixels and how they appear in After Effects, try opening d1circle.tif from the CH01 folder and experiment with the PAR toggle in any viewer panel (Composition, Layer, or Footage).

Your computer monitor, of course, displays square pixels, so any clip with a non-square PAR will look odd if displayed without compensating for the difference. Therefore, After Effects includes a toggle below the viewer panels to stretch the footage so that its proportions look correct (**Figure 1.18**) while the footage or composition itself isn't changed.

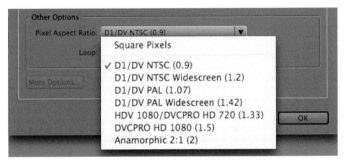

Figure 1.18 Listed are the non-square pixel video formats parsed by After Effects. Those with values above 1.0 use pixels that are wider than they are tall, making the image appear anamorphic—a.k.a. too skinny—when displayed using square pixels, without compensation.

With some digital formats such as DV, field order and pixel aspect are standardized and set automatically in After Effects. With other formats, it's best to know the correct field order and pixel aspect as specified by the camera or software that generated the image.

Source Formats

After Effects is capable of importing and exporting a wide array of footage formats, yet only a small subset of these recur typically in visual effects production. **Table 1.1** contains a run-down of common raster image formats, and some advantages and disadvantages of each.

Which formats will you use most? Probably TIFF and JPEG.

NOTES

One oddity of the PNG format is that it specifies that an alpha channel is saved and interpreted as Straight, with no explicit option to change the default.

TIFF offers lossless LZW compression, giving it an advantage over Photoshop, especially when you consider that TIFF can even store multiple layers, each with its own transparency. Other formats with lossless compression such as TGA don't support multiple bit-depths and layers like TIFF does. PNG is more limited and slower, but the file sizes are smaller.

TABLE 1.1 Raster Image Formats and Their Advantages

FORMAT	BIT DEPTH	LOSSLESS COMPRESSION	LOSSY COMPRESSION	ALPHA CHANNEL	OUTPUT FORMAT
TIFF	8/16/32 bit	Y	N	Y (multiple via layers)	Y
PNG	8/16	Y	N	Y (straight only)	Y
CIN/DPX	10	N	N	N	Y (Cineon 4.5 or DPX, see Cineon Settings)
CRW	12	N	N	N	N
EXR (non-native)	16/32	Y	N	Y	Y (downloadable plug-in)
JPG	8	N	Y	N	Y

JPEG is a lossy 8-bit format, but it's so useful for storing anything that doesn't have to be final high-quality that it has to be mentioned here. It is fast, standard everywhere and if you keep the quality at 7 or above (on the 0-9 scale used by After Effects), it's not always immediately obvious that there is any compression at all.

For film and computer graphics, it is normal to pass around CIN and DPX files (essentially the same format) and EXR, designed (and open-sourced) by ILM specifically to handle HDR renders with multiple channels of data (and these can be customized to contain useful information such as Z depth and motion data). More on these formats is found in Chapter 11, which also includes information on working with Camera Raw CRW images.

Photoshop Files

Although PSD files do not include even lossless compression, they do add a few features that allow you to work more easily between Photoshop and After Effects, making them highly useful in specific cases.

Although PSD and TIFF files are virtually indistinguishable when opened in Photoshop, only PSD can be imported as an After Effects composition. This is extremely useful for working with a matte painting or design that has been refined in Photoshop, but may want further tweaking when

TIP

To get the benefits of JPEG with options for higher bit depth, transparency and more, check out JPEG-2000, which was meant to supersede JPEG, then was not widely released due to apprehension about patent issues: http://jpeg.org/jpeg2000

TIP

Multi-channel OpenEXR plug-ins for After Effects, along with sample files and information on how to use them, can be found at http://www.fnordware.com/OpenEXR; they are also included on the book's disk.

it is put into motion in After Effects. In the Import File dialog, choose Composition or Composition (Cropped Layers) using the Import As pulldown menu (**Figure 1.19**).

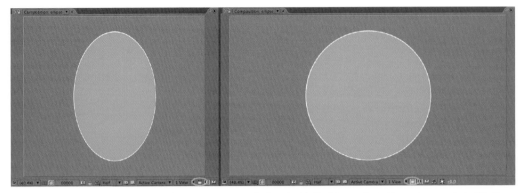

Figure 1.19 The same non-square pixel D1 aspect source, displayed with Pixel Aspect Ratio Correction toggled off (left) and on (right). The toggle for each is highlighted in green.

TIP

You can even create a new Photoshop layer in the context of a composition by choosing Layer > New > Adobe Photoshop File.

You can create a PSD file directly in After Effects (File > New > Adobe Photoshop File). Its dimensions will match that of the most recently opened composition, including title-safe and action-safe guides, and it is automatically included in your After Effects project.

Photoshop CS3 includes video layers; for the first time, not only can Photoshop work with moving images, but the PSD format can store them. This gives you new access to Photoshop's paint tools, which are fundamentally unique from those in After Effects. More about why you would want to work with video in Photoshop is included in Chapter 7, "Rotoscoping and Paint."

Composition Settings

It's normal to think that to begin working in After Effects, after you've imported some footage, you select Composition > New Composition and choose a preset in the Composition Settings dialog, along with the appropriate duration. I rarely do this.

To ensure that composition settings are exactly as they should be with the least effort, try one of the following:

▶ Use a prebuilt project template that includes compositions whose settings are already correct; duplicate and rename an existing template composition.

▶ Create a new composition by dragging its main footage (often the background plate) to the Create a New Composition icon (**Figure 1.20**).

Figure 1.20 Drag a source clip to the highlighted icon at the bottom of the Project panel to create a new composition with the clip's duration, pixel dimensions, pixel aspect, and frame rate. It's a reasonably foolproof way to match composition settings to a particular plate footage source.

The latter method automatically matches the pixel dimensions, Pixel Aspect Ratio, Frame Rate, and Duration all of which are crucial to get correct (although Duration is negotiable as long as it is not too short.)

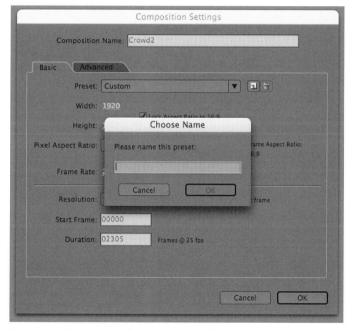

Figure 1.21 No preset matches what you need for your project? Create and save your own.

The Advanced tab in the Composition Settings dialog pertains to options for temporal and spatial settings (Chapter 4) and motion blur and 3D (Chapter 9, "The Camera and Optics").

NOTES

The term "plate" stretches back to the earliest days of optical compositing (and indeed, of photography itself) and refers to the source footage, typically the background onto which foreground elements are composited.

TIP

If there's no factory preset for footage you'll use repeatedly, by all means create your own and save it using the small icon adjacent to the Preset pulldown menu (**Figure 1.21**).

A 2K plate is the minimum typical horizontal film resolution: approximately 2000 pixels, or more precisely 2048 pixels in width. HD video, at 1920 pixels horizontal resolution, can also be considered a 2K format. Films are increasingly made with 4K effects plates—double the horizontal resolution, four times the overall pixels.

Previews and Viewers

How exactly does a professional work with footage in After Effects? This section offers some of the habits of highly effective compositors, to paraphrase a popular productivity guru. These strategies are particularly helpful when working with typically large format footage such as 2K film plates.

Resolution and Quality

There are several other effective ways to speed up previews and interactivity without ever setting a layer to Draft quality. Draft creates inaccurate previews by actually rounding off the numbers in calculating a mathematically precise operation such as a color key. Moreover, it is inconvenient, given the lack of a global toggle for layer quality (other than in the Render Queue).

To speed and lengthen previews, here are the methods I use, in rough order of preference:

▶ Lower viewer Resolution to Half, or in extreme cases, Quarter (**Figure 1.22**)

▶ Set a Region of Interest (ROI) if there are areas of frame that don't need attention

▶ Use Shift+RAM Preview to skip frames (default setting of 1 skips every second frame—details in "Caching and Previewing," below)

Figure 1.22 Keep the resolution (highlighted, right) matched to the current magnification setting (highlighted, left) to prevent over-rendering the current view (wasting your time) and slow RAM Previews.

Preferences > Display includes an toggle called Auto-Zoom When Resolution Changes. It's fine if you can get used to working this way; unfortunately, it's more common to want to change the Magnification (zoom) and want the resolution to match that setting, which this preference doesn't do.

Half resolution allows four times as much data to fill a RAM preview, and Shift+RAM Preview allows twice that much data. Thus a half-resolution preview of every other frame should be at least 8 times faster than at full resolution and motion, which can be saved for fine tuning and final render preparation.

To quickly change the display resolution in the Composition panel, use the keyboard shortcuts shown in **Table 1.2**.

TABLE 1.2 Display Resolution/Size Shortcuts

Resolution/Size	Keyboard Shortcut
Full	Ctrl+J/Cmd+J
Half	Ctrl+Shift+J/Cmd+Shift+J
Quarter	Ctrl+Shift+Alt+J/ Cmd+Shift+Option+J
Fit in viewer	Shift+/
Fit up to 100%	Alt+/ / Option+/

Hold down the **Spacebar** or activate the Hand tool (**H**) to move your view of a clip around. To zoom in and out, you can use

▶ **Ctrl+=/Cmd+=** and **Ctrl+-/Cmd+-**

▶ Zoom tool (**Z**); press **Alt/Option** to zoom out

▶ Comma and period keys

▶ Use a mouse with a scroll wheel; with the cursor over a viewer, the wheel zooms in and out

When focusing only on a particular section of the image, use the Region of Interest (ROI) tool (**Figure 1.23**), which lets you draw a rectangular preview region. Only the layer data needed to render that area is calculated and buffered, lengthening RAM previews.

TIP

With the cursor over a specific area of the frame, hold the **Option/Alt** key as you adjust the scroll wheel, and the viewer zooms around that point.

Figure 1.23 Region of Interest crops the active view region. You can even Crop Comp to Region of Interest (in the Composition menu) should a crop be exactly what you want.

NOTES

After Effects is a frame-based renderer; it generally calculates the entire frame even when you specify an ROI. Truthfully, it's quite a bit smarter than that, often ignoring elements entirely outside the ROI, but it won't deliver the speed boost of the equivalent feature in a scanline/tile-based renderer like Shake or Nuke.

Responsiveness

One major gotcha in After Effects is that UI interaction itself can be slowed down by the heavy processor activity of a big shot—so much so, in some cases, that even a simple attempt to drag a slider or move a layer position stutters to the point of non-interactivity. Here's a quick triage to solve the problem:

▶ **Enable OpenGL.** Preferences > Previews includes an Enable OpenGL toggle, which is off by default and unavailable on some systems. With it on, you can choose OpenGL-Interactive to get extra speed when, for example, positioning layers in 3D space. It only helps in specific cases, but in those cases it can make a huge difference for interactive setup.

▶ **Deactivate Live Update (Figure 1.24).** On by default, this toggle enables real-time update in the viewers as you adjust controls. Deactivate it and updates occur only when you release the mouse.

▶ **Hold Option/Alt as you make adjustments.** With Live Update on, this prevents views from updating. Deactivate Live Update and the behavior is inverted; the modifier keys instead enable real-time updates.

▶ **Activate Caps Lock.** If you don't mind working "blind" for periods of time, the caps lock key prevents updates to any viewer (**Figure 1.25**).

Figure 1.24 When Live Update is active, Composition and Layer panels update in real time as adjustments are made. Hold **Alt/Option** to prevent the views from updating (layers display as wireframes); with Live Update deactivated, this modifier causes the view to update in real time.

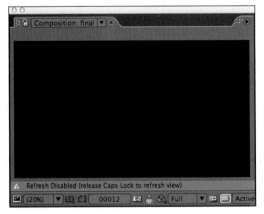

Figure 1.25 Caps Lock prevents view windows from updates; a prominent red border reminds you that it's on.

In general, the more responsive you can make your user interface, the better will be the result because you can make more decisions in a shorter period of time. Just leave time to double-check the result if you are in the habit of disabling viewers.

OpenGL in After Effects

OpenGL allows After Effects to use the graphics processor unit (GPU) to render elements in a composition, rather than the central processor unit (CPU), which is where all final-quality rendering is typically done. You get speedier interaction, particularly with 3D layers (a majority of OpenGL specifications apply to 3D), but the way the scene is drawn isn't as robust or as accurate; motion blur, for example, won't look right, and while the CPU has up to about 3 GB of RAM to use to create an image, the GPU can only have a fraction of that (at this writing all of my machines have 256 MB of VRAM, or graphics memory).

Thus you would only want to render with OpenGL enabled if it gave you a particular stylized look you wanted; instead, you will probably find that if you use it at all, it's most useful for setting up a complex 3D scene quickly.

OpenGL is disabled by default in After Effects because it can introduce instability (crashes). You can discover what OpenGL features are available on your system, and enable it in Preferences > Previews; click OpenGL Info to see a list of capabilities and which are supported (**Figure 1.26**).

TIP

Even if OpenGL is set to Always On, it is not employed in a RAM Preview. To preview with OpenGL, advance frames by dragging the CTI, using **Page Up/Page Down**, or by pressing the **Spacebar**. Spacebar previews become faster on the second pass, once texture data has buffered onto the display card.

Figure 1.26 Clicking OpenGL Info in Preferences > Previews opens this dialog. Texture Memory should be set approximately 40 MB below the total on Windows, as shown; on Mac, the correct memory setting is entered automatically. OpenGL is not supported on all versions of OS X 10.4, regardless of what card is installed.

NOTES

OpenGL can for various reasons become disabled even if your card fully supports it; it is not supported on OS X 10.4, regardless of hardware. If After Effects crashes with an OpenGL error, the feature will be disabled (un-checked in Preferences) the next time you start the application. If After Effects crashes on startup, you can remove OpenGL.aex from the plug-ins folder, and if that solves the crash problem, you should update the system OpenGL drivers before moving the plug-in back.

TIP

Nucleo Pro 2, from GridIron Software, goes even further to harness extra processor power, allowing you to cache precomps and pre-render individual layers in the background. Even with Multiprocessing now a part of After Effects, it can really help maximize what a single system can do with CS3.

Once you've enabled the feature, you can choose it in the Fast Previews pulldown menu along the bottom of the Composition viewer. There are two OpenGL options, Interactive and Always On; the former will help you with fast scene setup, especially in a complicated 3D scene, and the latter will give you the look of OpenGL at all times as you work.

Multiprocessing

New to After Effects CS3 is a Multiprocessing option that runs multiple processes to render more than one frame at a time. Off by default, you enable it via a toggle in Preferences > Multiprocessing; this dialog box contains only the single checkbox, accompanied by a long Description section.

This is one case where it's actually worthwhile to read the Description section. Not only is it customized for the system on which it appears, specifying how many processors are available and how they will be used, but it contains the following key tip (which reads the same on every system):

Each background process requires at least 400 MB of RAM. Reduce the Maximum RAM Cache Size in the Memory and Cache preferences to free RAM for the background processes.

In other words, lowering After Effects' RAM usage can greatly enhance performance. Assuming you heed this advice, there is no good reason not to enable Multiprocessing if your system supports it; previews and renders alike can be 80 to 100% faster per extra processor.

Caching and Previewing

The more Timeline footage you can cache into physical memory, the better. After Effects does this automatically as you navigate from frame to frame (**Page Up/Page Down**) or load a RAM preview (**0** on the numeric keypad). The green line atop the Timeline shows which frames are loaded.

Given that After Effects can only use a bit less than 3 GB of physical memory per session, you can do better. To extend the cache from physical memory (RAM) to physical media (ideally a high-speed local drive), enable Disk Cache in Preferences > Memory & Cache. This locks away a portion of your drive for use only by After Effects. A blue line shows frames loaded in the Disk Cache.

When you activate Enable Disk Cache, you must also specify a disk location; if in doubt just create a local folder with an intuitive name like AE Scratch. Even the default 2 GB (2000 MB) setting greatly extends available cache without occupying permanent disk space.

Two main questions usually come up regarding the Disk Cache:

▶ How can I make the application cache as much as possible?

▶ How do I preserve the cache once it is loaded?

The goal with caching, of course, is to get as close to real-time performance as possible. Disk Cache saves the time required to re-render a frame, but doesn't necessarily deliver real-time playback, and often is not invoked when you might think it should be.

If refined motion is not critical, use Shift+RAM Preview. Options in the pulldown menu (**Figure 1.27**) specify whether you preview every second frame, saving half the render time (Skip set to 1) or more (Skip 4 renders only every fifth frame, etc.).

Preview Settings

Sometimes a feature is hidden in plain sight, and so it is with Time Controls for a lot of people. Therefore allow me to point out additional options for RAM previews:

▶ **Frame Rate and Resolution.** It's normal to leave them on Auto, but these settings ensure that previews are always consistent.

▶ **Loop options.** Hidden among the playback icons atop Time Controls is a toggle controlling how previews loop. Use this to disable looping, or amaze your friends and supervisors with the "ping pong" option.

▶ **From Current Time** (Time Controls panel). Toggle it on and the work area is ignored; previews begin at the current time and roll through to the end of the comp.

▶ **Full Screen** (Time Controls panel). Self-explanatory and rarely used.

TIP

For maximum performance, no drive should be full beyond 90% of capacity.

TIP

The shortcut for Shift+RAM Preview is, naturally enough, **Shift+0** (on the numeric keypad). To set the Work Area to the length of any highlighted layers, use **Ctrl+Alt+B/Cmd+Option+B**— to reset the work area to the length of the comp, and double-click it.

Figure 1.27 The panel menu of Time Controls toggles RAM Preview and Shift+RAM Preview options.

TIP

To update an external preview device, press /.

▶ **Preferences > Video Preview** lets you specify an Output Device and how it is used (**Figure 1.28**). If you have a miniDV, DVCPro HD, or FireWire device attached with its own monitor, you can preview there even if the aspect ratio doesn't match (note the toggle to enable this). Third-party devices, such as PCI cards from Kona and Blackmagic, are supported as well.

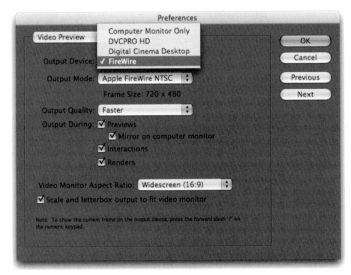

Figure 1.28 The items listed under Output Device in Preferences > Video Preview change according to the I/O and display hardware is installed on the system.

Customized Viewers

Custom, contrasting backgrounds are essential to a lot of effects work, such as keying and masking. You can customize the background color of the Composition viewer (**Ctrl+Shift+B/Cmd+Shift+B** or Composition > Background Color) or toggle the Transparency Grid icon beneath the Composition panel to evaluate edges in sharp relief.

What a lot of people don't consider is that *guide layers* enable a completely customizable background that will never show up in a render, nor when nested into another comp. You can insert background or reference footage, or create a custom gradient background (**Figure 1.29**). To make any layer a guide layer, context-click it in the Timeline and choose Guide Layer (Layer > Guide Layer).

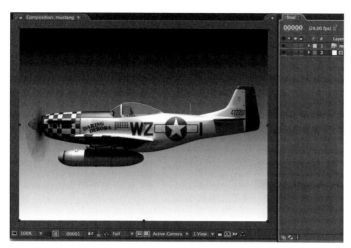

TIP

To create a basic gradient background, apply the Ramp effect to a solid layer.

Figure 1.29 The background is set as a guide layer, evident by the icon, a box of four small cyan guides, that appears beside the layer name.

Several other modes and toggles are available in the viewer panels. Some are familiar from other Adobe applications:

▶ **View > Show Grid** (**Ctrl+"**/**Cmd+"**) displays an overlay grid.

▶ **View > Show Rulers** (**Ctrl+R**/**Cmd+R**) not only displays pixel measurements of the viewer, it includes guides, which have several uses to compose an image.

▶ **Title/Action Safe** overlays determine the boundaries of the frame as well as its center point.

All of the above features can be accessed by a single pull-down menu beneath the viewer panel (the one that looks like a crosshair). To pull out a guide, choose Show Rulers and then drag from either the horizontal or vertical ruler. To change where the origin point (0 on each ruler) is, drag the crosshair from the corner between the two rulers.

Other Adobe conventions are View > Show Rulers (**Ctrl+R**/ **Cmd+R**) and the various Guides options under the View menu. I don't make use of guides much in After Effects, but I like the fact that, for example, when you create a new Photoshop file with After Effects, it includes guides showing the safe areas.

TIP

Use Preferences > Grids & Guides to customize your grid; the size, subdivisions and color are all fair game, and it's even possible to replace lines with dashes or dots for a lighter touch. You can also customize the Safe Margins in the Title/Action Safe overlay, even setting them to 0% to use only the center crosshair if you prefer.

To toggle visibility of individual Layer Controls such as masks, keyframes, and motion paths, use View > View Options (**Ctrl+Alt+U/Cmd+Option+U**), or just hide them all using View > Hide Layer Controls (**Ctrl+Shift+H/ Cmd+Shift+H**). There is also a toggle (next to Grid & Guide Options along the bottom of the viewer).

Throughout this book I encourage you to develop the habit of studying footage one color channel at a time. The Show Channel icon exists for this purpose, along with the corresponding keyboard shortcuts **Alt/Option+1** through **Alt/Option+4** (R, G, B, and A, respectively). An outline in the color of the selected channel helpfully appears around the viewer boundary (**Figure 1.30**).

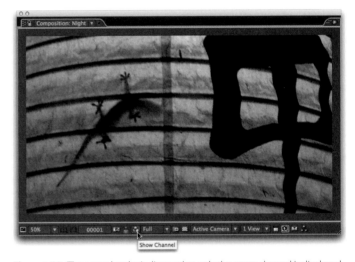

Figure 1.30 The green border indicates that only the green channel is displayed.

Effects & Presets

After Effects contains a lot of *effects*. These are filters (as they would be called in Photoshop) or processes that affect the appearance of a layer (or entire comp). Some provide bread-and-butter processes you probably use all the time, such as adjusting color with Levels or applying a blur. Others may be too esoteric or outdated ever to find their way into your workflow. A few are entirely unique to After Effects, including new ones developed by third-party (non-Adobe) software companies, with new ones coming along all the time.

At this writing I count about 200 effects plug-ins that ship with the application, and far more than that available on the open market. This book only covers a subsection of those 200, although it does so in depth, in many cases. The bottom line is

▶ It's likely that you'll use less than 10% of these effects something like 80–90% of the time, so there is no need to feel overwhelmed. You don't need to understand them all in order to use the most powerful ones.

▶ After Effects artists sometimes get a bad rap for using (or even buying) a plug-in to achieve an effect that can be done without it, if you know how.

Thus, where possible, this book goes deeply enough into the most essential effects plug-ins that it should help you understand which are the most useful and how you can use them together to create effects you might not have thought possible.

There are three basic ways to apply an effect to a layer:

▶ Choose it in the Effect menu

▶ Context-click the layer and choose it in the Effect context menu

▶ Choose it in the Effects & Presets panel, by double-clicking (or dragging and dropping) it.

The Effects & Presets panel is the most versatile method. It has options to display effects without their categories (**Figure 1.31**), as well as a search field to help you look for a specific effect by name, or for all the effects whose names include a specific word, such as "blur" or "channel."

TIP

Are you a MacIntel user with plug-ins from the pre-CS3 era? They won't work natively in After Effects CS3, but you can enable them by toggling Open in Rosetta in the Get Info dialog for Adobe After Effects CS3.app (in the Finder).

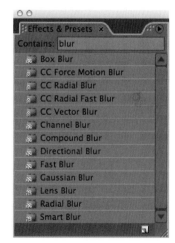

Figure 1.31 Type the word "blur" in the Effects & Presets search field and only effects with that text string in the name appear.

The Effects & Presets Panel

Each item in the Effects & Presets panel includes icon showing that it is one of the following types:

▶ an 8, 16 or 32 bit pixel effect (the highest possible bit depth is shown)

▶ an Animation Preset

▶ an Audio effect

▶ Missing

Effects that are capable of supporting 16 or 32 bits also operate at the standard 8 bits per channel. Chapter 11 contains more about the difference between bit depths and how to work with them.

The panel menu for Effects & Presets offers other unique ways to list its contents, options not available with standard menus, including the following toggles:

▶ Show only the effects that match the current project's bit depth (if 16 or 32 bpc)

▶ Alphabetical or Finder Folder order (as an alternative to the standard Categories found in the standard Effect menus

▶ Show Animation Presets

Animation Presets are sets of effects with custom default settings. You can use the ones that ship with After Effects or create your own. You can even browse the built-in ones from Adobe by choosing Browse Presets in the wing menu (or under the Animation menu); this opens the root folder containing them in Bridge, where selecting an individual .ffx file will also display an animated preview.

Animation presets are particularly useful when you're working with a team and sharing standardized practices. To save your own, in the Effect Controls window or the Timeline select whatever effects and properties you want to save and choose Animation > Save Animation Preset.

You can save an Animation Preset wherever you like, but for it to show up in the Effects & Presets palette automatically, save it to the Presets folder (the default location, found in the folder where the application itself resides). In a studio situation, a preset can be distributed to a number of users simply

TIP

Having trouble finding an item in Effects & Presets? Make sure you haven't set a display toggle in the panel menu that hides some of its contents—for example, Show 32 bpc-capable Effects Only mode, which excludes the majority of effects

NOTES

An animation preset file is recognizable by its .ffx file suffix; they can be found in the Plug-ins folder, within the same folder where the application itself is found (on Windows, this is a shortcut to the folder, which is stored one level deeper in the Support Files folder).

by placing it in this folder. The next time they restart After Effects or update the palette (using the Refresh List command in the wing menu), the preset is listed, ready for use.

Output: The Render Queue

The Render Queue is the main exit for your After Effects compositions. Although relatively intuitive, it contains some great features that are easy to miss, as well as a gotcha or two.

To place an item in the Render Queue, you can

► Use one of two keyboard shortcuts: **Ctrl+M** (**Cmd+M**) and the one I always tend to use, **Ctrl+Shift+/** (**Cmd+Shift+/**)

► Drag items from Project to the Render Queue

► Select Composition > Add to Render Queue

There are two key sections for each Render Queue item: Render Settings and Output Module. You can click on each to adjust settings manually, but as soon as you find yourself rendering more than one item with the same settings, you should choose, or as is likely necessary, create a template to save yourself one more opportunity for careless errors (the bane of the compositor's existence).

Render Settings: Pre-flight Checklist

Most of the items in the top Composition section of the Render Settings dialog (accessed by clicking on the current setting itself) correspond to settings in your composition and Timeline. Current Settings for each category uses whatever settings are used in the comp, but you can instead override with specific settings for Quality, Resolution, Proxies, Effects, Solo Switches, Guide Layers, and the Color Depth. There is even a checkbox to use the OpenGL renderer instead of the standard software method, if you like that look.

The Time Sampling section (center) has all to do with frames, fields, and overall frame rate and time span. Here you can introduce (or re-introduce) field order and pull-down to broadcast footage, control motion blur and frame blending (both further described in the next chapter).

TIP

You drag footage directly to the Render Queue, no comp required. After Effects makes one for you, rendering the footage as-is, which is efficient for quick file conversions (i.e. converting an image sequence to a Quicktime movie, or vice versa).

TIP

The output path you choose for the first of your active Render Queue items then becomes the default for the rest of them, should you wish to render several items to the same location.

NOTES

Most Render Settings are straightforward, offering either a Current or an override setting. Proxy Use is a little trickier, and is investigated in Chapter 4.

TIP

When rendering a still sequence, you can enable the Skip Existing Files toggle in Render Settings, and After Effects checks whether a frame already exists before rendering it. More on the use of this feature is found in Chapter 4.

In the bottom section, Options, After Effects defaults Use Storage Overflow toggled on; if your main render disk becomes full, the render doesn't have to fail if you have specified overflow volumes in Preferences > Output (**Figure 1.32**).

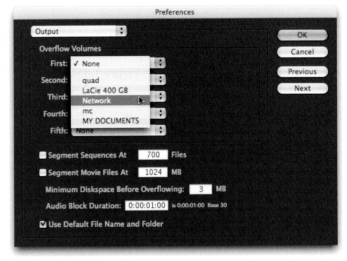

Figure 1.32 Storage overflow is insurance against failed planning; it's certainly preferable to a failed overnight render.

Render Settings, then, functions as a pre-flight checklist of the decisions needed to make a composition look as it should before the image is saved to disk; the actual save operation is handled in the Output Modules.

Output Modules: Making Movies

TIP

To render at a smaller size, it's best in most cases to scale down using a Stretch setting in the Output Module rather than a Resolution setting in the Render Settings (unless speeding up the render is more important than quality).

Output Modules do one thing only: convert a rendered frame into a particular video (or still) format with a given name. Included are options for which video and audio channels are included and at what size (or for audio, sample rate).

Output Module appears beneath Render Settings, item by item, because, as is detailed in Chapter 4, the visual order represents the order in which things actually happen. In this case, Render Settings are applied prior to frame actually being written using Output Module settings.

Several elegant and easily missed problem-solving tools are embedded in the Output Modules:

▶ You can add multiple Output Modules per Render Queue item (**Figure 1.33**).

▶ You can edit multiple Output Modules to a different preset by Shift-selecting the Output Modules themselves, rather than the Render Queue items (**Figure 1.34**).

▶ You can custom-number an image sequence beginning with the integer of your choice (**Figure 1.35**).

▶ Working with non-square pixels or letterboxing? Stretching and cropping output lets you change the pixel aspect without having to re-render.

▶ Post-Render Actions are available to import or replace the source composition. Chapter 4 describes optimal usage.

▶ A numbered image sequence must contain a string like [###] somewhere within its name (replaced, in this example, with a three-digit sequential number, one digit of padding for each # symbol).

Figure 1.33 It's easy to miss that you can add multiple Output Modules to a single render queue item, via Composition > Add Output Module. This can be an immense timesaver.

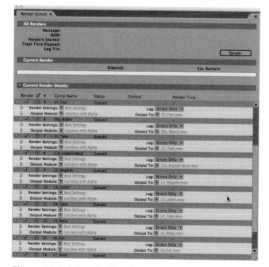

Figure 1.34 Select the first Output Module in the group and Shift-select the last, then change any of the selected ones and they all follow.

Output Module Settings

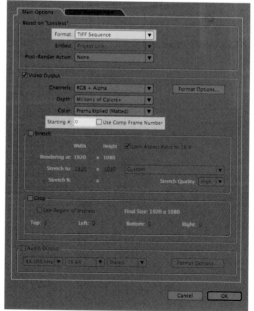

Figure 1.35 Custom-number a frame sequence by setting Use Comp Frame Number.

Creating your own Output Modules using the Make Template option at the bottom of the pulldown menu saves you the trouble of having to think of most of these options each time you render.

Optimized Output

Following are some suggested output settings (Render Settings and Output Modules) for specific situations:

- ▶ **Lossless output.** Use inter-frame compression (the default setting, Lossless, employs QuickTime with Animation/Most) for movie files; no individual pixel is altered by this form of "compression." TIFF with LZW is a good bet for still images.

- ▶ **Low-loss output.** QuickTime with Photo-JPEG at around 75% is the traditional favorite for test renders that are small and only lightly compressed, and that render quickly.

- ▶ **Online review.** This is a fast-changing area, but whatever format you choose, it is likely better to compress it outside of After Effects for multiple-pass encoding, which is key to your success with a format like H.264 or MPEG formats.

- ▶ **DV/HDV.** These are heavily compressed formats. You are stuck with them if you are shooting or delivering with them, but you don't need to use them at any other point in your process. Heed Stu Maschwitz's repeated advice in *The DV Rebel's Guide* (Peachpit Press, 2006); render once only: the final, directly from the source.

Obviously, there is much more to choosing your output settings than is covered here, including which source and delivery formats are demanded for your particular project.

Study a Shot like an Effects Artist

Seasoned visual effects supervisors miss nothing. The most trained eyes do not even need to see a clip twice to spot problems. In dailies on a feature film, nonetheless, a shot may loop for several minutes while the whole team gangs up on it, picking it apart. This is how shots in feature films can end up looking so good.

Photo-JPEG is universally available, even in older versions of QuickTime. Plus, at 100% it provides 4:4:4 chroma sampling, and at 75%, 4:2:2 (see Chapters 6 and 11 for more on chroma). New at this writing is Apple ProRes 422, introduced as part of Final Cut Pro 6, and delivering far less loss than Photo-JPEG without the compromises of H.264. Note that not all QuickTime compressors are not available with QuickTime for Windows.

Although After Effects cannot delivery multi-pass encoding via the Render Queue (despite the inclusion of Adobe Media Encoder for formats such as H.264) the Production Premium and Master Collection include it in Premiere Pro, via Adobe Media Encoder. See Chapter 4 for more about how to use this with After Effects.

You can and should scrutinize your shot just as carefully in After Effects. Specifically, throughout this book I encourage you to get in the following habits:

▶ Check the Info palette (**Figure 1.36**)

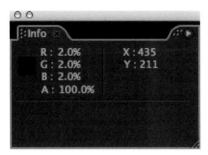

Figure 1.36 Whoops! The background level was meant to be black, but a glance at the Info palette with the cursor is over the background shows that it is actually 2% gray.

▶ Loop or rock and roll previews (**Figure 1.37**).

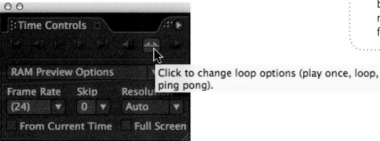

Figure 1.37 The three available settings for looping previews are highlighted in blue: Loop (the default, top), Ping-pong (center), or Play Through Once (bottom); toggle these by clicking on the icon.

▶ Zoom in to examine individual pixels, especially along any composited edges.

▶ Examine footage channel by channel.

▶ Slam the gamma and flash the blacks; details on how to use Levels on an adjustment layer like an investigative spotlight on your shot are included in Chapter 5, "Color Correction."

CLOSE-UP

Naming Conventions

Part of growing a studio is devising a naming scheme that keeps projects and renders organized. It's generally considered good form to

▶ Use standard Unix naming conventions (replacing spaces with underscores, intercaps, dashes, or dots).

▶ Put the version number at the end of the project name and the output file, and have them match. To add a version number to a numbered sequence, you can name the image sequence file something like foo_bar_[####]_v01.tif for version 1.

▶ Padding the numbers (adding zeros at the beginning) helps keep things in order as the overall number moves into multiple digits.

▶ After Effects doesn't like long file names; those above 32 digits are truncated in the Project panel and Timeline. Nonetheless, it's best to be explicit in the name about what is being rendered, e.g. pirates_precomp_colorkey03_forFinal_[####].tif

CLOSE-UP

What, exactly, is a QuickTime movie?

QuickTime is the most ubiquitous and universal playback format among video professionals, despite that it's an Apple format, not even installed by default on Windows. Not only that, but not all Mac-based media encoders for QuickTime are even available on Windows. Say what?

While still formats tend to offer a particular encoding option as part of the format itself, QuickTime is simply a container file that can hold arbitrary tracks of video, audio, still files, and more. Any of these tracks can have unique compression, frame rate, encoding, and bit depth. Sometimes, a given video or audio format is not available on a different machine or platform, even when it doesn't involve compression making QuickTime less universal than would ideal.

For example, Uncompressed 10-bit 4:2:2 is a useful Mac-only format; despite that the image is encoded but not compressed, as of this writing, the format cannot be read on a Windows machine; the movie will appear blank if played back.

The type of video encoding used when rendering a QuickTime is specified in Format Options under the Output Module Settings dialog. The dialog box is labeled Compression Settings and the pulldown menu Compression Type, but some choices involve encoding, not compression; the same goes for Audio.

Other moving image formats that seem to be related to QuickTime, such as .MP4 and .M4V, are more like sub-sets of it; they can play back without QuickTime Player installed, but they offer a more limited range of encoding and compression.

▶ Review your shot like the "bad cop," determined that there is something wrong that you cannot initially see, and try not to be hard on yourself when you find it.

▶ Approach your project like a computer programmer, trying to minimize the probability of a careless error (a "bug") invalidating the effort. Compositing and programming are more closely related than you might think; each consists of many logical decisions that hinge upon one another for a successful end result.

When I teach this subject in person, I add reminders of practices like these constantly. If you can do this for yourself, I guarantee beneficial results: a shot that is completed in fewer takes, with more of your own unique artistry in it. And that's what it's all about.

2

The Timeline

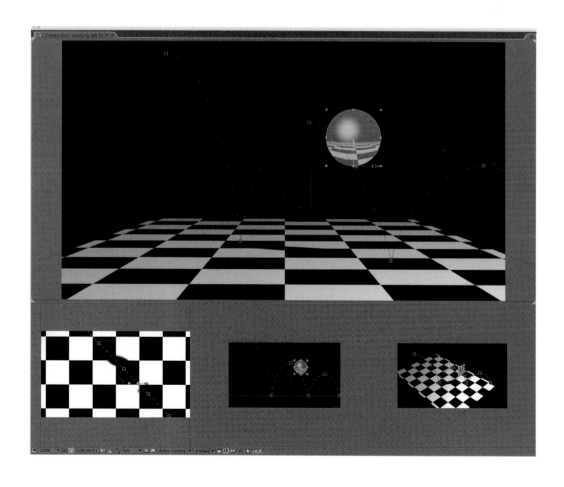

I've been a long time coming, and I'll be a long time gone. You've got your whole life to do something, and that's not very long.

–Ani DiFranco
(American singer, songwriter, and guitarist)

The Timeline

The Timeline is After Effects' killer application. More than any other feature, it extends After Effects unique versatility to a wide range of work. With the Timeline at the center of the compositing process, you can time elements and animations precisely as you control their appearance.

The Timeline panel is also a user-friendly part of the application, albeit one packed with hidden powers. By mastering its usage, you can streamline your workflow a great deal, setting the stage for more advanced work.

One major source of these hidden powers is the Timeline's set of keyboard shortcuts and context menus. These are not extras to be investigated once you're a veteran, but small productivity enhancers that you can learn gradually all the time. They actively build your momentum and confidence as an After Effects artist.

The Timeline makes render order explicit if you know how to view it. 2D layers render beginning with the lowest in the stack and ending with the top, while properties of each layer (visible by twirling down) render in top-to-bottom order. More about this can be found in Chapter 4, "Optimize the Pipeline."

Organization

The Timeline is a dynamic environment; as you work with it, you constantly alter not only its contents, but also your view of the environment itself. Its building blocks are layers organized into columns, and you determine which layers or columns are visible at any given time.

Column Views

You can context-click on any column heading to see and toggle available columns in the Timeline, but there are smarter ways to configure these than toggling all the time.

A minimal setup is shown in **Figure 2.1**. You can then augment or change the setup with the following tools:

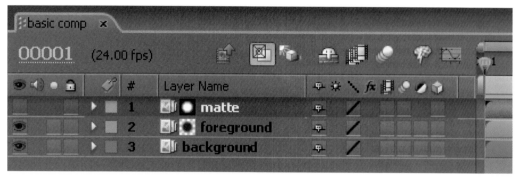

Figure 2.1 This basic column layout works when screen real estate is at a premium. The columns shown are useful virtually all of the time, and most of the rest are only a shortcut away.

▶ **Lower-left icons:** Most (but not quite all) of the extra data you need is available via the three toggles found at the lower left of the Timeline (**Figure 2.2**).

Figure 2.2 These icons at the lower left of the Timeline expand (or collapse) the most used columns: Layer Switches, Transfer Controls, and the various timing controls. The button to the right corresponds to the first two, toggling between them.

▶ **Layer Switches/Transfer Controls:** Save horizontal space (if you need it) using a built-in toggle between the modes represented by the first two lower-left icons. When only one of them is enabled, the F4 key or the Toggle Switches / Modes button which appears below the column will swap them.

▶ **Time Stretch:** The third lower-left icon toggles the timing columns (In, Out, Duration, and Stretch) together. It's easy to forget these even exist, given that layer Duration and In/Out are usually set to the layer bar itself, and Stretch isn't the usual way to retime a layer except in specific instances (detailed in "Manipulate Time," ahead).

TIP

If both Layer Switches and Transfer Controls are displayed, the F4 toggle hides both of them, maximizing horizontal space.

TIP

The general convention to rename an item anywhere in After Effects is to highlight it and press Return, instead of clicking and hovering (as can be done in the operating system).

▶ **Layer/Source:** You can (and often should) give a layer a custom name by selecting it, pressing Return, typing, and deselecting. The column heading switches from Source Name to Layer Name; click it to toggle them. Items in brackets in Layer Name mode still have the Source Name.

▶ **Parent:** On by default with no shortcut, this one is most likely to be visible when it's not needed. Not parenting in this comp? Context-click the column title and choose Hide This from the resulting menu.

▶ **AV Features/Keys:** AV Features are usually too useful to hide, and Keys comes along for free; its controls are embedded beneath AV Features when the layer is twirled down. Unless you are really desperate, leave these alone.

Unless your monitor is huge or you're not doing much keyframing, the game is to preserve horizontal space for keyframe data by keeping only the relevant controls visible.

Comments and Color

TIP

After Effects colors and their names can be edited in Preferences > Label Colors; version CS3 includes 16 unique color labels. Therefore the same label can have a different color on another system. Preferences > Label Defaults assigns specific colors to nine basic item types.

Ever try to make sense of someone else's project? You can make it easier for others—and even yourself—by color-coding layers and compositions, so everyone can see at a glance how comps are organized (**Figure 2.3**). Or, if you're creating a template or other project to hand off to others, or use again in the future, you can append comments to whole layers as well as specific points on the Timeline.

Figure 2.3 Each type of layer has a unique color, making it easy to discern among them.

Colors are assigned to specific types of layers according to Preferences > Label Defaults. Additionally, you may wish to call out special types of layers, such as track mattes and adjustment layers, with specific colors of your own choosing.

Comments are generally the least used column in the Timeline, but they let you offer full contextual explanations of the comp setup, with no character limit (although you may have to twirl down some properties to reveal the scroll bar). However, if the column is not made visible, neither are the comments.

Comments attached to layer markers are visible in the Layer view, where they require no extra space. To add one, highlight a target layer at a specific time and press the * key on the numeric keypad; a layer marker appears at the current time. Double-click it to open the Marker dialog. Add text to the Comment field and if the layer bar is visible, the result appears right on top of it.

Solo, Lock, and Shy

Several toggles on the A/V Features and Switches columns pertain to how layers are edited and viewed (or, in the case of audio, heard) as you work.

The round, white icon (**Figure 2.5**) in A/V Features is the Solo switch. Solo a layer, and you see only it; render a comp with a layer toggled solo, and the Solo Switches menu in Render Settings determines whether it outputs that way. By default, whatever visibility settings you have in the comp, including solo layers, are what render.

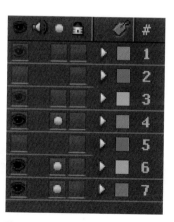

Figure 2.5 Three layers are solo, and the others behave as if deactivated; by default, the comp will also render this way.

NOTES

Included in the Redefinery folder on the book's disc is a script called rd_Commentron.jsx. It takes advantage of the long-text handling ability of the Comments fields in the Timeline and Project panels by duplicating information that is truncated in other fields, such as example, layer, and footage names that exceed 31 characters or other useful information.

TIP

New in After Effects CS3, you can add text to comp markers (Figure 2.4).

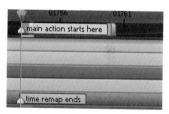

Figure 2.4 Comments can be added to layer or comp markers. In this case the layer marker is aligned to the comp marker, easy to do by holding down the Shift key to snap as you drag.

TIP

To change the visibility (rather than the solo state) of selected layers, use Layer > Switches > Hide Other Video.

TIP

To unlock a number of layers at once, use Layer > Switches > Unlock All Layers (**Ctrl+Shift+L / Cmd+Shift+L**).

NOTES

Shy layers can greatly reduce clutter in the Timeline, but if you ever lose a layer, take a close look at the Index numbers. If any are out of sequence, the missing number belongs to a layer that is now shy.

The Lock toggle is useful in situations when you know a layer is done and should not be touched; a locked layer can't even be selected, let alone edited.

Shy is a more elusive feature; toggle a layer to shy and nothing happens, until you also activate the Shy toggle for the entire composition (**Figure 2.6**). All shy layers disappear from the Timeline, although they still display in the comp itself, as before. This is a great way to keep only the layers you need in front of you.

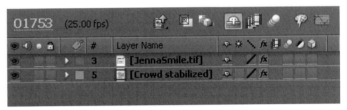

Figure 2.6 Layers 1, 2, and 4 from Figure 2.3 are shy; they still display in the comp viewer if visible, but I've made them invisible in the Timeline to leave only the layers I'm currently editing.

Navigation and Shortcuts

More than anywhere else in After Effects, the Timeline is *the* place where keyboard shortcuts—lots of them—allow you, the expert, to make changes via a single keyboard shortcut or a single click of the mouse, where a beginner might require several mouse clicks, or might not know that a given feature existed at all.

Time Navigation

Many users—particularly editors—learn time navigation shortcuts right away. Others primarily drag the Current Time Indicator, which can quickly become tedious. Here are some useful time navigation shortcuts:

▶ The **Home**, **End**, **Page Up**, and **Page Down** keys correspond to moving to the first or last frame of the composition, one frame backward, and one frame forward, respectively. Laptop users in particular may prefer **Ctrl/Cmd+left and right arrow** as an alternative to **Page Up** and **Page Down**.

▶ **Shift+Page Up** and **Shift+Page Down** skip ten frames backward or forward, respectively.

▶ **Shift+Home** and **Shift+End** navigate to the Work Area In and Out points, which can be set with the **B** and **N** keys, respectively. The **I** and **O** keys navigate to the beginning and end frames of the comp.

▶ Click on the current time status at the upper left of the Timeline to open the Go to Time dialog (press **Alt+Shift+J/Opt+Shift+J**).

▶ To navigate an arbitrary but precise number of frames or seconds (say, 48 frames following the current time), in the Go to Time dialog, replace the current time with your increment in the format +48, click OK, and After Effects calculates the increment for you.

If instead you need to navigate *backward* in time 48 frames, you can't simply enter −48 in the Go to Time dialog. If you do, you're transported to negative 48 (frames or seconds, either of which probably moves the indicator right off the Timeline—very confusing). Instead, you must use the format "+−48" to enter the offset; think of it as adding a negative number, rather than subtracting. It's weird, but it works.

Make Layers Behave

I was reviewing film-outs of shots from *The Day After Tomorrow* with the other artists at The Orphanage when my shot began to loop; it looked out a window at stragglers making their way across a snow-covered plaza and featured a beautiful matte painting by Mike Pangrazio. About two-thirds through the shot came a subtle pop. At some point, the shot had been lengthened, and a layer of noise and dirt I had included at approximately 3% transparency (for the window itself) had remained shorter in a sub-composition.

This is a primary reason some effects artists don't like to work with a timeline-based application; in other compositing programs, such as Shake, this would not inadvertently happen because static elements don't have a length unless you specify one.

NOTES

There's no need to add punctuation when entering time values into a number field in After Effects. 1000 is ten seconds (10:00) in Timecode mode or frame 1000 in Frames mode.

TIP

Go to Time used to have the shortcut Ctrl+Shift+G/Cmd+Shift+G, but Shape layers claimed this one for grouping shapes, so that After Effects would be consistent with other Adobe applications such as Illustrator. Think of the new shortcut (**Alt+Shift+J/Opt+Shift+J**) as "Jump" to help yourself remember it.

TIP

The add-a-negative number offset now operates in most number fields in After Effects (including Composition Settings).

To avoid the gotcha in which a layer ends up too short for its host composition when either is edited, some users prefer to make all of their comps longer (in duration) than they ever expect to need, and manage timing using only the Work Area settings.

The keyboard shortcut **Ctrl+/** **(Cmd+/)** adds selected items as the top layer(s) of the active composition.

To trim a composition's Duration to the current Work Area, choose Composition > Trim Comp to Work Area.

It can be annoying that the Work Area controls both preview and render frame ranges, because the two are often used exclusively of one another. By employing a separate "Render Final" composition that contains the Work Area for the final render, you can mess with your other composition Work Areas as much as you want without affecting the render range.

After Effects CS3 is more fluid and flexible in this respect than previous versions. Static elements such as stills and solids no longer have a fixed beginning or end, so you can always drag to extend them, and by default they extend the full length of the composition. If you lengthen the composition, however, you must still lengthen the layers themselves if you intend them to span the comp.

To add a layer beginning at a specific time, drag the element to the layer area; a second Time Indicator appears that moves with your cursor (horizontally). This determines the layer's start frame. If other layers are present and visible, you can also place it in layer order.

Here are some other useful tips and shortcuts:

▶ Navigate to the previous or next keyframe (or layer marker) by pressing **J** and **K**, respectively. This works for any visible keyframe or layer marker.

▶ To reset the Work Area to the length of the composition, double-click it; to set it to the exact length of the currently active layer, press **Ctrl+Alt+B**/**Cmd+Option+B**.

▶ Besides clicking on a layer to select it, you can enter the layer's index number using the numeric keypad.

▶ To select an adjacent layer without touching the mouse, use **Ctrl+Up Arrow** (**Cmd+Up Arrow**) to select the next layer up, and **Down Arrow** to select the next layer down.

▶ Add the **Alt** (**Option**) key to move a layer up or down in the stack, which you can also do with **Ctrl+]** and **Ctrl+[** (as in other Adobe applications). **Ctrl+Shift+]** moves a layer to the top of the stack and **Ctrl+Shift+[** moves it to the bottom.

▶ You can invert the layers currently selected: Context-click on a selected layer, and choose Invert Selection. (Locked layers are not selected, but Shy layers are selected even if invisible.)

▶ Duplicate any layer (or virtually any selected item) using **Ctrl+D** (**Cmd+D**). If you duplicate a layer and its track matte (Chapter 3, "Selections: The Key to Compositing"), they remain paired in layer order, above the source layers.

► For various reasons you might instead wish to split a layer (**Ctrl+Shift+D/Cmd+Shift+D**); the source ends and the duplicate continues from the current time. This is useful, for example, when you need one layer to straddle another in 2D order.

► To move a layer In point to the current time, use the [key, or press] to move the Out point. Add the **Alt** (**Option**) key to *set the current frame* as the In or Out point, trimming the layer.

► To slide a trimmed layer, preserving the In and Out points but translating the footage and its layer markers (but *not* keyframes), drag using the double-ended arrow you see over the area outside the In and Out points; it is visible when the layer has already been trimmed, making an edit handle available.

► To nudge a layer forward or backward in time (including its keyframes) use **Alt+Page Up/Page Down** (**Option+Page Up/Page Down**; hold **Option/Alt** with **Home** and **End** to move the layer's In point to the beginning of the comp, or the Out point to the end).

Often, you may add elements whose size or pixel aspect doesn't match those of the composition, yet which are meant to fill the frame (or one axis). No need to break open the Scale controls and guess; you can use the Fit to Comp shortcuts (which are included in the Layer > Transform menu).

The standard Fit to Comp, **Ctrl+Alt+F** (**Cmd+Option+F**) can be dangerous in that it ignores the aspect ratio of the layer, stretching X and Y scale individually to match each to the comp itself.

More commonly useful are the shortcuts for Fit to Comp on a single axis (X or Y), which retain the aspect ratio to scale the non-dominant axis. You can Fit to Comp Width (**Ctrl+Alt+Shift+H/Cmd+Option+Shift+H**), or Fit to Comp Height (twisting your fingers around **Ctrl+Alt+Shift+G/Cmd+Option+Shift+G**).

NOTES

There is even a preference controlling whether split layers are created above or below the source layer (Preferences > General; the toggle is labeled Create Split Layers Above Original Layer).

TIP

Double-click a keyframe and some rather cool hidden options present themselves for positioning and scaling relative to the comp (Figure 2.7).

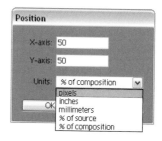

Figure 2.7 Need to position that layer relative to the composition, or to its source size? Double-click the keyframe and make use of this dialog; it's useful for other types of keyframes as well.

Timeline View Options

After Effects offers some useful workflow enhancements to help you work with keyframe data. These will help you work with timing more quickly, accurately and confidently.

▶ The **;** key toggles between a fully zoomed-in view of the current frame and a fully zoomed-out view of the whole Timeline.

▶ The slider at the bottom of the Timeline zooms in and out more selectively (**Figure 2.8**).

▶ If your mouse includes a scroll wheel, there's a cooler option: Not only can you scroll up and down the layer stack and Shift-scroll left and right in a zoomed Timeline view, but Alt-scrolling (Option-scrolling) dynamically zooms you in and out of time. Shift-scrolling navigates back and forth. Position your cursor over the Timeline panel to try these.

At the right edge of the Timeline is the Comp button (**Figure 2.9a**), which brings forward the Composition view associated with that Timeline. The Composition panel has a corresponding Timeline button (**Figure 2.9b**). Neither of these is strictly necessary, however; if you need to make either panel appear, or toggle between the two of them, use the backslash (\) key.

Figure 2.8 Absent a mouse scroll wheel, this click-and-drag interface at the bottom of the Timeline panel is probably the fastest method of zooming in and out.

TIP

The scroll wheel also zooms in and out of viewer panels when the cursor is placed over them, no modifier or selection needed.

TIP

The Current Time Indicator is capable of going where your Timeline panel cannot: to time frames previous to the first frame of the composition or beyond the last frame (usually because the trimmed area of a layer extends there). In such cases, the indicator disappears from the Timeline entirely. Have no fear. Clicking in the Time Ruler to place the indicator or using any of the time shortcuts outlined above recovers it.

Figure 2.9 Need to locate the Timeline related to the displayed composition, or vice versa? The shortcut for each is here, or simply use the \ on your keyboard. Also in this group is the Comp marker bin; drag comp markers from here.

Just above the Comp button is the Comp marker bin, where you can drag out a marker to a point on your Timeline. Markers are numbered sequentially, but new in CS3, you can double-click them to add names instead.

Replace a Layer or Composition

You can easily replace the source of a layer with an alternate take or a different element in the Project panel, keeping all of its settings and keyframes. Highlight the layer to be replaced in the Timeline and hold down the Alt (Option) key while dragging the new source to the Timeline. Or even easier, select both the existing layer and the new source and then press **Ctrl+Alt+/ (Cmd+Option+/)**.

You can even Alt/Option-drag one composition over another in the Project panel to replace its usage throughout the project.

Animation Methods

Twirl down any layer in the Timeline, and the Transform controls are revealed. Transforms are spatial data related to Position, Anchor Point, Scale, Rotation, and, um, Opacity. Opacity isn't really spatial transform data, but it's essential enough to be included with the spatial data.

▶ The keyboard shortcuts to reveal individual transforms are the first letter of each type: **P**, **A**, **S**, **R**, and, um, **T**—Opacity is the oddball again, because O is already in use as the Out point of a layer (mentioned above). Think of Opaci-"T."

▶ To reveal additional properties, hold down **Shift** when typing the letter shortcut; you can also toggle a property to hide in this manner.

A *property* in After Effects is a data channel under a twirled-down layer. Typically a property can be animated and has a stopwatch icon beside it which, when clicked, sets a keyframe at the current time.

TIP

Hold down the Shift key as you drag the Current Time Indicator to snap current time to comp or layer markers or visible keyframes.

TIP

To add a specific numbered comp marker, press Shift and one of the numbers at the top of your keyboard (not the numeric keypad): 1 through 0.

NOTES

Beware when replacing with source material of a different size or aspect; mask values are relative and scale to the dimensions of the new layer, but other values (transforms and effects settings) are absolute and, generally speaking, do not.

That by itself is simple enough. But there are, in fact, many different ways to animate a property in After Effects (**Figure 2.10**).

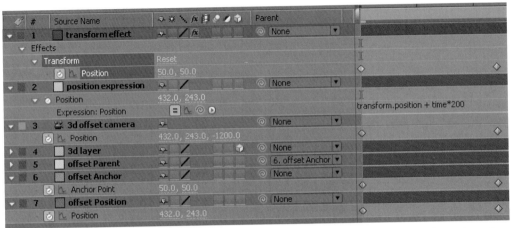

Figure 2.10 Each layer moves 200 pixels along the X axis over 24 frames; look carefully and you can see that each employs a unique method.

Suppose you wanted to move a layer 200 pixels along the X axis over 24 frames. After setting the first keyframe and moving the time indicator forward 24 frames, you could

▶ Drag the layer to the new position in the Composition viewer (holding the Shift key to constrain it to one axis)

▶ **Shift+Right Arrow** 20 times to move the layer exactly 200 pixels

▶ Enter the new value in the Timeline by highlighting the X Position numerical value and typing in the new number

▶ Drag the X Position numerical value to the right until it is 200 pixels higher (perhaps holding Shift to increment by ten pixels)

▶ Enter a numerical offset by highlighting the X Position numerical value and typing +200 (as was done with time, above)

▶ Copy and paste the Position keyframe from another layer, or another point in time (assuming one exists)

And those are just the options to keyframe-animate that one property. You could also create the same animation without keyframing Position values, by

▶ Keyframing the anchor point in the opposite direction (negative 200 pixel X value) over 24 frames

▶ Enabling 3D for the layer, adding a 50mm camera, and animating the camera moving 200 pixels, again in the negative X direction

▶ Parenting the layer to another layer with the transform animation

▶ Replacing the layer with a nested composition that already contains the layer and transform

▶ Assigning an expression to the Position channel that performs the animation without keyframes

If that's not crazy enough, you could even

▶ Apply the Transform effect to the layer and animate the effect's Position value

▶ Animate in real time via the cursor using Motion Sketch (I did say "crazy")

▶ Paste in a path (perhaps using a Mask or a Path from Photoshop or Illustrator) to the Position channel, adjusting timing as needed (this method defaults to creating a two-second animation)—again, crazy, but possible

Some of these options are clearly designed for other specific and most likely, more complex situations, such as parenting (under "Parent Hierarchy" later in this chapter) and expressions (Chapter 10).

Note that there is even a variety of ways to enter values while animating. You can

▶ Drag with the Selection tool (shortcut: **V**)

▶ Drag the Pan Behind tool to move the anchor point (shortcut: **Y**)

▶ Drag the Rotate tool (shortcut: **W**, which the documentation even points out is for "wotate")

You can also work directly with these values in the Timeline, whether by highlighting and entering values, or simply by dragging the value without highlighting. Try it.

Don't worry, you won't be tested on these. This list is here to spark your imagination and perhaps provide animation ideas you hadn't considered.

The Transform effect allows you to specify when transforms occur relative to effects. Normal transforms occur before effects, but this plug-in lets you interleave them with effects without precomping.

TIP

When dragging text in the Timeline or Effect Controls, hold down Shift to increment values at ten times the normal amount, or hold down **Ctrl+Alt (Cmd+Option)** to increment at one tenth the standard increment (usually a whole integer value, but this depends on the slider range, which you can edit; context-click the value in Effect Controls and choose Edit Value to adjust it).

Keyframes and the Graph Editor

The purpose of the Graph Editor is to give you maximum control over fine-tuning a keyframe animation, whether it consists of one animated property or several. If you're adjusting one property, you can take complete control of its animation; if several, you get a thorough comparison of timings.

Make Use of the Graph Editor

The simplest way to get started with the Graph Editor is to examine a sample project and to try messing around with it. To demonstrate the many features of this tool set, 02_graphEditor.aep in the accompanying disc's Chapter02 directory contains a simple animation, "bouncing ball 2d." A ball bounces across the frame, with a little bit of squash and stretch animation occurring from where it hits the bottom of the boundary

To enable the Graph Editor, click its icon in the Timeline (**Figure 2.11**).

Figure 2.11 This icon activates the Graph Editor.

A grid appears in the area previously occupied by the layer bars. At the bottom of this grid are the Graph Editor controls, labeled in **Figure 2.12**.

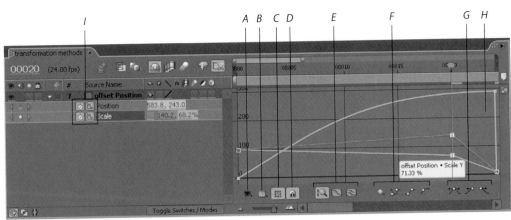

Figure 2.12 Components of the Graph Editor: (A) Show Properties, (B) Graph Options, (C) Show Transform Box, (D) Snap, (E) Zoom controls, (F) Keyframe controls, (G) Ease controls, (H) properties graphs, and (I) Graph Editor Set toggles.

Show Properties

By default, if nothing is selected, nothing displays; what you see depends on the settings in the Show Properties menu (the eye icon lower left). Three toggles in this menu control how animation curves are displayed:

▶ Show Selected Properties displays animation data only for selected properties

▶ Show Animated Properties displays all animated properties in a selected layer, whether they are selected or not

▶ Show Graph Editor Set displays properties whose Graph Editor Set toggle (next to the stopwatch and labeled I in Figure 2.12) is enabled

You may already have your own preference, but I consider Graph Editor Set to be the most versatile option. By specifying what properties you want to see, you ensure that only they are displayed, and you can freely mix and match selections from various layers without having to keep everything carefully selected.

TIP

It's easy to turn on Show Selected Properties and disable the other two, but the opposite configuration (disabling that Show Selected Properties and turning on the others), is a more powerful (less annoying) way to work because properties don't inadvertently appear and disappear as you work.

Graph Options

The real power of the Graph Editor has to do with how data is displayed, and there are options for displaying data that even advanced users miss. The Graph Options menu (labeled B in Figure 2.12) controls which components of the properties are displayed. For example, display only the Position data for ball and you might see something like the keyframe data in **Figure 2.13**.

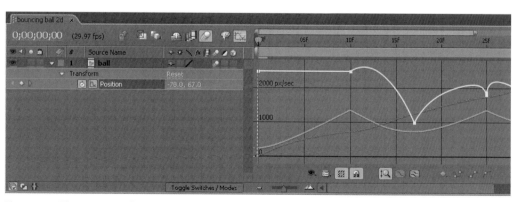

Figure 2.13 The 2D version of the bouncing ball animation is shown with the Speed graph active and the Value graph shown as a Reference graph.

Auto Select Graph Type selects Speed graphs for spatial properties and Value graphs for all others.

The Separate XYZ Position preset (in Animation Presets, in the Effects & Presets panel) uses expressions to set up separate spatial channels that can be timed independently of one another. This, however, can make life more complicated because it contains its own spatial properties which link to Position, and you must animate those to get the benefit.

Enable Show Reference Graph in the Graph Options and the actual spatial animation is displayed as curves, even though you normally edit motion paths in the viewer, and the Speed graph (the rate at which the layer animates) in the Graph Editor. For a bouncing ball animation, both contain vital information; as you edit speed to speed the ball toward the ground and slow it down in midair, you can move your cursor over the Value graph to see exactly where the ball is at a particular frame.

Switch to Edit Value Graph and you can actually grab a vertex belonging to a given axis and change its value. What you cannot do is offset it in time from the other axes; any temporal changes you make to a keyframe on X are also made to Y and Z.

The main use of the Reference graph is to get a property value at a specific time, which you can do by moving the cursor over the curve or simply by checking the Reference graph values displayed in gray at the right end of the Graph Editor (while values of the active graph are displayed left). If this is too much information at any point, toggle the Reference graph off (**Figure 2.14**).

Figure 2.14 A Reference graph as in Figure 2.13 can be overkill, cluttering the view if more than one property is active. The Speed graph shows rates of transition; in this case, each bounce of the ball is an abrupt shift in speed.

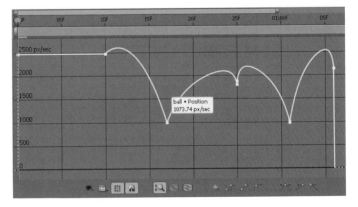

Show Graph Tool Tips is worth leaving on most of the time; values are displayed for any curve under the mouse, whether or not a keyframe occurs at that point in time.

At the bottom of the Graph Options menu is the Allow Keyframes Between Frames toggle. With this off, keyframes that you drag snap to precise frame values (as you would expect); turn it on and you can drag a keyframe to any point in time, should you need a keyframe to occur between frames. For example, you might want the moment when the ball hits not to be visible to match timing from a live shot. When you scale a set of keyframes using the

Transform Box, keyframes will often fall in between frames whether or not this option is enabled.

The Transform Box

The Transform Box lets you edit keyframe values in all kinds of wacky ways. Toggle on Show Transform Box and select more than one keyframe, and a white box with vertices surrounds the selected frames. Drag the handle at the right side left or right to speed or slow the entire animation, respectively, while the relative timing remains the same. Just as with mask transforms—covered in Chapter 3—dragging inside the box translates a set of keyframes, dragging the corners scales values. Additionally

▶ To offset the center of the Transform Box and thus the scale pivot, first drag the anchor to the desired pivot point, then (this is the important extra point) Ctrl-drag/Cmd-drag.

▶ To reverse keyframes, drag left/right beyond the opposite edge of the box (or simply context-click and choose Keyframe Assistant > Time-Reverse Keyframes).

▶ To scale the box proportionally, Shift-drag on a corner. To taper values at one end, Ctrl+Alt-drag (Cmd+ Option-drag) on a corner (**Figure 2.15**). To move one side of the box up or down, Ctrl+Alt+ Shift-drag (Cmd+Option+Shift-drag) on a corner. You can even skew the contents of the box by Alt-dragging (Option-dragging) on a corner handle.

NOTES

Take note of the second set of "Show" options – layer In/Out points, audio waveforms, layer markers and expressions, all features of the Layer view (most of them described in this chapter) can also be displayed in the Graph Editor to help avoid excessive toggling.

NOTES

The Snap button causes any keyframe you drag to snap to virtually any other visible marker in the Graph Editor, but it does not snap to whole frame values with Allow Keyframes Between Frames enabled.

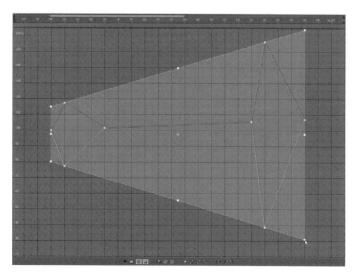

Figure 2.15 The Transform Box makes it possible to scale values proportionally. By Ctrl+Alt-dragging (Cmd+Option-dragging) on a corner, you can taper or expand values at one end of the selection area.

Flips and Flops

After Effects includes a Flop, as well as a Flip and a Flip + Flop in Animation Presets > Image – Utilities (search on any of these in the Effects & Presets panel). To "flop" a shot means to invert it horizontally, on the Y axis (a "flip" occurs on the X axis). The preset employs the Transform effect, which unfortunately is not compatible with 32 bpc mode; you can instead toggle Constrain Proportions for Scale and add a minus sign beside the X value (Figure 2.16).

Spatial interpretations, however, do not default to linear unless you enable Default Spatial Interpretation to Linear in Preferences > General. By default, a Bézier shape eases spatial transitions.

Mac users beware: The F9 key is used by the system for the Exposé feature, revealing all open panels in all applications. You can change or disable this feature in System Preferences > Dashboard & Exposé.

Figure 2.16 To flop a shot, be sure to uncheck Constrain Proportions before setting the X value to –100%.

Temporal Data and Eases

By default, After Effects offers linear temporal transitions between keyframes; a property proceeds from keyframe A to keyframe B at a steady rate, then from keyframe B to keyframe C at a separate but still steady rate, with an abrupt change of pace.

Experienced animators, anthropologists and economists alike recognize how rarely anything in nature proceeds in a linear fashion; natural motion is mostly arcs and curves. Think of a camera push: with a real camera operator moving that camera, a push starts and stops gently due to inertia and the human body, gradually moving at a more or less steady rate only at the middle of the transition. Thus the Easy Ease feature is your friend.

Easy Ease

Part of After Effects since around the time rapper Easy E was laid to rest (coincidence? Only a handful of guys named Dave know the truth), Easy Ease keyframe assistants ease transitions as follows:

▶ Context-click a keyframe and choose one of the Easy Ease options under the Keyframe Assistant submenu.

▶ Use keyboard shortcuts: **F9** applies Bézier interpolation, creating eases in and out of a keyframe, while **Shift+F9** creates an ease into the keyframe only, and **Ctrl+Shift+F9** (**Cmd+Shift+F9**) creates an ease out, maintaining a linear transition in.

▶ Click one of the Easy Ease buttons at the lower right of the Graph Editor (the ones that depict s-curved graph lines leading in and out of vertices).

For a camera push, you might add eases to the first and final frames, perhaps also adding intermediate keyframes with eases (disrupting the move to make it feel even more human and organic).

Figures 2.17a and **b** show the difference between a default linear camera push and one to which eases have been applied. The keyframes change from linear to Bézier type, and rate of motion is described by a curve instead of a straight line.

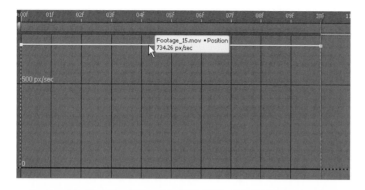

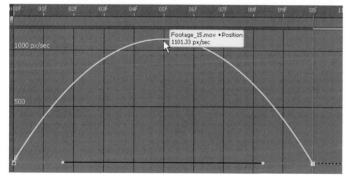

Figures 2.17a and b With no eases, the Speed graph for Position is flat, moving at a steady rate (a). Add eases (b), and it arcs from 0 (at the beginning and end of the move) to a higher value at the center peak of the ease.

You can (and often should) freely customize an ease using the Graph Editor. Select any keyframe and yellow Bézier handles extend to its left and right. To increase an ease, drag the yellow handle away from the keyframe; or inward toward the keyframe to reduce it. You don't even need Easy Ease.

NOTES

Hold keyframes solve problems any time you see unwanted in-between information creep into an animation; beware of this particularly with spatial animations, which can drift or even loop without holds.

Holds

A Hold keyframe prevents any change to a value until the next keyframe. Set it as follows:

▶ Context-click on the keyframe and choose Toggle Hold Keyframe.

▶ Use the shortcut **Ctrl+Alt+H (Cmd+Shift+H)**.

▶ Choose the Hold button below the Graph Editor (the one with the graph lines all at right angles).

In Layer Bar mode a hold is indicated by the square appearance on one or both sides of the keyframe. In the Graph Editor it appears as a flat horizontal line to the right of a keyframe.

To reposition a layer over time with no in-betweening whatsoever, begin by setting the first frame as a Hold keyframe; all keyframes that follow it in time will be Hold keyframes, signaled by their completely square appearance in layer bar mode or a series of right angles in the Graph Editor (**Figures 2.18a** and **b**). The result is that the property transitions instantly to the next held value, so for example, if you want to animate a layer's visibility on and off, set Opacity with Hold keyframes to 0% and 100%.

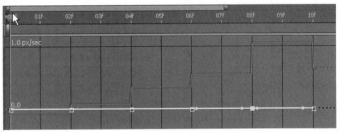

Figures 2.18a and b A series of Bézier keyframes have been converted to Hold keyframes, evident by the square shape at the right of each keyframe in the Layer Bar view (a) and right angles in the Graph Editor (b).

Spatial Data and Curves

When you are called upon to create a complex animation, the After Effects interface is up to it. I can't teach you to be a great animator, but I can focus on what you need to know to keyframe effectively and to avoid common pitfalls.

A closer look at the simple bouncing ball reveals a lot about animating spatial and temporal keyframes data (**Figures 2.19** to **2.22**). If this is new material and you are willing, try re-creating it yourself, as it reveals most of the fundamentals of expressing motion with keyframe animation.

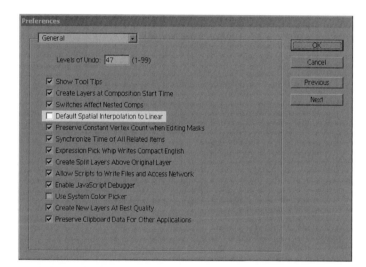

Figure 2.19a and b Under Preferences > General (**Ctrl+Alt+;** or **Cmd+Option+;**), Default Spatial Interpolation to Linear is off by default (a), producing this result (b) with three or more position keys.

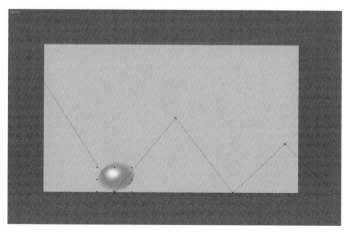

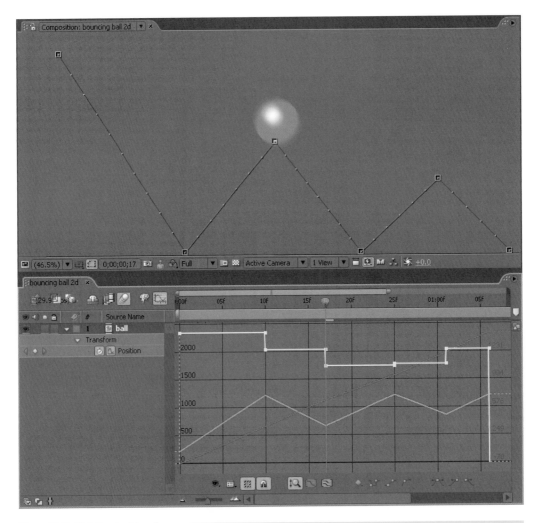

Figure 2.20 Click the check box for Default Spatial Interpolation to Linear, restart After Effects for the preference to take effect, and the result is three keyframes that are linear in both time and position.

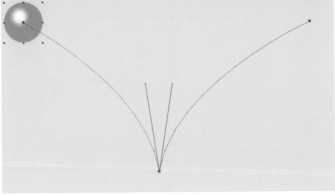

Figure 2.21 Hold down the Ctrl/Cmd key while clicking a spatial keyframe to activate its Bézier handles, then Ctrl/Cmd-click on one of the handles to "break" them. This enables you to form the V-shaped bounce shown here.

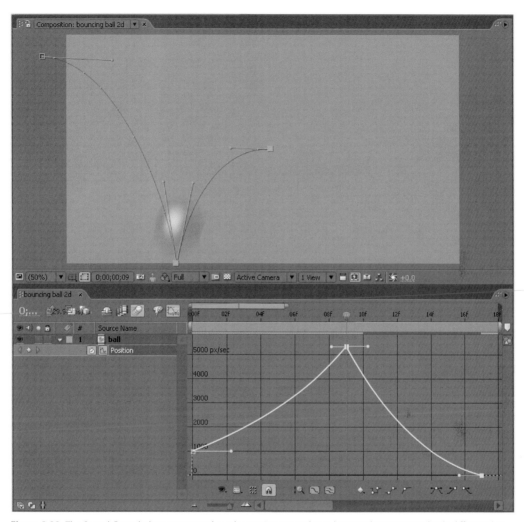

Figure 2.22 The Speed Curve below corresponds to the motion curve above, but it is showing completely different data and could have a very different shape without changing the motion. An ease has been applied to the final frame with the **F9** key; eases reduce speed to 0. The middle frame has the most abrupt shift of motion, for the bounce—it's the opposite of an ease.

In the (possibly likely) case that the need for a bouncing ball animation never comes up, what does this example show you? Let's recap:

▶ You can control a motion path in the Composition viewer, using Bézier tools and the Pen tool (described in detail in the next chapter).

▶ Realistic motion often requires that you shape the motion path Béziers and add temporal eases; the two actions are performed independently on any given keyframe, and in two different places (in the viewer and Timeline).

Animation can get a little trickier in 3D, but the same basic rules apply (see Chapter 9, "The Camera and Optics," for more).

Figure 2.23 The middle keyframe is set to rove and thus is now positioned in between frames; the arc of its motion is now even in and out of the keyframe.

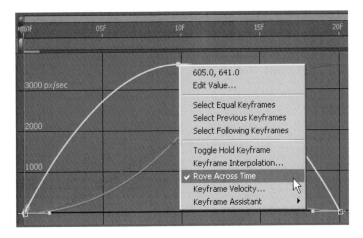

Three preset keyframe transition types are available, each with a shortcut at the bottom of the Graph Editor: Hold, Linear, and Automatic Bezier. Adjust the handles or apply Easy Ease and the preset becomes a custom Bezier Shape.

Copy and Paste Animations

There's more to copying and pasting keyframe data than you might think. If you ever want to see exactly how it is organized, try copying a set of keyframes and pasting the data into an Excel spreadsheet. This is also a great way to reformat keyframe data copied from other applications such as Shake or Maya.

CLOSE-UP

Roving Keyframes

Sometimes an animation must follow an exact path, hitting precise points, but progress steadily, with no variation in the rate of travel. This is the situation for which Roving keyframes were devised. Figure 2.23 shows a before and after view of the application of a roving keyframe to the animation in Figure 2.22; the path of the animation is identical, but the keyframes are now evenly spaced.

Copy keyframes from a particular property, then paste them with another layer selected, and they are automatically pasted to that layer's corresponding property, but always beginning at the current time; thus it's easy to relocate keyframes to another point in time, whether or not that's your intention.

If that target property doesn't exist, because it's part of an effect applied only to the source layer, After Effects adds the effect as well as the keyframes, just as you might expect.

Copy keyframes from a particular property and select a property with similar parameters; the animation data transfers to the new property, often very useful as long as you know it's happening. For example, apply a 2D Position keyframe to the Flare Center position of a Lens Flare effect by selecting the Flare Center property in the Timeline prior to pasting and the keyframes go to that property instead of Position.

That all means that you should pay attention to which item is currently selected when copying or pasting. **Figure 2.24** shows how easy it can be to miss that the Effect Controls panel is forward and has an effect highlighted, so that effect is copied, not the entire layer.

TIP

Enable a small lock icon that appears on the Effect Controls tab, and that effect remains visible even when you select a different layer. (This toggle also resides on the Composition and Layer tabs; its full use is described in Chapter 4.)

Figure 2.24 It's possible to have a different item selected in each panel, yet only one is the active item. If you were to press Delete in this case, the effect would be deleted because the Effect Controls panel is active.

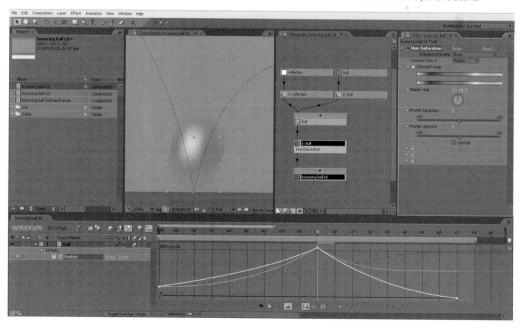

TIP

Ctrl/Cmd-click on a keyframe to reset its Temporal Interpretation to linear. Alt+Ctrl+K/Opt+Cmd+K opens the Keyframe Interpolation dialog where you can choose any Temporal or Spatial interpolation, or set a keyframe to rove.

If the result of a copy and paste ever seems strange, just undo and try again, carefully selecting exactly the thing you want to copy.

Layer vs. Graph

To summarize the distinction between Layer and Graph Editor views, in Layer view you can

▶ Block in keyframes with respect to the overall composition

▶ Establish broad timing (where Linear, Easy Ease, and Auto-Bezier keyframes are sufficient)

The Graph Editor is essential to

▶ Refine an individual animation curve

▶ Compare spatial and temporal data

▶ Scale animation data, especially around a specific pivot point

▶ Perform extremely specific timing (for example, a keyframe is needed between frames)

▶ Adjust keyframe values not at the current time (difficult in the layer view)

With either view you can

▶ Edit expressions

▶ Change keyframe type (Linear, Hold, Ease in, and so on)

▶ Make editorial/compositing decisions regarding layers (start/stop/duration, split layers, order—possible in both, easier in Layer view)

By no means, then, does the Graph Editor obviate use of the Layer view, where the majority of compositing and simple animation is typically accomplished.

Über-duper

More than anything, knowing shortcuts makes you a rapid-fire animator. This section is not only about the überkey, which is among the most useful shortcuts in all of After Effects, but also about taking control of keyframe data in general.

The überkey is available in two delicious flavors: **U** and **UU**. In the same 02_graphEditor.aep project, highlight the ball layer, and press a single **U**. All properties with keyframes (Position and Scale in this case) are revealed. Press **U** again to toggle, and they are concealed. When arriving cold at an animation you've never seen, or returning to one of your own, this is how you immediately find out where the keyframes are.

But wait, there's more. Now highlight the bg layer, which contains no keyframes whatsoever, and press **UU** (two Us in quick succession). All of the properties set to any value other than their default—including those with keyframes (none in this case)—are revealed.

The **U** shortcut is a quick way to find keyframes to edit or to locate a keyframe that you suspect is hiding somewhere. But **UU**—now *that* is a full-on problem-solving tool all to itself. It allows you to quickly investigate what has been edited on a given layer, is helpful when troubleshooting your own layer settings, and is nearly priceless when investigating an unfamiliar project. Highlight all of the layers in your comp, press **UU**, and you have before you all of the edits that have been made to all of the layer properties.

Dissect a Project

If you've been handed an unfamiliar project and need to make sense of it quickly, there are a couple of other tools to help you.

The Flowchart view offers a broad overview of the project's structure; it is enabled with the right-most button along the bottom of the Composition panel, via Window > Flowchart or using **Ctrl+F11**/**Cmd+F11**. You have to see it to believe it:

NOTES

The "überkey" plays of off Friedrich Nietzsche's übermensch—a man more powerful and important than others. It's one shortcut to rule them all.

TIP

To reveal only applied effects on a selected layer, use the E key. Or, if the überkey reveals effects and transforms and you want only the transforms, Shift+E toggles off revealed effects.

NOTES

What, if anything, is beyond the reach of the UU shortcut when analyzing a comp?

▶ Contents of nested compositions, which must be opened (Alt/Option-double-click) and analyzed individually

▶ Locked layers

▶ Shy layers remain hidden if the Shy toggle is on

▶ Settings not related to properties, such as Blending Modes and Motion Blur a nodal interface in After Effects (**Figure 2.25**), perhaps the least nodal of any of the major compositing applications.

Figure 2.25 Although After Effects is a layer-based application, the underlying logic of compositing and the flow of images and effects is clearly displayed in Flowchart. Interaction here is limited—there is no way to change the pipeline order or add nodes directly.

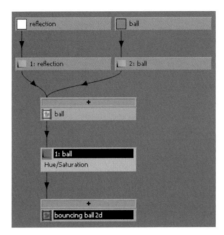

CLOSE-UP

Nerd-based Compositing

How exactly is the node view in After Effects more limited than what you'd find in a node-based compositor? Essentially, you can't make creative decisions there; it's useful for project analysis only, offering some insight into the order in which items render. It's also less "atomic": Properties and effects are grouped directly with layers instead of being listed as their own nodes, because their render order cannot be freely reconfigured as it can with nodes.

NOTES

In the panel menu you can choose your view; Left to Right fits well on a typical monitor. Whether you choose straight or curved connecting lines is up to you, but you can clean up the view by clicking this toggle holding the Alt/Option key.

This view shows how objects (layers, compositions, and effects) are used, and in what relationship to one another. The + button above a composition reveals its components; for the cleanest view, toggle layers and effects off at the lower left.

To investigate a project, start with the end composition and work your way backward; open any comp by double-clicking it in the Flowchart. Turn off the Shy toggle at the top if it's on, highlight all of the layers (**Ctrl+A/Cmd+A**), and press **UU** to reveal all altered properties. Now preview the composition, stopping at any frame where you have questions and investigating which settings and animations apply to that point in time. If you find a nested composition, open it (Alt/Option-double-click) and investigate. With some patience, you can make sense of even the most complicated project, one step at a time.

Keyframe Navigation and Selection

Although no shortcut can hold a candle to the überkey, there are several other useful Timeline shortcuts:

▶ **J** and **K** keys navigate backward and forward, respectively, through all visible keyframes (and layer markers, and Work Area boundaries).

- To select all keyframes for a property, highlight that property's name in the Timeline. To delete any keyframes not visible in the Timeline (those occurring before or after the comp), select all, then Shift-drag a rectangular selection around the ones you want to keep (the visible ones). Now delete.

- Context-click on a keyframe to Select Previous Keyframes or Select Following Keyframes. There is even an option to Select Equal Keyframes (those with an identical value).

- **Alt/Option+Shift+**the shortcut corresponding to a transform property (**P**, **A**, **S**, **R**, or **T**) sets the first keyframe, no need to click anywhere.

- Any stopwatch in the Effect Controls sets the first keyframe for an effect property at the current frame. However, if keyframes are already set, clicking the stopwatch deletes them.

- To add a keyframe without changing any value, context-click on the stopwatch in Effect Controls and choose Add Keyframe.

Read on; you are not a keyframe Jedi—yet.

Keyframe Offsets

To offset the values of multiple keyframes by the same amount in Layer view, select them all, *make certain that the Current Time Indicator is resting on a frame with one of the selected keyframes*, and drag text to offset. If instead, you edit one of these by typing in a new value, all keyframes will be set to that value—not, in most cases, what you want. The Graph Editor makes it easier to see what's happening.

Other tips for working with multiple keyframes include

- Nudge selected keyframes (one or many) forward or backward in time using **Alt+Right/Left Arrow** (**Option+Right/Left Arrow**), respectively.

- Deselect keyframes only using **Shift+F2**. Select all visible keyframes (without selecting their layers) using **Ctrl+Alt+A** (**Cmd+Option+A**).

TIP

J and K hit all revealed keyframes, so to navigate one property only, click the arrows that appear under A/V Features (the Keys column). Or reveal only the keyframes in that channel; J and K will ignore the rest.

NOTES

Multi-selection works differently with keyframes in the Layer Bar view than anywhere else in the application. To add or subtract a single frame from a selected group, Shift-click. Ctrl/Cmd-clicking on keyframes converts them to Auto-Bezier mode. This is not the case in the Graph Editor view.

TIP

Ctrl+Alt+A/Cmd+Option+A selects all visible keyframes while leaving the source layers, making it easy to delete them when, say, duplicating a layer but changing its animation.

TIP

The transform box in the Graph Editor offers an easy method for scaling keyframes temporally, but in Layer view you can instead select a set of keyframes, Alt-drag (Option-drag) on a keyframe at either end of the set, and the entire set is scaled proportionally in time (with the opposite end of the selected set acting as the stationary anchor).

TIP

Edit anchor points or set up a parent-child relationship *before* animating, if at all possible, to avoid offsetting keyframes and messing up the whole animation.

TIP

To adjust an anchor point or undo parenting without the automatic compensation from the application, hold down the Alt (Option) key as you make the change.

Spatial Offsets

The two most common ways to offset a transform animation—to edit its position, rotation, or scale from a point other than its center—are intuitive, easy to use, and well documented. In an individual layer, move the anchor point from the center to a specific point in the frame, typically using the Pan Behind tool (keyboard shortcut: **Y**). Details are in the "Anchor Point" section.

Alternatively, you can center several layers around the center point of a single layer by parenting them to that layer. The children take on all of the transforms of the parent layer (except Opacity, which, remember, isn't a real transform) plus whatever offsets they already have.

After Effects is generally designed to preserve the appearance of the composition when you are merely setting up animation, toggling 3D on, and so forth. Therefore editing an anchor point position with the Pan Behind tool triggers the inverse offset to the Position property. Parent a layer to another layer and the child layer maintains its position until you further animate either of them.

That's all clear enough. But reset an offset anchor point in the middle of a Position animation, and the Position keyframe at that point in time changes. Or undo parenting at a frame other than the one where you set it, and its Position value changes so that it appears to remain in the same place. I have used this to my advantage for 3D setup; I start with the camera at or near its default, toggle the layer to 3D and parent it to the camera, move the camera to some crazy faraway position where the layer is to appear and un-parent the layer.

Anchor Point

The most straightforward method to edit an anchor point in the Composition panel is to use the Pan Behind tool (**Y**); doing so offsets Position to maintain current appearance. For a similar result, you can edit anchor point values in the Timeline, but Position data is unaffected.

It can be difficult to edit animated anchor point data in the Composition viewer. Instead, activate the Layer viewer and change the View pull-down menu from Masks to Anchor Point Path (**Figure 2.26**).

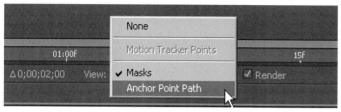

Figure 2.26 Masks, not Anchor Point Path, is the default Layer display mode. Change it as needed using this menu at the bottom of the Layer panel. Note that the bouncing ball examples included in 02_graphEditor.aep feature an offset (but not animated) anchor point, allowing squash and stretch animation to occur around the point of contact (at the base of the ball).

NOTES

The 02_graphEditor.aep project used for the bouncing ball animation earlier in this chapter includes an anchor point offset to the base of the ball; this allows the scaling involved for squash and stretch in the bounce to occur around the point of contact.

Parent Hierarchy

A parent-child relationship is set up by choosing the target parent layer from the child's pull-down menu in the Parent column of the Timeline, or by dragging the pickwhip adjacent to that menu to the target parent layer.

Parenting "sticks" even when you change layer order or duplicate or rename the parent. You can select all of the children of a parent layer by context-clicking it and choosing Select Children. To remove parenting from all selected layers, choose None from the pull-down menu of any one of them.

To move layers relative to a point that is not represented in any current layer, you can add a null object (for the shortcut, go to Layer > New > Null Object). Null objects are actually 100 x 100 pixel layers that do not render. They possess all of the normal transform controls and can contain effects (and Masks for that matter, which are completely useless in null objects). Contained effects can be used by expressions as reference for other settings; more on this in Chapter 10, "Expressions."

NOTES

If you've ever worked with 3D animation, you are probably already aware how usefully parenting solves all kinds of animation puzzles, even just during setup. For example, you can array layers in a circle by parenting one layer, rotating the parent, parenting the next layer, rotating again, and so on.

Motion Blur

Motion blur is essential to most realistic animated shots. If a layer and/or the camera is animated at a sufficiently high velocity, and the Motion Blur toggle is enabled at the Layer and Composition levels, then, for free, realistic blur is added to match the apparent motion of the scene, using settings you control.

Motion blur is the natural result of movement that occurs while a camera shutter is open, causing the image to smear. This can be the result of moving objects, or of movement of the camera itself. Far from something to avoid, however, motion blur not only can be aesthetically quite beautiful, it also helps create persistence of vision, the means by which the eye detects motion, and thus it is often more natural relaxing to the eye.

All of this helps explain why efforts to eliminate motion blur from a sampled image have tended to seem faddish and strange, although new cameras, from high-speed live-event HDTV to the Red camera, are capable of almost eliminating it. Who knows, along with grain, motion blur may become more of an arbitrary artistic choice as viewers adapt to 21ˢᵗ century electronic imaging.

After Effects offers control over how long and precisely when the camera shutter is open, via the Composition Settings dialog's Advanced tab (**Figure 2.27**). This latest version of After Effects offers major improvement to the quality and default effectiveness of motion blur.

You might not notice motion blur with your naked eye, but it does occur—watch a ceiling fan in motion, and then follow the individual blades with your eye; depending on how closely you can follow its movement, you will see more or less blur.

Figure 2.27 The Shutter Angle and Shutter Phase settings on the Advanced tab of the Composition Settings dialog control the appearance of motion blur.

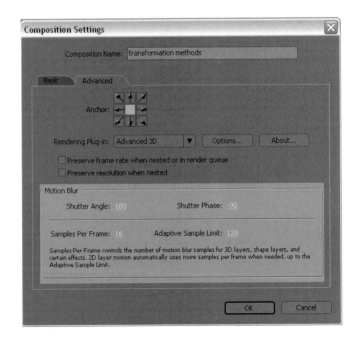

Shutter Angle controls how long the shutter is open; a higher number (up to a maximum of 720) means more blur. Shutter Phase controls at what point, during a given frame, the shutter opens. The new Samples Per Frame and Adaptive Sample Limit settings permit you to refine the look of the blur, to make it appear smoother and less "steppy" (at the expense of extra process cycles naturally), as in **Figure 2.28**.

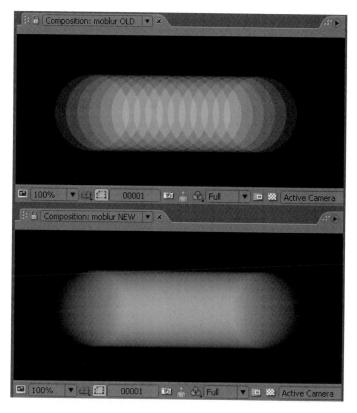

Figure 2.28 By raising Samples per Frame from the default shown in Figure 2.27, you can finally avoid steppy motion blur when creating fast motion in After Effects. This setting determines the minimum number of samples; Adaptive Sample Limit determines the maximum.

The Virtual Camera Shutter

Using a real, physical camera, the shutter setting (along with the aperture) determines the amount of light passed onto the film or video pickup. Low-lit scenes are blurrier because the shutter remains open longer, allowing it to gather more light. Other scenes will be deliberately taken with a slow shutter (and the aperture closed down) to produce, streaky, smeary blur, which, if taken with a high-quality video pickup or film, can look quite lovely.

Unlike an actual camera, After Effects is unconcerned with the need to gather light, and it does not produce (or even emulate) any other lens effects associated with a high or low shutter angle setting (nor the Aperture setting on a 3D camera, explored in Chapter 9). Therefore, by opening the aperture, you mimic only the desirable part—the blur itself.

What the Settings Mean

A physical film camera employs an angled mechanical shutter that opens in a circular motion anywhere between a few degrees and a full 360 degrees (an electronic shutter behaves differently, but never mind about that—it's the metaphor that's important here). Theoretically, 360 degrees provides the maximum open aperture, and thus the greatest amount of blur a shot would contain; After Effects doubles this ceiling for cases where you simply want more.

A camera report can help determine this setting, although you can typically eyeball it by zooming in on an area where background and foreground elements should be blurred with the same motion and matching them (**Figures 2.29a** and **b**). If your camera report includes shutter speed, you can calculate the Shutter Angle setting using the following formula:

shutter speed = 1 / frame rate * (360 / shutter angle)

Figures 2.29a and b In 2.29a, the default Shutter Angle setting of 180 degrees appears too heavy for the white solid masked and tracked over the front hubcap. In 2.29b, Shutter Angle was cut down by 50% (to 90 degrees). In this case, blur has simply been eye-matched to that of the moving truck.

NOTES

180 Shutter Angle and -90 Phase are the default settings in After Effects CS3. However, the defaults change to whatever was set most recently, saved in Preferences.

Setting Shutter Phase to -50% of Shutter Angle is useful when motion tracking and should probably be the default. When motion blur is added to the tracked layer, the track stays centered, instead of appearing offset.

This isn't as gnarly as it looks, but if you dislike formulas, think of it like this: If your camera takes 24 frames per second, but Shutter Angle is set at 180 degrees, then the frame is exposed half the time (180/360 = ½) or ¹⁄₄₈ of a second. If the camera report shows a ¹⁄₉₆ of a second exposure, Shutter Angle should be 90 degrees.

Shutter Phase determines when the shutter opens.

A setting of 0 opens the shutter and starts the blur at the beginning of the frame while the default −90 setting (with a 180° Shutter Angle setting) causes half the blur to start before the frame (blurring the layer in the frame) and half to follow it.

Manipulate Time

After Effects is quite flexible when working with time. You can retime footage or mix and match speeds and timing using a variety of methods, each of which is useful for a particular set of situations.

Absolute (Not Relative) Time

After Effects measures time in absolute (not relative) terms, using seconds (rather than frames, whose timing and number changes according to how many there are per second). If time were measured using the total number of frames, or frames per second, changing the frame rate would pose a problem. Instead, at the very deepest level, After Effects is entirely flexible about frame rate.

So, you can change the frame rate of any comp on the fly, and the keyframes maintain their position in actual time. The timing of an animation won't change, only the number of frames per second used to display it (**Figure 2.30**).

Motion Blur without Motion

You get motion blur for free with any layer animated in After Effects and toggled to generate it. However, there is no built-in provision to generate motion blur for footage that contains motion but insufficient blur—a 3D element, say, or footage shot with a high shutter speed. Directional Blur can help, until you deal with footage whose directionality isn't uniform (as is typical with natural motion). At that point, consider Reel Smart Motion Blur from RE:Vision Effects. This plug-in uses optical flow technology (for which the founders won a Technical Achievement Academy Award) to sample the motion in the scene and generate or enhance motion blur, with powerful controls to allow for transparency and sub-sampling. A demo is included on the book's disc.

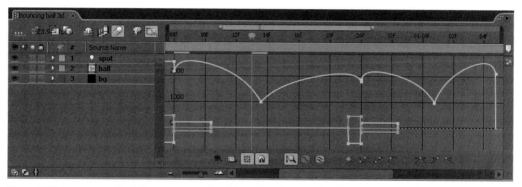

Figure 2.30 The composition's frame rate was altered from 29.97 fps to 24 fps after keyframes were set. All frames following the first one now fall in between the whole frames represented by the grid, but the timing of the animation itself, measured in seconds, is unchanged.

Likewise, footage (or a nested composition) whose frame rate does not match that of the current composition displays in absolute time, even if the beginning of each frame matches up only at the one-second mark.

This should make sense to musicians who know how to beat 3 against 4, or other polyrhythms, creating elaborate syncopations, against the steady beat of the metronome. In After Effects, one second is one beat of that metronome.

NOTES

If time was measured as frames, or frames per second, a change to the frame rate would offset keyframes. Instead, After Effects consistently evaluates time in seconds; keyframes are allowed to fall between frames if necessary to keep the overall timing consistent.

Figure 2.31 The highlighted icon reveals and conceals Time Stretch settings.

Stretching a layer does not "stretch" the timing of any applied keyframes; you can use the Graph Editor to stretch keyframes to match, or precompose the layer with its keyframes prior to Time Stretch to guarantee that the animation lines up.

Time Stretch

Time Stretch lets you alter the duration (or speed) of a source clip; provided you don't need to animate the rate of change (in which case only Time Remap will do).

The third of the three icons at the lower left of the Timeline reveals the In/Out/Duration/Stretch columns (**Figure 2.31**).

You can

▶ Edit the In or Out point: **Ctrl+Shift+comma** (**Cmd+Shift+comma**) stretches the In point to the current frame, **Ctrl+Alt+comma** (**Cmd+Option+comma**) stretches the Out point to the current time

▶ Change the duration of the layer

▶ Alter the stretch value from 100%

Alternatively, specify these settings in the Time Stretch dialog, activated by clicking the Duration or Stretch value, or choose Layer > Time > Time Stretch (**Figure 2.32**).

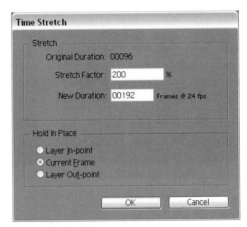

Figure 2.32 You can set an alternate Duration or Stretch Factor in the Time Stretch dialog. It's easy to miss that you can specify the pivot point: In point, Out point, or current time.

Frame Blending

The noticeable side effect of lengthening or shortening a source clip is that motion becomes choppier as frames repeat (or skip). Unless the stretch value factors evenly into 100% (say, 50% or 200%), the repeating or skipping occurs in irregular increments, typically causing a distracting lurching motion.

Enable Frame Blending for the layer and the composition, and After Effects averages the adjacent frames together to create a new image on frames that fall in between the source frames.

There are two basic modes for Frame Blending. Frame Mix mode overlays adjoining frames, essentially blurring them together. Pixel Motion mode uses optical flow techniques to track the motion of actual pixels from frame to frame, creating new frames that are something like a morph of the adjoining frames. Confusingly, the icons for these modes are the same as Draft and Best layer quality, respectively, yet there are cases where Frame Mix may be preferable.

Figure 2.33 shows where the mode is located. Whether the result is acceptable depends on a few predictable criteria. It may appear too blurry, too distorted, or contain too many noticeable frame artifacts, in which case either Frame Mix is preferable, or the Timewarp effect, because it offers control over how the frame blend happens, explained in detail below.

Time Reversal and Freeze Frame

A layer's timing can be reversed with a simple shortcut: Highlight the layer, and press **Ctrl+Alt+R** (**Cmd+Option+R**) or choose Layer > Time > Time-Reverse Layer to set the Stretch value to –100%. The layer's appearance alters to remind you that it is reversed (**Figure 2.34**).

Figure 2.34 The candy striping along the bottom of the layer indicates that the Stretch value is negative and the footage will run in reverse.

The Layer > Time > Freeze Frame command applies the Time Remap effect and sets a Hold keyframe at the current time.

TIP

Frame blending is available not only on layers with time stretching but with any footage that comes in at a frame rate other than that of the composition.

NOTES

The optical flow in Pixel Motion and the Timewarp effect was licensed from The Foundry. The same underlying technology is also used in Furnace plug-ins for Shake, Flame, and Nuke.

Figure 2.33 These toggles enable Frame Mix or Pixel Motion mode for a retimed layer.

Time Stretch and Nested Compositions

If you apply Time Stretch (or Time Remap) to a nested composition, the nested comp behaves as if it now has the main composition's frame rate. Keyframe animations are resliced to fit the new rate instead of adhering to the old one.

You can instead force After Effects to use the frame rate of the embedded composition. On the Advanced tab of the Composition Settings panel of the *nested* comp, toggle Preserve Frame Rate When Nested or in Render Queue (**Figure 2.35**). This forces After Effects to use only whole frame increments in the underlying composition, just as if it were imported footage with that frame rate.

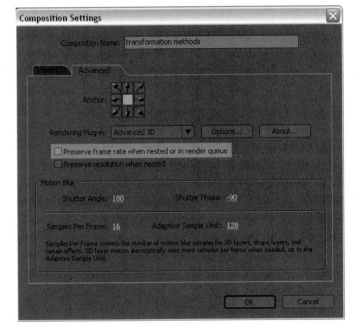

Figure 2.35 If you need a subcomposition to run at a different rate than the master composition, checking the highlighted box in the subcomp prevents After Effects from resampling keyframes at the master comp's rate.

An alternative method to force a given layer to a particular frame rate, whether or not it is a nested composition, is to apply Effect > Time > Posterize Time, entering the desired rate (any value lower than the source rate).

Time Remap

However, once you're comfortable with Time Remap, you may find that you let go of the Time Stretch feature set altogether. The philosophy behind Time Remap is elusively simple: Time has a value, just like any other property, so you can keyframe it, ease in and out of it, loop and ping-pong it, and generally treat it like any other animation data.

Figures 2.36a, b, and **c** show sample timelines that contain typical uses for Time Remap. You needn't go completely nuts rolling footage back and forth, ramping the frame rate up and down, although you can of course do just that. From *The Matrix* to *300*, it's noticeable how accustomed audiences have become to fluid, stylized timing treatments over the past decade or so.

TIP

The final Time Remap keyframe is one greater than the total timing of the layer (in most cases a nonexistent frame) to guarantee that the final source frame is reached, even when frame rates don't match.

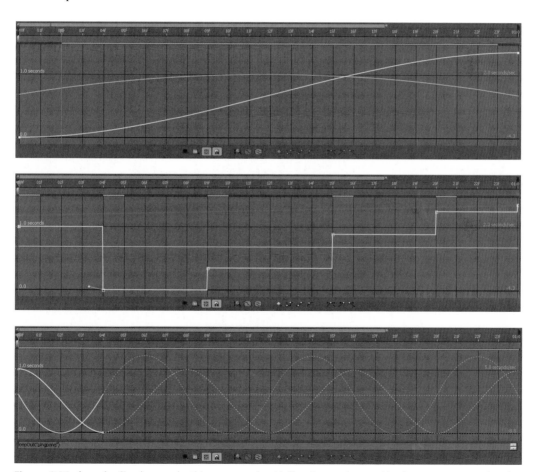

Figures 2.36a, b, and c Simple, everyday things you can do with Time Remap, shown with reference curves: speed up the source with eases (a), progress through a series of stills selected from the moving clip using Hold keyframes (b), and loop the source using a simple expression (c).

TIP

Beware when applying Time Remap to a layer whose duration exceeds that of the composition; either default keyframe may be hidden beyond the Timeline boundaries. You can add keyframes at the layer in and out points, click Time Remap to highlight all keyframes, deselect the added ones, and delete the rest.

TIP

To reverse a clip via Time Remap, highlight all keyframes by clicking on the Time Remap property name. Next, context-click one of the highlighted keyframes, and select Keyframe Assistant > Time-Reverse Keyframes.

You can set Time Remap by selecting it under the Layer menu or using the shortcut (**Ctrl+Alt+T**/**Cmd+Option+T**). This reveals two keyframes, at the beginning and one frame beyond the end of the layer. Time remapped layers have a theoretically infinite duration, so the final Time Remap frame effectively becomes a hold keyframe for the remaining layer duration.

Time Remap can take a little while to understand in complex situations, but it is useful in a more daily way for retimes with eases, holds, time loops (discussed in Chapter 10), or time reversal. Once you've done a few of these, the more complicated stuff becomes easier.

Timewarp

Although The Foundry's amazing Furnace plug-ins are not, at this writing, available for After Effects, Adobe did license one component of Furnace: Kronos, the retiming tool. It's the technology in Pixel Motion, and the Timewarp effect offers actual control over the way that Pixel Motion works with footage.

Timewarp can be used to speed up, slow down, or (like Time Remapping) dynamically animate the timing of a clip. When you speed up a clip with Timewarp, it can add the appropriate amount of motion blur (if so enabled under the Motion Blur settings of the effect).

Most of the time, however, Timewarp is used to slow footage down, creating new in-between frames, and to do this, a particular extra bit of setup is required. By default, Timewarp is set with a speed of 50.00, or 50% (half) of the original speed. Apply it directly to a footage layer and you'll find that the layer ends halfway through the retime operation. There's no way to extend the length of the original footage layer unless you either precompose it into a longer composition or enable Time Remapping. Leave the Time Remap keyframes at their defaults, as they are overridden by Timewarp's Speed or Source Frame property. You determine which of these two criteria to animate in Timewarp with the Adjust Time By setting.

Like Pixel Motion mode, Timewarp employs optical flow, tracking individual pixels via a matrix of vectors. There's no option to see or control those vectors directly, but you can influence how footage is analyzed as follows:

▶ The biggest improvement you can make to the result is to give Timewarp a mask specifying a given layer of movement. **Figure 2.37a** shows a typical case where this is helpful. Specify which portions of the footage are sampled using the **Matte Channel**, **Matte Layer**, and **Source Crops** options.

TIP

By default, Timewarp uses Pixel Motion as the Method setting, and it's hard to imagine changing this setting other than to temporarily compare what is happening with the source (Whole Frames) or a simple blend without optical flow (Frame Mix).

Figures 2.37a and 2.37b In this shot, the camera viewpoint revolves around the subject (a), and Timewarp has no way of distinguishing foreground and background elements, so they tend to tear. You can help guarantee success by providing a traveling foreground matte (b).

▶ The **Warp Layer** control sets another layer as a target for the Timewarp operation. This is vital when you are working footage that would be difficult for Timewarp to analyze without first adjusting its contrast or luminance, or keying it, but those adjustments don't belong in the final shot.

▶ The **Tuning** section contains controls to specify how many vectors Timewarp uses (**Vector Detail**) and how much smoothing to add (**Global** and **Local Smoothing**, **Iterations**), as well as **Filtering**, **Error Threshold**, and **Block Size** settings. It's incorrect to assume that the best result will always come from raising Vector Detail, Smoothing, and Filtering, although in many cases it will help, even though it may slow image processing considerably.

TIP

Timewarp isn't the only optical flow option for After Effects users; before it ever existed, there was Twixtor from RE:Vision Effects, which may very well yield preferable results more easily. To explore whether this is the case with a given shot, try the demo version, available on this book's disc.

Image tearing and pixel artifacts are the most common problems when using Timewarp. To solve these, specify a matte if at all possible. Next, you can increase Filtering from Normal to Extreme (although, even if Extreme helps, you may want to leave Filtering on Normal until it's time to render, as Extreme will slow things down considerably). You can even increase the amount of smoothing on the Global (all vectors) and Local (single vector) level.

Increasing Error Threshold from the default of 1.00 results in fewer motion vectors and more blending, so it will also help with image tearing. However, a scene with heavy grain or other high-frequency detail will actually be improved by lowering this setting so that it is ignored.

Finally, you can increase Vector Details right up to the maximum setting of 100 and reduce Block Size from the default of 6.0, but this can be inadvisable when analyzing fast motion, where the vectors will not be spread across a wide enough matrix to track it.

Just like color keying (Chapter 6, "Color Keying") successful retiming with optical flow requires that you learn to balance an interdependent set of adjustments, and to give the effect what it needs, source-wise, to maximize the possibility of success. And just as with keying, there is a third-party plug-in alternative that some users may prefer (see tip on this page).

In Conclusion

The elegance and logic of the After Effects Timeline is not always evident to the new user, but this chapter taught you that shortcuts and other workflow enhancements help streamline what might otherwise be tedious or exacting edits. The Timeline and Graph Editor, once mastered, give you the control you need over the timing and placement of elements.

If this chapter's information seems overwhelming on first read, keep coming back to it so that specific tips can sink in once you've encountered the right context to use them.

3

Selections:
The Key to Compositing

I'm fixing a hole where the rain gets in
And stops my mind from wandering
Where it will go.

—John Lennon and Paul McCartney

Selections: The Key to Compositing

A particle physicist works with atoms, bakers and bankers each work with their own types of dough, and compositors work with selections—many different types of selections, potentially thousands, each derived uniquely.

If compositing were simply a question of taking pristine, perfect foreground source A and overlaying it onto perfectly matching background plate B, there would be no compositor in the effects process; an editor could accomplish the job before lunchtime.

Instead, compositors break sequences of images apart and reassemble them, sometimes painstakingly, first as a still frame and then in motion. Often, it is one element, one frame, or one area of a shot that needs special attention. By the clever use of selections, a compositor can save the shot by taking control of it.

This chapter focuses on how a layer merges with those behind it. Then Section II, "Effects Compositing Essentials," and in particular in Chapters 6 and 7, examines particular ways to refine selections, create high-contrast mattes, and pull keys.

Many Ways to Create Selections

After Effects offers a number of ways to create selections. Here are the most common.

Pull a Matte

Not only keying out the blue or green from an effects film shoot (**Figure 3.1**), but also high-contrast, or *hi-con*, *mattes*, are created by maximizing the contrast of a particular channel or area of the image. Other types of mattes exist as well, such as the elusive *difference matte*. Chapter 6, "Color Keying," discusses pulling mattes—the process of creating automated selections using pixel data—in depth.

Import with Alpha Channel

Alpha and transparency channels are accurate selections that are included for free with computer-generated footage (typically 3D animations, **Figure 3.2**). They make life easier until you run into problems with alpha channel interpretation, described in Chapter 1, "Compositing in After Effects." At that point, the fact that After Effects is not explicit about alpha interpretation can actually make life more difficult.

This is something to watch for not only when you interpret alpha on import but also when applying effects to layers with an alpha. The "Alpha Channels and Premultiplication" section later in this chapter offers the lowdown on how to deal with edge multiplication.

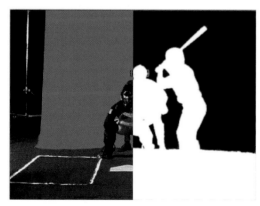

Figure 3.1 This split-screen image shows a blue-screen shoot (left) and the resulting matte. (All baseball images courtesy of Tim Fink Productions.)

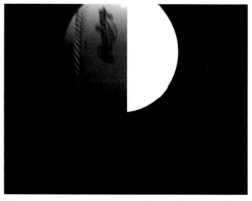

Figure 3.2 A computer-generated baseball's color and alpha channels.

Mask

A mask is a vector shape that determines the opaque and transparent areas of an image (**Figure 3.3**). This chapter introduces the fundamentals of creating and combining masks. A follow-up discussion in Chapter 7, "Rotoscoping and Paint," focuses specifically on *rotoscoping*, the art of animating selections over time.

Masks are generally created by hand, one vertex at a time, or beginning with a simple primitive shape such as an ellipse. After Effects can also generate them automatically by examining the raster data of an image, using Layer > Auto-trace.

Figure 3.3 This split-screen view shows the garbage matte mask that was added to remove areas of the stage not covered by the blue screen.

Auto-trace creates detailed and accurate outlines using the contrast of the image, overall or on individual color channels. With all but the very simplest shots, lots of overlapping outlines are created—dozens, typically—too many for effective rotoscoping (**Figure 3.4**).

Figure 3.4 The result of Auto-trace on a complex image is interesting but with these settings would likely have only abstract artistic applications.

Blending Modes

Blending modes (e.g. Add, Multiply, Screen) combine color channels mathematically, pixel by pixel, in ways that mimic real-world optics (**Figure 3.5**). Inexperienced compositors will sometimes use selections where blending modes are preferable; expert compositors are good at combining both.

You can also use selections combined with blending modes to get the best of both worlds.

This chapter focuses in-depth on the modes most relevant to effects compositing and gets into the nitty-gritty of what they are actually doing as they combine pixel data.

Figure 3.5 Blending modes are the preferred way to composite elements that are composed predominantly of light rather than matter, such as fire.

Effects

Several effects create or refine transparency selections. Section II explores many of these in detail. Effects such as Levels and Curves include control of the transparency (alpha) channel, and effects in the Channel submenu work with the alpha channel directly.

Combine Techniques

Even an ordinary effects shot will typically combine more than one of the above techniques; for example, you will often apply a garbage matte prior to a color key, or enhance the effect of a blending mode by adding a hi-con matte.

The art is in knowing which approach to apply for a given situation, how to apply it, and when to try something else. No single technique is as sophisticated as the result of combining and refining them together, sometimes in clever and unexpected ways.

Compositing: Science and Nature

What exactly is happening in a simple A over B composite? Is it just like placing one object on top of another, like laying a drawing on your desk? A over B makes intuitive sense, but to master compositing, it helps to know what is going on—not only in the virtual world of software but the physical or "real" world, and beyond that, the equally real physical world of optics.

These three worlds do not always operate according to the same rules, and while it might seem like the digital artist re-creates, as faithfully as possible, what is happening in the natural world, it is the world of optics, the way that the camera sees the world, that a compositor is actually trying to emulate. And edge detail between objects, in particular, distinguishes these worlds rather sharply.

Bitmap Alpha

A *bitmap selection channel* is one in which each pixel is either fully opaque or fully transparent. This is the type of selection generated by the Magic Wand tool in Photoshop. You

NOTES

As is detailed further in Chapter 6, the Color Key and Luma Key effects also generate bitmap selections, making them tools largely to be avoided.

can feature or blur the resulting edge, but the initial selection contains no semitransparent pixels.

This type of selection may have an occasional use, but it belongs to the world of computers, not nature (or optics). An edge made up of pixels which are either fully opaque or invisible cannot describe a curve or angle smoothly, and even a straight line looks unnatural in a natural image if it completely lacks edge thresholding (**Figure 3.6**).

Feathered Alpha

Although it's easy enough to see that a bitmap edge does not occur in nature, it's hard to imagine that hard objects should have transparent, feathered edges. Examine the edge of this book. Do you see a soft, semitransparent edge? Of course not.

But now study an image of the same thing, and you'll find it isn't razor sharp in its hardness, either. It so happens that semitransparent edge pixels are the digital approximation for overlapping edges in optics because they solve two problems in translating the world of objects to the world of pixels:

▶ They come closer to describing organic curves (**Figure 3.7**).

▶ They mimic optics behavior, the way light and objects interact when viewed through a lens.

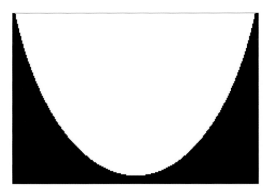

Figure 3.6 400% magnification shows the flaws of a curved or angled shape described by only bitmap pixels, those that are either fully transparent or opaque.

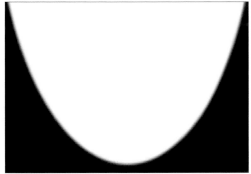

Figure 3.7 Ah—better. Even at 400%, a feathered and anti-aliased edge more properly describes a smooth, soft curve.

The first point is intuitive enough once you've gained some experience working with *raster images*, digital images made up of pixels. The second point is easier to miss.

Study a digital photo with no compositing whatsoever close-up (**Figures 3.8a and b**). In the digital image, areas at the edge of objects become a fine wash of color combining the foreground and background. This is what happens to light as it travels around objects in the physical world and then through the lens of the camera.

Geek Alert: The Compositing Formula

So, what *does* happen when you layer a raster image with semitransparent alpha over an opaque background image? The foreground pixel values are multiplied by the percentage of transparency, which, if not fully opaque, reduces their value. The background pixels are multiplied by the percentage of opacity (the inverse of opacity), and the two values are added together to produce the composite. Expressed as a formula, it looks like

$(Fg * A) + ((1-A)*Bg) = Comp$

With real RGB pixel data of R: 185, G: 144, B: 207 in the foreground and R: 80, G: 94, B: 47 in the background, calculating one edge pixel only might look like

$[(185, 144, 207)\ 3\ .6] + [.4\ 3\ (80, 94, 47)] = (143, 124, 143)$

The result is a weighted blend between the brightness of the foreground and the darker background.

Other effects compositing programs, such as Shake, do not take this operation for granted the way that After Effects and Photoshop do. You can't simply drag one image over another in a layer stack—you must apply an Over function to create this interaction. Is there a difference? Not until you add to the discussion the operations that go along with an Over, in particular premultiplication, which is detailed later in this chapter.

Figures 3.8a and b This image (a) has no compositing. Natural softness is apparent along hard edges (b) despite that they are in focus.

Opacity

The real world also informs After Effects' handling of opacity, which can seem illogical, as in the following quiz.

Take two identical layers, no alpha/transparency information for either layer. Set each layer to 50% Opacity, and the result does not add up to 100%. Here's why.

A lead developer on the After Effects team once described the program's opacity calculations as follows: Imagine you have a light which is 1, and place a 50% transparent filter (say, a sheet of vellum) in front of it. Half the total light is permitted through the vellum (0.5 * 1 = 0.5). Put another 50% transparent sheet of vellum on top of that. Now half of half the light shows through (0.5 * 0.5 = 0.25). You can theoretically repeat ad infinitum without reaching 0% light transmission, at least in a pure digital environment.

Hence, and in some tangential relationship to Zeno's Paradox, After Effects mimics how transparency behaves in the real world. This is *not* how opacity settings are handled in many alternative compositing applications, and so it often takes users of such programs as Shake by surprise, but the operation is by design.

NOTES

Zeno's Paradox goes something like this: Suppose I wish to cross the room. First, of course, I must cover half the distance. Then, I must cover half the remaining distance. Then, I must cover half the remaining distance. Then I must cover half the remaining distance, and so on forever. The consequence is that I can never get to the other side of the room.

Alpha Channels and Premultiplication

One major source of confusion and even occasional derision with After Effects has to do with its handling of alpha channels and premultiplication. After Effects has a persistent concept of the alpha channel as part of every image, and this channel is expected always to be un-multiplied within After Effects, whether it originated that way or not. Thus premultiplication is set on import, in the Interpret Footage dialog, and you are more or less expected not to consider edge multiplications until it's time to render.

This works surprisingly well given the correct import settings, but it doesn't free you from the need to understand premultiplication and how problems with edges may be related to it.

Premultiplication Illustrated

Premultiplication exists for one reason only: so that rendered images look nice, with realistic, anti-aliased edges against a neutral background, *before they are composited.*

All premultiplication does is composite the foreground against the background, so that the edges and transparency blend as well into that solid color (typically black) as they would against the final background.

When you ask After Effects to "guess" how to interpret the footage (on import, by choosing Guess in the Interpret Footage dialog, or pressing **Ctrl+F/Cmd+F**), it looks for repeated pixels indicating a solid color background and the difference between that background color and the foreground in the edge pixels.

What does it mean to have the background multiplied into the edge pixels? Revisit "Geek Alert: The Compositing Formula," and imagine the background value to be 0,0,0; edge pixels are multiplied by 0 (they turn pure black) and are added to the source, weighted by the percentage of transparency as determined by the corresponding alpha channel pixel. The overall effect is to darken semitransparent edge pixels if the background is black, to lighten them if it's white, and to really wreak havoc with them if it's any other color.

The close-ups in **Figures 3.9a** and **b** show a section of the same foreground image with the alpha interpreted properly and with it misinterpreted. A misinterpreted alpha either fails to remove the background color from the edge pixels, or removes color that should actually be present.

Figures 3.9a and b Motion blur and a white background clearly reveal improper edge multiplication, especially when compared with the correct version (a). There is dark matting all around the edges, including areas of the canopy meant to be translucent, and around the blur of the propeller (b).

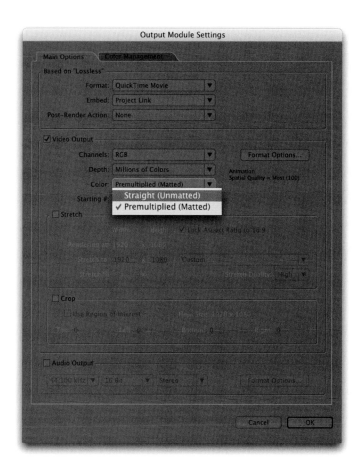

Figure 3.10 Although premultiplied alpha is typically the default setting, the Color pull-down menu in Output Settings can be used to generate straight alphas.

Most computer-generated images are premultiplied, unless specific steps are taken to counteract the process. The Video Output section of the Output Module Settings for items in the Render Queue includes a pulldown to specify whether you render with Straight or Premultiplied alpha; by default, it is set to Premultiplied (**Figure 3.10**).

You may find these artifacts presenting themselves although you've carefully managed alpha channel interpretation on import; nonetheless, elements have black fringing. Your job depends on getting to the bottom of this. There are two basic ways this can occur:

▶ An alpha channel is misinterpreted in Interpret Footage (see "Getting It Right on Import")

▶ Edge multiplication occurs within a composition, probably unintentionally, by applying a matte and adding a background (see "Solving the Problem Internally")

Unfortunately, artists who misunderstand the underlying problem will resort to all sorts of strange machinations to fix the black edge, ruining what may be a perfectly accurate edge matte.

TIP

To see any alpha channel displayed in straight alpha mode (all pixels with any transparency displaying as pure white), choose RGB Straight from the Show Channel pull-down menu, below the Composition and Layer panels (**Alt+Shift+4/ Option+Shift+4**).

Getting It Right on Import

A preference in Preferences > Import determines what happens when footage is imported with an alpha channel; if this is set to anything other than Ask User (the default), you may not know how alpha channels are being interpreted, particularly with the Guess option enabled (**Figure 3.11**).

Guess can be wrong if the factors it expects in a premultiplied alpha are there in a straight image or vice versa. Thus it is preferable not to trust to automation.

NOTES

With a premultiplied image, After Effects attempts to guess not only the setting but also the color of the background; generally this will be black or white, but watch out for situations where a 3D artist has become creative and rendered against canary yellow or powder blue. For that reason, there is an eyedropper adjacent to the Matted with Color setting (Figure 3.11).

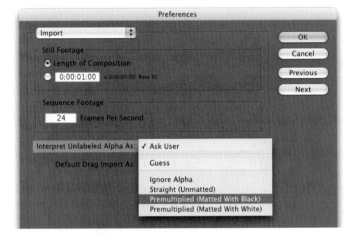

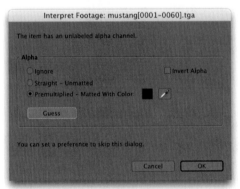

Figures 3.11a and 3.11b Import preferences default to Ask User about alpha channel interpretation (a); this presents the Interpret Footage dialog (b) which includes a button marked Guess that will typically get the setting right, or generate a beep in cases of uncertainty.

When in doubt, examine your footage without the alpha applied: If you see a solid background that is neither pure black nor white and After Effects isn't detecting it, use the eyedropper.

Fundamentally, though, as an effects compositor you need to be able to examine your images and spot the symptoms of a misinterpreted alpha: dark or bright fringing in the semi-opaque edges of your foreground.

Solving the Problem Internally

The really gnarly fact is that premultiplication errors can be introduced within a composition, typically by applying a matte to footage that is already somehow blended—multiplied—with a background.

If you see fringing in your edges, you can try the Remove Color Matting effect (**Figures 3.12a** and **b**). This effect has one setting only, for background color, because all it does is apply the unpremultiply calculation (the antidote to premultiplication) in the same manner that it would be applied in Interpret Footage.

TIP

Remove Color Matting will not work properly on a layer with a track matte; be sure to precompose the layer and its track matte prior to applying Channel > Remove Color Matting.

TIP

UnMult, originally created by John Knoll and available free from Red Giant Software (and included on this book's disc), is useful in tricky situations in which Remove Color Matting won't do the job because there is no alpha channel. It uses the black areas of the images to create transparency and remove premultiplied black from the resulting transparent pixels.

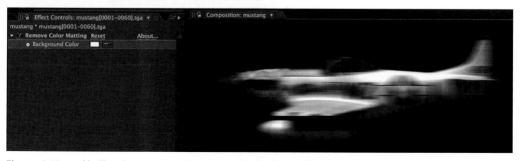

Figures 3.12a and b The plane was matted against a white background, but transparency has been applied via a track matte (the equivalent of a straight alpha), so white fringing appears against black (a). Remove Color Matting with Color set to pure white corrects the problem (b), but only when applied to a precomp of the image and matte.

TIP

Shape layers are a new addition to After Effects CS3. These are directly related to masks; they are drawn with the same tools (**Figure 3.13**). Generally, if a selected layer can receive a mask, then After Effects draws a mask by default; otherwise, it creates a new Shape layer, generally to serve as a design element in a motion graphics project, rather than to define transparency, although it can be used as a track matte. More about Shape layers is found below.

Masks

Although hand-created and animated for the most part, masks open up all kinds of possibilities in After Effects. Masks are the principal method for defining transparency regions in a clip without regard to actual pixels because they are vector shapes. This section lays down the basics for smart use of masks.

Typical Mask Workflow

Masks are the principal non-procedural method to define transparency in a layer, using vector shapes. There are five basic automated shapes and the Pen tool (**G**) for drawing free-form. The **Q** key activates and then cycles through the basic mask shapes.

Figure 3.13 If an image is selected in the Timeline, selecting a shape tool in the toolbar and dragging in the viewer creates a mask (and so there are five basic mask shapes where previously there were two); otherwise, a new Shape layer is added with its own properties.

Figure 3.14 Use this toggle in the Layer viewer to disable a mask; as long as it's selected, it's still visible.

A mask can be drawn in either the Composition or Layer viewer. Layer makes it easier to draw while continuing to look at the source; you can toggle Render with Masks Selected in the pull-down menu to disable all mask selections (**Figure 3.14**). Composition allows you to see the layer in context, but if a layer is, for example, rotated in 3D space, it can be difficult to draw or adjust a mask; an ideal compromise in such cases is to open the Layer and Composition views side-by-side.

When drawing with a mask tool

▶ Double-click the Mask tool (in the Tools palette) to set the boundaries of the mask shape to match those of the layer.

▶ Use **Shift** to constrain the shape; **Ctrl/Cmd** draws the shape from the center.

▶ The Mask Shape dialog is useful in rare cases where your mask requires exact dimensions. Access it by clicking the underlined word "Shape" under Mask options (**M** with the layer highlighted).

▶ Double-click the shape itself to activate Free Transform mode, which enables you to offset, rotate, or scale the entire mask shape (**Figure 3.15**). As always, hold down **Shift** to keep the scale proportional, snap the rotation to 45-degree increments, or constrain movement to one axis.

▶ Highlighting a layer with a mask and pressing **MM** (the **M** key twice in rapid succession) reveals the full Mask options for that layer.

TIP

Even if your mask can't be completed with one of the five preset shapes, it can be helpful to use them as a starter and then edit with the Pen tool if they are anything like what you're trying to draw.

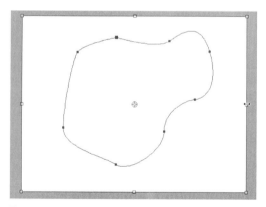
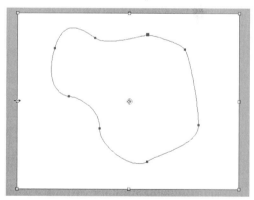

Figure 3.15 How do you flip a mask symmetrically in After Effects? Enable View > Show Grid and View Snap to Grid, then double-click the Rectangular Mask tool to create a second mask that is the exact size of the layer. Select both masks, then double-click a point to set the Free Transform tool. Now drag the handles at the image boundaries to the opposite sides, deleting the layer-sized mask when you're done.

TIP

The Mask Expansion feature has many uses; you can, for example, create an edge selection with boundaries of your choice. Expand a mask, duplicate it, and set the duplicate to Subtract with a negative Mask Expansion value.

▶ Feather is applied to the entire mask, and is always centered around the mask path (half the amount of feather is applied inside and outside the mask). Big, soft masks are useful for all kinds of lighting, smoke, and glow effects, detailed throughout this book (**Figure 3.16**).

▶ Press the **F** key to solo the Mask Feather property.

▶ Mask Expansion expands or (given a negative value) contracts the mask area, often a preferable alternative to redrawing a mask.

Keyboard shortcuts help eliminate a lot of the fuss and bother that comes with masking in After Effects.

Figure 3.16 The Feather of this mask is set roughly equal to its radius, creating a big, diffuse gradient in the shape of the mask (in this case, elliptical), useful for many types of lighting effects.

Bézier Masks

By default, the Pen tool creates Bézier shapes; learn the keyboard shortcuts and you can fully edit a mask without ever clicking anywhere except right on the mask.

I sometimes draw a Bézier mask first as straight lines only, clicking to place points at key transitions and corners. Once I've completed the basic shape, with the Pen tool still active, I can go back point-by-point and edit the shape, because I have instant access to all of the mask shortcuts shown in the Pen Tool pulldown:

▶ Click on a point with the Pen tool active to delete it (look for the minus "-" sign in the cursor).

▶ Click on a segment between points with the Pen tool active to add a point (a plus sign in the cursor).

▶ Alt/Option-click on a point with the Pen tool to enable the Convert Vertex tool (which looks like a caret): Apply it to a point with no handles, and you can drag out to create handles. Apply it to a point with handles, and you cancel the handles.

▶ Click on a Bézier handle with the Pen tool to break the center point of the Bézier, enabling you to adjust the handles individually.

▶ Context-click on the mask path to enable the context menu of options for that mask, including Mask settings found in the Timeline, the ability to specify a First Vertex (detailed below), and Motion Blur settings for the mask, which can be toggled on or off separate from the layer itself.

▶ Hold down **Ctrl/Cmd** to enable the Selection tool, then double-click the shape to activate free transform. Alternatively, you can always switch to the Selection tool by pressing **V**. The **G** and **V** keys enable the Pen and Selection tools, respectively, at any time.

▶ Click on a point with the Pen tool active to delete it (look for the minus "=" sign in the cursor).

▶ To deselect the current mask and start a new one without switching tools, use **F2** or **Ctrl+Shift+A** (**Cmd+Shift+A**) to deselect the active mask.

TIP

Standard in all Adobe mask tools, including After Effects: as you draw a mask, to move a vertex into exact place after drawing it, keep the mouse button down and hold the spacebar; you can freely move the vertex until you release the spacebar, and if the mouse is still held you can drag out tangent handles. Toggle between the two modes as often as necessary.

Shape Layers

Because the focus of this book is realistic visual effects more than abstract motion graphics, the Shape tools don't get as much attention here as they might in a book that assumed you to be a visual designer rather than an effects artist. Like the Type tools, Shape isn't essential to effects work, where masks are the bread and butter.

However, if you fully understand what makes a Shape layer unique from a masked solid, it may help you discover creative uses for it (and in any case, most of us actually fall somewhere on the spectrum between pure realism and abstraction in our work). Try creating some shapes, then create a solid and with it selected, try selecting the same shapes as masks for that solid. Here's what you discover:

▶ There are five basic shapes, equally available as Shape layers or mask paths, with a key difference: when you create a Star, Polygon, or Rounded Rectangle as a mask its vertices can be edited as normal Béziers. A shape's points cannot themselves be edited; instead, you edit the entire shape either by adjusting existing properties in the Timeline or by adding new ones—some of which, such as Pucker & Bloat, Twist, or Zig Zag, will deform the entire shape.

▶ Shapes all have two basic characteristics: Fill and Stroke, each optional and editable. With a Shape active, Alt/Option-click on Fill and Stroke in the toolbar to cycle through the options (also available in the Timeline).

▶ Shapes can be instanced and repeated in 2D space.

The last point may be the most significant: Consider shapes when you need a repeatable pattern of some type, such as the film sprockets in **Figure 3.17**. You could create something like this using masks as well, but a Shape layer has the advantage of letting you edit a single set of parameters and apply it to the entire pattern. There is no 3D repeat option—that will have to wait for a future version of the software.

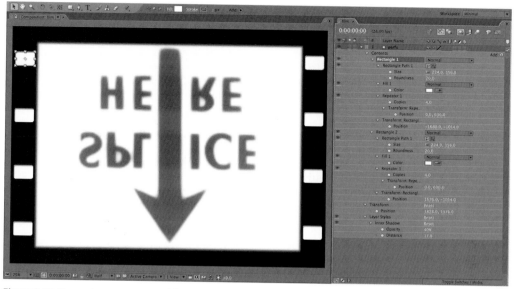

Figure 3.17 It's easy to create a repeatable pattern such as these film sprocket holes using a shape and the Repeater property, although it results in a lot of editable properties that can appear confusing. Here I've even added an Inner Shadow Layer Style to give a little feeling of depth and dimension.

Combining Multiple Masks

By default, all masks are drawn in Add mode, meaning that the contents of the mask are added to the layer selection, and the area outside all of the masks is excluded. There are other options for combining them, however; the five primary mask modes are

▶ **Add:** The default mode; adds the opacity values to the image as a whole, including masks higher in the stack (**Figure 3.18**).

▶ **Subtract:** Subtracts opacity values from areas which overlap with masks higher in the stack or from the image as a whole if no other masks precede it (**Figure 3.19**).

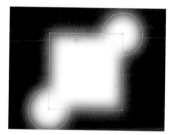

Figure 3.18 Add mode combines the luminance values of overlapping masks.

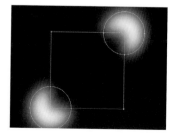

Figure 3.19 Subtract mode is the inverse of Add mode.

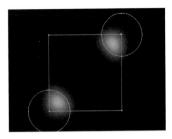

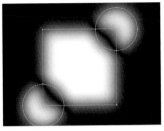

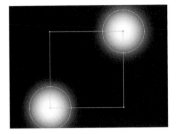

Figure 3.20 Intersect mode adds only the overlapping areas of opacity.

Figure 3.21 The inverse of Intersect, Difference mode subtracts overlapping areas.

Figure 3.22 With None mode, the mask is effectively deactivated.

TIP

In Preferences > User Interface Colors, enable Cycle Mask Colors and each new mask you create automatically uses the next color of the 16 listed in Preferences > Label Colors (which you can also customize). It's much easier to work with several masks on one layer when they're not all yellow.

▶ **Intersect:** Combines only the areas of opacity that overlap (intersect), with masks higher in the stack (**Figure 3.20**).

▶ **Difference:** Subtracts overlapping areas (**Figure 3.21**).

▶ **None:** Has no effect on the image whatsoever; this is like turning off or disabling the mask. It can be useful as a placeholder or for effects that use masks (**Figure 3.22**).

Two variables change the above mask interactions in somewhat mind-bending ways. A toggle labeled Inverted sits adjacent to the mask mode pull-down menu. Inverting an Add mask is straightforward enough; all of the areas outside the mask are selected, instead of those inside. The Mask Opacity property (revealed by twirling open the mask) lets you dial back the strength of a mask; setting any mask other than the first one to 0% is like disabling it.

TIP

When rotoscoping (masking an animated shape, detailed in Chapter 7) it is wise to employ multiple masks, as attempting to animate a complex shape that does not move in a single direction can become cumbersome, or even impossible.

The behavior of Mask Opacity works a little differently for the first mask. A single Add mask set to 0% Mask Opacity causes the entire layer to disappear. That's logical, because otherwise setting that mask to, say, 50% would have to cause 50% of the area outside the mask to reappear. However, if the first mask is set to Subtract, setting Mask Opacity to 50% does just that—instead of the area inside the mask reappearing, the rest of the scene becomes 50% transparent. I call this a bug, and the development team has acknowledged that it only stays this way for backward compatibility; the workaround is to start with a full-frame mask set to Add mode, then add a Subtract mask. Generally speaking, it's easier to understand masks if the first mask is set to Add, whether it is inverted or not.

Overlapping Transparency

"Density" is traditionally a film term describing how dark (opaque) the frame of film is at a given area of the image. It is therefore the inversion of opacity or alpha values; the higher the density, the less light is transmitted. In the digital world we sometimes speak of masks and alpha channels as having "density," and overlapping semitransparent areas must be managed to avoid having the densities build up in undesirable ways.

When combining masks that have semitransparent areas, either because the opacity of the masks is less than 100% or, as in the examples shown here, because the edges are heavily feathered, two overlapping pixels each with 50% transparency would become fully opaque, not usually the desired behavior. That's when Lighten and Darken modes come into play.

Figures 3.23a and **b** show the result of using each of these modes; they prevent mask densities from building up the way that they do with the other modes. No pixel within the combined masks will have a value greater or lesser than the same pixel in the overlapping masks; either the lighter or the darker of the two will be represented.

TIP

Trouble keeping multiple masks organized? Name them in the Timeline (Return key, then type), change the color if it could be more visible, and lock masks you're not using. You can even context-click on the mask you're editing and choose Mask > Lock Other Masks, and if overlapping masks are still too much in your way, Mask > Hide Locked Masks.

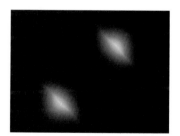

Figures 3.23a and b A Darken (a) or Lighten (b) mask uses only the darker (lower) or lighter (higher) value, respectively, for overlapping pixels.

Remember that masks render from top to bottom, so each mask's mode applies to its relationship with the layers above it. Thus applying these modes to the top mask in the stack has no effect.

Masks in Motion

Ahead of Chapter 7's more detailed discussion of rotoscoping, here are the basics to put a mask in motion.

Interpolation Basics

You can set a temporal ease on a mask keyframe (and adjust it in the Graph Editor), but there is no corresponding spatial curve to adjust, as there is with Position keyframes. Each point will travel in a linear fashion to its next keyframed position. Thus in order to precisely mask an object traveling in an arc, you must set many more keyframes than for an object traveling in a single direction.

Despite that After Effects now lets you apply expressions to a mask (see Chapters 7 and 10 for more on this), there's no way to get at the translation data of the mask points directly, and thus you can't translate a group of mask keyframes together. As soon as you move, rotate, or scale it, your selection snaps to the current keyframe only.

You can instead duplicate the layer being masked and use it as an alpha track matte for an unmasked source of the same layer, in which case you're free to transform (or even motion track) the duplicate using the normal layer transforms. This may seem like a less-than-perfect solution, but Chapter 7 elucidates how working this way can also make rotoscoping in After Effects much faster and more efficient.

Moving, Copying, Pasting, and Masks

You can freely copy a mask path from one source (a different mask, a different keyframe in the same mask animation, or even another Adobe application that uses mask paths such as Illustrator, or Photoshop) and paste it into an existing Mask Path channel, but beware of the following situational rules:

▶ **With no Mask Path keyframes in the source or target:** Copying the mask and pasting it to another layer automatically either creates a new mask, or applies it to any mask that is selected.

▶ **Source mask contains Mask Path keyframes, target has none:** Highlighting the mask (not the specific keyframes) and pasting creates a new mask as if pasting from time 0. Highlighting any or all Mask Path keyframes pastes a new mask with keyframes starting at the current time.

▶ **Target layer contains masks (with or without keyframes):** To paste Mask Path keyframes into a particular mask at a particular time, highlight the target mask before pasting. Highlighting the target Mask Path property highlights any keyframes and replaces them, effectively deleting the previous shape.

When you need to replace a specific mask path at a specific keyframe, there is a somewhat hidden feature in the Layer panel to make it less of a blind operation than the final option above. The Target pulldown along the bottom of the window lets you choose an existing mask as the target; you can start drawing a new mask anywhere in the frame and it replaces the shape in the target mask layer (**Figure 3.24**).

If the target layer has different dimensions than the source, a mask stretches to maintain its relationship to the boundaries of that layer when copied and pasted. This is an advantage when the target is different sized but identically proportioned.

Figure 3.24 This pull-down menu along the bottom of the Layer panel makes it easy to create a new mask path that replaces the shape in the target mask. If the target mask has keyframes, After Effects creates a new keyframe wherever the new shape is drawn.

First Vertex

When pasting in shapes or radically changing the existing mask by adding and deleting points, you may run into difficulty lining up the points. Hidden away in the Layer > Mask (or Mask context) menu, and available *only with a single vertex of the mask selected*, is the Set First Vertex command. If your mask points twist around to the wrong point during an interpolation, setting the First Vertex to two

Smart Mask Interpolation (available via a panel in the Window menu) is designed to help you transition between two radically different shapes. It's not too essential to normal masking and rotoscoping, but if you're ever out of luck with normal mask vertex interpolation, you could check it out, with the help of the online documentation.

NOTES

Traditional optical compositing—covering all movies made prior to the 1990s—was capable of bi-packing (multiplying) and double-exposing (adding) two source frames (layers). Many sophisticated effects films were completed using only these two "blending modes."

points that definitely correspond should help straighten things out. This also can be imperative for effects that rely on mask shapes, such as the Reshape tool (described in Chapter 7).

Blending Modes: Compositing Beyond Selections

After Effects includes 34 blending modes, each created with a specific purpose (**Figure 3.25**)—although no one is quite sure in what context Dancing Dissolve was ever useful (and I'm only half joking). For effects work, moreover, the majority of them are not particularly recommended.

Figure 3.25 With 34 blending modes to choose from, it's virtually guaranteed that less experienced users will be easily overwhelmed and compelled to play hunt and peck. You will likely use a small subset of these 90% of the time.

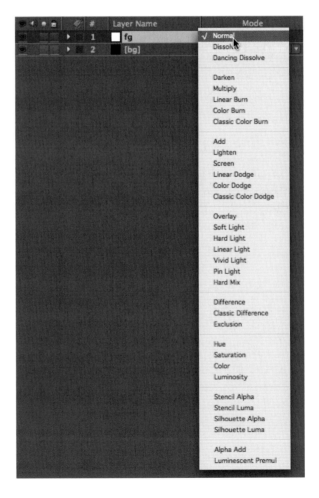

So how do you tell which are the useful ones? Once you understand how your options work, you can make informed compositing decisions instead of relying on trial and error.

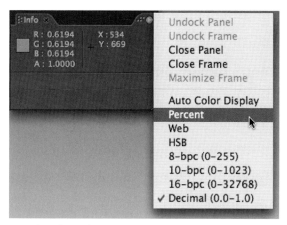

Figure 3.26 The Info panel can display pixel values in several optional modes (accessed via the panel menu). Shown here are decimal values with the cursor on medium gray. Visible decimal values are "normalized" to the range of 0.0 to 1.0, which makes calculations more straightforward than 0 to 255, the standard 8-bit range (or the even more obtuse 0 to 32768 for 16-bit). Select a color mode for the Info palette via its wing menu; whatever mode you select is thereafter also used by the Adobe Color Picker.

To help you understand what the various blending modes are doing, **Figures 3.27** through **3.33** blend a grayscale gradient over a fully saturated background. Contextual examples using these blending modes follow in the next section.

Figure 3.27 Blending in this figure is set to Normal for purposes of comparison with those that follow.

NOTES

These mathematical descriptions of blended pixel values use a color range normalized to 1; in other words, the full range of pixel values is described as 0 to 1 instead of 0 to 255, as it typically appears in your color controls. A medium gray on any channel is 0.5 instead of 128, pure white is 1, and pure black is 0 (**Figure 3.26**). This makes it much simpler to show the calculations that are actually used to create the blended pixels, because the internal math typically is based this way. For information about overbright values, which have a value greater than 1, see Chapter 11, "32 Bit HDR Compositing and Color Management."

NOTES

Blending modes are all based on mathematical operations for combining pixels in the layer containing the given blending mode and the pixels behind it—either below it in the stack, if all the layers are 2D, or positioned behind it in 3D space, if all the layers are 3D.

Add and Screen

Add and Screen modes both brighten the foreground image while making darker pixels transparent. Screen yields a subtler blend than Add in normal video color space, but does not work correctly with linear color (details in Chapter 11).

Add mode is every bit as simple as it sounds; the formula is

$$newPixel = A + B$$

where A is a pixel from the foreground layer and B is a background pixel. The result is clipped at 1 for 8- and 16-bit pixels.

Add is incredibly useful with what After Effects calls a Linearized Working Space, where it perfectly re-creates the optical effect of combining light values from two images. It is useful for laying fire and explosion elements shot in negative space (against black) into a scene, adding noise or grain to an element, or any other element that is made up of light and texture (**Figures 3.28a**, **b**, **c**, and **d**).

NOTES

Linear Dodge and Add are identical blending modes; the former is merely Photoshop's term for the latter.

Figures 3.28a, b, c and d Add mode (a) takes the source foreground element, the fire shot against a black background (b), and adds its pixel values channel by channel to the background (c), causing the pure black pixels to disappear completely (d).

Screen mode has an influence similar to Add mode's, but via a slightly different formula. The pixel values are inverted, multiplied together, and the result is inverted:

$$newPixel = 1-((1-A) * (1-B))$$

Once you discover the truth about working linearized with a 1.0 gamma, you understand that Screen is a workaround, a compromise for how colors blend in normal video space. Screen is most useful in situations where Add would blow out the highlights too much—glints, flares, glow passes, and so on (**Figure 3.29**).

NOTES

In Screen mode, fully white pixels stay white, fully black pixels stay black, but a midrange pixel (0.5) takes on a brighter value (0.75), just not as bright as would be with Add (1).

Figure 3.29 The difference between Screen and Add (Figure 3.28) may be subtle in printed figures until you look closely; notice there's less brightness in the "hottest" areas of the fire.

Multiply

Multiply is another mode whose math is as elementary as it sounds; it uses the formula

$$newPixel = A * B$$

NOTES

To fully comprehend the difference between Add and Screen requires an understanding of a linearized working space, which is offered in Chapter 11.

Keep in mind that this formula uses color values between 0 and 1 to correspond to the colors on your monitor. Multiplying two images together, therefore, actually has the effect of reducing midrange pixels and darkening an image overall, although pixels that are full white in both images remain full white.

Multiply or Add has the inverse effect of Screen mode, darkening the midrange values of one image with another. It emphasizes dark tones in the foreground without replacing the lighter tones in the background, useful to create for texture, shadow, or dark fog (**Figure 3.30**).

Figure 3.30 Dark smoke (actually a grayscale fractal noise pattern) is multiplied over the background, darkening the areas that are dark in either the foreground or background further.

NOTES

Overlay and the various Light modes do not work properly with values above 1.0, as can occur in 32 bpc linearized working spaces (see Chapter 11).

NOTES

Reversing layer order and swapping Overlay for Hard Light yields an identical result.

Overlay and the Light Modes

Overlay uses Screen or Multiply, depending on the background pixel value. Above a threshold of 50% gray (or .5 in normalized terms), Screen occurs, and below the threshold, Multiply. Hard Light operates similarly, instead using the top layer to determine whether to screen or multiply, so the two are inverse effects.

These modes, along with Linear and Vivid Light, can be most useful for combining a layer that is predominantly color with another layer that is predominantly luminance, or contrast detail (**Figure 3.31**). Much of the lava texturing in the Level 4 sequence of *Spy Kids 3-D* was created by using Hard Light to combine a hand-painted color heat map with moving fractal noise patterns.

  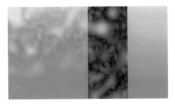

Figure 3.31 Overlay and its inverse, Hard Light, are useful for combining color and texture. Here, an instant lava lamp texture was created using the components shown at the right: a solid with Fractal Noise applied set to Overlay mode on top of a red-to-yellow gradient.

Difference

Difference inverts a background pixel in proportion to the foreground pixel. It can help you line up two identical layers, which is helpful while working even if you rarely use it for final output (**Figure 3.32**).

Figure 3.32 The selection area in the foreground is identical to the background; when they are perfectly aligned, all pixels cancel out to black.

HSB and Color Modes

The Hue, Saturation, and Brightness modes each combine one of these values (H, S, or B) from the foreground layer with the other two from the background layer. Color takes both the hue and saturation from the top layer, using only the luminance (or brightness of) from the underlying background (**Figure 3.33**).

Figure 3.33 Setting a deep-blue-colored solid to Color mode and overlaying it on the plate footage has the effect of tinting the colors in the image blue. Artistic uses of this mode are explored in Chapter 12, "Light."

NOTES

Stencil Alpha and Silhouette Alpha are useful to create custom edge mattes as well as a light wrap effect, demonstrated in Chapter 12.

These modes are often useful at an Opacity setting below 100%, to combine source HSB values with ones that you choose.

Stencil, Silhouette, Preserve Transparency

Commonly overlooked, Stencil and Silhouette blending modes operate only on the alpha channel of the composition. The layer's alpha or luminance values become a matte for all layers below it in the stack. Stencil makes the brightest pixels opaque, and Silhouette the darkest.

Suppose instead you have a foreground layer that is meant to be opaque only where the underlying layers are opaque, as in **Figure 3.34**. The small highlighted checkbox, labeled Preserve Underlying Transparency, makes this happen, much to the amazement of many who've wished for this feature and not realized it was already there.

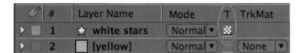

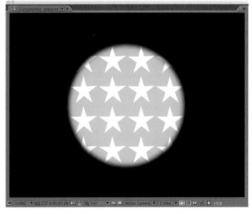

Figure 3.34 Among the hardest-to-find and most-easily-forgotten features in the Timeline is the Preserve Underlying Transparency toggle, highlighted. This recreates behavior familiar to Photoshop users, where a layer's own transparency only applies where it intersects with that of the underlying layer, one more way to avoid track mattes or precomping.

Alpha Add and Luminescent Premultiply

Alpha Add and Luminescent Premultiply are blending modes that affect semitransparent edge pixels only.

Just as two overlapping layers with 50% opacity are not fully opaque when layered together (see "Opacity"), the same behavior applies to semitransparent pixels. Just as the name implies, Alpha Add directly adds transparency pixels, so, for example, two 50% opaque pixels combine to become 100% opaque (**Figures 3.35a** through **d**).

TIP

Alpha Add is useful when recombining two layers that have been matted from a single object.

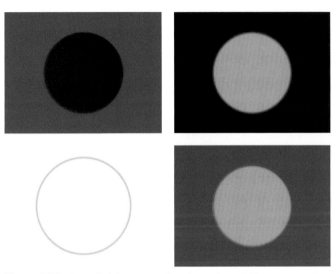

Figures 3.35a through d It seems as though matting an object over another with the exact inverse matte (a, b) would result in a fully opaque image. Instead, edge pixels form a semitransparent halo (c). Alpha Add does just what the title implies, adding the alpha values together so that inverse pixels add up to 100% transparency throughout the image (d).

Why would you combine a layer with itself, inverting the alpha? You probably wouldn't. But you might combine two layers with overlapping transparency that would require this method—for example, two parts of the same layer.

Luminescent Premultiply is one method to remove premultiplication on the fly from source footage, retaining bright values in edge pixels that are otherwise clipped. Premultiplication over black causes all semitransparent pixels to become darker; removing it can cause them to appear dimmer than they should.

TIP

Luminescent premultiply can be useful in cases where an element with transparency has been created against a black background within After Effects, bypassing the opportunity to remove premultiplication on import.

Track Mattes

Track mattes allow you to use the alpha or luminance information of one layer as the transparency of another layer (**Figure 3.36**). It's a simple enough concept, yet one that is absolutely fundamental as a problem-solving tool for complex composites.

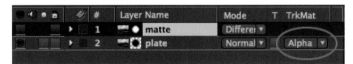

Figure 3.36 The alpha of layer 1 is set as the alpha of layer 2 via the highlighted pull-down menu. The small icons to the left indicate which is the image and which is the matte.

The perceptual difference between an alpha channel and a track matte isn't, for the most part, too difficult to grasp. In both cases, you have pixels with a value (in 8-bit color space) between 0 and 255, whether a grayscale alpha channel or three channels of color. With color, the three channels are simply averaged together to make up a single grayscale alpha. With 16 and even 32 bpc, it's finer increments in the same range.

To set a track matte, place the layer that contains the transparency data directly above its target layer in the Timeline and choose one of the four options from the Track Matte pull-down menu:

▶ **Alpha Matte:** Uses the alpha channel of the track matte layer as if it were the alpha of the underlying target layer

▶ **Alpha Inverted Matte:** Does the same as Alpha Matte but inverts the result, so that the lighter areas of the alpha are transparent and the darker areas are opaque

▶ **Luma Matte:** Uses the luminance data of the track matte layer (the relative brightness of the red, green, and blue channels combined) as if it were the alpha of the underlying target layer

▶ **Luma Inverted Matte:** Does the same as Luma Matte but inverts the result, so that the lighter areas of the alpha are transparent and the darker areas are opaque

Share a Matte

Node-based compositing programs all make it possible for a single node to provide transparency to as many others as is needed. After Effects also has a one-to-many capacity, but it generally means precomping and reusing the nested composition in several places. The point here is that in After Effects, each track matte needs to be a layer in the composition. To share it dynamically among several layers—allowing you to change the matte and have the change affect them all the same way—requires either that the matte be precomposed and all the changes made in the precomp, or that you use expressions to link essential properties together (this being the more complicated and limited approach, but one that avoids precomping).

By default, visibility of the track matte layer is disabled when you activate it from the layer below by choosing one of these four modes, which is generally desirable. Some clever uses of track mattes leave them on; for example, by matting out the bright areas of the image and turning on the matte, setting it to Add mode, you could naturally brighten those areas even more.

Track mattes solve a lot of compositing problems. They also help overcome limitations of After Effects. For example, it's not possible to track a mask in After Effects. But it is possible to apply the mask to a track matte instead, and then to track that layer (instead of the mask itself). Chapter 8, "Effective Motion Tracking," discusses this in detail; it can change rotoscoping in After Effects from nearly impossible to easy. Any procedural matte that you create using techniques described in Chapter 6 can be applied as a track matte rather than directly on a layer; this allows you, for example, to create a matte with Keylight without having it change the color of the matted layer.

Gotchas

Even an advanced user has to pay attention when working in a composition with track mattes. They are exceptional in certain ways that can bite you. Unlike parented layers, track mattes do not stay connected with their target if moved around; instead, if you move a layer that has a track matte set to it without moving the matte along with it, the layer will use whatever layer is above it. Move it to the top of the composition and it will use no track matte until you add another image above it, but at that point you may have forgotten all about having applied the track matte in the first place.

After Effects does at least help you in certain ways. Duplicate a layer (**Ctrl+D**/**Cmd+D**) with a track matte activated and it moves up two layers, above the track matte layer. Include the track matte when you duplicate and

NOTES

If the layer to which the track matte is applied already has an alpha channel, then the new selection area created by the track matte is opaque only in the areas that intersect.

it also moves up two layers, so layer order is preserved (**Figure 3.37**).

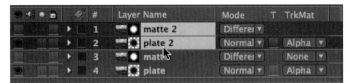

Figure 3.37 Select and duplicate the layers from Figure 3.41, and the two new layers leapfrog above to maintain the proper image/matte relationship.

NOTES

If there seems to be some doubt as to whether edits you are applying to the track matte are properly affecting the target, be scientific about it. First crank up the effect applied to the track matte, so it's obvious whether it is applied or not. If it's not, you must precompose the track matte layer; this forces it to render prior to track matting.

Render Order

Render order when using track mattes can be tricky. In most cases, adjustments and effects that you apply to the matte layer are calculated prior to creating the target matte, but in other cases you must first precompose for applied effects and adjustments to activate prior to application of the track matte.

And what happens when you apply a track matte to another track matte? Generally speaking, this will not work and the practice should be avoided. It will work in some cases, however, and the user interface does not prohibit doing so. A better idea is certainly to precompose the first instance of track matting and apply the second track matte to that nested composition.

The next chapter looks in depth at solving issues related to render order such as these; you'll begin to see how to use the Timeline as a visual problem-solving tool for such situations.

4

Optimize the Pipeline

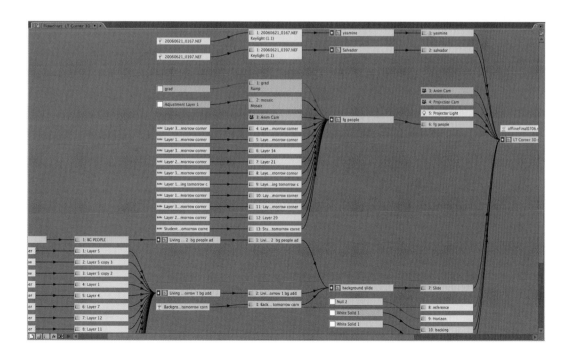

Build a system that even a fool can use and only a fool will want to use it.

–George Bernard Shaw

Optimize the Pipeline

This chapter examines how image data flows through an After Effects project in detail. That may not sound gripping until you find you are able to work faster and solve thorny problems as a result.

At times, you must be the digital compositor version of a master chef—someone who knows what has to be finished before something else can be started, and what can be prepped and considered "done" before it's time to serve the final result. At other times, you find yourself thinking more like a programmer, able to isolate and "debug" elements of a project. This chapter helps you artistically and technically, as if the two can be separated.

Once you

- ▶ Understand how to use multiple compositions
- ▶ Know when to precompose
- ▶ Know how to optimize rendering time

you will find the After Effects experience closer to what you might call "real-time." Efficient rendering, however, depends on well-organized compositions and the ability to plan for bottlenecks and other complications.

Multiple Compositions, Multiple Projects

It's easy to lose track of stuff when projects get complicated. This section demonstrates

- ▶ How and why to create a project template
- ▶ How to keep a complex, multiple-composition pipeline organized
- ▶ Shortcuts to help orient you quickly

These tips are especially useful if you're someone who knows compositing well but find After Effects disorienting at times.

Project Templates

I'm always happiest with a project that is well organized, even if I'm the only one likely ever to work on it. Keeping the Project panel well organized and tidy can clarify your ability to think about the project itself.

Figure 4.1 shows a typical project template containing multiple compositions to create one final shot. Considering the days or even weeks of takes that can be necessary, this level of organization can be a lifesaver. Here are some criteria to use when creating your own:

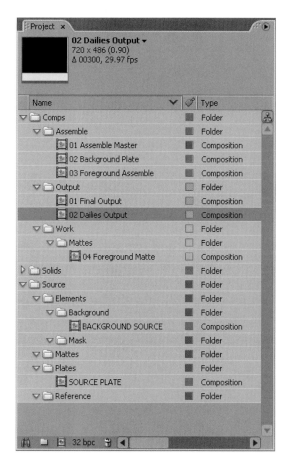

Figure 4.1 Here's how a visual effects shot might be organized. There are two basic categories of folders (Source and Comps) and preconfigured compositions numbered to appear in correct render order. This template and a simplified version of it are included on the book's disc.

▶ Create folders to group specific types of elements, such as Source, Precomps, and Reference.

▶ Number the Master comps; that way they show up in order atop the Project panel and their order can more easily be discerned elsewhere.

▶ Create a dedicated Final Output comp preset to the exact format and length of the final shot. No edits happen here, nor previews, so that the work area and any other settings cannot inadvertently be set wrong at render time.

▶ Add any useful guide layers. These could include masks for various delivery formats and preset adjustment layers with Levels set to high contrast (for checking black and white level matches; more on these in "Guide Layers") (**Figure 4.2**).

Figure 4.2 A film project can include preset layers such as these. Nonrendering guide layers show the holdout areas for that film's delivery formats, as well as a Levels adjustment, normally off, to "slam" the gamma (more about that in Section II). There can be a color correction specified as not to be edited (if it's part of the overall look), as well as precomped foreground and background layers.

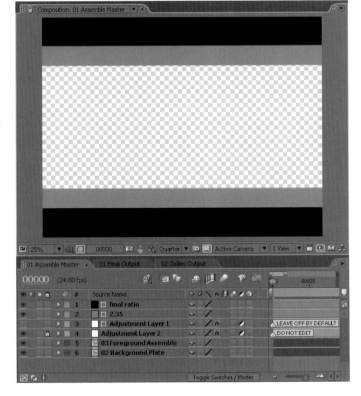

▶ Organize a Source folder and create a composition for each source clip used in the shot. Just as with the Final Output comp, no edits go into this comp; this makes it easier to cleanly replace versions of source footage, should that become necessary.

▶ If sharing the project as a template, optionally add a locked placeholder layer to key comps explaining how to use them.

The basic elements of a Master comp, source comps, and a render comp seem useful on a shot of just about any complexity, but the template can include a lot more than that: custom expressions, camera rigs, Color Management settings, and recurring effects setups.

Tabbed Timelines

The Timeline is great for timing, but once your project requires multiple nested comps, you can begin to lose your sense of the big picture and find yourself hunting for a given comp. Here's how to avoid that.

First of all, and most obviously, close Timeline palettes that aren't currently essential (with any Timeline highlighted, choose **Ctrl+Alt+A/Cmd+Opt+A**). Or close them all, reopen the master composition, and Alt/Option-double-click on any precomp you need to edit, repeating as necessary to drill several comps deep. The reopened tabs now follow, right to left, the basic render order.

To edit the Timeline of a nested comp while looking at the master or another later one, enable the lock icon at the upper left of the viewer you want to remain active. Now that viewer is displayed and previewed no matter which Timeline is forward.

Alternatively, you can work viewing a precomp or layer and always preview a master view using the Always Preview This View toggle at the lower left of the Composition panel. Not everyone—myself included—uses this feature, because of the unwelcome surprise of discovering it's still on when it should be off.

TIP

Why place source footage in its own precomp prior to working with it? One typical scenario is retransfer of film. An initial one-light initial transfer of film footage will not match pixel-for-pixel with a retransfer for color or exposure correction, but they could be carefully lined up in this comp, obviating problems with masks or other pixel-specific edits.

TIP

To navigate quickly forward or backward through a set of open comp tabs, press Alt+Shift+ comma or Alt+Shift+period (Option+Shift+ comma or Option+Shift+period on a Mac). You can remember them as the < and > keys, as if they were arrows.

TIP

To quickly split the view and create two viewers side-by-side, one locked, try Ctrl+Alt+Shift+N (Cmd+Option+Shift+N).

The Project/Comp Relationship

Because After Effects has you organize source elements in one place (the Project panel) and work with them in another (Timeline), it's helpful to know all the various ways to work with them in synchronicity.

Besides numbering compositions and organizing them into folders in the Project panel, as recommended earlier, context-clicking is most helpful:

▶ Select any item in the Project panel and adjacent to its name by the thumbnail at the top of the panel is a small pull-down caret, along with the number of times, if any, the item is used in a comp (**Figure 4.3**)

Figure 4.3 Click the caret next to the total number of times an item is used to see a list of where it is used.

▶ Context-click any item in the Project panel and choose Reveal in Composition, then the name of any composition in which that item appears (**Figure 4.4**).

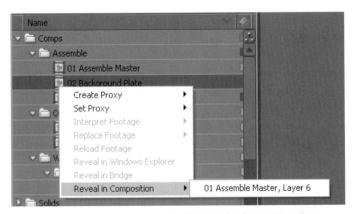

Figure 4.4 Context-click any item, and under Reveal in Composition choose from a list, if applicable; that Timeline opens with the item selected.

▶ Context-click any footage, comp or solid item in the Timeline and choose Reveal Layer Source in Project to see that item highlighted in the Project panel (**Figure 4.5**).

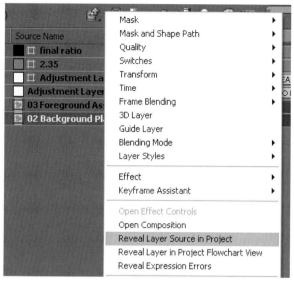

Figure 4.5 Context-click any footage item in the Timeline and you can choose to reveal it either in the Project panel or in Flowchart view.

Figure 4.6 Find the empty area below the layers in the Timeline and context-click; you can reveal the current comp in the Project panel.

▶ Context-click in the empty area of a Timeline and choose Reveal Composition in Project to see the current composition highlighted in the Project panel (**Figure 4.6**).

Alt/Option-double-click any composition nested in the Timeline to open its Timeline (simply double-clicking it only reveals it as a layer).

▶ New in CS3, the Open Parent Composition button atop the Timeline allows you to reveal the current composition in any other Timelines in which it might appear (**Figure 4.7**).

Figure 4.7 This button, a new addition to After Effects CS3, displays a list of comps in which the open comp is nested.

TIP

It's rather obvious, but descriptive composition names really help make sense of things. For example, you can begin the name of the Master comp with 00, the first nested comp 01, and so on, followed by a descriptive name in a standard format, such as 03_pcomp_smokeElement and so on (underscores are largely optional, a sometimes useful Unix convention to keep names as a single string).

Precomping and Composition Nesting

Precomping is often regarded as the major downside of compositing in After Effects, because it obscures vital information from view. Artists will let a composition become completely unwieldy, with dozens of layers, rather than bite the bullet and precomp. Yet precomping is an effective way to solve problems and optimize a project, provided you plan things out a little.

Just to get our terms straight, *precomping* is the action of selecting a set of layers in a composition and assigning them to a new subcomp. Closely related to this is *composition nesting*, the action of placing one already created composition inside of another.

Typically, you precomp by selecting the layers of a composition that can and should be grouped together and choosing Precompose from the Layer menu (keyboard shortcut **Ctrl+Shift+C**/**Cmd+Shift+C**).

Two options are presented, the second one unavailable if multiple layers are selected: to leave attributes (effects, transforms, masks, paint, blending modes) in place or transfer them into the new composition.

Why Do It?

Precomping is both the solution to most problems, and something of a necessary evil in a timeline-based application like After Effects.

Besides preventing a composition from containing so many layers that you can't display them all at once, there are some good reasons to precomp:

▶ To reuse a set of elements as one: If you ever find yourself making the same adjustments to two different layers, or even anticipate doing so, it's generally more effective and foolproof to adjust simultaneously using a single precomp.

▶ To fix render order problems: Because you cannot change the order in which effects, masks and transforms occur, precomping is sometimes the only way.

For example, should you wish to blur inside a mask, without affecting the mask selection itself, precomp the blurred element, then mask the nested composition.

▶ To keep the Master comp well organized: Not only is it tidier to have fewer layers in top-level comps, grouping together elements that are interrelated influences how you think about the composite.

▶ Because an element or a set of layers is essentially done: If you can finish some part of your shot, particularly if it's a render-intensive portion such as a color key or retime, precomping that part gives you the option of pre-rendering it, thus enhancing interactivity thereafter. It also helps remind you that you no longer need to consider editing that portion of the project.

If you're already comfortable with the idea of precomping, focus on the last point. This chapter describes the advantages to finishing an element, if only for the time being, instead of always keeping options open. Most "real-time" compositing systems rely heavily on the equivalent of pre-rendered subcomps.

Gotchas

Precomping several layers together can solve problems, but it can also create new ones. Common gotchas include

▶ You want some but not all properties to be precomped.

▶ It can be a pain to undo in order to restore precomped layers to the master composition.

▶ You must deal with the all-or-nothing behavior of blending modes and 3D layers, depending on the Collapse Transformations setting.

▶ It can be unclear how motion blur, frame blending, and collapsed transformation switches in the master composition affect nested comps.

▶ Layer timing (duration, In and Out points) and dimensions can become constraints.

Following are some useful strategies to work with these situations.

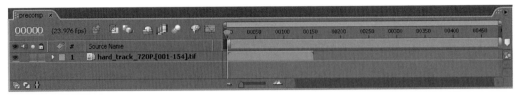

Figures 4.8 After Effects artists get in the habit of using compositions that are longer than the shot is likely ever to be, because it's much easier to shorten a nested composition than it is to lengthen it.

 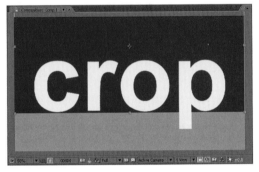

Figures 4.9a and b The nested comp has a blue background and the leg of the letter "p" extends outside its boundaries (a); a simple quick-fix is to enable Collapse Transformations, and the boundaries of the nested comp are ignored (b).

> **TIP**
>
> When adjusting timing use shortcuts: Alt/Option+[or] trims a layer's start or end point, respectively, to the current time, and [or] (no modifier) moves the current start or end point, respectively, to the current time. A script that uses the In and Out points of precomposed layers is included on the disk: preCompToLayerDur.jsx from Dan Ebberts at www. motionscript.com.

Boundaries of Time and Space

Each composition in After Effects contains its own fixed timing and pixel dimensions, and a couple of strategies help avoid making this an issue:

▶ Make source compositions longer than the shot is ever anticipated to be to avoid truncating timing (**Figure 4.8**).

▶ Enable Collapse Transformations for the nested composition to ignore its boundaries (**Figures 4.9a and b**).

These two simple rules will cover many situations, but Collapse Transformations has extra benefits and complications of its own.

Collapse Transformations

By default, Switches Affect Nested Comps is enabled in General Preferences. Any time you enable frame blending or motion blur in a master composition, those switches are also respected and passed through from any nested composition. 3D position data and blending modes, on the other hand, can be ignored if Collapse Transformations is not enabled (**Figure 4.10**). Enable it and these features behave as if the precomposed layers resided in the Master comp.

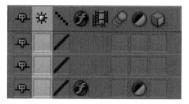

Figures 4.10 This switch (highlighted) has two roles (and two names). With a nested composition layer, it is a Collapse Transformations toggle. Enable it, and blending modes and 3D positions from the nested comp are passed through as if they were not precomposed at all. (Its other role, Continuously Rasterize, applies only to vector layers such as Adobe Illustrator files.)

CLOSE-UP

Grow Bounds

Sometimes enabling Collapse Transformations/Continuously Rasterize is not desirable—for example, if you set up 3D layers in a subcomp and don't want them affected by a camera in the Master comp. This can lead to a gotcha where effects that expand the pixel area occupied by that layer (such as blurs and distortions) are cut off at the edges of the nested composition (Figure 4.11a). By adding the Grow Bounds effect prior to the effect that needs more pixel area, you avoid this problem (Figure 4.11b).

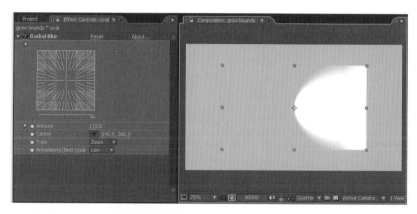

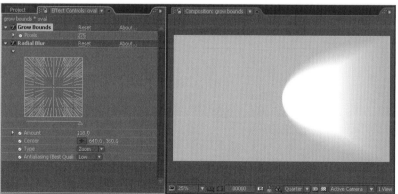

Figures 4.11a and b The half-oval layer has been precomposed, and a Radial Blur is cut off at the edges of the layer (a). Precomping would restore the other half of the oval, but Grow Bounds (b) just enlarges the boundaries of the layer so the blur is not truncated.

Collapse Transformations prevents the application of a blending mode on the collapsed layer. Apply any effect to the layer (even disable it) and After Effects must render the collapsed layer (making it what the Adobe developers call a *parenthesized* comp), a side benefit of which is that blending modes become available. 3D data, however, is no longer preserved in this scenario.

Nested Time

After Effects is less rigid than most digital video applications when working with time. All compositions in a given project need not use the same frame rate, and as has been shown you can change the frame rate of an existing composition on the fly, and keyframes retain placement relative to overall time.

With power comes responsibility, of course, so pay particular attention when you

TIP

Annoyed to find sequences importing at the wrong frame rate for your project? Change the default Sequence Footage Frames per Second under Preferences > Import.

▶ Import an image sequence

▶ Create a new composition from scratch

▶ Embed a composition with a given frame rate into another with a different frame rate

In the first two cases you're just watching out for careless errors, but in the third, you might have reason to combine two compositions with different frame rates, in which case After Effects will treat the frame rate of the embedded comp as if it were that of the master. When instead you actually want the nest frame rate preserved, set it on the Advanced tab of the Composition Settings dialog.

Advanced Composition Settings

In addition to the Motion Blur settings introduced in Chapter 2, "The Timeline," and detailed in Chapter 8,"Effective Motion Tracking," Composition Settings: Advanced contains two Preserve toggles that influence how time and space are handled when the composition is nested into another.

Preserve Frame Rate maintains the frame rate of the composition wherever it goes—into another composition with a different frame rate, or into the Render Queue with different frame rate settings. So if a simple animation cycle looks right at 4 frames per second, it won't be expanded across the higher frame rate but preserve the look of 4 fps.

Preserve Resolution When Nested controls concatenation of transforms. Typically, if an element is scaled down in a precomp and the entire composition is nested into another comp and scaled up, the two operations are treated as one, so that no data loss occurs via quantization. If the data in the subcomp is to appear pixilated, as if it were scaled up from a lower-resolution element, this toggle preserves the big pixel look.

Adjustment and Guide Layers

Two special types of layers that don't render, adjustment and guide layers, offer vitally useful applications, that might not be immediately apparent.

Adjustment Layers

An *adjustment layer* is itself invisible, but it can contain effects that affect all layers below it in the stack. It is a fundamentally simple feature with many uses. To create one, context-click in an empty area of the Timeline, and choose New > Adjustment Layer (or do the same from the Layer menu). Or, the Adjustment Layer toggle will make any layer behave as an adjustment layer (**Figure 4.12**).

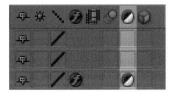

Figure 4.12 Any pixel layer becomes an adjustment layer by toggling this switch. Creating a new adjustment layer simply creates a white solid the size of the comp with this switch toggled on.

Adjustment layers allow you to apply effects to an entire composition without precomping it, simply by adding the layer to the top of the composition. That by itself is pretty cool, but there's more. Move the adjustment layer down the stack and layers above it are unaffected. Change its timing and the effects appear only on frames within the adjustment layer's In/Out points.

Furthermore you can time or effectively dial back any effect in an adjustment layer simply using Opacity. Many effects do not themselves include so direct a control, even when it makes perfect sense to do so. Colorize your scene using Hue/Saturation, and the supervisor says, "Dial it back 50%." Set the adjustment layer's Opacity to 50%, or even dial it up and down before the supe's very eyes. Impressive.

NOTES

Effects that work specifically with the alpha channel have no effect on the alpha channel of adjustment layers, instead affecting the alphas of the layers below. This is consistent with the general principle that an adjustment layer affects other layers, not itself.

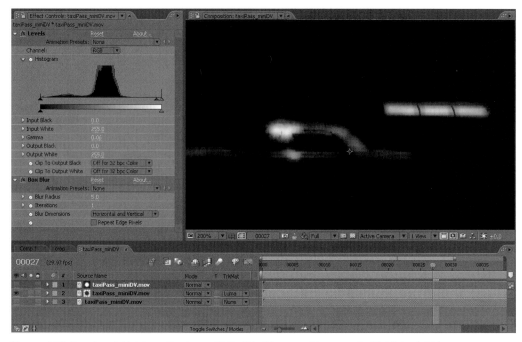

Figures 4.13 One clever trick is to matte a layer with itself, in this case to bloom out the highlights (which appear quantized in the source). A Levels effect in the matte holds out just the brightest highlights, and the matte itself is then blurred, as well as the image layer below it (here, the background is turned off for clarity).

Maladjusted

There are only a couple of major gotchas to watch out for with adjustment layers. Always keep in mind that their timing and Transform properties still apply.

In other words, make sure that your adjustment layer starts at the first frame of the comp and extends to the last frame of the comp (or the start and end frames of the portion for which you need it); otherwise its effects will pop on and off unexpectedly. And if you set any transforms to the adjustment layer, make sure they are intentional, as the boundaries of these layers are still respected in the rendering process. Finally, if you enlarge a composition you will probably have to resize any adjustment layers as well.

You can also apply mattes or masks to adjustment layers, delineating specific holdout areas; just as the entire layer can have variable transparency, so can any individual pixel. There are even clever tricks you can do by matting a layer with itself (**Figures 4.13**).

Guide Layers

Like adjustment layers, *guide layers* are normal layers with special status. A guide layer appears in the current composition but not in any subsequent compositions or the final render (unless you specifically override this functionality in Render Settings). Common uses include

▶ Foreground reference clips

▶ Temporary backgrounds to check edge transparency

▶ Text reminders (specific render instructions? Add a text layer with a bullet-pointed list in the render comp and set it as a guide layer)

▶ Adjustment layers that are used only to check images (described further in the next chapter); a layer can be both an adjustment and a guide layer

Any image layer can be made a guide layer either by context-clicking it or by choosing Guide Layer from the Layer menu. Within the current comp, you'll notice no difference (**Figure 4.14**). You can still apply effects to this layer or have other layers refer to it, and it is fully visible. Nest this composition in another composition, however, and the guide layer disappears.

NOTES

If you decide you want guide layers to appear at render time, there is a toggle to do so in Render Settings. This does, of course, sort of defeat the whole purpose, but at least the option exists.

Figure 4.14 A gradient can be an excellent background for evaluating a matte; to ensure that it never ends up in a render, however, make the background a guide layer.

Render Pipeline

To become an expert compositor is to precisely understand the order in which actions are performed on an image, also known as the render pipeline. For the most part render order is plainly displayed in the Timeline and follows consistent rules:

▶ 2D layers are always calculated from bottom to top of the layer stack.

▶ Layer properties (masks, effects, transforms, paint, and type) are always calculated from top to bottom (as indicated when layer properties are twirled down).

▶ 3D layers are calculated based on their distance from the camera (coplanar 3D layers respect stacking order and behave relative to one another as 2D layers).

TIP

3D calculations are precise well below the decimal level, but do round at some point. Coplanar 3D layers can thus introduce rendering errors and should generally be avoided by precomping them in 2D.

Figure 4.15 Just because After Effects lacks a tree/node interface doesn't mean you can't see the render order in the Timeline easily. Layer properties render in top to bottom order (as shown here: Motion Trackers, then Masks, Effects, and finally Transforms).

TIP

The Transform effect offers an alternative method to transform a layer, allowing you to transform before a given effect is applied instead of precomping (because transforms otherwise always follow effects).

TIP

Apply an Add mask to a layer set as a Luma Track Matte and the areas outside the mask contain the equivalent of solid black (transparent) pixels.

In a 2D composition, After Effects starts with the bottom layer, calculates any adjustments to it in the order properties are shown, top to bottom, then calculates adjustments to the layer above it, composites the two of them together, and so on up to the top layer of the stack, while the properties of an individual layer render top to bottom (**Figure 4.15**).

So, while effects within layers always calculate prior to transforms, by applying an effect to an adjustment layer above, you guarantee that it is rendered after the transforms of all layers below it.

Track mattes (and blending modes) are applied last, after all other layer properties (masks, effects, and transforms) have been calculated. And before a track matte takes effect, its own mask, effect, and transform data are applied. Therefore, you don't generally need to pre-render a track matte just because you've edited it.

As was mentioned in the previous chapter, it's best not to apply a track matte to another track matte. Sometimes this works, and the UI seems to condone it by not specifically prohibiting it; however, it's inconsistent, so precomping is recommended instead.

Optimize Previews and Renders

I'm sometimes able to surprise other artists with the speed and interactivity that can be squeezed out of After Effects, even working on complex, high-definition shots. My secret?

As I work, I organize portions of my master comp that I consider finished into their own subcomps, and if they require any render cycles at all, I pre-render them.

It is astonishing how many veteran compositing artists waste time redundantly re-rendering simply by failing to commit to decisions. For example, take an effects shot based on a blue-screen key: Not to pre-render the keying operation before assembling the shot adds several seconds to each frame update and minutes or even hours to a render. After Effects does its best to cache nested image data and to ignore areas with no relevant pixel data, but it's mere artificial intelligence, no match for your own.

Following are features to help you optimize a complex project for playback, beyond simple image caching as was covered in the "Caching and Previewing" section in Chapter 1. These are all features that are easy to miss or misunderstand.

Post-Render Options

Tucked away in the Render Queue panel, but easily visible if you twirl down the arrow next to Output Module (**Figure 4.16**), is a menu of three post-render actions. After the render is complete, you can choose

▶ **Import:** Simply Imports the result

▶ **Import & Replace Usage:** Keeps the source comp but replaces its use—or that of any other element you choose instead—in the project

▶ **Set Proxy:** Adds a proxy to the source comp (or any other item you specify)

> **TIP**
>
> The Info panel can show you what exactly is rendering at any time. To view these descriptive updates, choose Preferences > Display and check Show Rendering in Process in Info Panel and Flowchart.

Figure 4.16 Twirl down the arrow beside the Output Module settings for a Render Queue item and you reveal options to perform actions following the render. Note the pickwhip allowing you to specify any element for replacement.

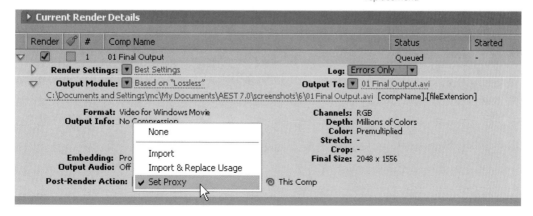

TIP

If you choose Import & Replace Usage and then need to change back, Alt/Option-drag the source comp over the replacement clip in the Project. This operation works just the same as Alt/Option-dragging footage over a highlighted item in the Timeline but replaces usage throughout the project.

With either of the latter two, the Pickwhip icon adjacent to the menu can be clicked and dragged to whatever item in the Project panel needs replacement, so that if you've already created a pre-render or proxy, you can replace it.

Proxies have the best potential to speed up your work on a heavy project, but their implementation is a little complicated.

Proxies and Pre-Renders

Any visual item in your Project panel can be set with a *proxy*, which is an imported image or sequence that stands in for that item. Its pixel dimensions, color space, compression, and even its length can differ from the item it replaces; for example, you can use a low-resolution, JPEG-compressed still image to stand in for a full-resolution, moving image background.

To create a proxy, context-click an item in the Project panel and choose Create Proxy > Movie (or Still). A render queue item is created which automatically renders at Draft quality and half-resolution; the Output Module settings create a video file with alpha, so that transparency is preserved, and the Post-Render Action uses the Set Proxy setting.

Figure 4.17 shows how a proxy appears in the Project panel. Although the scale of the proxy differs from that of the source item, transform settings within the comps that use this item remain consistent with those of the source item, so that it can be swapped in for final at any time. This is what proxies were designed to do, to allow a low-resolution file to stand in, temporarily and nondestructively, for the high-resolution final.

Figure 4.17 The black square icon to the left of an item in the Project panel indicates that a proxy is enabled; a hollow square indicates that a proxy is assigned but not currently active. Both items are listed atop the Project panel, the active one in bold.

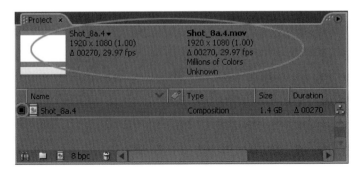

By default, the source file or composition is used to render unless specifically set otherwise in Render Settings > Proxy Use. Choosing Use Comp Proxies Only, Use All Proxies, or Current Settings options (**Figure 4.18**) allows proxies to be used in the final render. To remove them from a project, select items with proxies, context-click (or go to the File menu), and choose Set Proxy > None.

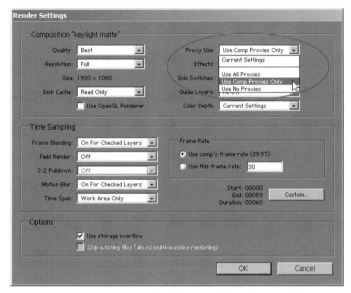

Figure 4.18 Use Comp Proxies Only offers you the best of both worlds with proxies. Source footage can employ low-resolution stand-ins that do not appear in the final render, while source compositions use fully rendered stand-ins that can save gobs of rendering time thereafter. Some users prefer to use the Current Settings option and manage proxy use in the Project panel.

Similar to proxies, but with a different intended use, are pre-rendered elements. With a composition selected, choose Composition > Pre-render and a moving image file is set to render at Best quality, full resolution; the Import and Replace Usage is set for the Output Module.

Use this one for any precomp that is render intensive and completed (or at least in some stage of completion). I recently worked on a project that reused several extremely high-resolution 3D layers, and pre-rendering them at the proper resolution, then rendering the final using the proxies, was the only way to complete the render in hours instead of days.

Precomp Proxies

Nucleo Pro is an After Effects plug-in from Gridiron Software (www.gridironsoftware.com) that optimizes After Effects' previewing workflow and performance on a multicore (multiprocessor) system. New in version 2 are Precomp Proxies, an optimized hybrid of proxies and pre-rendered compositions with a good deal more freedom and convenience than either. When a composition is marked as a Precomp Proxy, Nucleo pre-renders a full-resolution proxy in the background while you continue to work, saving it in a cache automatically so you don't even have to manage the render.

Multiprocessing

New to After Effects CS3 is a built-in Multiprocessing option. Disabled by default because it degrades performance if not set up properly, the toggle can be found under Preferences > Multiprocessing. Beneath the toggle is a long description of how this option operates on your specific system (**Figure 4.19**). For each additional processor detected, a process is opened to render nonsequential frames for RAM Previews and final renders. With this option enabled, you will notice frames turning green in the Timeline out of order as a preview is created.

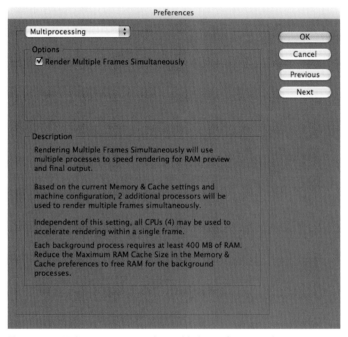

Figure 4.19 Multiprocessing must be enabled in Preferences, where copious instructions are included as to how it will operate on the given local system.

TIP

On the Mac, background processes do not open under Rosetta even if the main application does (see page 33 for more information on Rosetta).

A process is effectively a second (or third, fourth, maybe even eighth) version of After Effects opened in the background. The preference window adds a statement that each process needs a minimum amount of RAM, and directs you to lower the Maximum RAM Cache Size in Preferences > Memory & Cache as needed. As a rule of thumb, divide the number of "additional" processors into 100% and use that value; so with a quad-core machine, use a setting of 33%.

Disk Cache

As frames cache to RAM, a green bar draws in above them in the Timeline to let you know that they are saved into physical memory. When the cache is full, any new frame added to it replaces an earlier cached frame. However, there is a way to get more frames into the cache, by changing the settings in Preferences > Memory & Cache.

If you don't want to risk strange side effects by messing with the default Maximum Memory Usage and Maximum RAM Cache, a more stable and reliable option is Enable Disk Cache. Toggle this switch (off by default) and a Choose Folder dialog opens—you have to assign a specific disk location.

The optimal disk cache for video is on your fastest and least-fragmented drive; a system that has been set up for nonlinear editing is most likely to have a dedicated external drive just for this purpose. As a general rule of thumb, an external drive will be preferable if you have one; if you're on a laptop, keep in mind that the amount of disk cache that you assign is physical disk space you won't be able to use until you disable this option.

The Timeline indicates that a frame is cached to disk by drawing a blue bar above it. The entire cache is purged automatically when you quit After Effects, but if you have a need to clear the cache while the application is open, choose Edit > Purge > Image Caches.

The Conformed Media Cache section of Memory & Cache is new in CS3; playback of formats that used to be slow, such as audio and MPEG video, is now much speedier thanks to these elements being cached for optimum preview performance in this location. This is always on; you can change the location or clean the cache as needed.

Network Renders

A single system, even one with multiple processor cores, can do only so much to render an After Effects project. If your studio is large enough that it includes a render network, however, After Effects can make use of it to good effect.

NOTES

After Effects compares the speed of caches to the time required to re-render a frame; if the round-trip to the cache is slower than rendering the frame on the fly, the cache cannot be activated for that frame.

There are two basic network render options. File > Watch Folder looks in a given folder for projects ready to be rendered; these are set up using the Collect Files option. It's okay on small, intimate networks, but it has to be set up manually on each machine. The help topic Rendering on the Network: Using a Watch Folder page includes everything you need to know, so there's no reason to reiterate setup here.

On a network of more than a few machines Watch Folder is superseded by such third-party rendering solutions as Rush Render Queue (http://seriss.com/rush/). These programs run scripts that manage the process of rendering on multiple machines (**Figure 4.20**). The better applications among them, Rush included, are capable of far more than just straight-ahead renders; you can for example have one render wait until a certain time or for another one to complete before commencing.

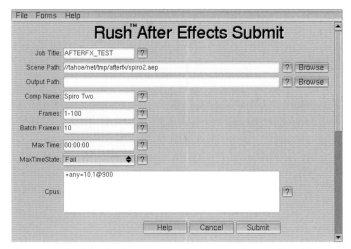

Figure 4.20 Rush Render Queue may not have a pretty front-end, but it's pretty sophisticated; this Submit panel allows you to specify which boxes will pick up the render, at what priority, how many to use, and how much time to give each of them to render before timing out. At big studios, this is indispensable.

This type of software is not generally even implemented via a standard installer; required instead are the implementation skills of a system administrator or equivalent technical expert. Most larger facilities have just such a "geek" on staff, and many advanced After Effects users are themselves capable of setting this up in smaller studios.

Multiple applications and aerender

All that the third-party render management applications are doing, behind the scenes, is sending commands to aerender, a command-line application that controls the After Effects render queue. You can do the same thing yourself, directly, although with Multiprocessing enabled you may find few reasons to do so.

On either platform, open up a command line in the terminal. On the Mac, this means opening the Terminal application; on Windows, it's Start > Run, and then type cmd and press Enter. Now on either platform, find aerender in the Adobe After Effects CS3 folder (nested in the Support Files folder on Windows) and drag it to the terminal window (or *shell*) and press Enter. The full usage manual for this command is displayed. Most helpful are the examples at the bottom. The arguments shown in quotes can be added (without the quotes) after the main command as shown in the examples, with a space between each argument.

Alternatively, you can open multiple versions of After Effects including the UI. Although memory intensive, this allows you to actually investigate, compare, and edit two projects at once.

On a Mac, all you need to do is locate Adobe After Effects 7.0.app in the Finder (most likely in Applications/Adobe After Effects 7.0) and duplicate it (**Cmd+D**). You now have two versions of the application that will open separately, and you are free to render a project in one version while continuing to work in the other. One downside is that it can be hard to tell the two of them apart (unless you hack the icon of one of them), although the duplicate application will retain whatever name you give it (Adobe After Effects 7.0 copy.app by default).

On Windows, you can open a second version of After Effects from the command line, assuming you have some basic DOS navigation skills. From the Start menu, choose Run, type cmd, and click OK. In the DOS shell that opens, navigate to the location of AfterFX.exe and then enter AfterFX.exe -m (that's "m" as in "multiple"). Voilà, a second version initializes. If you know how to write a DOS

NOTES

You can run After Effects from the Terminal in OS X and the same —m flag operates in Unix. It's just simpler for most Mac users to work directly in the Finder, but this has the advantage of saving the disk space otherwise required by the extra instance of the application.

batch script, you can create a .bat file that does all of this for you with a double-click.

Note that this is not an officially sanctioned activity, and that it's a good idea not to work on the same project that is rendering so that you don't trip yourself up inadvertently saving over your own work in the wrong application. Note also that you are not limited to running just two copies at a time, but for most systems, this is a sensible limit.

To prevent the two copies of After Effects from competing with one another, you can even lower the priority of the background copy of the application so that full interactivity is maintained as you continue to work in the forward copy. This is easily done on a Windows system: Open the Task Manager (**Ctrl+Alt+Del**), click on the Processes tab, locate the background application, and right-click to decrease the Set Priority setting. On the Mac, this involves use of the nice command in Terminal (man nice to learn more); the trick is getting the path to After Effects entered correctly, which, like DOS, is beyond the scope of this book.

Adobe Media Encoder

Also new in After Effects CS3 is Adobe Media Encoder, a dedicated render application for certain media formats, including Flash Video, H.264, MPEG-2 and Adobe Clip Notes. Choose one of these in Output Module Settings and the Encoder reveals many specialized options having to do with that particular format.

Owners of Adobe Production Premium or Master Collection can also access Media Encoder from Premiere Pro, where it can perform multipass encoding (essential for the best quality compression). Because the render queue fundamentally works one frame at a time only, this capability does not exist in After Effects.

Project Optimization

Finally, to finish Section I of this book, a clean sweep of preferences, memory management settings and what do to if After Effects crashes.

CLOSE-UP

Clip Notes

One final very cool addition to CS3 when working with client feedback is Clip Notes, one of the formats rendered by Media Encoder. This feature is uniquely Adobe; it lets you create an Acrobat PDF file with the rendered composition embedded at the center of the page, the rest of which is preformatted for comments that maintain their relationship to clip timing even when reimported into After Effects. Make sure that you have the latest version of Adobe Reader or Acrobat, and be prepared to follow the copious instructions carefully.

Setting Preferences and Project Settings

The preference defaults have changed in version 7.0 and you may be happy with most of them. Here, however, are a few you might want to adjust that haven't been mentioned yet:

▶ **Preferences > General > Levels of Undo:** The default is 32, which may be geared toward a system with less RAM than yours. I set mine to 47; something around there usually gives me enough undos. Setting it to the maximum value of 99 won't bring the application to a grinding halt, but it may shorten the amount of time available in RAM Previews.

▶ **Preferences General:** Check the options Allow Scripts to Write Files and Access Network to use some of the scripts included with this book. Use System Color Picker may be preferable on a Mac, but not so in Windows XP (at this writing I can't comment on Vista).

▶ **Preferences > Display:** Go ahead, set Disable Thumbnails in Project Panel on a project of any substantial size. If you never look at the thumbnails at the top of the Project panel, you might as well disable the feature. Otherwise, be prepared for situations in which you wait for it to update, especially over a network.

▶ **Preferences > User Interface Colors:** You may wish to darken the UI using the User Interface Brightness slider. In the same dialog, consider turning on Cycle Mask Colors so that multiple masks applied to a layer automatically have different colors.

▶ **The Secret Preferences:** Hold down Shift while opening the Preferences dialog and you'll see an extra "Secret" category of Preferences at the bottom of the drop-down list. These relate to memory management, covered in the next section.

TIP

To restore Preferences to their defaults, hold down **Alt+Ctrl+Shift/ Option+Cmd+Shift** immediately after launching After Effects, and click OK on the prompt. Press down **Alt/Option** while clicking OK, and you're asked if you want to delete your shortcuts file as well (otherwise, they remain).

Hack Shortcuts or Text Preferences

After Effects Shortcuts and Preferences are saved as text files which are fully editable and relatively easy to understand, although if you're not comfortable with basic hacking (learning how code works by looking at other bits of code) I don't recommend it. The files are located as follows:

Windows: Documents and Settings\[user profile]\ Application Data\Adobe\After Effects\8.0\

Mac OS: Users/[user profile]/Library/Preferences/ Adobe/Adobe After Effects/8.0/

The names of the files are

> Adobe After Effects 8.0 Prefs
> Adobe After Effects 8.0 Shortcuts

These can be opened with any text editor that doesn't add its own formatting and works with Unicode. The default applications, TextEdit on the Mac and Notepad on Windows, are acceptable, although there are more full-featured alternatives. Make a safety copy before editing by simply duplicating the file (any variation in the file name causes it not to be recognized by After Effects). Revert to the safety by giving it the original file name should any-thing start to go haywire after the edit.

The Shortcuts file includes a bunch of comments at the top (each line begins with a # sign). The Shortcuts them-selves are arranged in a very specific order that must be preserved, and if you add anything, it must be added in the right place. You can add the line

```
"NewEffectsLayer" = "(Cmd+Option+Y)"
```

or on Windows

```
"NewEffectsLayer" = "(Ctrl+Alt+Y)"
```

between "NewDebugComp" and "NewLight"—this gives you a shortcut to create a new adjustment layer. If you under-stand this basic format, you can change other shortcuts to be what you like. For example, if you don't like the fact that Go To Time was changed in CS3 (apparently to align it with other Adobe applications) search for "GoToTime" and make your changes to the shortcut in quotes after the = sign; "(Alt+Shift+J)" becomes "(Ctrl+G)" on Windows, "(Opt+Shift+J)" becomes "(Cmd+G)" on Mac (but make sure to change the Group shortcut to something else).

Be extra careful when editing Preferences—a stray character in this file can make After Effects unstable. Most of the contents should not be touched, but here's one example of a simple and useful edit (for studios where a dot is preferred before the number prefix instead of the underscore), change

```
"Sequence number prefix" = "_"
```

to

```
"Sequence number prefix" = "."
```

In other cases, a simple and easily comprehensible numerical value can be changed:

```
"Eye Dropper Sample Size No Modifier" = "1"
"Eye Dropper Sample Size With Modifier" = "5"
```

and in many cases the value after the = is a binary yes/no value, expressed as 0 for no or 1 for yes, so if you're nostalgic for how the After Effects render chime sounded in its first several versions, find

```
"Play classic render chime" = "0"
```

and change the 0 to a 1. Save the file, restart After Effects, and invoke nostalgic memories of past renders.

Memory Management

One area of major improvement in After Effects 7.0 is that the application can handle more physical memory (RAM) than previous versions.

In OS X, After Effects can now see and use more than 2 GB of RAM. Theoretically the amount of space available is 4 GB, but because the system reserves some of that space, it is more like 3.5 GB. Your machine may have more total memory than this, but most applications on a Mac are still limited to 32-bit 4 GB address spaces.

On Windows XP, the maximum amount of memory supported for a single application is 4 GB (again, using 32-bit 4 GB address spaces). According to Microsoft, however, "The virtual address space of processes and applications is still limited to 2 GB unless the /3GB switch is used in the

TIP

A fantastic script for specifying your own modifier keys called "KeyEd Up" has been developed specifically for After Effects CS3 by Jeff Almasol, author of other scripts included with this book. Because Jeff is now an Adobe employee, his scripts are posted at adobe.com and were not made available for the book's disc.

On the Mac: Force a Crash

One benefit of After Effects has historically been that it is among the most stable applications in its category, and when it does crash, it attempts to do so gracefully, offering the option to save before it exits. The new auto-save options, if used properly, further diminish the likelihood that you are ever likely in danger of losing project data.

For OS X users, there is an extra feature that may come in handy if the application becomes unresponsive but does not actually crash.

▶ Open Terminal, and enter ps –x (then press Return) to list all processes. Scan the resulting list for After Effects and note its PID (Process ID) value.

▶ Now enter kill –SEGV ### where "###" is replaced by the After Effects PID value. This causes the application to crash with a save opportunity.

Boot.ini file." Editing this file is out of the scope for this book, so check out www.microsoft.com/whdc/system/plat-form/server/PAE/PAEmem.mspx for specific information.

On either platform, extra memory (beyond what the application can use) will come in handy when running more than one version of the application, when using Nucleo (which simulates running multiple versions of After Effects), or, obviously, when running other applications simultaneously.

Some users have found in certain situations that renders that fail due to out-of-memory errors will succeed if the image cache is emptied more aggressively than usual. If you want to try this, hold down the Shift key when opening any category of Preferences, and the Secret category is revealed in the pull-down menu. You can check Disable Layer Cache and specify the number of frames after which the cache will be purged (1 being the most aggressive setting). You can also check Ignore Sequence Rendering Errors, which will continue rendering even if out-of-memory errors occur. Under normal circumstances, neither should be necessary; this option exists only for desperation situations in which renders fail due to memory errors.

Create a Shot

You've reached the end of Section I (assuming you're reading this book linearly, that is) and should now have a firm grasp on getting the most out of the After Effects work-flow. Now it's time to focus more specifically on the art of visual effects. Section II, "Effects Compositing Essentials," will teach you the techniques, and Section III, "Creative Explorations," will show you how they work in specific effects situations.

Avanti.

SECTION II

Effects Compositing Essentials

5

Color Correction

*I cannot pretend to be impartial about the colors.
I rejoice with the brilliant ones, and am genuinely
sorry for the poor browns.*

—Winston Churchill

Color Correction

No skill is as essential for a compositor as the ability to authoritatively and conclusively take control of color, such that foreground and background elements seem to inhabit the same world, shots from a sequence are consistent with one another, and their overall look matches the artistic direction of the project.

The compositor, after all, is typically the last one to touch a shot before it goes into the edit. Inspired, artistic color work injects life, clarity, and drama into standard (or even substandard) 3D output, adequately (or even poorly) shot footage, and flat, monochromatic stills. It draws the audience's attention where it belongs, never causing them to think about the compositing at all.

Good compositors are credited with possessing a "good eye," but color matching is a skill that you can practice and refine even if you have no feel for adjusting images— indeed, even if you consider yourself color blind.

And despite that new color tools appear each year to refine your ability to dial in color, for color matching in After Effects, three color correction tools do most of the heavy lifting: Levels, Curves, and Hue/Saturation (and because Levels and Curves overlap in their functionality, in many cases you're just choosing one or two of the three). These endure (from the earliest days of Photoshop, even) because they are stable and fast, and they will get the job done every time—just learn how to use them, and keep practicing.

A skeptic might ask:

▶ Why these old tools with so many cool newer ones?

- ▶ Why not use Brightness & Contrast to adjust, you know, brightness and contrast, or Shadow and Highlight if that's what needs adjustment?

- ▶ What do you mean I can adjust Levels even if I'm color blind?

This chapter holds the answers to these and many more questions. First, we'll look at optimizing a given image using these tools, and then move into matching a foreground layer to the optimized background, balancing colors. The goal is to get you away from hacking away, to build skills that eliminate some of the guesswork and enable artistry.

This chapter introduces topics that resound throughout the rest of the book. Chapter 11, "32 Bit HDR Compositing and Color Management," deals specifically with HDR color, and then Chapter 12, "Light," focuses on specific light and color scenarios, while the rest of Section III describes how to create specific types of effects shots.

Optimized Levels

What constitutes an "optimized" clip? What makes a color corrected image correct? Let's look at what is typically "wrong" with source footage levels and the usual methods for correcting them, laying the groundwork for color matching. As an example, we'll balance brightness and contrast of a *plate* image, with no foreground layers to match.

Levels

Levels may be the most-used tool in After Effects, and yet it's rare to find detailed descriptions of how best to use it. It consists of five basic controls—Input Black, Input White, Output Black, Output White, and Gamma—each of which can be adjusted in five separate contexts (the four individual image channels R, G, B, and A, as well as all three color channels, RGB, at once). There are two different ways to adjust these controls: via their numerical sliders or by dragging their respective carat sliders on the histogram. The latter is the more typical method for experienced users.

NOTES

The term *"plate"* stretches back to the earliest days of optical compositing (and indeed, of photography itself) and refers to the source footage, typically the background onto which foreground elements will be composited. A related term, *"clean plate,"* refers to the background with any moving foreground elements removed; its usage is covered in the following chapter.

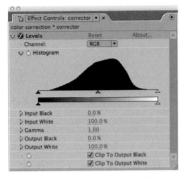

Figure 5.1 Possibly the most used "effect" in After Effects, Levels consists of a histogram and five basic controls per channel; the controls are typically adjusted using the triangles on the histogram, although the corresponding numerical/slider controls appear below.

Two check boxes at the bottom of the Levels effect controls specify whether black and white levels "clip" on output. These are checked on by default, and until you work in HDR (Chapter 11), you might as well ignore their very existence; they handle values beyond the range that your monitor can display.

Contrast: Input and Output Levels

Four of the five controls—Input Black, Input White, Output Black and Output White (**Figure 5.1**)—determine brightness and contrast, and combined with the fifth, gamma, they offer more precision than is possible with the effect called Brightness & Contrast.

Figures 5.2a and **b** show a Ramp effect applied to a solid using the default settings, followed by the Levels effect. Move the black caret at the lower left of the histogram— the Input Black level—to the right, and values below

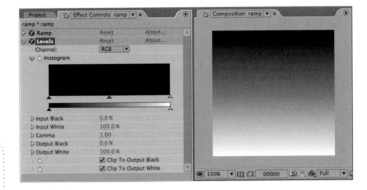

Figures 5.2a and b Levels is applied to a layer containing a Ramp effect at the default settings, which creates a smooth gradient from black to white (a); this will be the basis for understanding what the basic color correction tools do. You can create this for yourself or open 05_colorCorrection.aep, which also contains the image (b).

its threshold (the numerical Input Black setting, which changes as you move the caret) are pushed to black. The further you move the caret, the more values are "crushed" to pure black.

Move the Input White carat at the right end of the histogram to the left, toward the Input Black caret. The effect is similar to Input Black's but inverted: more and more white values are "blown out" to pure white (**Figure 5.3**).

TIP

Compositing is science as well as art, and so this section employs a useful scientific tool: the control, which is a study subject that eliminates random or hidden variables. This control for the Levels effect is a grayscale gradient I generated with the Ramp effect. You can often set up similar experiments to clarify your understanding of computer graphics applications.

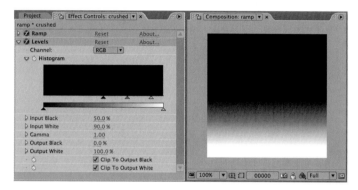

Figure 5.3 Raising Input Black and lowering Input White has the effect of increasing contrast at either end of the scale; at an extreme adjustment like this, many pixels are pushed to full white or black (in an 8-bpc or 16-bpc project).

CLOSE-UP

Why Not Brightness & Contrast?

The Brightness & Contrast effect is like training wheels compared to Levels. It contains two sliders, one for each property. Raising the Contrast value above 0.0 causes the values above middle gray to move closer to white and those below the mid-point to move closer to black, in proportion. Lower it and pixels turn gray. The Brightness control offsets the midpoint of any contrast adjustment, allowing a result like that in Figure 5.4.

So what's the problem? Almost any image needs black and white adjusted to a different degree, and Brightness & Contrast allows this only indirectly; this can make adjustment a game of cat and mouse, as illustrated in **Figures 5.5a, b**, and **c**. Add to that the fact that there is no histogram or individual Channel control, and it becomes a lot like playing the piano with mittens on.

Either adjustment effectively increases contrast, but note that the midpoint of the gradient also changes if one is adjusted further than the other. In Figure 5.3 Input Black has been adjusted more heavily than Input White, causing the horizon of the gradient to move closer to white and more of the image to turn black. You can re-create this adjustment with Brightness & Contrast (**Figure 5.4**), but to do so you must adjust both contrast and brightness, with no direct control of the midpoint (gamma) of the image.

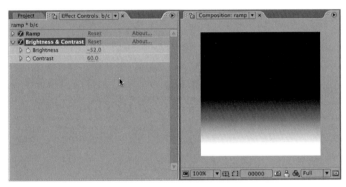

Figure 5.4 You can use Brightness & Contrast to match the look of Figure 5.3's gradient, mostly because it has no gamma adjustment.

Figures 5.5a, b, and c The source (a) was balanced for the sky, leaving foreground detail too dark to make out. Raising Brightness to bring detail out of the shadows makes the entire image washed out (b); raising Contrast to compensate completely blows out the sky (c). Madness.

TIP

You can reset any individual effect control by context-clicking it and choosing Reset. You know it's individual if it has its own stopwatch.

Reset Levels (click Reset at the top of the Levels effect controls) and try the same experiment with Output Black and Output White, whose controls sit below the little gradient. Output Black specifies the darkest black that can appear in the image; adjust it upwards and the minimum value is raised.

Similarly, lowering Input White is something like dimming the image, cutting off the maximum possible white value at the given threshold. Adjust both and you effectively reduce contrast in the image; with them close together, the gradient becomes a solid gray (**Figure 5.6**).

Note that you can even cross the two carets; if you drag Output White all the way down, and Output Black all the way up, you have inverted your image (although the more straightforward way to do this typically is to use the Channel: Invert effect).

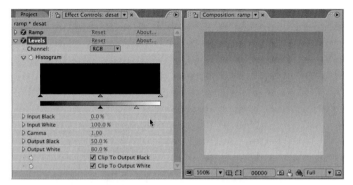

Figure 5.6 Raising Output Black and lowering Output White reduces contrast in the dark and light areas of the image, respectively; they will come into play in the Matching section.

Evidently the Input and Output controls have the opposite effect on their respective black and white values, when examined in this straightforward fashion. However, there are even situations where you would use them together.

As is the case throughout After Effects, the controls are operating in the order listed in the interface. In other words, raising the Input Black level first crushes the blacks, and then a higher Output Black level raises all of those pure black levels as one (**Figure 5.7**). It does not restore the black detail in the original pixels; the blacks remain crushed, they all just become lighter.

If you're thinking, "So what?" at this point, just stay with this—the controls are being broken down to build up an understanding.

Figure 5.7 Black and white levels crushed by adjusting the Input controls aren't then brought back by the Output controls, which instead simply limit the overall dynamic range of the image, raising the darkest possible black level and lowering the brightest possible white.

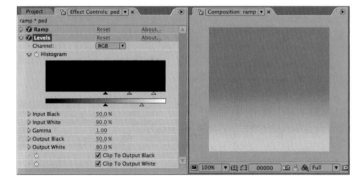

Brightness: Gamma

As you adjust the Input Black and White values, you may have noticed the third caret that maintains its place between them. This is the Gamma control, affecting midtones (the middle gray point in the gradient) at the highest proportion and black and white, not at all. Adjust it over the gradient and notice that you can push the grays in the image brighter (by moving it to the left) or darker (to the right) without changing the black and white levels.

Many images have healthy contrast, but a gamma boost gives them extra punch. Similarly, an image that looks a bit too "hot" may be instantly adjusted simply by lowering gamma. As you progress through the book, you will see that it plays a crucial role not only in color adjustment but also in the inner workings of the image pipeline itself (more on that in Chapter 11).

In most cases, the histogram won't itself offer much of a clue as to whether the gamma needs adjusting, or by how much (see "Problem Solving using the Histogram," for more on the topic). The image itself provides a better guide for how to adjust gamma (**Figure 5.8**).

So what is your guideline for how much you should adjust gamma, if at all? I first learned to adjust too far before dialing back, which is especially helpful when learning. An even more powerful gamma adjustment tool that scares most novice artists away is Curves (more on this later).

By mixing these five controls together, have we covered everything there is to know about using Levels? No—because there are not, in fact, five basic controls in Levels (Input and Output White and Black plus Gamma), but instead, five times five (RGB, Red, Green, Blue, and Alpha).

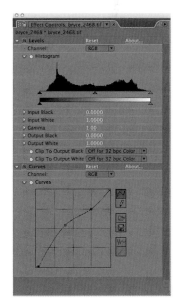

Figure 5.8 The image from Figure 5.2 is improved with a boost to gamma using Curves (explained ahead); the indication that this is a good idea comes not from the histogram, which looks fine, but from the image itself, which lacks foreground detail.

CLOSE-UP

Geek Alert: What Is Gamma, Anyway?

It would be so nice simply to say, "gamma is the midpoint of your color range" and leave it at that. The more accurate the discussion of gamma becomes, the more obscure and mathematical it gets. There are plenty of artists out there who understand gamma intuitively and are able to work with it without knowing the math behind it or the way the eye sees color midtones, but here's the basic math, just in case.

Gamma adjustment shifts the midpoint of a color range without affecting the black or white points. This is done by taking a pixel value and raising it to the inverse power of the gamma value, like so:

$$\text{newPixel} = \text{pixel}^{(1/\text{gamma})}$$

You're probably used to thinking of pixel values as being 0 to 255, but this formula works only if they are *normalized* to 1. In other words, all 255 values occur between 0 and 1, so 0 is 0, 255 is 1, and 128 is .5—which is the "normal" way the math is done behind the scenes.

Why does it work this way? Because of the magic of logarithms: Any number to the power of 0 is 1, any number to the power of 1 is itself, and any fractional value (less than 1) raised to a higher power approaches 0 without ever reaching it. Lower the power closer to 0 and the value approaches 1, again without ever reaching it. Not only that, but the values distribute proportionally, along a curve, so the closer an initial value is to pure black (0) or pure white (1) the less it is affected.

To try this for yourself, all you need is After Effects and a Web browser. Create a 255×255 comp and switch the Info panel to Decimal values (in the panel menu). Enter a Gamma value of .25, divide that value into 1 (result is 4) and at www.google.com search on .5^4, then check to see if the result matches the value you see by placing your cursor over the center of frame. Now try a gamma value of 2.0; divide it into 1 and you get .5, go to Google and try searching on .5^.5. The values will line up.

Individual Channels for Color Matching

In baseball, most hitters are "hackers," unable to discern when to swing at a pitch in the fraction of a second when it approaches the plate. A very few gifted hitters, even at the professional level, can actually discern a pitch as it approaches the plate at 90+ miles per hour; Barry Bonds is the ultimate example, and I say that not only as a beleaguered Giants fan. If you color correct images without looking at individual color channels, you're only hacking, but if you develop the habit of adjusting on individual color channels, you'll swing like Barry (with or without the stimulants).

Many After Effects artists completely ignore that pull-down menu at the top of the Levels control that isolates red, green, blue, and alpha adjustments, and even those who do use it once in a while may do so with trepidation; how can you predictably understand what will happen when you adjust the five basic Levels controls on an individual channel? The gradient again serves as an effective learning tool to ponder what exactly is going on.

Reset the Levels effect applied to the Ramp gradient once more. Pick Red, Green, or Blue in the Channel pull-down of Levels and adjust the Input and Output carets. Color is introduced into what was a purely grayscale image. With the Red channel selected, by moving Red Output Black inward, you tint the darker areas of the image red. If you adjust Input White inward, the midtones and highlights turn pink (light red). If, instead, you adjust Input Black or Output White inward, the tinting goes in the opposite direction—toward cyan, in the corresponding shadows and highlights. As you probably know, on the digital wheel of color, cyan is the opposite of red, just as magenta is the opposite of green and yellow is the opposite of blue (a sample digital color wheel and a visual guide to how levels adjustments operate on individual channels are included on the book's disc).

Gradients are one thing, but the best way to make sense of this with a real image is to develop the habit of studying footage on individual color channels as you work. This is the key to effective color matching, detailed ahead.

Along the bottom of the Composition panel, all of the icons are monochrome by default save one: the Show

Channel pulldown. It contains five selections: the three color channels as well as two alpha modes. Each one has a shortcut that, unfortunately, is not shown in the menu: **Alt+1** through **Alt+4** (**Option+1** through **Option+4**) reveal each color channel in order. These shortcuts are toggles, so reselecting the active channel toggles RGB. A colored outline around the edge of the composition palette reminds you which channel is displayed (**Figure 5.10**).

Try adjusting a single channel of the gradient in Levels while displaying only that channel. You are back on familiar territory, adjusting brightness and contrast of a grayscale image. This is the way to work with individual channel adjustments, especially when beginning or if at all color blind. As you work with actual images instead of gradients, the histogram can show you what is happening in your image.

The Levels Histogram

You might have noticed the odd appearance of the histogram applying Levels to a default Ramp. If you were to try this setup on your own, depending on the size of the layer to which you applied Ramp, you might see a histogram that is flat along the top with spikes protruding at regular intervals (**Figures 5.9a** and **b**).

Same Difference: Levels (Individual Controls)

Both Levels and Levels (Individual Controls) accomplish the exact same task. The sole difference is that Levels lumps all adjustments into a single keyframe property, which expressions cannot use. Levels (Individual Controls) is particularly useful to

▶ Animate and time Levels settings individually

▶ Link an expression to a Levels setting

▶ Reset a single Levels property (instead of the entire effect)

Levels is more commonly used, but Levels (Individual Controls) is sometimes more useful.

TIP

An often overlooked feature of Levels is that it allows direct adjustment of brightness, contrast, and gamma of the grayscale transparency channel (Alpha Channel). More on this in Chapter 6, "Color Keying."

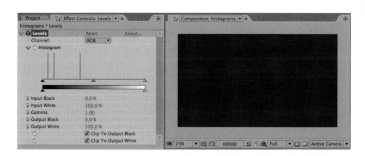

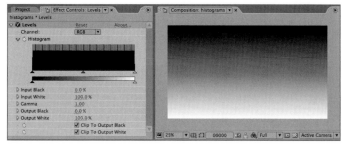

Figures 5.9a and b Strange-looking histograms. A colored solid (a) shows three spikes, one each for the red, green, and blue values, and nothing else. With Ramp (b) the distribution is even, but the spikes at the top are the result of the ramp not being an exact multiple of 255 pixels, causing certain pixels to recur more often than others.

The histogram is exactly 256 pixels wide; it is effectively a bar chart made up of 256 single pixel bars, each corresponding to one of the 256 possible levels of luminance in an 8-bpc image (these levels are displayed below the histogram, above the Output controls). In the case of a pure gradient, the histogram is flat because luminance is evenly distributed from black to white; if spikes occur in that case, it's because the image is not exactly 255 pixels high (or some exact multiple of 256, minus one edge pixel because the Ramp controls default to the edges of the layer), making it slightly uneven at 8 bits per channel.

In any case, it's more useful to look at real-world examples, because the histogram is useful for mapping image data that isn't plainly evident on its own. Its basic function is to help you assess whether any color changes are liable to help or harm the image. There is in fact no one typical or ideal histogram—they can vary as much as the images themselves, as seen back in Figure 5.8.

Despite that fact, there's a simple rule of thumb for a basic contrast adjustment. Find the top and bottom end of the RGB histogram—the highest and lowest points where there is any data whatsoever—and bracket them with the Input Black and Input White carets. To "bracket" them means to adjust these controls inward so each sits just outside its corresponding end of the histogram (**Figure 5.10**).The result stretches values closer to the top or bottom of the dynamic range, as you can easily see by applying a second Levels effect and studying its histogram (**Figure 5.11**).

Try applying Levels to any image or footage from the disc and see for yourself how this works. First crush the blacks (by moving Input Black well above the lowest black level in the histogram) and then blow out the whites (moving Input White below the highest white value). Don't go too far, or subsequent adjustments will not bring back that detail—unless you work in 32-bpc HDR mode (Chapter 11). Occasionally a stylized look will call for crushed contrast, but generally speaking, this is bad form.

Black and white are not at all equivalent, in terms of how your eye sees them. Blown-out whites are ugly and can be

TIP

Moving Input White and Input Black to the edges of the histogram is similar to what the Auto Levels effect does. If that by itself isn't enough to convince you to avoid using Auto Levels, or the "Auto" correctors, consider also that they are processor intensive (slow) and resample on every frame (so the result is not consistent from frame to frame, which isn't generally what you want).

TIP

Footage is by its very nature dynamic, so it is a good idea to leave headroom for the whites and foot room for the blacks until you start working in 32 bits per channel. Headroom is particularly important when anything exceptionally bright—such as a sun glint, flare, or fire—enters frame.

Figure 5.10 Here is a perfect case for bringing the triangle controls corresponding to Input Black and Input White in to bracket the edges of the histogram, increasing contrast and bringing out vibrant colors without losing detail.

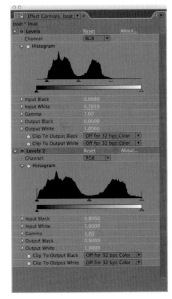

Figure 5.11 Adding a second Levels effect to this image's histogram only reveals the result of the prior adjustment; levels now extend to each end of the contrast spectrum.

a dead giveaway of an overexposed digital scene, but your eye is much more sensitive to subtle gradations of low black levels. These low, rich blacks account for much of what makes film look like film, and they can contain a surprising amount of detail, none of which, unfortunately, would be apparent on the printed page.

The occasions on which you would optimize your footage, making it look best, by raising Output Black or lowering Output White controls are unusual, as this lowers dynamic range and the overall contrast. However, there are many uses in compositing for lowered contrast, to soften overlay effects (say, fog and clouds), high-contrast mattes, and so on. More on that later in this chapter and throughout the rest of the book.

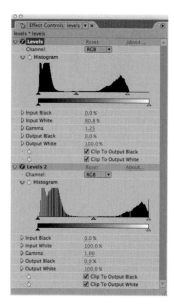

Figures 5.12a and b In the first instance of Levels (a), Gamma is raised and the Input White brought in to enhance detail in the dark areas of the foreground (b). The second instance is applied only to show its histogram.

Problem Solving using the Histogram

As you've no doubt noticed, the Levels histogram does not update as you make adjustments. After Effects lacks a panel equivalent to Photoshop's Histogram palette, but you can, of course, apply a Levels effect just for the histogram, if only for the purposes of learning (as was done in Figure 5.11).

The histogram reveals a couple of new wrinkles in the backlit shot from Figure 5.5, now adjusted with Levels to bring out foreground highlights (**Figures 5.12a** and **b**). At the top end of the histogram the levels peak into a spike. This may indicate clipping and a loss of image detail.

Many current displays, and in particular flat-panels and projectors, lack the black detail that can be produced on a good CRT monitor or captured on film. The next time you see a projected film, notice how much detail you can see in the shadows and compare.

At the other end of the scale is the common result of a Gamma adjustment: a series of spikes rising out of the lower values like protruding hash marks, even though a 16-bpc project prevents quantization. Raising Gamma stretches the levels below the midpoint, causing them to clump up at regular intervals. As with crushing blacks and blowing out highlights—the net effect is a loss of detail, although in this case, the spikes are not a worry because they occur among a healthy amount of surrounding data. In more extreme cases, in which there is no data in between the spikes whatsoever, you may see a prime symptom of overadjustment, *banding* (**Figure 5.13**).

Figure 5.13 Push an adjustment far enough and you may see quantization, otherwise known as banding in the image. Those big gaps in the histogram are expressed as visible bands on a gradient. Switching to 16 bpc from 8 bpc is an instant fix for this problem in most cases.

Banding is typically the result of limitations of 8-bit color, and 16-bit color mode was added to After Effects 5.0 specifically

Figure 5.14 An entire project can be toggled from the default 8-bit color mode to 16-bit mode by Alt-clicking (Option-clicking) the project color depth toggle in the Project panel; this prevents the banding seen in Figure 5.13.

to address that problem. You can switch to 16 bpc by Alt-clicking (Option-clicking) on the bit-depth identifier along the bottom of the Project panel (**Figure 5.14**) or by changing it in File > Project Settings. Chapter 11 explains more.

Perfecting Brightness with Curves

Curves rocks. I heart curves. The Curves control is particularly useful for gamma correction, because

- ▶ Curves lets you fully (and visually) control how adjustments are weighted and roll off.

- ▶ You can introduce multiple gamma adjustments to a single image or restrict the gamma adjustment to just one part of the image's dynamic range.

- ▶ Some adjustments can be nailed with a single well-placed point in Curves, in cases where the equivalent adjustment with Levels might require that you coordinate three separate controls.

It's also worth understanding Curves controls because they are a common shorthand for how digital color adjustments are depicted; the Curves interface recurs not only in all of the other effects compositing packages but also in more sophisticated tools within After Effects, such as Color Finesse (discussed briefly later in this chapter).

Curves does, however, have drawbacks, compared with Levels:

- ▶ It's not immediately intuitive, it can easily yield hideous results if you don't know what you're doing, and there are plenty of artists who aren't comfortable with it.

- ▶ Unlike Photoshop, After Effects doesn't offer numerical values corresponding to curve points, making it a purely visual control that can be hard to standardize.

- ▶ Without a histogram, you may miss obvious clues about the image (making Levels more suitable for learners).

The most daunting thing about Curves is clearly its interface, a simple grid with a diagonal line extending from lower left to upper right. There is a Channel selector at the top, set by default to RGB as in Levels, and there are some optional extra controls on the right to help you draw, save, and retrieve custom curves. To the novice, the arbitrary map is an unintuitive abstraction that you can easily use to make a complete mess of your image. Once you understand it, however, you can see it as an elegantly simple description of how image adjustment works. You'll find the equivalent Curves graph to the Levels corrections on the book's disc.

Figure 5.15 shows the more fully featured Photoshop Curves, which illustrates a little better how the controls work.

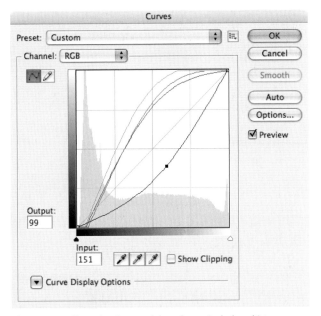

Figures 5.15 Photoshop's more deluxe Curves includes a histogram, built-in presets, displays of all channels together, and fields for input and output values for a given point on the curve.

Figures 5.16a through **d** show some basic Curves adjustments and their effect on an image. **Figures 5.17a** through **f** use linear gradients to illustrate what some common Curves settings do. I encourage you to try these on your own.

Figure 5.16a The source image.

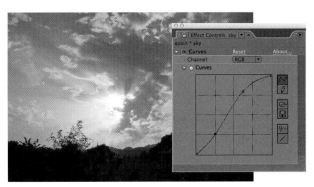

Figure 5.16b An increase in gamma above the shadows.

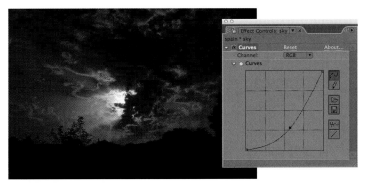

Figure 5.16c A decrease in gamma.

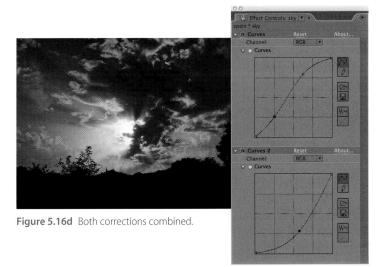

Figure 5.16d Both corrections combined.

Figures 5.16a through d What you see in an image can be heavily influenced by gamma and contrast.

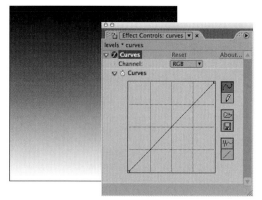

Figure 5.17a The default gradient and Curves setting.

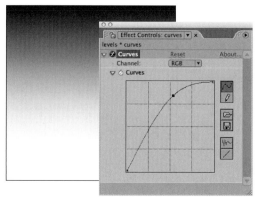

Figure 5.17b An increase in gamma.

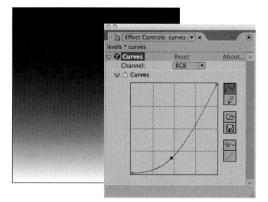

Figure 5.17c A decrease in gamma.

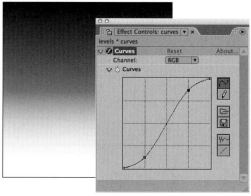

Figure 5.17d An increase in brightness and contrast.

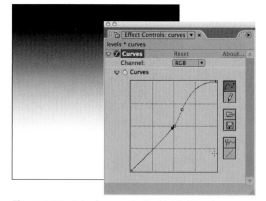

Figure 5.17e Raised gamma in the highlights only.

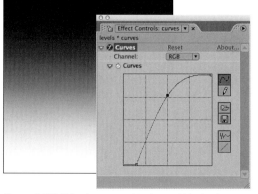

Figure 5.17f Raised gamma with clamped black values.

Figures 5.17a through f This array of Curves adjustments applied to a gradient shows the results of some typical settings.

More interesting are the types of adjustments that only Curves allows you to do—or at least do easily. I came to realize that most of the adjustments I make with Curves fall into a few distinct types that I use over and over, and so those are summarized here.

The most common adjustment is to simply raise or lower the gamma with Curves, by adding a point at the middle of the RGB curve and then moving it upward or downward. **Figure 5.18** shows the result of each. This produces a subtly different result from raising or lowering the Gamma control in Levels because of how you control the roll-off (**Figure 5.19**).

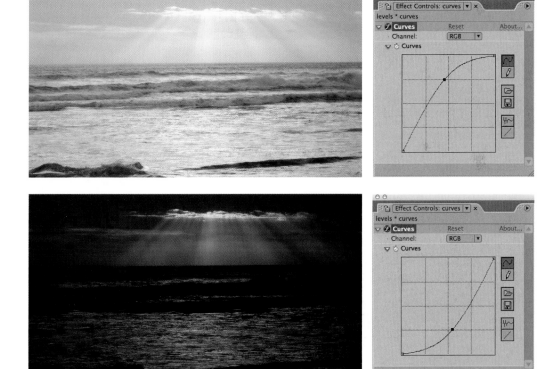

Figure 5.18 Two equally valid gamma adjustments employ a single point adjustment in the Curves control. Dramatically lit footage particularly benefits from the roll-off possible in the highlights and shadows.

Figure 5.19 Both the gradient itself and the histogram demonstrate that you can push the gamma harder, still preserving the full range of contrast, with Curves rather than with Levels, where you face a choice between losing highlights and shadows somewhat or crushing them.

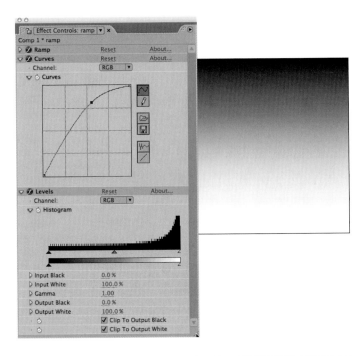

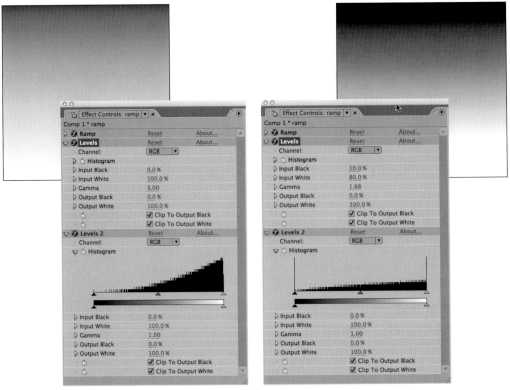

Figure 5.16b weights the gamma adjustment to the high end by adding a point to hold the shadows in place. The classic S-curve adjustment, which enhances brightness and contrast and introduces roll-offs into the highlights and shadows (**Figure 5.20**) is an alternative method to get the result of the double curves in Figure 5.16d.

Some images need a gamma adjustment only to one end of the range—for example, a boost to the darker pixels, below the midpoint, that doesn't alter the black point and doesn't brighten the white values. Such an adjustment requires three points (**Figure 5.21**):

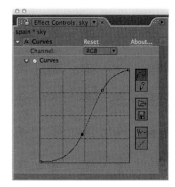

Figure 5.20 The classic S-curve adjustment: The midpoint remains the same, but contrast is boosted.

Figure 5.21 The ultimate solution to the backlighting problem presented back in Figure 5.5: Adding a mini-boost to the darker levels while leaving the lighter levels flat preserves the detail in the sky and brings out detail in the foreground that was previously missing.

- ▶ One to hold the midpoint
- ▶ One to boost the low values
- ▶ One to flatten the curve above the midpoint

A typical method for working in Curves is to begin with a single point adjustment to adjust gamma or contrast, then modulate it with one or two added points. More points quickly become unmanageable, as each adjustment changes the weighting of the surrounding points. Typically, I will add a single point, then a second one to restrict its range, and a third as needed to bring the shape of one section back where I want it. The images used for the figures in this section are included as single stills on the book's disc for your own experimentation; open 05_colorCorrection.aep to find them.

Just for Color: Hue/Saturation

The third of three essential color correction tools in After Effects is Hue/Saturation. This one has many individualized uses:

▶ Desaturating an image or adding saturation (the tool's most common use)

▶ Colorizing images that were created as grayscale or monochrome

▶ Shifting the overall hue of an image

▶ De-emphasizing, or knocking out completely, an individual color channel

All of these uses recur in Chapters 12 through 14, to create monochrome elements, such as smoke, from scratch.

NOTES

Chapter 12 details why Tint, not Hue/Saturation, is the right tool to convert an entire image to grayscale.

The Hue/Saturation control allows you to do something you can't do with Levels or Curves, which is to directly control the hue, saturation, and brightness of an image. The HSB color model is merely an alternate slice of RGB color data. All real color pickers, including the Apple and Adobe pickers, handle RGB and HSB as two separate but interrelated modes that use three values to describe any given color.

In other words, you could arrive at the same color adjustments using Levels and Curves, but Hue/Saturation gives you direct access to a couple of key color attributes that are otherwise difficult to get at. To desaturate an image is essentially to bring the red, green, and blue values closer together, reducing the relative intensity of the strongest of them; a saturation control lets you do this in one step, without guessing.

Often is the case where colors are balanced but merely too "juicy," and lowering the Saturation value somewhere between 5 and 20 can be a direct and effective way to make an image adjustment come together (**Figure 5.22**). It's essential to understand the delivery medium as well, because film is more tolerant and friendly to saturated images than television.

Figure 5.22 For footage already saturated with color, even a subtle boost to gamma or contrast can send saturation over the top. There's no easy way to control this with RGB tool, such as Levels and Curves, but moving over to the HSB model allows you to single out saturation and dial it back.

The other quick fix that Hue/Saturation affords you is a shift to the hue of the overall image or of one or more of its individual channels. The Channel Control menu for Hue/Saturation includes not only the red, green, and blue channels but also their chromatic opposites of cyan, magenta, and yellow. When you're working in RGB color, these secondary colors are in direct opposition, so that, for example, lowering blue gamma effectively raises the yellow gamma, and vice versa.

The HSB model includes all six individual channels, which means that if a given channel is too bright or over-saturated, you can dial back its Brightness & Saturation levels, or you can shift Hue toward a different part of the spectrum without unduly affecting the other primary and secondary colors. This is even an effective way to reduce blue or green spill (Chapter 6).

More Color Tools and Techniques

This section has laid the foundation for color correction in After Effects using its most fundamental tools. The truth, of course, is that there are lots of ways to adjust the color levels of an image, with new ones emerging all the time. Alternatives used to create a specific look—layering in a color solid, creating selections from an image using the image itself along with blending modes, and more—are explored in Section III of this book.

TIP

When in doubt about the amount of color in a given channel, try boosting its Saturation to 100%, blowing it out—this makes the presence of that tone in pixels very easy to spot.

TIP

One alternative usage of these basic color correction tools is to apply them via an adjustment layer, because you can then dial them back simply by adjusting the layer's opacity, or hold them out from specific areas of the image using masks or track matte selections.

TIP

The previous edition of this book mentioned that Adobe Premiere Pro includes a Three-Way Color Corrector that is supported with an equivalent effect in After Effect. This effect appears only if applied in a Premiere Pro project that you then import into After Effects, however, where it then lacks the color wheel UI. This effect is still not directly available in After Effects CS3.

NOTES

Chapter 12 includes a "roll your own" recipe and Animation Preset for cheap and cheerful three-way color correction.

Color Finesse

Color Finesse is a sophisticated color correction system included with After Effects Professional; unfortunately, it runs as a separate application, and does not allow you to see your corrections in the context of a composite, making it more suitable for overall color adjustments. Furthermore, it is made up mostly of tools that resemble the ones described in the preceding section, so you'd still want to master them. And although I love the way it allows easy isolation and adjustment of specific secondary color ranges, I rarely use it for compositing because of how separate it is from the After Effects workflow (other ways of isolating color for adjustment are revealed throughout Section II of the book).

Three-Way Color

What has been sorely missing from After Effects is a three-way color corrector, typically featuring color wheels to adjust three distinct color ranges: shadows, midtones, and highlights. Look at any contemporary feature film or major television show and you're likely to find strong color choices that strongly deviate from how the original scene must have looked: In an ordinary day-lit scene the shadows might be bluish, the midtones green, and the highlights orange.

A third-party tool, Magic Bullet Colorista, has recently been released by Red Giant Software to make this type of correction quick and intuitive in After Effects (**Figure 5.23**);

Figure 5.23 The hot After Effects plug-in for color work as of this writing is Colorista; the simple and intuitive color wheels make it easy to perform radical color surgery such as this day-for-night effect (detailed in Chapter 12).

a demo version is included on the book's disc. This type of tool can be essential to finish the color look of a project, although the more tried-and-true tools will work every time when matching colors, discussed next.

Color Matching

Having examined the color correction tools in depth, it's now time for the bread and butter of compositing: to match foreground and background elements so that the scene appears to have been taken with the same basic light conditions.

Although it requires artistry to do well, this is a learnable skill with measurable objective results. The process obeys such strict rules that you can do it without an experienced eye for color. Assuming the background (or whatever source element you're matching) has already been color-graded, you even can satisfactorily complete a shot on a monitor that is nowhere near correctly calibrated.

How is that possible?

As with so much visual effects work, the answer is derived by correctly breaking down the problem. In this case, the job of matching one image to another obeys rules that can be observed channel by channel, independent of the final, full-color result.

Of course, effective compositing is not simply a question of making colors match; in many cases that is only the first step. You must also obey rules you will understand from the careful observation of nature described in the previous chapter. And even if your colors are correctly matched, if you haven't interpreted your edges properly (Chapter 3) or pulled a good matte (Chapter 6), or if such essential elements as lighting (Chapter 12), the camera view (Chapter 9), or motion (Chapter 8) are mismatched, the composite will not succeed.

These same basic techniques will work for other situations in which your job is to match footage precisely—for example, color correcting a sequence to match a *hero* shot (the one determined to have the right color juju), a process also sometimes known as *color timing*.

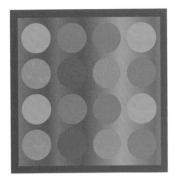

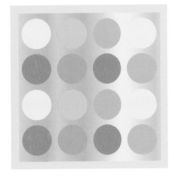

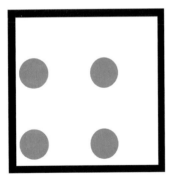

Figures 5.24a, b, and c There are no yellow dots in 5.24a, and no blue dots in 5.24b; the four dots shown in 5.24c are identical to their counterparts in the other two images.

The Fundamental Technique

Integration of a foreground element into a background scene often follows the same basic steps:

1. First match overall contrast without regard to color, using Levels. When matching the black and white points, pay attention to atmospheric conditions.

2. Next, study individual color channels and use Levels to match the contrast of each channel (as needed—not all images contain so fundamental a color imbalance).

3. Match the color of the midtones (gamma), channel by channel, using Levels or Curves. This is sometimes known as *gray matching* and is easiest when an object in the background scene is known to be colorless gray (or something close).

4. Evaluate the overall result for other factors influencing the integration of image elements—lighting direction, atmospheric conditions, perspective, grain or other ambient movement, and so on (all of which and more are covered in this book).

The overall approach, although not complicated or even particularly sexy, can take you to places your naked eye doesn't readily understand when looking at color. Yet, when you see the results, you realize that nature beats logic every time.

The sad truth is that even an experienced artist can be completely fooled by the context of the image. **Figures 5.24a, b**, and **c** show an example in which seeing is most definitely *not* believing. Therefore you should not feel that working channel by channel is some kind of crutch. The results of your color adjustments will undoubtedly be challenged by other members of your production team, and when it comes time to review them channel by channel, it's pretty cool to be able to say you got it right.

Ordinary Lighting

We begin with a simple example: inserting a 3D element lit with ordinary white lights into a daylight scene. As you can see in **Figure 5.25**, the two elements are close enough in color range that a lazy or hurried compositor might be tempted to leave it as is.

Figure 5.25 An unadjusted foreground layer (the plane) over a day-lit background.

With only a few minutes of effort, you can make the plane look as though it truly belongs there. Make sure the Info palette is somewhere that you can see it, and for now, choose Percent (0–100) in that palette's wing menu to have your values line up with the ones discussed here (you can, of course, use whatever you want, but this is what I'll use for discussion in this section).

This particular scene is a good beginner-level example of the technique because it is full of elements that would appear monochromatic under white light; next we'll move on to scenes that aren't so straightforward. The background is dominated by colorless gray concrete, and the foreground element is a silver aircraft.

Begin by looking for suitable black and white points to use as references in the background and foreground. In this case, the shadow areas under the archways in the background, and underneath the wing of the foreground plane, are just what's needed for black points—they are not the very darkest elements in the scene, but they contain a similar mixture of reflected light and shadow cast onto similar surfaces, and you can expect them to fairly nearly match. For highlights, you happily have the top of the bus shelter to use for a background white point, and the top silver areas of the plane's tail in the foreground are lit brightly enough to contain pure white pixels at this point.

Figure 5.26 shows the targeted shadow and highlight regions and their corresponding readings in the Info palette. The shadow levels in the foreground are lower (darker) than those in the background, while the background shadows have slightly more red in them, giving the background warmth absent from the unadjusted foreground. The top of the plane and bus shelter each contain levels at 100%, or pure white, but the bus shelter has lower blue highlights, giving it a more yellow appearance.

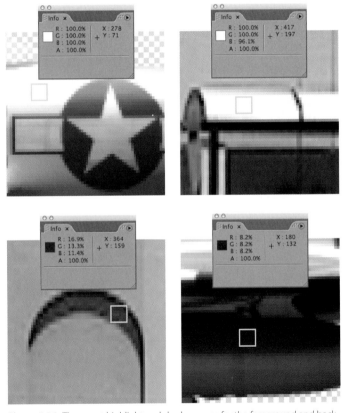

Figure 5.26 The target highlight and shadow areas for the foreground and background are outlined in yellow; levels corresponding to each highlight (in Percent values, as set in the panel menu) are displayed in the adjacent Info palette.

To correct for these mismatches, apply Levels to the foreground and move the Output Black slider up to about 7.5%. This raises the level of the blackest black in the image, lowering the contrast.

Having aligned contrast, it's time to balance color. Because the red levels in the background shadows are higher than blue or green, switch the Composition panel to the red channel (click on the red marker at the bottom of the panel or use the **Alt+1/Option+1** shortcut), causing a thin red line to appear around the viewer. You can now zoom in on an area that shows foreground and background shadows (**Figure 5.27**).

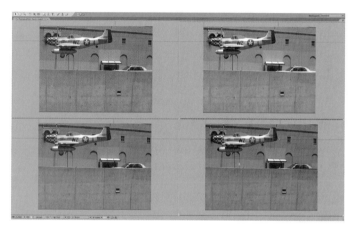
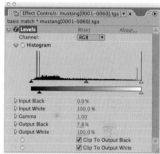
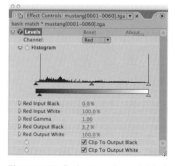
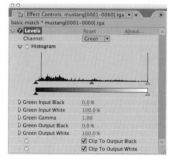
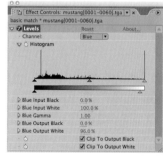

Figure 5.27 Evaluate and match black and white levels; start with RGB and then work on each color channel individually. In this case the image is "green matched:" The RGB adjustment is all that is needed for the green channel (often the best channel to match using RGB instead of its individual channel).

Black levels in the red channel are clearly still too low in the foreground, so raise them to match. Switch the Channel pop-up in Levels to Red, and raise Red Output Black slightly to about 3.5%. You can move your cursor from foreground to background and look at the Info palette to check whether you have it right, but the great thing about this method is that your naked eye usually evaluates variations in luminance correctly without the numerical reference.

Now for the whites. Because the background highlights have slightly less blue in them, switch to the blue channel (clicking the blue marker at the bottom of the Composition panel or using **Alt+3**/**Option+3**). Pull back slightly to where you can see the top of the bus shelter and the back of the plane. Switching Levels to the blue channel, lower the Blue Output White setting a few percentage points to match the lower blue reading in the background. Back in RGB mode (**Alt+3**/**Option+3** toggles back from blue to RGB), the highlights on the plane take on a more sunlit, yellow quality. It's subtle, but it seems right.

What about the midtones? In this case, they're taking care of themselves because both the foreground and background are reasonably well balanced and these corrections are mild.

Figure 5.28 displays the result, with the same regions targeted previously, but with the levels corrected. To add an extra bit of realism, I also turned on motion blur, without yet bothering to precisely match it (something you will learn more about in Chapter 8, "Effective Motion Tracking"). You see that the plane is now more acceptably integrated into the scene.

Work on this composite isn't done either; besides matching the blur, you can add some sun glints on the plane as it passes, similar to those on the taxi. On the other hand, you can tell that the blur on the plane is too heavy for the pilot's absence from the cockpit to be noticeable, a good example of how an initial pass at a composite can save a lot of extra work.

> **TIP**
>
> The human eye is more sensitive to green than red and blue. Often, when you look at a shot channel by channel, you will see the strongest brightness and contrast in the green channel. For that reason, a sensible approach to matching color may be to get the overall match in the ballpark so that the green channels match perfectly, and then adjust the other two channels to make green work. That way, you run less risk of misadjusting the overall brightness and contrast of your footage.

Figure 5.28 This is a better match, particularly in the shadow areas; motion blur helps sell the color adjustment as well.

Dramatic Lighting

Watch a contemporary feature film objectively for color and you may be shocked at how rare ordinary day-lit scenes such as the plane example are. Dramatic media—not just films but television and theater—use color and light to create mood, to signify key characters and plot points, and more.

Therefore a scene dominated by a single color, such as **Figure 5.29**, is much more commonly found in dramatic films than it is in your everyday family snapshots. One of

Figure 5.29 This is the unembellished source lighting of this shot. (Image courtesy Shuets Udono via Creative Commons license.)

the main reasons films take so long to shoot is that the cinematographer and lighting director require the time and resources to get the lighting the way it needs to be to create an image that is both beautiful and serves the story.

The foreground element added in **Figure 5.30** clearly does not belong in this scene; it does not even contain the scene's dominant color, and is white-lit. That's fine; it will better demonstrate the effectiveness of this technique.

Note that both the foreground and the background elements have some areas that you can logically assume to be flat gray. The bridge has concrete footings for the steel girders along the edges of the road, while the can has areas of bare exposed aluminum.

NOTES

This section discusses colors expressed as percentages; to see the same values in your Levels effect, use the wing menu of the Info palette to choose Percent for the Color Display.

Figure 5.30 Not only is it clear that the can does not belong in the color environment of the background, the mismatch is equally apparent on each color channel.

To play along with this game, open the project 05_colorMatching2.aep and apply Levels to the foreground layer in the "before" composition ("after" is the final comp to which you can refer as needed once you've tried this on your own).

Switch both your Composition view (**Alt+1**/**Option+1**) and the Channel pulldown in Levels to Red. I'll warn you now that the most challenging thing about this technique will be remembering to keep both settings on the same color channel, which is why using a four-up setup as shown in Figure 5.33 is probably worth the trouble.

Now, let's pretend that the red channel is a black-and-white photograph in which you're using the red channel of the Levels effect to match the foreground to the background. Clearly, the foreground element is far too bright for the scene. Specifically, the darkest silver areas of the can are way brighter than the brightest areas of the concrete in the background. Therefore, adjust the gamma down (to the right) until it feels more like they inhabit the same world; in my example, I've adjusted Red Gamma way down to 0.67. Now cut down the red highlights a little; bring Red Output White down to about 92.5% or whatever looks right to you. The end result should look like a black-and-white photo whose elements match (**Figure 5.31a**).

Now move the Levels Channel and Composition view (**Alt+2**/**Option+2**) over to green. Green is the dominant color here, and its black contrast and brightness are much higher in the background. Therefore, raise Green Input Black to about 12.5% (for the contrast) and Green Gamma to something like 1.3 (**Figure 5.31b**). Better than copying my levels, try to find these on your own.

Finally, switch Levels and the Composition viewer (**Alt+3**/**Option+3**) to the Blue channel. Whoa; there is almost no match here. The can is way brighter and more washed out than the background. Again the Input Blue Level must come up, to about 17.5%, but this time gamma has to come way down, ending up at about 0.45%. Now the can looks believably like it belongs there (**Figure 5.31c**).

It's strange to make all of these changes without ever looking at the result in full color. So now, go ahead and do that. Astoundingly, that can is now in range of looking like it belongs in that scene; defocus it slightly with a little fast blur and add a shadow and you start to believe it. Make any final contrast adjustments on the Levels RGB Channel, and

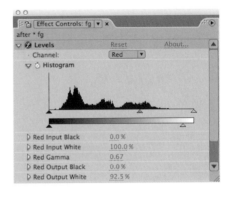

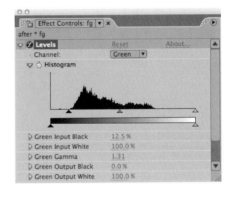

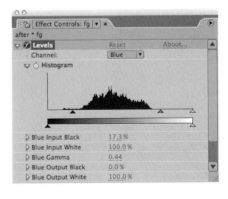

Figures 5.31a, b, and c It's actually fun to pull off an extreme match like this channel-by-channel. The Levels settings used were not really derived from the histogram, but by a mixture of looking for equivalent black/white/midpoints in the image, as well as just analyzing whether the result looks like a convincing black and white image on each channel.

you have an impressive result that required no guesswork whatsoever (**Figure 5.32**).

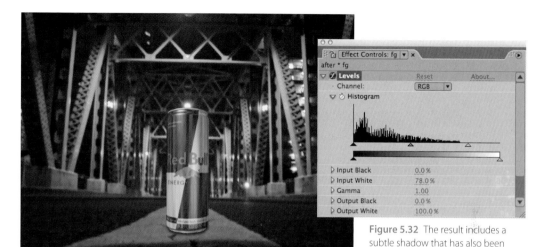

Figure 5.32 The result includes a subtle shadow that has also been color matched as well as a final adjustment to the white contrast.

When There's No Clear Reference

The previous examples have contained fairly clear black, white, and gray values in the foreground and background elements. Life, of course, is not always so simple.

Figure 5.33 is a scene that lacks any obvious gray values to match; the lighting is so strong, it's hard to tell what color anything in the scene was originally, or whether there were any neutral black, white or gray items in the scene.

Figure 5.33 What the heck is going on here? Again, the source image is as it was shot. Examine some of your favorite films and you may find scenes lit this dramatically; the eye quickly becomes accustomed to strong shifts of color, but the color can also be used to strike a subconscious chord. (Image courtesy Jorge L. Peschiera via Creative Commons license.)

It's often a good idea to take a break when trying to finalize fine color adjustment. When you come back, even to a labored shot, you regain an immediate impression that can save you a lot of noodling.

The technique still works in this case, but it may require more in the way of trial and error, or artist's intuition. Looking at each individual color channel, only green is even close to a plausible match right off the bat; the red channel contains blown-out whites, and the blue channel is so dark (and grainy) it hardly exists.

Once again, just try to get the brightness and contrast adjusted, working channel by channel, and you get an initial result something like **Figure 5.34**. Considering how subjective the adjustments are by necessity in this case, this isn't half bad; and fine adjustments to the RGB channel can bring it where it needs to go.

Figure 5.34 This one requires as much intuition as logic, but adjusting it channel by channel still yields a striking result.

The ability to match color without seeing an image in full color is so powerful that it can seem almost magical the first few times you try it. Why, then, do so few artists work this way? I would have to say that laziness and ignorance are the main culprits here. Switching channels seems like a pain, and few untrained artists clearly realize that color works like this.

Gamma Slamming

Maybe you've seen an old movie on television—the example I think of first is *Return of the Jedi* (before the digital re-release)—in which you see black rectangular garbage mattes dancing around the Emperor's head, inside the cloak, that you obviously shouldn't be seeing. *Jedi* was made prior to the digital age, and some of the optical composites worked fine on film, but when they went to video, subtleties in the black levels that weren't previously evident suddenly became glaringly obvious.

Don't let this happen to you! Now that you know how to match levels, put them to the test by *slamming the gamma* of the image. To do this, you need to make a couple of adjustment layers. I usually call one slam up and the other slam down, as in the examples. Be sure that both of these are guide layers so that they have no possibility of showing up in your final render.

To slam up, apply Curves with the gamma raised significantly (**Figure 5.35**). This exposes any areas of the image that might have been too dark to distinguish on your monitor; if the blacks still match with the gamma slammed up, you're in good shape.

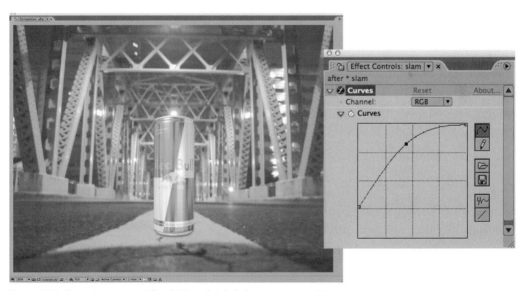

Figure 5.35 Slamming gamma is like shining a bright light on your scene. Your black and midtone levels should still match when viewed at these extremes.

Similarly, and somewhat less crucial, you can slam down by lowering the gamma and bringing the highlights more into the midrange (**Figure 5.35**). All you're doing with these slams is stretching values that may be difficult for you to distinguish into a range that is easy for you to see.

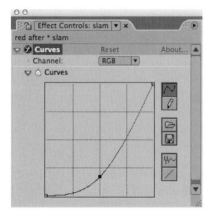

Figure 5.35 If in doubt about the highlights in your footage, you can also slam the gamma downward. Here, the slam makes it clear that the highlight reflected in the can is not as bright or bloomed as the overhead lights, and a lack of grain in the foreground becomes apparent. Grain matching is detailed in Chapter 9, "The Camera and Optics."

NOTES

You can try the Exposure control found at the lower right of every viewer window to slam the image and check levels; just scrub the numerical setting up and down, clicking the adjacent icon to reset when you're done. This approach requires no additional steps and does not render; however, it does not affect contrast, only luminance.

This method is useful anywhere that there is a danger of subtle discrepancies of contrast; you can use it to examine a color key, as you'll learn in the next chapter, or a more extreme change of scene lighting.

Beyond the Basics

This chapter has covered some of the basics for adjusting and matching footage. Obviously there are exceptional situations, some of which occur all of the time: depth cueing, changes in lighting during the shot, backlighting, interactive light and shadow. There are even cases in which you can, to some degree, relight a shot in After Effects, introducing light direction, exchanging day for night, and so on. These topics and more are covered in depth in Chapter 12.

6

Color Keying

Slow down, I'm in a hurry.

—Franz Mairinger (Austrian Equestrian)

Color Keying

Color keying was first devised in the 1950s as a clever means to combine live-action foreground footage and backgrounds that could come from virtually anywhere. As of 2007, the tools to do this are more powerful than ever, but the overall process still remains full of pitfalls—pitfalls that won't likely be overcome until some other means evolves to define precise areas of transparency in foreground footage (and several contenders are in some form of development).

The process goes by many names: color keying, blue screening, green screening, pulling a matte, color differencing, and even chroma keying, a term that really belongs to analog color television, a medium defined by chroma and heavily populated with weather forecasters.

The purpose of this chapter is to help you not only with color keying of blue- and green-screen footage but with all cases in which pixel values (hue, saturation, and/or brightness) stand in for transparency, allowing compositors to effectively separate foreground from background based on color data.

All of these methods extract luminance information that is then applied to the alpha channel of a layer (or layers). The black areas become transparent, the white areas opaque, and the gray areas gradations of semi-opacity; it's the handling of these gray areas that typically determines the success or failure of a matte.

Good Habits and Best Practices

Before we get into detail about specific keying methods and when to use them, here is some top-level advice to remember when creating any kind of matte:

For those reading nonlinearly, this chapter extends logically from fundamental concepts about mattes and selections in Chapter 3, "Selections: The Key to Compositing."

Novices often wonder if a background must be blue or green to be keyed. The answer is no, although specialized tools, such as Keylight, work with only the digital primaries red, green, or blue. It also happens that blue and green are primary colors not dominant in human skin tones, and most foreground elements (costumes and props), while they might be blue or green, tend to be less purely so. That's the hope, anyhow…

▶ **Use a bright, saturated, contrasting background** (**Ctrl+Shift+B/Cmd+Shift+B**) such as yellow, red, orange, or purple (**Figures 6.1a, b**, and **c**). If the foreground is to be added to a dark scene, a dark shade is okay, but in most cases bright colors better reveal matte problems. Solo the foreground over the background you choose (**Figure 6.2**).

Figures 6.1a, b, and c The background influences what you see. Against black, almost no detail is visible (a). Checkerboard reveals shadows (b), but flaws in the matte are clearest with a bright, solid, contrasting background (c). (Source footage courtesy Pixel Corps.)

▶ **Protect edge detail.** This is the name of the game (and the focus of much of this chapter); the key to winning is to isolate edges as much as possible and focus just on them so as to avoid crunchy, chewy mattes (**Figure 6.3**).

Figure 6.2 The keyed layer can be soloed at any time, revealing it against the background of your choice.

Figure 6.3 A coyote ugly, chewy matte (this one exaggerated for effect) is typically the result of clamping the foreground or background (or both) too far.

▶ **Keep it simple, and be willing to start over.** Artists spend hours on keys that could more effectively be redone in minutes, simply by beginning in the right place. There are many complex and interdependent steps involved with creating a key; if you start to feel cornered, don't stay there.

▶ **Constantly scan frames and zoom into detail.** When possible, start with a tricky area of a difficult frame; look for motion blur, fine detail, excessive color spill, and so on, and keep checking various areas in various modes (**Figure 6.4**).

Figure 6.4 A glimpse of the alpha channel can reveal even more problems, such as faint holes in the foreground, which should be solid white. This is the matte from Figure 6.1.

▶ **Break it down into multiple passes.** This is the single most important concept overlooked by beginners. In the vast majority of cases, a successful matte incorporates at least two passes: a core matte whose foreground is 100% opaque and a second edge pass.

I encourage you to review this list again once you've explored the rest of this chapter.

Linear Keyers and Hi-Con Mattes

There are cases in which edge detail is not a factor because an element does not need to be completely isolated; for example, you might create a holdout area of an image using a *high-contrast* (*hi-con*) matte. To specify one area of a clip for adjustment, a *linear key* will often do the trick.

Linear keyers are relatively simple and define a selection range based on a single channel only, be it red, green or blue, or even just overall luminance. They're useful in a wide variety of cases outside the scope of blue- and green-screen shots, although the underlying concepts are also operative when working with such high-level tools as Keylight.

The most useful linear keyers are

▶ Extract

▶ Linear Color Key

The keyers to be avoided at all times are

▶ Luma Key

▶ Color Key

Extract and Linear Color Key

Extract is useful for *luminance (luma) keying*, using the black and white points of an image or any of its individual channels. Linear Color Key is a more appropriate tool to isolate a particular color (or color range).

Extract

Extract employs a histogram to help isolate thresholds of black and white; these are then graded with black and white softness settings. You can work with averaged RGB luminance, or access histogram controls for each of the color channels.

One of the three color channels nearly always has better defined contrast than overall luminance, which is merely an average of the three. Either green or red is typically the brightest and most contrasty channel, while blue generally has lower contrast and higher noise (**Figures 6.5a, b**, and **c**).

TIP

Color Key and Luma Key cannot calculate semi-opaque threshold areas of a matte; Edge Thin and Edge Feather controls instead crudely choke, spread, and blur a pure bitmap. There is seriously no reason ever to use them, so it's unfortunate that they have the more memorable names.

CLOSE-UP

When, Exactly, Is Linear Keying Useful?

Keying using a single channel (or the average of multiple channels) is useful to

▶ Matte an element using its own luminance data, in order to hold out specific portions of the element for enhancement. For example, you duplicate a layer and matte its highlights to bloom them (see Chapter 12, "Light").

Figures 6.5a, b, and c The red channel contains the strongest foreground contrast (a); the green channel (b) shows that the matte contains some green; although it may not be clear at this size, the blue channel (c) is noisier than the other two, typical of digital images and one reason why green screens became popular in the digital era.

Extract is interactive and easy to use, a cousin to Levels. Its histogram shows the likely white or black thresholds on each channel. You bring in the White Point or Black Point (the upper of the small square controls below the histogram), then threshold (soften) that adjustment with the White Softness or Black Softness controls (the lower of the small squares). It is intuitive and relatively easy to use.

Figure 6.6 This grayscale conversion (using Tint) of the channels shown in Figures 6.5a, b, and c weights the three channels according to how the eye sees them. The result appears closest to, but not identical to green.

CLOSE-UP

All Channels Are Not Created Equal

If you set an RGB image as a luma matte, the red, green, and blue channels are averaged together to determine the luminance of the overall image. However, they are not weighted evenly, because that's not how the eye sees them (**Figure 6.6**).

If you find yourself wanting to use a particular channel as a luma matte, use Shift Channels (**Figure 6.7**).

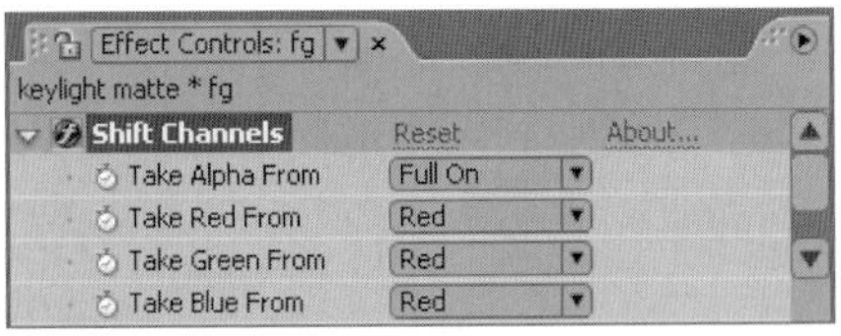

Figure 6.7 Shift Channels shifts all channels to red. Alpha is set to Full On as a precaution against transparency data, which should not be used for a luma matte.

Linear Color Key

Linear Color Key offers direct selection of a key color using an eyedropper tool. The default color is blue (ironic given that blue-screen keying is exactly the wrong thing to do with this tool, given the alternatives). The default 10% Matching Softness setting is arbitrary and defines a rather loose range. I often end up with settings closer to 1%.

Note that there are, in fact, three eyedropper tools in the Linear Color Key effect. The top one defines Key Color, and the other two add and subtract Matching Tolerance. The eyedroppers work directly on either of the adjacent thumbnail images, as well as in the Layer panel (double-click the layer and choose Linear Color Key in the View pulldown, **Figure 6.8**). For whatever reason the eyedropper tools don't work consistently in the Composition viewer.

Figure 6.8 Linear Color Key can matte a non-primary color range; in this case, the magenta sign on the bus is selected. (Source footage courtesy Pixel Corps.)

You can use RGB, Hue, or Chroma values to match color values. RGB will usually do the trick, but in unusual situations, sample each option before you start fine-tuning. You can adjust Tolerance, which specifies how close the colors have to be to the chosen value to be fully matted, and Softness, which then grades the threshold, softening the edges according to how close the color values are to the target range.

The default setting for the Key Operation is to Key Colors, which is straightforward enough. You might guess, therefore, that the other option, Keep Colors, would simply invert the result. In fact, Keep Colors was designed for cases in which the first instance of the effect eliminates something you want to bring back. First instance, you ask? That's right, you have the opportunity to recover foreground colors despite that they've already been keyed out: Add a second copy of Linear Color Key targeting a second range, set to Keep Colors.

Difference Mattes

A *difference matte* is simple in principle: Frame two shots identically, the first containing the foreground subject, the other without it (commonly called a *clean plate*). Now, have the computer compare the two images and remove everything that matches identically, leaving only the foreground subject. Great idea.

TIP

To set up a second instance of Linear Color Key to Keep Colors, you should temporarily turn off the first instance (set to Key Colors) in order to set the color to keep using the eyedropper (**Figure 6.9**). Alternatively, work in Layer view.

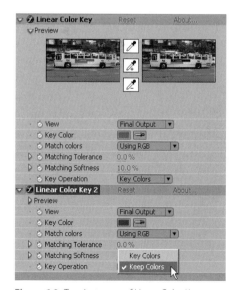

Figure 6.9 Two instances of Linear Color Key: The first is set to Key Colors, the second set to Keep Colors.

Luma Mattes

In the interest of full disclosure, I often use track mattes (as detailed in Chapter 3) with a duplicate of the layer, instead of the luminance keys described here, applied directly to the layer. With a track matte, I can use Levels to work with color ranges on all channels, in order to refine transparency. Other artists may consider this approach more cumbersome, preferring to work with a single layer and an effect, so the choice as always is yours.

The hand-to-hand green-screen shots in this chapter (such as Figure 6.10) include tracking markers on the background. These are intended to provide dimensional perspective for 3D camera tracking (a.k.a. match moving), which otherwise might not be possible. More on match moving is included at the end of Chapter 8, "Effective Motion Tracking."

In practice, of course, there are all sorts of criteria that preclude this from actually working very well, specifically

▶ Both shots must be locked off or motion stabilized to match, and even then, any offset—even by a fraction of a pixel—can kill a clean key.

▶ The foreground element may be rarely entirely unique from the background; low luminance areas, in particular, tend to be hard for the Difference Matte effect to discern.

▶ Grain, slight changes of lighting, and other real-world variables can cause a mismatch to two otherwise identical shots. Raising the Blur Before Difference setting helps correct for this, but only by introducing inaccuracy.

To try for yourself, begin with a locked-off shot containing foreground action, ideally one in which a character enters the frame (such as the footage used for Figure 6.10, included on your DVD). Duplicate the layer, and lock off an empty frame of the background using Layer > Time > Freeze Frame. Apply Difference Matte to the other layer. Adjust Tolerance and Softness; if the result is noisy, try raising the Blur Before Difference value.

Figures 6.10a, b, and **c** show the likely result of attempting to key this footage using only Difference Matte. It's not a terrible way to isolate something when clean edges are not critical, but it cannot compare with more sophisticated methods for removing a solid color background.

Figures 6.10a, b, and c This effects shot (a) includes a clean plate (b); and the alpha channel of a Difference Matte effect (c) demonstrates that this is not an effective way to key a foreground. Unwanted features such as the tracking markers disappear, however, so this matte could be combined with a regular green-screen key.

Blue and Green Screen Keys

Back in the day, the alternatives to the rather pedestrian Color Difference Key in After Effects were third-party plug-ins, and for a few years there were two choices: Ultimatte for After Effects (now AdvantEdge, Ultimate Corporation) and Primatte Keyer (Red Giant Software, formerly from Pinnacle Systems, and before that, Puffin Designs).

Beginning with version 6.0 Professional, an alternative was included free with After Effects: Keylight. Its reputation was already well established prior to its inclusion in After Effects, having even earned it a Technical Achievement Award from the Academy of Motion Picture Arts and Sciences. The competition has by no means disappeared (I personally remain a big fan of Primatte) but Keylight is part of After Effects, so it's the main focus of this chapter.

Keylight is useful in many keying situations, not just studio-created blue- or green-screen shots. For example, you can use Keylight for removal of a murky blue sky (**Figure 6.11**). You wouldn't use Keylight to pull a luminance key, however, or when simply trying to isolate a certain color range within the shot; its effectiveness decreases the further you get from the three primary colors.

Keylight is most typically employed to a back-plate shot against a uniform, saturated, primary color background. It is used when preservation of edge detail is of utmost importance—in other words, most typically (but not exclusively) when working with footage that was specifically shot to be keyed against a screen of blue or green.

NOTES

When I label Color Difference Key "pedestrian," I speak as someone who matted hundreds of shots with it, back before there were alternatives in After Effects. Its methodology is fundamental and can be replicated using basic channel math and Levels controls. It provides the exact methodology that was used for early digital composites, which themselves mimicked optical compositing methods.

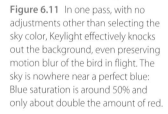

Figure 6.11 In one pass, with no adjustments other than selecting the sky color, Keylight effectively knocks out the background, even preserving motion blur of the bird in flight. The sky is nowhere near a perfect blue: Blue saturation is around 50% and only about double the amount of red.

Steps to a Perfect Key

Figure 6.12 shows a process tree that outlines the steps detailed below. No two complex shots are the same, but something like this approach should help you pull a good matte, regardless of the tools used. The next section reprises these steps, specifically using Keylight.

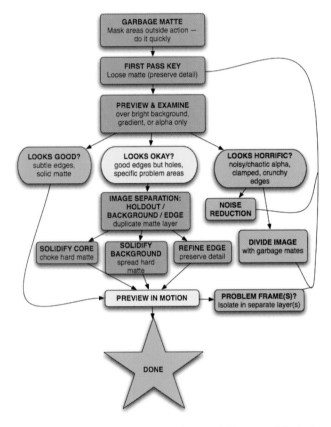

Figure 6.12 This chart summarizes steps that can yield a successful color key. It is also included as a PDF (keyingFlowchart.pdf) on the book's disc.

The basic steps are

1. **Garbage matte** any areas of the background that can easily be masked out. "Easily" means no articulated matte (don't animate individual mask points). As a rule of thumb, limit this to what you can accomplish in about 20 minutes or less (**Figure 6.13**).

Figure 6.13 The quick-and-dirty garbage matte is your friend for eliminating unwanted parts of the stage.

2. Attempt a **first pass** quickly, keeping this matte on the loose side (preserving as much edge detail as possible) to be refined later.

3. **Preview** this at full resolution, in full motion, against a bright primary color. In rare cases, you're done, but before you throw up your arms in victory, switch to a view that clearly displays the alpha channel. Note any obvious holes in the foreground or areas of the background that have failed to disappear, as well as any noise in the solid areas of the matte (**Figure 6.14**).

If things look noisy and chaotic in the alpha channel or the edges are clamped and chewy, you can

▸ Start over and try a new pass

▸ Apply noise reduction to the plate, then start over (see "Noise Suppression" later in this chapter)

▸ Articulate or track garbage/holdout mattes to isolate problem portions of the footage (see "Typical Keying Challenges")

Figure 6.14 A quick diagnosis of Keylight's first pass at this shot: The shadows must be keyed out because they extend outside the garbage matte area (and right off the set). This in turn has an effect on fine detail such as motion blur and hair, so these areas (hands, hair) may require their own holdout mattes.

TIP

Just in case I'm not yet succeeding in beating you over the head with it: the most effective way to improve a difficult matte is to break down plate footage into separate passes when keying to prevent problems local to one area from compromising the entire selection.

CLOSE-UP

Holdout Mattes

A *holdout matte* isolates an area of an image for separate treatment. You can think of a color key as an edge matte surrounded by two holdout mattes: one for the core, one for the background.

The question then arises as to how these mattes are combined, which is explored in depth in the "Keylight" section.

4. If necessary, **separate the plate for multiple passes**. At the very least, it's often useful to create a solid core and a completely transparent background so that you can focus only on the edge (detailed in the next section), but you may also need to separate individual parts of a layer for a separate keying pass, such as hair or a fast-moving, motion blurred limb.

5. **Refine the edge.** Zoom in on a challenging area of the foreground edge (200% to 400%), and refine the key to try to accommodate it, using strategies outlined in the following sections. Challenging areas may include

   ▶ Fine detail such as hair

   ▶ Motion blurred foreground elements

   ▶ Cast shadows

   You must also watch out for, and consider rotoscoping, foreground features that can threaten an effective key, such as

   ▶ Areas of the foreground that reflect the background color

   ▶ Edge areas whose color nearly matches the background

   ▶ Areas of poor contrast (typically underlit regions of the shot)

6. **Preview the shot in full motion.** Again, note holes and noise that crop up on individual frames, and use the strategies outlined in "Typical Keying Challenges" to overcome these problems. Approaches you may employ at this stage are

   ▶ Adding holdout mattes (typically masks), either for the purpose of keying elements individually or roto-scoping them out of the shot (**Figure 6.15**)

   ▶ Holding out the matte edge only, for the purpose of refining or blurring it (see "Matte Problems")

   Ironically, the lazy single-pass approach either leads to a poor result or much more work, overall, as you struggle to make all areas of your shot play nice with one-size-fits-all settings.

You can follow along with the steps using the blueScrn_mcv_HD.mov footage included in this chapter's Pixel Corps folder on the book's disc. Completed versions of several of the examples from this chapter are contained in the 06_colorKey. aep project.

Figure 6.15 It may seem tedious and cumbersome to create individual holdout mattes for things like hair or heavy motion blur, but you could waste hours trying to eliminate the shadows while retaining the detail in one pass; an acceptable roto-matte might take 10 or 20 minutes.

Keylight

After Effects CS3 features version 1.2 of Keylight for After Effects; its usage is more or less identical to that of the previous version (the big changes are under the hood, such as support for the Intel Mac).

The first decision in Keylight is most important: sampling a color for the Screen Colour setting (Keylight reveals its UK origins at Framestore CFC with that u). More information to help you make an effective choice lies ahead in "The Inner Workings of Keylight" section.

In the best-case scenario, you create any necessary garbage mattes and then

1. Use the Screen Colour eyedropper to sample a typical background pixel. View defaults to Final Result so you get a matte instantly; set the background to a bright color and solo the plate layer, or examine the alpha channel (**Alt+4/Option+4**).

2. If in doubt about the Screen Colour setting, turn the effect off and set another instance, repeating as necessary until you have one that eliminates the maximum

unwanted background (**Figures 6.16a**, **b**, and **c**); you can then delete the rest.

CLOSE-UP

The Eyedropper and the Info Panel

With the Info panel active, sample a pixel in After Effects, either using an eyedropper tool or simply by moving your cursor around a viewer. The Info panel then displays the value that belongs to the exact pixel underneath the selection point of the cursor (the lower-left corner of the eyedropper, the upper-left corner of the pointer).

As in Photoshop, the After Effects eyedropper samples only the color state of a pixel; transparency of any given pixel is always evaluated as if 100%.

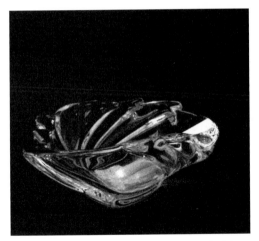

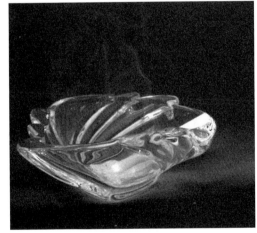

Figures 6.16a, b, and c Even with well-shot, high-definition source (a), it is imperative to get the Screen Colour setting right to preserve all of the transparent detail in this shot. Choosing a darker background color (b) creates a more solid initial background, but a lighter color selection (c) preserves far more detail. (Source footage courtesy Pixel Corps.)

Now, as needed, look for areas to refine.

3. Switch View to Status. Opaque pixels display white, transparent pixels black, and those containing transparency are gray (**Figure 6.17**). It's an exaggerated version of the alpha channel that shows where your matte is not solid.

Figure 6.17 Sample a background pixel near the center of the image for a good initial key, as seen in the Status matte. The black areas are already completely transparent, the white areas opaque, and the gray pixels constitute the areas of focus; they are the semitransparent regions.

4. Still in Status view, try Screen Balance at settings of 5.0, the default 50.0, and 95.0, and choose whichever one yields the best-looking matte. You might evaluate this based on edge softness or firmness of the foreground matte (**Figure 6.18a** and **b**).

Figures 6.18a and b This initial result, with a Screen Balance of 95 (a), seems in Status view to be inferior to a setting of 5 (b), but a look at the color channel shows the default 95 setting to yield a subtler initial matte edge.

5. If the background is not solid black, you have the option to boost Screen Gain until the gray mostly disappears in Status view. Use this as sparingly as possible, preserving gray at the edges of the foreground. If gray remains in the background, but separate from the foreground such that you can eliminate it with a garbage matte, do so (**Figure 6.19**).

Figure 6.19 A light touch is best with Screen Gain; some artists (me, much of the time) never raise it above the default value of 100, although settings up to 105 or 110 are often acceptable. Don't use it to remove anything like the noise in the lower left corner, which is easily solved instead with a garbage matte.

NOTES

Keylight in general and Despill Bias in particular can enhance the appearance of graniness, particularly of 4:2:2 or other compressed source. If you notice that the keyed foreground appears grainier than the source, reset Despill Bias, and if that doesn't help, apply the keyed layer as a track matte instead.

6. Now, another optional step (that I often skip): For spill correction, you can set the Despill Bias using its eyedropper. Sample an area of the foreground that has no spill and should remain looking as is (typically a bright and saturated skin tone area).

In the ideal scenario, your matte is now complete. If not (**Figure 6.20**), this is a decision point to divide the plate. Following are the most basic useful steps for doing so. Before taking these steps, you can revert Screen Gain to 100 to loosen the basic matte.

Figure 6.20 Nice edges—it's the core of this matte that needs to be a little firmer.

As you may know, the Keylight toolset exists in other compositing applications as well. The Shake implementation of Keylight has the same underlying technology but it has one key addition missing from the After Effects version: inputs for a garbage matte and holdout matte. If you can create these procedurally such that they completely avoid the edge area, this allows you to consider them done and then focus only on the edge, which is all that matters.

I was inspired by what I call the Three Pass Method of shake to devise the following workflow to achieve the same in an After Effects precomp, with as few extra steps as possible. I encourage you to try it out, and let me know if your mattes are improved as a result of focusing exclusively on the edge.

NOTES

Keylight includes its own controls for adding holdout areas to mattes via the Inside Mask and Outside Mask controls. You draw a mask, set it to None, and then select it under Inside Mask or Outside Mask. This works for garbage mattes, but it's not a substitute for duplicating the layer to combine multiple keys.

7. Create a precomp containing the Keylight layer with the Move All Attributes option checked. Rename the layer Edge. Duplicate this layer (with Keylight applied), rename it Background, and solo it. For clarity's sake, turn off effects for Edge for the moment.

8. Create a background matte that is purely transparent and well separated from the edge, as follows. Mask in any needed overall garbage matte. Raise Clip Black just enough to remove gray pixels from the background in Status view, then lower the Clip White setting just above the same number (**Figure 6.21**).

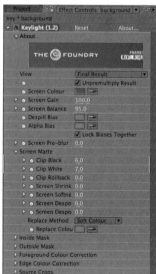

Figure 6.21 Screen Gain can always be left at 100 for the edge matte (ideal) if the background is matted separately. A garbage matte eliminates the corner noise.

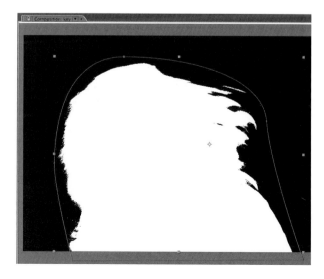

9. Expand the matte either by raising the Screen Shrink/ Grow value or by applying Simple Choker and lowering the Choke Matte setting. Make sure that the selection is completely outside the edge, separated by at least a few pixels; to check this, switch to Final Result view and set the layer's blending mode to Stencil Alpha (**Figure 6.22**).

Figure 6.22 Look closely at the edges; the matte from Figure 6.21 has been expanded so that it doesn't touch them, and the layer is set to Stencil Alpha so that the matte is passed through.

10. Duplicate the original Edge layer again, solo the duplicate, rename it Core and make sure Keylight is enabled. In Status view, lower Clip White until the foreground is completely opaque. Raise Clip Black to a value just below the same number (**Figure 6.23**).

Figure 6.23 The core matte, like the background matte, is chewy but solid, and is choked so as not to touch the edges.

11. Shrink the matte either by lowering the Screen Shrink/ Grow value or by applying another effect such as Simple Choker and raising the Choke Matte setting. Make sure that the selection is completely within the edge, separated by at least a few pixels, then switch to Final Result view and set the layer's blending mode to Stencil Alpha. The result is a matte of the edge only (**Figure 6.24**).

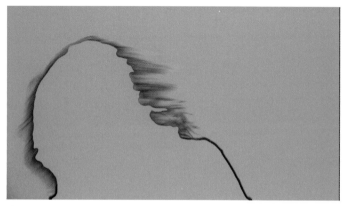

Figure 6.24 Thanks to the combination of Stencil Alpha for the background matte and Silhouette Alpha for the foreground, only the crucial part of the matte, the edge, remains. The core can be switched back to Normal blending for the final version.

12. Refine the key of the edge layer, preview each layer in motion to ascertain that they don't contain errors, and switch the blending mode of the core layer to Normal when you're done.

This procedure may still leave particular areas needing to be separated with mattes for individual attention—the edge of the hair, for example, might be keyed separately from the body, with an articulated matte (described in detail in the next chapter) to define each.

Get the Best Out of Keylight

So your matte now either looks pretty good or has at least one obvious problem. If you think it's looking good, focus in on a few details, and note if there are any problems with the following in your full-motion preview:

▶ Hair detail: Are all of the "wispies" coming through? (**Figure 6.25a**)

▶ Motion blur or, in unusual cases with a defocus, lens blur: Do blurred objects appear chunky or noisy, or do they thin out and partially disappear? (**Figure 6.25b**)

▶ Screen contamination areas: Do holes remain in the foreground? (**Figure 6.25c**)

▶ Shadows: Are they keying as desired (usually all or nothing)? (**Figure 6.25d**)

Figures 6.25a through d Fun challenges you may encounter when pulling a color key include wispy hair (a), motion blur (b), contamination of foreground elements by the background color (c), and shadows (d).

Figure 6.25a

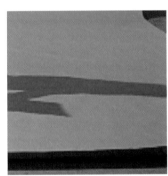

Figure 6.25b

Figure 6.25c

Figure 6.25d

Alternatively, you may discover something fundamentally wrong with your matte, including

▶ Ill-defined foreground/background separation or semitransparency throughout the foreground or background

▶ *Crunchy*, *chewy*, or *sizzling* edges (feel free to invent your own such terms)

TIP

You can switch a RAM Preview to Alpha Channel view (**Alt+4/Option+4**) without losing the cache. Not only that, but the alpha will preview at speed, in full motion.

- ▶ Other noise in the matte
- ▶ Edge fringing or an overly choked matte
- ▶ Errors in the spill suppression

Keylight anticipates these issues, offering specific tools and techniques to address them. Before delving into those (in the "Focusing In" section), here's how Keylight actually operates.

The Inner Workings of Keylight

A few decisions are absolutely essential in Keylight; most of the rest compensate for the effectiveness of those few. This section offers a glimpse into the inner workings of Keylight, which will greatly aid your intuition when pulling a matte.

The core of Keylight involves generating the *screen matte*, and as has been mentioned, the most essential step is the choice of screen color. From that, Keylight makes weighted comparisons between its saturation and hue and that of each pixel, as detailed in **Table 6.1**.

TABLE **6.1** How Keylight Makes Its Key Decisions

Compared to Screen Color, Pixel Is	Keylight Will
Of a different hue	Consider it foreground, making it opaque
Of a similar hue and more saturated	Key it out completely, making it transparent
Of a similar hue, but less saturated	Subtract a mathematically weighted amount of the screen color and make it semitransparent

The lesson contained in Table 6.1 is that a healthy background color is of a reasonably high saturation level and of a distinct hue.

Those sound like vague criteria, not easily met—and it's true, they are somewhat vague and often not met. That's why Keylight adds the Screen Gain, Screen Balance, and Despill and Alpha Bias controls. Screen Gain emphasizes the saturation of the background pixels, and Screen Balance delineates the background hue from the other primary colors. The Bias controls color-correct the foreground.

NOTES

These top five controls (from Screen Colour to Alpha Bias) differ from those below them in that they work on the color comparison process itself, rather than the resulting matte. You can adjust them without adding any processing load whatsoever, and they work together to yield the ideal matte; the rest of the controls merely correct the result.

Screen Gain

One major enemy of a successful color key is muddy, desaturated colors in the background. A clear symptom that the background lacks sufficient intensity is when areas of the background are of a consistent hue, yet fail to key easily. Similarly, a clear symptom that your foreground is contaminated with reflected color from the background is that it appears semi-opaque. In either case, Screen Gain becomes useful.

Screen Gain boosts or reduces the saturation of each pixel before comparing it to the screen color. This effectively brings more desaturated background pixels into the keying range if raised or, if lowered, knocks back pixels in the foreground containing the background color.

A Rosco Ultimatte Blue screen contains quite a bit of green—much more than red, unless someone has lit it wrong. Ultimatte Green screens, meanwhile, are nearly pure green (**Figure 6.26**).

Figure 6.26 The Rosco colors: Ultimatte Blue, Ultimatte Green, and Ultimatte Super Blue. Blue is not pure blue, but double the amount of green, which in turn is double the amount of red. Ultimatte Green is more pure, with only a quarter the amount of red and no blue whatsoever. Lighting can change their hue (as does converting them for print in this book).

Screen Balance

That takes care of saturation, but what about hue (the actual green-ness or blue-ness of the background and foreground) and how pure is it? Keylight is designed to expect one of the three RGB color values to be far more prevalent than the other two in order to do its basic job. It is even more effective, however, if it knows whether one of the two remaining colors is more prevalent, and if so, which one.

Screen Balance allows you to alert Keylight to this fact.

On this theory, you would employ a balance of 95% with blue screens and leave it at 50% for green screens, and in version 1.1v1 of Keylight, that is exactly how the plug-in sets Screen Balance depending on whether you choose a blue or green Screen Colour setting.

The more generalized recommendation from The Foundry, however, is to set it "near 0, near 100, and compare" these to the default setting of 50 to evaluate which one works best. In other words, imagine there are three settings (instead of 100) and try 5%, 50%, and 95%.

Bias

The Bias settings, Despill Bias and Alpha Bias, color correct the image in the process of keying, by scaling the primary color component up or down (enhancing or reducing its difference from the other two components).

As mentioned, a couple of things have changed with these settings in this new version. They are no longer tied together by default, and The Foundry recommends that in most cases you leave Alpha Bias at the default. They also both now operate via eyedroppers rather than value sliders, and it is recommended that you click the Despill Bias eyedropper on a well-lit skin tone that you wish to preserve; despill pivots around this value.

Focusing In: Clean-Up Tools

Once you are satisfied that you have as good an edge matte as possible, you are ready to zoom in on a detail area and work on solving specific problems.

If you see an area that looks like a candidate for refinement, save (so that you can revert to this as your ultimate undo point), zoom in, and create a region of interest around the area in question.

Now take a look at some common problems you might encounter and the tools built into Keylight that solve them.

Holes and Edges

The double-matte method (core and edge) shortcuts a lot of the tug of war that otherwise exists between a solid foreground and subtle edges. Even with this advantage, both mattes may require adjustments to the Clip White or Clip Black controls.

The game is to keep the largest possible difference (or *delta*, if you prefer) between these two settings. The closer the two numbers approach one another, the closer you are to a bitmap alpha channel, in which each pixel is pure

TIP

I have found, to my dismay, that keyed footage can become significantly grainier as the result of adjusting Despill Bias. I highly recommend that you compare before and after versions of foreground plate footage if you use this feature, and if the result is adding grainy noise to your footage, reset Despill Bias and try a different despill method (see "Spill Suppression").

TIP

Increment and save your project after creating a good basic matte, should you wish to revert after further changes.

TIP

Remember that with a scroll wheel on your mouse, you can hold down **Alt/Option** to zoom around the point where you place the cursor.

black or white—a very bad thing indeed (**Figure 6.27**). The delta between the Clip values represents the area where all of your gray, semitransparent alpha pixels live, so the goal is to offer them as much real estate as possible.

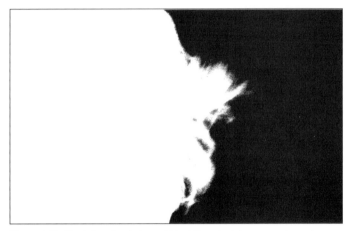

Figure 6.27 Here's how her hair would look if you hadn't separated an edge matte for the hair. This is the very definition of a "chewy" matte—you can see individual, contrasty pixels.

If you push the Clip controls too far and need a way out of that corner without starting over, raise the Clip Rollback value. This control restores detail only to the edge, and only what was there in the original matte operation (with those top five controls). Used in moderation, and with a close eye on the result, it can be effective.

Clip Rollback works as follows: Its value is the number of pixels from the edge that are rolled back. The edge pixels reference the original, unclipped screen matte. So if your edges were looking nice and soft on the first pass and removing noise from the matte hardened them, this tool can restore the subtlety.

Noise Suppression

Are your mattes sizzling? Keylight includes a Screen Pre-blur option that you should apply only in a zoomed-in view (to closely examine the result) and only with footage that has a clearly evident noise problem, such as source shot on miniDV. Essentially, this option blurs your source footage before keying it, so it adds inaccuracy and is something of a desperation move. The footage itself does not appear blurred, but the matte does.

A better alternative for a fundamentally sound matte is Screen Softness, found under the Screen Matte controls. Screen Softness blurs the matte itself after the key has been pulled and the matte created, so it has a much better chance of retaining detail. As was shown in Chapter 3, edges in nature are always slightly soft; so used to a modest degree (considering that it is introducing error into your key), this control can enhance the realism of a matte (**Figures 6.28a** and **b**).

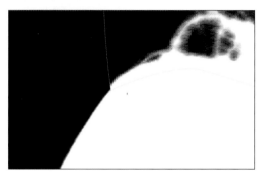 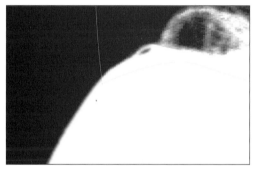

Figures 6.28a and b The softer hair matte and the harder matte around the torso don't line up, and the torso has an unrealistically hard border (a). Adding Screen Softness and a positive Shrink/Grow adjustment can fix this (b).

A more drastic approach, when softening and blurring cannot reach larger chunks in the footage, is using the Despot cleanup tools. Crank these up, and you'll definitely notice undesirable blobbiness in your matte. For this reason, I don't trust these controls and usually leave them alone.

A better approach, particularly with miniDV and HDV footage (which, by the way, are both guaranteed to add undesirable noise and are typically not recommended for blue-screen and green-screen shoots), is to

Chroma Sampling: The 411 on 4:1:1

Most digital video images aren't stored as RGB but Y′CrCb, the digital equivalent of YUV. Y′ is the luminance or brightness signal; Cr and Cb are color-difference signals (roughly corresponding to red-cyan and blue-yellow).

Unfortunately, as you might imagine, this type of compression is less than ideal for color keying; hence the recommended approach here for softening the effect of color quantization particularly in common formats such as miniDV.

1. Convert the footage to YUV using Channel Combiner (the From pull-down). This will make your clip look very strange, because your monitor displays images as RGB. Do not be alarmed (**Figure 6.29**).

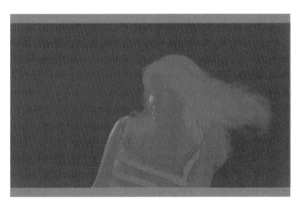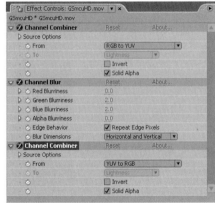

Figures 6.29 This is how an image converted to YUV should look on an RGB monitor—wrong. The round-trip around a Channel Blur appears in the Effect controls (but the second Channel Combiner effect is temporarily disabled, hence the strange look).

2. Apply Channel Blur to the green and blue channels only, at modest amounts (to gauge this, examine each channel as you work—press **Alt+2/Option+2** or **Alt+3/ Option+3** while zoomed in on a noisy area). Make sure Repeat Edge Pixels is checked.

3. Round-trip back from YUV to RGB, using a second instance of Channel Combiner.

4. Apply Keylight, and breathe a sigh of relief.

Fringing and Choking

Sometimes, despite all best efforts, your extracted matte contains extra, unwanted edge pixels (fringing), or the keyed subject lacks subtle edge detail because the matte is choked too far.

Keylight does offer the Screen Grow/Shrink control for such situations. On the other hand, if you find yourself having to shrink or expand your matte, it may be a symptom of other problems. Faced with the need to choke or

NOTES

YUV is the digital version of the broadcast video color space. It is used in component PAL television and is functionally similar to YIQ, the NTSC variant. In After Effects YUV, the red channel displays the luminance value (Y) of the shot, while the green and blue channels display blue and red weighted against green (U and V).

spread a matte (another way of saying shrink or grow), you might first go back and try the initial key again, possibly breaking it down further into more component parts (say, separating the hair) using holdout masks. More information on choking and spreading follows below.

Spill Suppression

Keylight suppresses *color spill* (foreground pixels contaminated by reflected color from the background) when the matte is initially pulled, as part of the keying operation. Thus spill-kill can be practically automatic if you pull a good initial key.

When is this not what you want? First of all, when it's an unwanted by-product. There are situations when parts of the foreground that you want to keep are close enough in color range to the background that their color is suppressed. **Figure 6.30** shows a scene shot with a green screen out the window in which the interior of the set is also meant to be of a greenish cast, all of which was carefully decided and lit on set.

Figure 6.30 A green-lit set with a green screen out the window: Things like this happen all the time. Applying the matte to the plate with spill suppression limited to areas (such as the top of the monitor) that are reflecting the green screen solves this problem.

TIP

You can use Keylight for spill suppression only. Follow the same steps as you would to key the footage, but do not adjust any controls below Despill Bias (which you should select using the eyedropper on a representative area of skin tone or equivalent). Change the View setting to Corrected Source; the footage is keyed but the alpha channel remains unaffected.

Adjustments to the matte can also expose areas of the clip that aren't spill suppressed. These areas are indicated by the green pixels in the Status view (as in Figure 6.21); spill suppression of these pixels may now be off. In such cases, you specify a Replace Method setting; Soft Colour set to medium gray is a good choice if the only affected pixels are at the edge. It is a cheat, but it may make your key look better by gently desaturating pixels that might otherwise pop.

Finally, spill suppression can lead to other undesirable effects on plate footage. In **Figure 6.31**, notice how the whole shape of the girl's face seems to change due to the removal of highlights via spill suppression. Even worse, as mentioned earlier, something about the spill suppression operation in Keylight also seems to enhance the graininess of footage in many cases.

Figures 6.31 Her face doesn't even look the same without the highlights reflected with the green. Even worse, at this magnification it's easy to see that the amount of grain noise has increased significantly. It's a definite case for pulling the matte on one pass and applying spill suppression separately.

Should Keylight's spill suppression become unwieldy or otherwise useless for any of the above reasons, there is an easy out. Create a nice matte without worrying about spill, precompose the result, and apply it as an alpha matte to the foreground source. Color spill can be removed on a separate pass without adversely affecting the plate footage.

Keylight itself also includes additional spill suppression tools, under the Edge Colour Correction heading (as well as the overall Foreground Colour Correction). Beneath each is a check box to enable it, but nothing changes until you adjust Saturation, Contrast, or Brightness below the check box (or, alternatively, the Colour Suppression and Colour Balancing tools). If necessary, soften or grow the edge to increase the area of influence.

Typical Keying Challenges

As you must know by now, because I've seized every opportunity thus far to drill it into your head, the number one solution to most matte problems is to break the image being matted into multiple sections rather than trying to get one matte in one pass. You can divide the matte as follows:

▶ Core and edge matte (hard and soft matte)

▶ Holdout masks for particular areas of the frame (useful if lighting varies greatly within the frame, or if one area contains a particularly challenging element, such as hair or motion blur)

▶ Temporal split (if light conditions change as the shot progresses)

All other tricks fall short if you're not willing to take the trouble to do this. And now for some more bad news.

On Set

No matter how advanced and well paid you may be, your time is likely to be far cheaper than that of a full crew on set. That means—shocking, I know—you'll have the opportunity to fix things in post that should have been handled differently on set. You could call it job security (but that sounds so cynical); however you think of it, it's bound to be part of your job.

If you're fortunate enough to be supervising the effects shoot (I recommend it for the craft services alone), you can do all sorts of things to ensure that the footage will key successfully later on.

A hard *cyclorama*, or *cyc* (pronounced like "psych"), painted a uniform key color is far preferable to a temp cloth background. If you can't rent a stage that has one, the next best thing might be to invest in a roll of floor covering and paint it, to get the smooth transition from floor to wall, as in **Figure 6.32** (assuming the floor is in shot). Regarding the floor, don't let anyone walk across it in street shoes, which will quickly contaminate it with very visible dust. There are white shoe-cover booties often used specifically to avoid this, but it can be a losing battle.

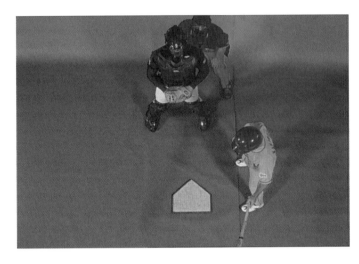

Figure 6.32 On a set with no hard cyclorama, you can create the effect of one—the curve where the wall meets the floor—using blue-screen cloth instead. It doesn't behave as well (note the hotspot on the curve), but it will certainly do in a pinch and is much preferable to removing the seam caused by the corner between the wall and floor. (Image courtesy Tim Fink Events and Media.)

Assuming you begin with a correct-colored, footprint-free background with as few seams and other variations as possible, the most important concerns are to light it correctly, balancing the foreground and background lighting.

This job is, of course, best left to a professional, and any kind of recommendations for a physical lighting setup are beyond the scope of this book. But, hey, you're going to spend more time examining this footage than anyone else, so here are a few things to keep in mind as the on-set effects supervisor:

▶ Light levels on the foreground and background should match. A spot light meter tells you if they do.

▶ Diffuse lights are great for the background (often a set of large 1 K, 2 K, or 5 K lights with a silk sock covering them), but fluorescent lights will do in a pinch. With fluorescents you just need more instruments to light the same space. Kino Flo lights are a popular option as well (**Figure 6.33**).

CLOSE-UP

The Right Color

The digital age lets shooters play fast and loose with what they consider a keyable background. You may be asked (or try on your own) to pull mattes from a blue sky, from a blue swimming pool, or from other monochrome backgrounds.

How different must the background color be from the foreground? The answer is "not very." Red is worth avoiding simply because human skin tones contain a lot of it, but a girl in a light blue dress or a soldier in a dress blue uniform often keys just fine from a blue screen (although spill suppression will require special attention).

Figure 6.33 Diffuse white lighting that causes no hotspots in the background is ideal.

▶ Maintain space between the foreground and background. Ten feet is ideal.

▶ Avoid dark unwanted shadows like Indiana Jones avoids snakes, but by all means light for shadows if you can get them and the floor is clean. Note that this works only when the final shot also has a flat floor.

▶ Shoot exteriors outside if possible, using portable backgrounds such as solid color cloths and carpets. You lose the controlled environment of the studio, but the quality of broad daylight can be difficult and expensive to re-create on set. There's just no key light as big as the sun.

▶ Record as close to uncompressed as possible. Even many low-end HD cameras allow you to record uncompressed directly to a disk array and avoid the pitfalls of heavily compressed tape formats.

If the setup permits, bring along a laptop with After Effects on it and with some representation of the scene into which the footage you're taking is going to be keyed. This can be enormously helpful not only to you but to the gaffer and director of photography, to give them an idea of where to focus their efforts.

Finally, once the lighting has been finalized and before action is called on the shot, ask the camera operator to shoot a few frames of clean plate—the background with

NOTES

Many computer graphics artists shoot environment reference of a set, either using a camera capable of taking ultra-wide angle photos (using a circular fisheye lens), or by aiming the camera at a reflective silver ball (known in garden shops as a gazing ball). Not only does this provide reference for the lighting setup, but it can be used to re-create HDRI lighting in 3D software.

no foreground characters or objects to be keyed out later. There are all sorts of ways to make use of this, and it's easy to forget; if you do, try to get it at the end of the setup, or the end of the day.

Matte Problems

There are specific tools to help you manipulate any matte that needs help. You may simply need to loosen or choke a matte edge.

Minimax is powerful, but not as precise as Matte Choker or Simple Choker. It operates in whole pixel increments to choke and spread pixel values, so the result isn't necessarily subtle. It provides a quick way to spread or choke pixel data, particularly without alpha channel information (since it can also operate on individual channels of luminance).

Simple Choker allows you to choke or spread alpha channel data (via a positive or negative number, respectively) at the sub-pixel level (use decimal values). That's all it does. If you push it hard, it behaves better than the Screen Shrink/ Grow control in Keylight, which starts to look blobby. Matte Choker seems more deluxe than Simple Choker (it's not stuck with that "Simple" label) but it merely adds softness controls that can just complicate a bad key. Don't be afraid to "settle" for Simple Choker: It's no monkey wrench.

Edge Selection

Earlier in this chapter the three-pass method for deriving a matte was introduced; this is one way to derive an edge matte when its specifically the edge pixels you need to select for adjustment. However, the simplest method to get an edge matte is probably as follows:

1. Apply Shift Channels. Set Take Alpha From to Full On and all three color channels to Alpha.

2. Apply Find Edges (often mistaken for a useless psychedelic effect because, as with Photoshop, it appears in the Stylize menu). Check the Invert box (**Figure 6.34**).

TIP

A useful third-party alternative to Minimax is Erodilation from ObviousFX (www.obviousfx.com). It can help do heavy choking (eroding) and hole-filling (dilating) in situations where the Simple Choker, well, chokes, and its controls are simple and intuitive (choose Erode or Dilate from the Operation menu and the channel—typically Alpha).

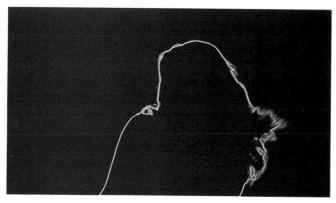

Figure 6.34 You can use this selection to blur the background and foreground together along the edge via an adjustment layer. Beware that the bottom edge is included in the matte; don't let this bite you if your frame has no *padding* (non-visible area at the edge of frame).

Minimax is useful to help choke or spread this edge matte. The default setting under Operation in this effect is Maximum, which spreads the white edge pixels by the amount specified in the Radius setting. Minimum chokes the edge in the same manner. If the result appears a little crude, an additional Fast Blur will soften it (**Figure 6.35**).

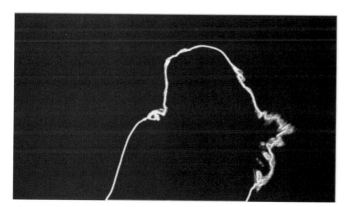

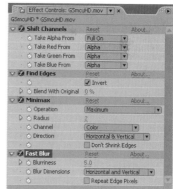

Figure 6.35 Need thicker, softer edges? A quick Minimax set to the default Maximum allows you to specify a Radius by which the white area will grow. If the result looks a little chunky, a quick Fast Blur will soften it back.

▶ Apply the result via a luma matte to an adjustment layer. You should not need to precompose before doing so.

Now what? Fast Blur will soften the blend area between the foreground and background, another way around a chewy matte that doesn't harm the overall image. A Levels adjustment will darken or brighten the composited edge to better blend it. Hue/Saturation can be used to desaturate the edge, similar to using a gray edge replacement color in Keylight.

Matte Holes

Holes can appear in solid areas of a matte: in the background because of uneven lighting, seams, dirt on the floor, or in the foreground, usually because of reflections from the background (especially the floor). No built-in tool in After Effects deals with these procedurally, but there's a great third-party tool called Alpha Cleaner, part of the Key Correct set (formerly Miracle Alpha Cleaner in Composite Wizard). Because it is an automated solution, it will occasionally fill holes that should remain unfilled, such as the little triangular gap that can open up under outstretched arms (**Figure 6.36**).

Thus matte holes present a situation in which you may have to rotoscope. It's often not as bad as you think it will be; the painstaking part of keying is defining the edge, and holes can often be fixed using crude masks or by tracking in paint strokes (each covered in the next two chapters, respectively).

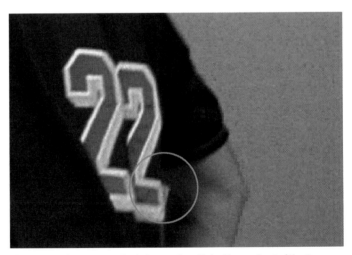

Figure 6.36 An automated solution, such as Alpha Cleaner (part of the Key Correct Pro pack), fills holes in the foreground matte but may have side effects, closing needed holes such as this tiny gap under the arm.

Matte Fringe

Visible fringing around the edge of a feathered matte can appear when a matte is applied via a track matte. Whether to avoid Keylight's heavy processing of spill and grain or to build a multilayer matte, you have seen a few reasons to work this way.

One solution to fringing is hidden away in the Channel menu. Remove Color Matting (a difficult name to remember which could instead be "un-premultiply") is designed specifically to remove background color from premultiplied edges (if the distinction eludes you, review Chapter 3).

Remove Color Matting uses black as the default Background Color (usually the right setting), and this is the only user-adjustable parameter in this effect. You can instead use the eyedropper to sample a background color. If the fringing is bright colored, a white or gray background may have been premultiplied.

Color Spill

Color spill need not be a big deal. If you're not happy with the spill suppression in Keylight (or another keyer), you can apply the matte as an alpha track matte to the source footage and pursue alternative options.

Sometimes the Spill Suppressor tool that is included with After Effects will do the trick. It uses a simple channel multiplication formula to pull the background color out of the foreground pixels. All you need to do is select a sample from the background color (you can even copy your original choice of screen color from Keylight, but it mostly matters whether you choose blue or green) and leave the setting at 100%.

If even Spill Suppressor has undesirable side effects, then it may be advisable to apply Hue/Saturation and target the specific hue that is causing you problems, either desaturating or shifting it. Select the color of the spill under Channel Control—say, Blues (for some reason they're all plural).

TIP

The free Unmult plug-in from Red Giant Software is included on this book's disc. It differs from Remove Color Matting in that it only works with black backgrounds, and it adds actual transparency to pixels based on how much black they contain.

Channel Range contains two color spectrums with a set of controls between them (**Figure 6.37**). These control the actual range of a given hue. The inner hash marks control the range affected by the controls below; the region between those and the outer, triangular markers is the threshold area.

Figure 6.37 The hash marks and triangles under the upper gradient of the Channel Range control the core and threshold of the affected hue range; the result is reflected in the lower gradient. This is often an effective method to remove spill.

For the best result, turn off Keylight or any other matte operations and work directly with the plate. Set the Saturation for the channel (Blue Saturation or Green Saturation) to –100%. Move the inner and outer hash marks outward until the background is completely gray; the foreground inside the edges should appear unaffected. Re-enable the matte, now without spill.

Conclusion

Keylight is a powerful tool that should offer the results you're after. Primatte Keyer is also a great option (included as a demo on the book's disc). Sometimes, however, there's no way to avoid plain old manual labor. The next chapter offers hands-on advice for situations where procedural keying can't accomplish everything, and you have to work by hand.

7

Rotoscoping and Paint

It's a small world, but I wouldn't want to paint it.

—Steven Wright

Rotoscoping and Paint

Why roto something painstakingly by hand if a matte or motion track lets the computer do it for you? It's always preferable to use a procedural solution when you can. Inevitably, though, it's sometimes necessary to animate a mask or paint some frames. *Rotoscoping* (or roto) is the art (although not everyone would call it that) of drawing on a shot frame by frame, generally using masks. Cloning and filling using paint tools are variations on this task.

After Effects is not famed as a rotoscoping tool, and while third-party tools to create and track masks and paint continue to evolve, masks and paint in After Effects CS3 are largely unchanged from the previous version.

If you've determined that no procedural method for keying (Chapter 6, "Color Keying") or tracking (Chapter 8, "Effective Motion Tracking") a matte will help your shot, here are some guidelines for roto and paint:

▶ Keep it simple. Use as few points as possible per mask, or as few paint strokes as you can. Put these in motion with as few keyframes as possible (the next section has specifics).

▶ Paint is a last resort; it's virtually always slower and more painstaking than animating masks, when that's an alternative, although a quick clone or well-placed paint stroke in a matte gap can save you time.

▶ Review constantly at full speed. The next section offers some new tips to help you do just that.

▶ Combine strategies. Effective rotoscoping may mix keying (whether color keying or a *hi-con matte*, Chapter 6), tracking, animated masks, and paint. Break the shot down, starting with the strategy that gains the most ground quickest.

It can be satisfying to knock out seamless roto, especially if you can avoid fighting the tools.

NOTES

"Rotoscoping" was invented by Max Fleischer, the animator responsible for bringing Betty Boop and Popeye to life, and patented in 1917; it involved tracing over live-action movement, a painstaking form of motion capture. The term has come to stand for any tracing of movement frame-by-frame in a moving image.

NOTES

"Keyframing" began at Disney, in the 1930s, where top animators would create the key frames—the top of the leap, the moment of impact—and lower-level artists would add the in-between frames thereafter. With a computer, you are the one creating the keyframes, leaving the computer itself to create the in-betweens as much as possible.

Articulated Mattes

Keep it simple, keep it quick; the simpler and quicker your masking process, the better (and more satisfying) the result.

The previous edition advocated rotoscoping in the Layer viewer, but thanks in part to e-mail correspondence with a reader (check the acknowledgments for details) I have rethought that stance when articulating mask shapes. The paint tools, however, operate only in Layer view (more on that later).

To roto effectively, you can play a game called "preserve the RAM cache." To win, you need to prevent the sequence that is being rotoscoped from constantly re-rendering, which is exactly what happens each time you draw a mask shape directly on a frame.

Instead, try the following steps, beginning with a plate shot that needs roto:

1. Create a comp containing only the plate (you can drag the source to the new Composition icon in the Project panel).

2. Add a solid layer above the plate; you can make it white and name it Mask although neither is essential.

3. Turn off the solid layer so only the plate layer is displayed.

4. Lock the plate layer (this is important).

5. Create a RAM Preview of the entire comp or a section to roto (by specifying a shorter work area).

6. Select the solid (still hidden) and your masking tool of choice (Pen or a shape); draw a selection on the first frame.

7. Press **M** to reveal Mask Path and create a keyframe.

8. Proceed to another point in time and edit the shape to update the selection.

9. Note that the green bar in the Timeline is still displayed—the RAM cache remains because the layer is locked. Press the Spacebar (not RAM Preview) to see the mask interpolate over the footage at full speed.

With this setup, you can make further adjustments and add more masks without disturbing the RAM buffer, so that as you use the **Page Up** and **Page Down** keys to quickly check adjacent frames, update is instantaneous. When it comes time to apply the masks, you can either apply the solid as a track matte or copy the masks and keyframes to the plate layer itself.

There are a few things to watch out for:

▶ This method works best with layers that have not been transformed; you can precomp to get back to the source footage if necessary. You can fine-tune masks in the context of the comp, if necessary.

▶ When working with a large scene, turn off layers you don't need and limit the work area or Region of Interest.

▶ You may need to select and lock all layers other than the one where you're drawing the masks.

Having laid down the basic groundwork for how to quickly preview masks over footage, we now turn our attention to making best use of the tools themselves.

Rotobeziers

Rotobezier shapes are designed to animate a mask over time; they're like Bézier shapes (discussed in Chapter 3, "Selections: The Key to Compositing") without the handles, which means less adjustment and less chance of pinching or loopholes when points get close together (**Figure 7.1**).

Figure 7.1 Bézier handles are a bad mix with animation; for each point, three points must be managed for each vertex, and crimping inevitably results when handles cross.

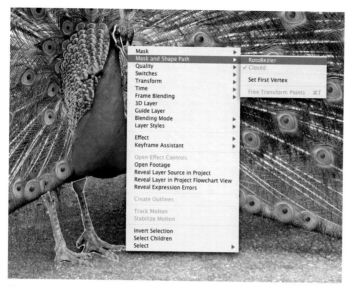
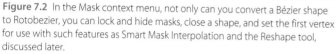

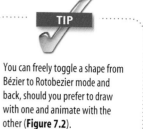

You can freely toggle a shape from Bézier to Rotobezier mode and back, should you prefer to draw with one and animate with the other (**Figure 7.2**).

Figure 7.2 In the Mask context menu, not only can you convert a Bézier shape to Rotobezier, you can lock and hide masks, close a shape, and set the first vertex for use with such features as Smart Mask Interpolation and the Reshape tool, discussed later.

Rotobeziers aren't universally beloved, partly because it's difficult to draw them accurately in one pass. Activate the Pen tool (**G** key) and check the Rotobezier box in the Tools menu, then click the layer to start drawing points; beginning with the third point, the segments are by default curved at each vertex (**Figure 7.3**).

Figure 7.3 Your first pass with Rotobeziers can just hit the key transitions quickly. Place a point at the apex of each curve, as well as at each corner.

The literal key to success with Rotobeziers is the **Alt/Option** key. At any point as you draw the mask, or once you've completed and closed it by clicking on the first point, hold **Alt/Option**. A double-ended arrow icon appears, the Adjust Tension pointer. Dragging it to the left increases tension, making a vertex a sharp corner (**Figure 7.4a** and **b**), like collapsed Bézier handles. Drag in the opposite direction, and the curve rounds out. You can freely add or subtract points as needed by toggling the Pen tool (**G** key; look for the cursor to change, adding a plus or minus sign beside it).

TIP

If the Selection tool (**V**) is active, **Ctrl+Alt** (**Cmd+Option**) activates the Adjust Tension pointer.

 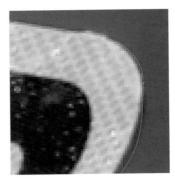

Figures 7.4a and b Alt/Option-drag a point anywhere between full tension (a) and no tension (b).

The hardest thing to accept about Rotobeziers is that the first pass at the shape is usually wrong, and each point you add changes the shape around adjacent points. You can instead draw regular Béziers, get the still shape right, then context-click the mask and toggle Mask and Shape Path > Rotobezier. This lets you leverage the real strength of Rotobeziers, using them for animation.

Strategies for Complex Shapes

Specific strategies make effective roto of complex organic shapes possible, regardless of tools:

▶ Use multiple overlapping masks instead of a single mask on a complex, moving shape (**Figure 7.5**).

CLOSE-UP

Work Quickly

A summary of mask shortcuts:

▶ To replace a Mask shape, in Layer view select the shape from the Target menu and start drawing a new one; whatever you draw replaces the previous shape. Beware: The first vertex point of the two shapes may not match, creating strange in-between frames. To set the first vertex point, context-click on any mask vertex.

Figure 7.5 Rotoscoping a complex shape that needs articulation over time? Divide it into individual shapes, each with a dozen or less vertices, so as to avoid headaches.

One key to working quickly is to intentionally create overlapping, separate mask shapes for different parts of your masked area that you know will move independently, or be revealed and concealed (in this case, because of a simple perspective shift). A shape with 20 or more points will be difficult to manage over time.

▶ Define a shape beginning on a frame where it can be drawn with the fewest possible points, adding more points as needed as you go. As a rule of thumb, no articulated mask should contain more than a dozen or so points.

▶ Go through the clip and look for the natural keyframe points, where a change of direction, speed, or shape begins or ends, and block in keyframes before you animate them.

Block in and refine the first shape, then refine as necessary. Check the result at full speed against a contrasting background, just as you do with color keys. Then move on to the next shape. Following are more strategies to help you work with masks in After Effects.

TIP

Enable Cycle Mask Colors in Preferences > User Interface Colors to generate a unique mask color with each new mask. You can customize the color if necessary to make it visible by clicking its swatch in the Timeline.

Overcome Mask Limitations

As mentioned earlier, masks in After Effects haven't evolved as a feature in quite some time. Here are some common limitations, followed by tips to work around them.

▶ There is no direct way to apply a tracker directly to an After Effects mask, let alone track individual mask points (although you are welcome to try a script called RotAE at aenhancers.com which attempts this; just search on the keyword RotAE).

▶ You can't translate multiple mask keyframes at once; even if you select multiple keyframes, the move is applied only at the current frame.

▶ After Effects lacks the ability to specify whether a feather is applied to the inside or outside of a mask, nor can you vary feather settings on a per-vertex basis (**Figure 7.6**).

▶ Adding points to an animated mask has no adverse effect on adjacent mask keyframes. Delete a point, however, and it is removed from all keyframes, usually deforming them (hence the tip above to start with the simplest shape).

TIP

Preferences > General includes a preference, on by default, to preserve a constant vertex count when editing masks. Practically the only reason to disable this is if you're creating keyframes on every frame, with no in-betweens.

Figure 7.6 This mask has no threshold to match the motion blur of the shot. After Effects lacks per-vertex mask feather, but animate the mask and enable motion blur, and you create the feathering effect automatically (Figure 7.13). For per-vertex feather or filtering, check out PV Feather from RE:Vision Effects (www. revisionfx.com).

▶ There is no dedicated morphing tool in After Effects. The tools to do a morph, however, do exist, along with solid deformation tools generally.

The following sections elaborate upon the above points in depth.

Tracking and Translating

One workaround for the lack of a mask tracker is described in the next chapter: if the movement comes from camera motion, you can essentially stabilize the layer, animate the mask in place, and then reapply motion to both.

You can also apply a motion track to a separate layer containing the mask and apply the layer as a track matte (**Figure 7.7**). Or, if you're merely trying to translate a mask with many keyframes, since you can't multiselect and nudge multiple mask keyframes, you can instead move an entire track matte layer containing them.

New in After Effects CS3, you can link mask shapes together directly with expressions. Alt/Option-click the Mask Path stopwatch, then use the pickwhip to drag to the target Mask Path. Only a direct link is possible, no mathematical or logical operations, so all linked masks behave like instances of the first.

Figure 7.7 The green holdout area is a corner-pinned mask to which a track can be applied (and a corner-pin track can even track the deformation as it moves across a frame). The same idea works in any case where a simple mask shape can be tracked without need to deform drastically over the course of the shot.

Mask Motion Blur

To mask motion blur would seem to be something of a nightmare, as its edges defy careful observation. It's not easy by any means, but masks respect the motion blur settings of the composition; a masked element in motion can be set with motion blurred edges that obey the same composition settings as any other animated element.

That means you have a chance of matching the motion blur using a mask whose contours would fit the shape of the object in its stationary state (**Figure 7.8**). To make the mask work with the moving element is a matter of getting the composition's Shutter Angle and Shutter Phase settings to match. (For details, see Chapter 2, "The Timeline.")

Figure 7.8 Putting a rotoscope mask in motion via keyframes allows motion blur to come along for the ride, simplifying the problem posed in Figure 7.6.

This may leave you with edge problems to cleverly conceal, whether by choking, further blurring the edges, forcing them to the background color, and so on.

Morph

Let's talk about morphing—that's right, that craze of the early '90s, the breakout success by PDI, the Bay Area company that would go on to do *Shrek*, on Michael Jackson's *Black or White* video.

Thing is, morphing can come in handy, without being so blatant and obvious, if you consider it a concealing tool. It's useful when you don't want anyone to notice a transition between two objects or even a transition between one object and itself at a different point in time. Or heck, go crazy morphing together members of your extended family to see if you look anything like the result.

What exactly is a morph? It is, quite simply, a combination of two warps and a dissolve. Given two images, each with a corresponding shape (say, the features of the face), you warp the source image's face shape to the face shape of the target, warp the target from something that matches the source to its face shape, fading the target in over the source.

After Effects has no tool called "Morph," and for a long time, the program offered no good way to pull off this effect. However Reshape is a warping tool that lays the groundwork for simple morphs. You can build these up into more complex morphs, with separate individual transitions occurring to create an overall transition.

Reshape

Unfortunately, creating a morph with Reshape is nowhere near a one-button process. This book generally steers away from step-by-step recipes in favor of helping you solve larger problems creatively, but in this case, it's easy to get confused. So here is a step-by-step, using a demonstration of my own resemblance transitioning to that of my evil twin (**Figure 7.9**):

Figure 7.9 Me and my evil twin, and that awkward adolescent phase in between.

1. Start with two elements that have some basic similarities in their relative position of features. The subtler the distortion required, the more you can get away with.

2. Isolate the two elements you will be morphing from their backgrounds to prevent contamination. If you're working with elements shot against a blue screen, key them out first. Otherwise, mask them. In my example, I created masks for each layer.

3. Ascertain that the two layers are the same size in the X and Y dimensions and as closely aligned as possible. If they are not, precompose one layer to match the other. *This step is important because it will make matching the source and target masks much, much simpler.* Name the two layers Source and Target (as they are in the example) if it helps you follow along.

4. Choose matching sections from your two clips for the duration of your transition (say, 24 frames). If you have still elements, no worries. The closer your moving elements are to still, the more likely you'll get a clean result.

Figures 7.10 The outline of each head is carefully masked. These two masks need not correspond to one another; they are defining the boundary for the Reshape effect and can have differing numbers and orders of points. This mask prevents Reshape from pulling bits of background into the morph region.

NOTES

As of version 7.0, mask names are copied along with masks; the copied mask in step 8 remains named me in the new layer.

5. Draw a mask around the boundary that is going to morph in both layers. Be as precise as possible, erring to the inside if at all (**Figure 7.10**). This could be the masks created in step 2, if you created masks there. It need not be active; if you don't need it to mask out the background, set it to None. Rename each mask something descriptive like outer (the name used in my example).

6. Create a mask around the area of the Source layer that is the focus of the morph. In my example, the focus is facial features: the eyes, nose, and mouth (**Figure 7.11**). Make this mask as simple as you can; use Rotobeziers and as few points as will work to outline the features in question.

7. Set the mask mode to None; this mask is your first shape, you don't need it to influence the layer at all; you will use it for the Reshape effect only. Give it a name (mine is called me).

8. Copy this mask shape and paste it in the Target layer. If the two layers are the same dimensions, it should be an identical size and position as it was in the Source layer.

9. Duplicate the mask. Give it a different color and rename it. In my case, I called the mask it.

10. First scale and rotate, then if necessary move individual points (as little as possible!) so that the it mask surrounds the equivalent area of the Target layer that me does of the source: in my example, the eyes, nose, and mouth.

11. Copy the resulting it mask shape, and paste it to the Source layer to create a new, third mask.

12. You now have three masks for each of the Source and Target layers. Now apply the Reshape effect to each layer.

13. Starting with the Source layer, set the Source Mask (me), the Destination Mask (it), and the Boundary Mask (outer). Set Elasticity to Liquid (you can experiment with other settings later if need be). Set Interpolation to Smooth.

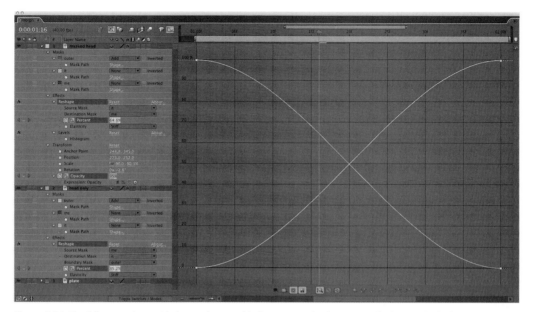

Figure 7.11 The full setup along with the top layer enabled at 100% and color corrected. It begins the final animation at 0% Opacity, reaching 100% at the end of the transition.

14. At the first frame of the morph transition, still in Source, set a keyframe for Percent (at the default, 0.0%, meaning no reshaping is occurring). At the last frame, set Percent to, you guessed it, 100.0%. Now sit back and wait for the gruesome transformation. Don't worry about how it looks yet.

15. Repeat steps 12 and 13 for the Target layer, with the following changes: Set Source Mask to it and Destination Mask to me. The Percent keyframes should be set to 0.0 at the *last* frame of the transition (where it is keyframed to 100.0 on the Source layer) and, you guessed it, 100.0 at the first frame.

16. You've created the warps, now you just need the cross dissolve. Set an Opacity keyframe for Target at the last frame of the transition (leaving it at the default 100.0%), and then add a 0.0% Opacity keyframe at the first frame.

You should now be ready to preview. The preview may take a long time to build the first frame; subsequent frames render much more quickly, so be patient. The main question to resolve is whether the features line up properly;

TIP

The Correspondence Points in Reshape can be raised from the default of 1 to make the distortion more precise (and in some cases, less twisted). The downside is that this slow effect thus becomes even slower. Better to simplify what you're attempting to do with your masks and fix things there; raise this value only as a last resort.

TIP

If at any point during setup it becomes difficult to interact with the UI because After Effects is taking so long updating a frame, enable Caps Lock on your keyboard to prevent any further frame rendering until you're done.

if not, you must adjust the source and destination mask shapes accordingly, watching the median frame to see whether the changes are improving matters.

At this point my example may be looking good in terms of the face transition, but, of course, I've made life hard on myself by transitioning from a head of one size to a larger one, and the edges just kind of fade in. Therefore—and this is where it can get really complicated—I add a second morph, using the same steps as before, but all new masks.

Why complicated? Why new masks? These two questions are interrelated. If you set a second Reshape effect, the key is to avoid influencing the result of the first Reshape effect at all. Therefore, on the second instance the Boundary mask should be the boundary of the object *minus the area occupied by the original source and destination masks*. My second set of shapes covers the ears and top of the head, but avoids the area of the previous masks completely (**Figure 7.12**).

NOTES

Because I know this is complicated, I've included the source project and the final result as projects on the book's DVD-ROM. Please do not use the result as the centerpiece of your horror feature.

Figure 7.12 The full setup to do more than one morph on a single image quickly becomes pretty gnarly. Here are two non-overlapping holdout areas containing two sets of transition curves. This setup also takes exponentially longer to render.

Now, a quick look at a detail I left out (by having you duplicate the Source and Destination masks in step 9, for example, rather than draw them from scratch).

First Vertex and Target Mask

The Reshape tool heavily relies on the First Vertex to determine which point on the source mask corresponds to which on the destination mask. In this morph example, it is easiest to duplicate the source mask to create the destination mask to automatically satisfy the two criteria most essential for a smooth Reshape effect:

▶ Placement of the First Vertex corresponds on both masks

▶ Each mask has the same number of points

If either is not fulfilled, Reshape will execute some not-so-nice compensatory measures, probably deforming the in-between frames in undesirable ways. The easiest solution is usually to duplicate the source mask and edit it, keeping the same number of points. The next easiest method would be to draw a new mask with the same number of points, in the same direction (clockwise or counterclockwise), and to set the First Vertex where you need it (by context-clicking on the mask and choosing Select First Vertex from the menu).

To draw a new mask, go to the Layer viewer and choose Masks from the View pulldown (**Figure 7.13**). If the layer has a mask, a Target pulldown appears along the bottom of the viewer. Choose the mask you want to replace from this menu and draw or paste a new one (**Figure 7.14**). If the Mask Path has keyframes, it will deform from the previous mask shape to the new one, and if the First Vertex and vertex direction match, the transition will be clean.

Figure 7.13 The View menu specifies what is active in the Layer panel; the Render checkbox determines whether that particular step is displayed, or the source.

Figure 7.14 Choose a mask from the Target menu and draw a new mask (or paste in a mask shape). The target mask shape will be replaced; this is predominantly useful with a keyframed Mask Shape.

Puppet

Reshape is old-school compared with the Puppet tools, in many ways the most interesting addition to After Effects CS3. To get started with Puppet, select a layer (preferably a foreground element with a shape defined by transparency, such as an alpha channel or mask), add the Puppet Pin tool (**Ctrl+P/Cmd+P**) by clicking points on areas you want to animate. Click two points, drag the third, and behold: The layer is now pliable in a very organic, intuitive way.

Just because I could, I created a pretzel (**Figures 7.15a** and **b**). Puppet can be used for much subtler stuff, but this example clearly demonstrates something previously impossible in After Effects.

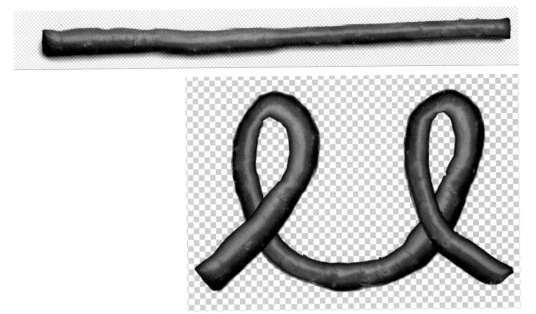

Figures 7.15a and 7.15b Just to show I could, I made myself an ultra-long pretzel in Photoshop and then deformed it into the familiar shape (without worrying about realistic nuances such as light direction). Puppet can really deform stuff.

Here are the basic steps to create a deformation animation:

1. Use the Puppet Pin tool to add three pins to a foreground layer. Experimentation will tell you a lot about where to place these, but they're very similar to the places on a marionette where the wires connect: the center, joints, and ends.

2. Move one of them, and observe what happens to the overall image.

3. Add points as needed to further articulate the deformation.

4. To animate by positioning and timing keyframes: Expose the numbered Puppet Pin properties in the Timeline (UU); these have X and Y Position values matching many other properties in After Effects.

5. To animate in real time: Hold **Ctrl/Cmd** as you move your cursor over a pin, and a stopwatch icon appears; click and drag that pin and a real-time animation of your cursor movement records from the current time until you release the mouse. You can specify an alternate speed for playback by clicking Record Options in the toolbar.

Try these steps with virtually any matted image and see what happens; you'll quickly get the feel for how Puppet is used. To refine the result, you have some options.

In the toolbar is a toggle to show the mesh. The mesh not only gives you an idea how Puppet actually works, it can be essential to allow you to properly adjust the result. I like to leave it on.

Expansion and Triangles use defaults that are often just fine for a given shape. Raising Expansion can help clean up edge pixels left behind in the source. Raising Triangles makes the deformation more accurate, albeit also slower. The default number of triangles varies according to the size and complexity of the source.

More Tools

The Puppet Pin tool does the heavy lifting, but **Ctrl/Cmd+P** cycles through two other Puppet tools that help in special cases.

The pretzel example requires specific control over which parts of the deformation overlap as two regions cross; this is handled by the Puppet Overlap tool. The mesh must be displayed to use Puppet Overlap, and you apply the

TIP

To animate an image from its initial position once you've already deformed it, create keyframes for the pins that have moved, go to the frame that should have the initial position, and click Reset for those pin properties. Only keyframes at the current time are reset.

TIP

Pins disappeared? To display them, three conditions must be satisfied: the layer is selected, the Puppet effect is active and the Puppet Pin tool is currently selected.

Overlap point on the original, undeformed mesh shape, not the deformation (**Figure 7.16**).

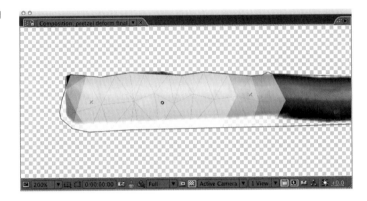

Figure 7.16 The Puppet Overlap tool lets you specify an area of the mesh that you wish to specify be in front or behind other parts of the mesh; a pretzel shape has just this type of need for over/under relationships.

Overlap is not a tool you animate (except perhaps its numerical settings, which are found in the Timeline). Instead, you place it at the center of the area that should overlap others and then adjust the settings as to how much "In Front" it's meant to be and its Extent (how far from the pin this overlap area reaches). You can leave the In Front setting at the default until you start mixing more than one overlap; the higher the value, the closer to the viewer (and negative values will be further away than those with no setting, which default to 0).

The Starch tool prevents an area from deforming. It's not meant to anchor a region of the image but instead to sit between animated pins, preventing the highlighted area (expanded or contracted with the tool's Extent setting) from being squished or stretched (**Figure 7.17**).

Figure 7.17 You would expect such a grotesque extension of the fingers to distort the fingernails and back of the hand, the darker areas show where Starch pins are preventing areas of the mesh from deformation..

Paint and Cloning

Paint is generally a last resort when roto is impractical, and for a simple reason: Paint work is typically painstaking, and more likely to show flaws than approaches involving masks. Of course, there are exceptions. The ability to track clone brushes offers a huge advantage over masks, which are not so easy to track, and painting in the alpha channel is akin to masking with paint.

For effects work, paint controls in After Effects have at least a couple of predominant uses:

▶ Clean up an alpha channel mask by painting directly to it in black and white

▶ Clone Stamp to overwrite part of the frame with alternate source

Once you fully understand the strengths and limitations of paint, you can come up with your own uses.

Paint Fundamentals

Two panels, Paint and Brush Tips, are essential to the three brush-based tools in the Tools palette—Brush, Clone Stamp, or Eraser. These can be revealed by choosing the Paint Workspace (**Figures 7.18a, b,** and **c**).

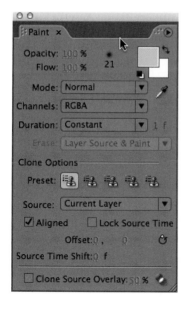
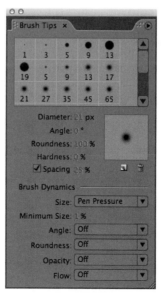

Figures 7.18a, b, and c Use the keyboard shortcut **Ctrl+B** (**Cmd+B**) to cycle through the three basic brush tools (a, above); to their right is a toggle that reveals (or hides) the Paint and Brush Tips panels (b and c, left and right).

239

The After Effects paint functionality is patterned after Photoshop, but with a couple of fundamental differences. After Effects offers fewer customizable options for its brushes (you can't, for example, design your own brush tips). More significantly, Photoshop's brushes are raster based, while After Effects brushes are vector based, allowing them to be edited and animated at any stage.

Suppose that you have an alpha channel in need of a touch-up; for example, the matte shown in **Figure 7.19** is a difficult key without matte cleanup, due to tracking markers and shadows. With the Brush tool active, go to the Paint palette and set Channels to Alpha (this palette remembers the last mode you used); the foreground and background color swatches in the palette become grayscale, and you can make them black and white by clicking the tiny black-over-white squares just below the swatches. To see what you are painting, switch the view to the Alpha Channel (**Alt+4/Option+4**); switch back to RGB to check the final result.

Figure 7.19 Touch up an alpha channel matte (for example, remove a tracking marker): In the Paint palette, select Alpha in the Channels menu, then display the alpha channel (**Alt/Option+4**).

When using the paint tools:

- ▶ Brush-based tools operate only in the Layer panel

- ▶ Brushes include a Mode setting (analogous to Transfer Modes)

- ▶ With a tablet, you can use the Brush Dynamics settings, at the bottom of the Brush Tips palette, to set how the pressure, angle, and stylus wheel of your pen affect strokes

- ▶ The Duration setting and the frame where you begin painting are crucial

- ▶ Preset brushes and numerical settings for properties such as diameter and hardness (a.k.a. feather) live in the Brush Tips panel.

Much more fun and interactive than the Brush Tips panel are the following shortcuts. With the brush tool active in the Layer viewer:

- ▶ Hold **Ctrl/Cmd** and drag to scale the brush

- ▶ Add the **Shift** key to adjust in larger increments, and **Alt/Option** for fine adjustments

- ▶ With the mouse button still held, release **Ctrl/Cmd** to scale hardness (an inner circle appears representing the inside of the threshold, **Figure 7.20**)

- ▶ Alt/Option-click to use the eyedropper (with brushes) or clone source (with the clone brush)

By default, the Duration setting in the Paint menu is set to Constant, which means that any paint stroke you create on this frame continues to the end of the layer. For cleaning up an alpha channel, this is typically not a desirable setting because you're presumably painting stray holes in your matte here and there, on single (or just a few) frames. The Single Frame setting confines your stroke to just the current frame on which you're painting, and the Custom setting allows you to enter the number of frames that the stroke will persist.

TIP

The older Vector Paint effect (Pro only) remains useful for painting in the context of a comp viewer, but it won't clone, and it's not intuitive; I prefer to open two viewers (Comp and Layer).

TIP

There is a major gotcha with Constant (the default mode): Paint a stroke at any frame other than the first frame of the layer, and it does not appear until that frame during playback. It's apparently not a bug, but it is certainly an annoyance.

Figure 7.20 Modifier keys (**Ctrl/ Cmd** to scale, **Alt/Opt** to feather, all with mouse button held) let you define a brush on the fly. The inner circle shows the solid core; the area between it and the outer circle is the threshold (for feathering).

The other option, Write On, records your stroke in real time, re-creating the motion (including timing) when you replay the layer; this stylized option can be useful for such motion graphics tricks as handwritten script.

The Brush Tips panel menu includes various display options and customizable features: You can add, rename, or delete brushes, as well. You can also name a brush by double-clicking it. Brush names do not appear in the default thumbnail view except via tooltips when you move your cursor above each brush.

For an alpha channel, you will typically work in Single Frame mode (under Duration in the Paint panel), looking only at the alpha channel (**Alt+4/Option+4**) and progressing frame by frame through the shot (pressing **Page Down**).

After working for a little while, your Timeline may contain dozens of strokes, each with numerous properties of its own. New strokes are added to the top of the stack and given numerically ordered names; to select one to edit or delete, you may more easily find it using the Selection tool (**V**) to directly select it in a viewer panel.

Cloning Fundamentals

When you clone moving footage, the result retains grain and other natural features that still images lack. Not only can you clone pixels from a different region of the same frame, you can clone from a different frame of a different clip at a different point in time (**Figures 7.21a, b,** and **c**), as follows:

▶ **Clone from the same frame:** This works just as in Photoshop. Choose a brush, Alt/Option-click on the area of the frame to sample, and begin painting. Remember that by default, Duration is set to Constant, so any stroke created begins at the current frame and extends through the rest of the composition.

▶ **Clone from the same clip, at a different time:** Look at Clone Options for the offset value in frames. Note that there is also an option to set spatial offset. To clone from the exact same position at a different point in time, set the Offset to 0, 0 and change the Source Time.

TIP

As in Photoshop, the **X** key swaps the foreground and background swatches with the Brush tool active.

NOTES

The Aligned toggle in the Paint panel (on by default) preserves 1:1 pixel positions even though paint tools are vector-based. Nonaligned clone operations tend to appear blurry.

Figures 7.21a, b, and c Clone source overlay is checked (a) with difference mode active, an "onion skin" that makes it possible to line up precisely two matching shots (b and c). Difference mode is on, causing all identical areas of the frame to turn black when the two layers are perfectly aligned.

▶ **Clone from a separate clip:** The source from which you're cloning must be present in the current composition (although it need not be visible and can even be a guide layer). Simply open the layer to be used as source, and go to the current time where you want to begin; Source and Source Time Shift are listed in the Paint panel and can also be edited there.

▶ **Mix multiple clone sources without having to reselect each one:** There are five Preset icons in the Paint panel; these allow you to switch sources on the fly and then switch back to a previous source. Just click on a Preset icon before selecting your clone source and that source remains associated with that preset (including Aligned and Lock Source Time settings).

That all seems straightforward enough; there are just a few things to watch out for, as follows.

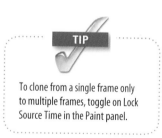

TIP

To clone from a single frame only to multiple frames, toggle on Lock Source Time in the Paint panel.

NOTES

Clone is different from many other tools in After Effects in that Source Time Shift uses frames, not seconds to evaluate the temporal shift. Beware if you mix clips with different frame rates, although on the whole this is a beneficial feature.

Tricks and Gotchas

Suppose the clone source time is offset, or comes from a different layer, and the last frame of the layer has been reached—what happens? After Effects helpfully loops back to the first frame of the clip and keeps going. This is dangerous only if you're not aware of it.

Edit the source to take control of this process. Time remapping is one potential way to solve these problems; you can time stretch a source clip or loop it intentionally.

You may need to scale the source to match the target. Although temporal edits, including time remapping, render before they are passed through, other types of edits—even simple translations or effects—do not. As always, the solution is to precompose; any scaling, rotation, motion tracking, or effects to be cloned belong in the subcomposition.

Finally, Paint is an effect. Apply your first stroke and you'll see an effect called Paint with a single checkbox, Paint on Transparent, which effectively solos the paint strokes. You can change the render order of paint strokes relative to other effects. For example, you can touch up a green-screen plate, apply a keyer, and then touch up the resulting alpha channel, all on one layer (**Figure 7.22**).

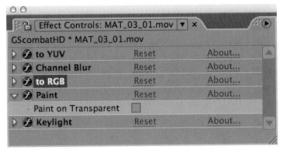

Figure 7.22 Paint strokes and effects are interleaved; touch-up of the plate occurs after compression artifacts related to 4:2:2 sampling are removed (see previous chapter) but before Keylight is applied.

The View pull-down menu in the Layer panel (**Figure 7.23**) lists, in order, the paint and effects edits you've added to the layer. To see only the layer with no edits applied, toggle Render off; to see a particular stage of the edit—after the first paint strokes, but before the effects, say—select it in the View menu, effectively disabling the steps below it. These settings are for previewing only; they will not enable or disable the rendering of these items.

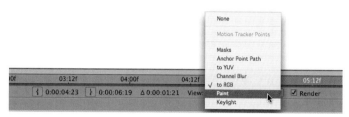

Figure 7.23 The Layer panel's View pull-down menu is a useful method for soloing paint strokes in the overall effects pipeline.

You can motion track a paint stroke. To do so requires the tracker, covered in the next chapter, and a basic expression; this topic is fully covered in Chapter 10, "Expressions."

Wire Removal

Wire removal and rig removal are two common visual effects needs. Generally speaking, *wire removal* is cloning over a wire (typically used to suspend an actor or prop in mid-air). *Rig removal*, meanwhile, is typically just an animated garbage mask over any equipment that appeared in shot.

Some rotoscoping applications have dedicated wire-removal tools, but in After Effects, you're on your own. However, wire removal need not be a painstaking process in After Effects simply because there's no dedicated tool for it. There are several creative approaches that can work; if the ends of the wire are trackable, you can track position and rotation and apply these to a null, which would be the parent of a masked element to replace the wire. This specific instance, with an example, is demonstrated in the following chapter.

Rig removal is often aided by tracking motion, because rigs themselves don't move, the camera does. The key is to make a shape that mattes out the rig, then apply that as a track matte to the foreground footage and track the whole matte (see Chapter 8).

Photoshop Video

Photoshop CS3 offers an intriguing Adobe alternative to the After Effects vector paint tools; for the first time ever, it's possible to work with moving footage in Photoshop. The After Effects paint tools are heavily based on those in Photoshop, but with one key difference: Photoshop strokes are bitmaps (actual pixels), those from After Effects are vectors. This makes it possible to use custom brushes, as are common in Photoshop (and which are themselves bitmaps). There's not as much you can do overall with the stroke once you've painted it as in After Effects, but if you like working in Photoshop, it's certainly an option. After Effects can open Photoshop files containing video.

Dust Bust

This is as nitty-gritty as rotoscoping gets. For various reasons, even on the highest budget visual effects film, the shooting and transfer process introduces flaws visible on a frame-by-frame basis: Dust and scratches make their way onto the pristine master. Most of these flaws can be corrected only via frame-by-frame cloning, sometimes known as *dust busting*. If you've carefully read this section, you already know what you need to know to do this work successfully, so get to it.

Conclusion

And so, like rain, into every effects artist's life a little rotoscoping must fall. The tools outlined here are mostly sufficient for the type of rotoscoping work that compositors will have to do. Dedicated rotoscope artists would likely choose software other than After Effects to ply their trade, or perhaps employ Silhouette as an After Effects plug-in. As long as rotoscoping isn't your stock in trade, however, the After Effects tools will usually allow you to finish the shot without having to look for other software.

The next chapter completes the picture by adding motion tracking to your areas of expertise. As mentioned, motion tracking plus rotoscoping can equal a shortcut around tedious tasks.

8

Effective Motion Tracking

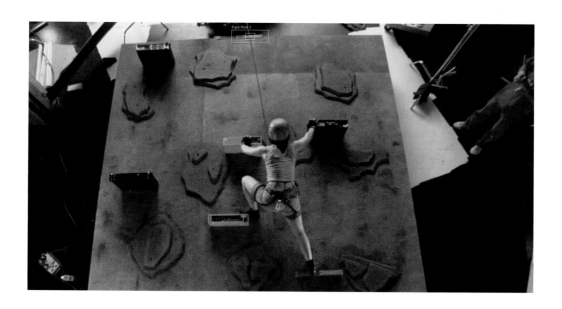

Even if you're on the right track, you'll get run over if you just sit there.

—Will Rogers

Effective Motion Tracking

The After Effects tracker helps you precisely capture two-dimensional motion in source footage and apply it to target layers (Track Motion) or remove camera motion from a shot (Stabilize Motion). Click a button and match motion more precisely than would be possible by hand.

Skill counts, however, as the After Effects tracker is not fully automated, and it is fallible; you should understand its criteria and how to

▶ Choose effective initial track points

▶ Customize settings based on the particular challenge

▶ Rescue tracks that seem to have gone astray (or abandon and restart, provided you understand what to try instead)

▶ Handle motion blur

▶ Apply motion tracking indirectly, using a 3D camera

This chapter addresses these techniques and more.

Once you've nailed down the essentials, you can move on to some elegant uses of the tracker. For example, you can

▶ Use the After Effects 3D camera as if it were a physical camera, matching objects you insert in the scene to the scene motion automatically

▶ Procedurally smooth a camera move (beyond simply stabilizing a static shot)

▶ Use a simple expression to continue tracking an object that becomes occluded (the track area moves offscreen or otherwise disappears)

▶ Bring three-dimensional depth to effects even though After Effects does not import 3D meshes

Don't forget, the tracker's uses go beyond those clearly spelled out in the Tracker Controls panel (which can always be revealed by choosing it in the Window menu, although it appears automatically upon applying a track).

The Essentials

There's no point in learning about all the cool tricks you can perform with the tracker if you're still fighting it for a good basic track. If you still find your tracks going astray after reviewing the After Effects documentation (if you haven't read it, at least skim Motion Tracking in the Adobe Help Center, **F1**), read on and don't despair. Just because it is automated doesn't mean that it's automatic; you sometimes have to come to a certain "understanding" with this feature set.

Tracking is a two-step process: The tracker analyzes the clip and stores its analysis as a set of layer properties that don't actually do anything. They must be applied to take effect. Both steps, setting the tracking target and applying the track, occur in the Tracker Controls panel.

Choose a Feature

There are trackers that don't require you to choose track points (predominantly dedicated third-party 3D and planar trackers, discussed later in this chapter). After Effects, however, relies on you to choose a feature that will track effectively, and it is the most important choice for a successful track (**Figure 8.1**).

Figure 8.1 You set After Effects tracking points in the Layer panel, via the Tracker Controls panel.

TIP

Search and feature regions don't have to be square! Widen the feature region to match a wide, short target feature. With unidirectional motion—say, a left-to-right pan—widen the search region and offset it to the right.

Make sure the feature you plan to track

▶ Contrasts in color, luminance, or saturation from the surrounding area

▶ Has defined edges entirely within the feature region

▶ Is identifiable throughout the shot

▶ Does not have to compete with similar distinct features within the search region at any point during the track

▶ Is close to the area where the tracked object or objects will be added

To find a good candidate for tracking, look for "corners" in your image—places where two or more edges meet (**Figures 8.2a, b**, and **c**).

Figures 8.2a, b, and c High-contrast, clearly defined corners that maintain shape and lighting are optimal (a), track regions that are likely to have any type of motion in them (b) less so, and features that are themselves likely to move least of all (c); these points are also non-planar, explained later).

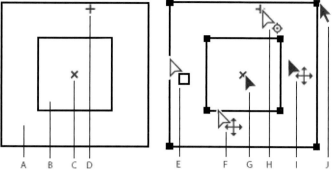

Figure 8.3 Many interactive controls are clustered close together in the tracker. Identified here are: A. Search region, B. Feature region, C. Keyframe marker, D. Attach point, E. Move search region, F. Move both regions, G. Moves entire track point, H. Move attach point, I. Move entire track point, J. Resize region. Zoom in to ensure you're clicking the right one.

WARNING

Be forewarned: The tracker controls contain several draggable items in close proximity to one another (**Figure 8.3**). Watch carefully for the correct icon before clicking and dragging.

The search region should include only the area in which the feature will appear on the very next frame—no more, and certainly no less. Be generous when setting this region, but don't give the tracker any reason to search where there is no helpful detail (**Figure 8.4**).

Figure 8.4 The bus travels from screen right to left, so I offset the search region (the outer box) to the left of the feature region (inner box). Customizing the track regions in this manner speeds up the track and reduces the margin of error considerably.

NOTES

Tracks slow down (requiring more processor cycles) in direct proportion to their size. Although systems are relatively fast and capable these days, large feature or track regions can be excessively slow.

No Good Reference Point in Sight

Sometimes you get lucky, and you discover a trackable feature right where the target layer belongs. A successful track here is almost like returning to the shoot and placing the object directly on set.

At other times, however, you may not find very many suitable features in a shot, or a feature may exit frame at an inconvenient moment (one potential solution to this is described in "Extend a Track"). In such cases, you can edit the attach point, that little x in **Figure 8.5**. The attach point defaults to the center of the feature region, but you can offset it anywhere in the frame.

NOTES

If the best target feature changes or even disappears as the shot progresses, look for strategies later in the chapter for dealing with this.

Figure 8.5 You may need to zoom way in to see controls such as the attach point, which has been offset in this case to the low contrast corner. This solves a common problem: a more trackable feature is nearby, but not exactly where the track point needs to be.

This chapter will show you how to more or less ignore the attach point by using nulls and parenting instead, which let you offset this point and do all sorts of other useful things when tracking. This isn't how the documentation would have you do it, but it tends to solve more problems.

Tracker Options

Prior to version 6, the After Effects tracker was rather notorious. With default settings geared toward slow systems rather than optimal results, it was practically guaranteed not to produce a good track. Simply clicking Play after setting tracking regions now often yields an effective result.

Nevertheless, defaults will take you only so far. The tracker is packed with plenty of powerful options designed for specific scenarios that, sooner or later, you are bound to encounter.

Track types

It's easy enough to get an idea of the types of tracks available in After Effects: Just have a look at the Track Type menu (**Figure 8.6**). But what exactly are the differences?

Stabilize and *Transform tracking* are virtually identical until applied. Clicking Edit Target shows the singular difference between them: Stabilize tracks are always applied to the *anchor point of the tracked layer*. Transform tracks are applied to the *position of a layer other than the tracked layer*.

Figure 8.6 The various available track types are set in the Tracker Controls panel.

Using Stabilize, the animated anchor point (located at the center of the image by default) moves the layer in opposition to Position. Increasing the anchor point's X value (assuming Position remains the same, which it does when you adjust the Anchor Point value directly in the Timeline) moves the layer to the left, just as decreasing the Position value does.

Corner Pin tracking is something else altogether—essentially a cheat to skew a rectangular source so that its four corners appear to translate in 3D space. This is not true 3D tracking in any sense. Instead, Corner Pin tracking applies data to a 2D layer via the Corner Pin plug-in, animating its 2D corner values. Imagine replacing a sign on the side of a moving bus (something you can attempt later in the chapter), and you get the idea. Corner pins are classically used for adding a plane (monitor screen content, billboard, and so on) to a framed area of a source shot.

TIP

You can, and likely should, use Stabilize, exclusively, even when tracking elements to match a background scene. Methodology follows in the "2.5D Tracking" section.

There are two types of Corner Pin tracking. Both generate four points of data, one for each corner of the target layer, but Parallel Corner Pin does so with only three track points. This works as long your target is perfectly rectangular and remains so throughout the shot—a shot of a door, head-on, with the camera at a perpendicular angle, for example. In most cases, you use Perspective Corner Pin (**Figures 8.7**).

Figure 8.7 The basic corner pin setup. Offsetting a corner like the lower right typically does not work, as the offset doesn't scale.

TIP

A Corner Pin track simultaneously tracks the deformation of a rectangular area, applying the result to the four corners of the Corner Pin effect, and Position tracks the entire layer. When perspective doesn't change much, it's often best to remove most of the Corner Pin keyframes for a smoother result.

Raw tracks generate track data only, graying out the Edit Target button. What good is track data that isn't applied anywhere? It can be used to drive expressions or saved to be applied later. It's no different than simply never clicking Edit Target; the raw track data is stored within the source layer (**Figure 8.8**).

Rotation and Scale

Additionally tracking rotation and scale data is straightforward enough, employing two track points instead of one. Typically, the two points should be roughly equidistant from the camera due to the phenomenon of parallax.

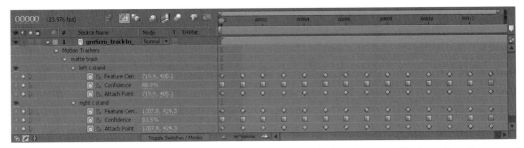

Figure 8.8 Each motion track generates raw data, whether or not it is specified as a Raw track. The data is found here, under Motion Trackers. As shown, the track and its points can be named for future reference, useful on a difficult track requiring multiple attempts.

Imagine where in Z space the object belongs and track points that are both at that relative depth. Otherwise no bag of tricks—not offsets, not 3D extrapolation—is likely to help.

When tracking rotation and scale, features being tracked typically change from frame to frame (they rotate and scale). In Motion Tracker Options you'll find the Adapt Feature on Every Frame setting, which is like restarting the track on each and every frame. This is not a good default because, theoretically at least, it adds a greater margin of error over time, but it can solve tracks of features whose appearance changes over the course of the shot. If you know that a feature being tracked is going to change its orientation, or size, or color, or the like over the course of the shot, consider enabling it; for example, try it using the tracker on one of the dolly or zoom shots included with this chapter's project.

If a track keeps slipping going forward, try starting at the end of the clip and tracking in reverse (note that the "play" icons in Tracker Controls go both directions (**Figure 8.9**).

TIP

Tracking in reverse is particularly useful when tracking an object moving away from the camera, whose features and track region otherwise diminish to the point of being untrackable. Adapt Feature on Every Frame is an effective option in this case as well.

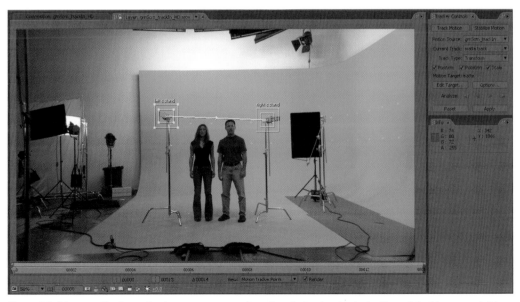

Figure 8.9 When tracking items that become more prominent later in the shot (as do the C stands in this camera dolly), try tracking in reverse. The tracker does a much more effective job of tracking a large pattern as it gets smaller, than the opposite.

Confidence

Below the Adapt Feature check box is a pull-down menu that sets After Effects' mysterious Confidence settings. Take a closer look at the properties listed under a track point (**Figure 8.10**); Confidence contains data showing how accurate the track is at a given frame. My experience is that good tracks tend to stay in the 80% to 100% region, ideally above 90%, and a major problem returns Confidence values of 30% or less.

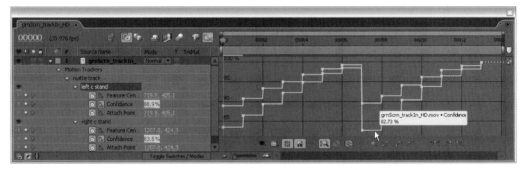

Figure 8.10 Revealing Confidence graphs in the Graph Editor clearly shows where the tracker's confidence has been shaken, so to speak. Just because a frame has low confidence doesn't mean there's a problem, although in this case it is clear that specific frames seem to have slipped, where the graph drops drastically.

After Effects can take specific actions as the track is created, depending on the Confidence settings at the bottom of Motion Tracker Options (**Figure 8.11**). You can assign the track to continue no matter what or to simply stop tracking if confidence drops so that you can manually reset the track at that frame. The Extrapolate Motion option is there for tracked features that disappear for a few frames, retaining more or less steady motion while out of view.

Figure 8.11 The menu at the bottom of Motion Tracker Options (accessible via the Tracker palette) specifies what to do when the Confidence rating drops below a certain threshold during the track.

The default setting Adapt Feature If Confidence Is Below 80% is effective in many cases; this is the setting with which you're most likely to get lucky and have the track solved without much extra managing.

Other Options

The rest of the Motion Tracker Options (**Figure 8.12**) determine how footage is examined and analyzed.

Instead of luminance, you can track RGB (for contrasting colors of a similar luminance) or Saturation (for the unlikely scenario of extraordinarily high and low color saturation but flat color and contrast). Luminance is preferable most of the time, provided you can locate the aforementioned "corners" with strong bright/dark contrast.

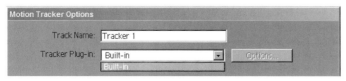

Figure 8.12 These tracker options control what is analyzed and how.

For me, Track Fields serves as a reminder to instead separate them on import (either way, make sure you're working with individual fields if they exist). Likewise, you set Process Before Match to pre-blur or pre-sharpen (Enhance) a clip, but the need may indicate that your footage needs degraining or, conversely, is too blurry to track effectively in After Effects.

NOTES

Motion Tracker Options optimistically includes a Plug-in pulldown but no one outside of Adobe has shown up for the party (**Figure 8.13**).

Figure 8.13 Nothing to click here, move along…

When Tracks Go Wrong

The feature you're tracking changes as the shot progresses, and the tracker suddenly jumps to a different, similar feature within the search region. You didn't set Stop Tracking if Confidence drops—or maybe it didn't drop. You pounce on the Stop button in the tracker controls (**Figure 8.14**). Now what? The tracker has created a few frames' worth of bad data.

Figure 8.14 When the tracker suddenly loses its way for a few frames, stop the track, move current time back to the last good frame, and restart. In many cases, depending on the Confidence setting (Figure 8.10), this will solve whatever problem occurred on the previous pass.

It's no big deal! Just drag the Current Time Indicator (in the Layer panel) back to the last correctly tracked frame and click Play. In so doing, you have reset the Feature Region contents, so there is a higher likelihood that the tracker will succeed without changing anything. If not, and the tracker continues to drift, the next line of defense is Adapt Feature on Every Frame:

TIP

To reveal the current track in the Timeline with the Track Controls active, use the SS (show selected) shortcut.

▶ If an object briefly passes in front of the track target, set Extrapolate Motion, using the Confidence threshold at which the track went astray (found in the Timeline).

▶ If a feature changes its shape, color, or luminance during the shot, try Adapt Feature.

▶ If neither of the above helps, Stop Tracking may be your best option; you can manually reset the track point when it fails.

Remain flexible, be creative about your choice of points, and be prepared to start over if things aren't working too well.

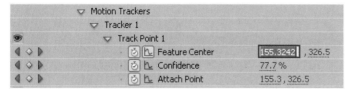

Figure 8.15 Curious about accuracy of the tracker? Highlight a keyframe and you can see that it's accurate to $^1/_{10,000}$ of a pixel.

Match Motion Blur

Don't neglect the possibility of motion blur! It can be your friend until it appears unwanted, like a malingering house-guest, impossible to ignore. Notice that:

▶ Foreground layers may need motion blur to match the background plate

▶ A stabilized layer may have motion blur that is no longer desirable

Figure 8.16 Easily overlooked, the Motion Source pull-down menu is a one-stop location for all layers in the Timeline containing motion tracks.

The solution to the former problem is relatively simple, and the methodology is similar to that of color matching (as in Chapter 5, "Color Correction"). Zoom into an area of the image that would have well-defined contours were there is no motion blur—a solid object with well-defined, high-contrast edges, if possible. Enable motion blur for tracked foreground layers, and eye-match the length of the

Subpixel Motion

The key feature of the After Effects tracker is sub-pixel positioning, on by default in Motion Tracker Options. You could never achieve this degree of accuracy manually; most supposedly "locked off" scenes require stabilization despite that the range of motion is less than a full pixel; your vision is actually far more acute than that.

As you watch a track in progress, the trackers move in whole pixel values, bouncing around crudely, but unless you disable subpixel positioning, this does not reflect the final track, which is accurate to $^1/_{10,000}$ of a pixel (four places below the decimal point, **Figure 8.15**).

If you need to reapply a track and can't find it, look in the Motion Source pull-down menu of the Tracker Controls (**Figure 8.16**). Layers that can accept tracks are black, and those with track data show up in the Current Track menu.

Previous tracks can be found in the Current Track pulldown in Tracker Controls; to delete individual points or whole tracks, go to layer properties.

blur, adjusting accordingly via the Composition Settings panel (**Ctrl+K/Cmd+K**), Advanced tab (**Figure 8.17**).

Figure 8.17 This panel is not interactive; to eye-match motion blur may involve reopening it more than once.

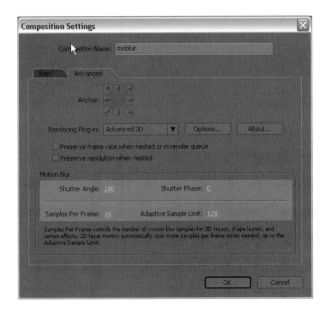

The latter problem, of removing existing blur, is more formidable. Even if you could easily do this in After Effects, footage that is heavily blurred will probably exhibit other problems when stabilized, such as a visible gutter area around the tracked image (**Figure 8.18**). The best solution is probably to forgo a completely locked stabilization in favor of smoothing the camera motion, but leaving some of the movement (see "Smooth a Moving Camera").

Figure 8.18 Extreme stabilization opens gaps around the repositioned layer, which can be fixed only by scaling and repositioning the shot; this often accompanies heavy motion blur on the source plate, which will in any case sink the result.

Use Nulls to Solve Transform Problems

Having difficulty placing your track correctly? Nulls are often the solution. It can be disconcerting to apply a track to a layer and see it repositioned, rotated, or scaled from its correct placement. There's a relatively easy (and easily overlooked) fix: Apply the track to a null, then parent the target layer to the null—no further finagling needed.

Figures 8.19a through **d** shows a particularly fiendish rig removal that was aided by the use of tracked nulls. One

TIP

Applying tracking data to a null is a universally good idea for a few reasons. For example, you can also lock it, preventing you from inadvertently nudging one of its keyframes.

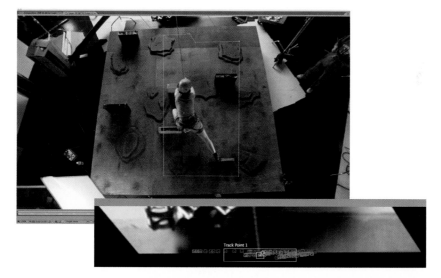

Figures 8.19a, b, c, and d Obviously it is essential that the rope reach the edge of the frame, yet the set does not (a). The point where the rope meets the edge of the set can be tracked, however (b), and a two-point mask with a Stroke effect added to replace it (c). The final image has motion blur applied, offsets to the shape of the added rope animated as needed, and the colors carefully matched, selling the effect (d).

section of the moving rope that was not over the set had to be replaced and matched to the movement of the rest of the rope. The problem area was isolated and the movement of the rope along its edges tracked, then a substitute rope section was created using Stroke. By parenting this to the null containing the motion, motion blur was created procedurally as well, selling the final shot.

As you'll see in the next section, and again in the next chapter, nulls are particularly useful to animate a 3D camera, given that it has no anchor point and cannot be the target of a motion track. Parenting a camera to a null is the most sensible and straightforward method to apply tracker data to it.

If you prefer not to add a null object layer, if only because it's just one more layer to manage, there is, of course, an alternative: Apply an expression to offset the tracked transform data. If that sounds tempting, check out Chapter 10, "Expressions." Most users will find the use of nulls simpler and more convenient.

2.5D Tracking

Say you need to track an arbitrary number of overlaid elements into a scene, matching the movement of a camera. You might expect to track each layer individually or parent one to another (if that would even work, given that parenting changes the center of a rotation or scale transform). Instead, on many shots you can have the benefits of 3D tracking without a 3D tracker.

The key is to stabilize the background layer and then parent a camera to that stabilization, restoring the motion. The motion of the source camera is captured and applied to a virtual camera, so that any elements you add to the scene pick up on that motion. It's quite cool.

The AE Camera as a Tracking Tool

Suppose you need to add an arbitrary number (more than one, or more as you go along, and so on) of foreground layers to a background plate with camera motion: CG objects, color corrections, effects with hold-out masks, you name it. Applying track data to each of those layers individually would be a time-consuming headache.

Instead, the following method allows you to stabilize the background scene, add static foreground elements and then reapply the scene motion:

1. With the background layer selected, choose Stabilize Motion (either by context-clicking the layer or choosing it from the Animation menu).

2. Stabilize the layer for Position, Rotation, and Scale, using two points equidistant from the camera.

3. The stabilized layer offsets and rotates in the frame (**Figure 8.20**). Return to the first frame of the track (quite possibly frame 0 of the comp). Turn on the stabilized layer's 3D switch.

4. Add a 3D camera (context-click in an empty area of the Timeline); in the Camera Settings, give it a name like trackerCam, use the 50mm preset, and click OK.

NOTES

A 50 mm camera lens in After Effects offers a neutral perspective; toggle any layer to 3D and it should appear the same as in 2D.

Figure 8.20 Gaps open up around the edges of the image as the track points are held in place.

5. Parent the camera layer to the stabilized layer (**Figure 8.21**).

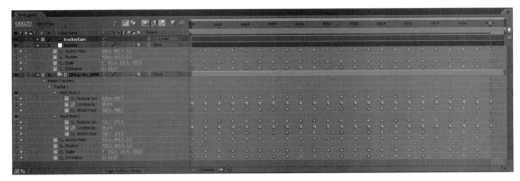

Figure 8.21 The relevant Transform properties have been copied and pasted to a null, to which the camera is then parented.

Everything now appears back to normal, with one intriguing twist: any new item added to the scene picks up the scene motion as soon as you toggle its 3D switch. Any layer that shouldn't follow the track, such as an adjustment layer, can remain 2D (**Figure 8.22**).

Figure 8.22 Extra layers for a new clock face, child's artwork along with a shadow are added as 3D layers, so they pick up the motion of the scene as captured by the tracked camera.

Any layer that is equidistant from camera with the motion track points has a Z-depth value of 0. Offsetting layers is tricky as there is no frame of reference for where they should be placed in Z space—not even a grid. (**Figure 8.23**).

Figure 8.23 A 3D camera opens the possibility to reposition layers in 3D space, such as the matte painting outside the window, far back in Z space, and the sheet of paper sitting on the file cabinet, closer to the camera. Getting view angle and relative distances correct can be tricky, however, especially with the foreground item, which may instead require a 3D track from third-party software.

This section is entitled 2.5D tracking because, after all, although it uses 3D space and a 3D camera, the tracking points and layers are themselves two-dimensional. Therefore any 3D offset that you introduce with this method is only approximately accurate; sometimes that's good enough, but sometimes you need a real 3D camera solution (detailed in the last section of this chapter).

Smooth a Moving Camera

Once you've succeeded in sampling the motion of a scene and have applied it to an After Effects 3D camera, you also have the option to modify the motion, including the ability to use built-in tools to smooth bumpy camera motion. This option doesn't officially exist in After Effects, yet it's no

NOTES

Oddly enough, this technique even works with a shot that contains a zoom; to some extent even layers that are offset in 3D space create believable parallax, although with just two track points it is difficult to get a result that is as stable as a 3D track (using outside software), which generally contains far more track points.

mere hack; it can really can allow you to apply stabilization while retaining camera motion.

Figure 8.24 features an aerial shot of Silicon Valley and downtown San Jose (look closely and you can spot Adobe headquarters in that shot). To stabilize a shot like this, pay attention to where the viewer's attention will be, because that's the area that you want to stabilize. Objects in the near foreground move more than those in the distance, and so you can't stabilize both—you have to choose. In this case, the viewer is likely to be looking for the near-horizon (the downtown area) to appear stable and will accept more motion in the foreground.

Figure 8.24 This section features aerial footage shot from a Cessna aircraft, leading to extensive camera wobble even with an experienced pilot flying as smoothly as possible. The camera is parented to a null containing the same Anchor Point data as the stabilized plate, but with a smooth operation applied to it.

The camera has no data of its own to smooth; its motion is derived only from being parented to the stabilized layer. You don't want to apply a smooth to that source layer either, as the smoothing effect will be derived from the difference between that layer's motion and that of the camera. Ideally, you would like to be able to adjust the amount of smoothing after applying it, too.

Therefore, create a null named Stabilizer, or something like that, enable 3D and then paste the Anchor Point data. Figure 8.24 shows the setup, including the smooth operation applied as an expression (**Figure 8.25**), which is vastly superior to any reliance on The Smoother (**Figure 8.26**).

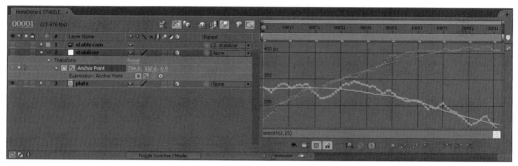

Figure 8.25 The Graph Editor has been set to display curves for the initial and smoothed tracking data (the Anchor Point property itself as well as the expression each has its Graph Editor Set icon enabled). The default **smooth** expression settings don't do much, but after specifying a wider sample and more iterations, a smooth curve appears—just the result sought.

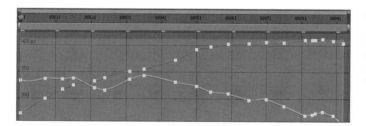

Figure 8.26 Avoid The Smoother, a relic from the pre-expressions days. It is a "black box" tool with only one adjustable property, and it does its work by destroying keyframe data— the result is always fewer keyframes.

The main problem with The Smoother is that it's a one-shot deal: Once you've applied it, you can undo or delete it, but you cannot adjust it. The Smoother is a destructive edit: It changes the keyframe data to which it is applied. Even if you want to adjust it, there is only one setting, for Tolerance; only by trial and error can you know how that setting will influence the track. Expressions are completely nondestructive and offer several adjustable properties.

To apply a smooth expression

1. Alt/Option-click on the Anchor Point stopwatch of the layer to which the camera is parented.

2. With the default expression (anchorPoint) still highlighted, go to the Expressions menu and under Property choose the smooth default: smooth(width = .2, samples = 5, t = time).

3. In most cases, you will discard the third argument and the code hints, and adjust the width and samples settings to be more powerful, such as: smooth(2, 48).

The expression works as follows: it gives a command (smooth) followed by three settings known as *arguments*. The third one, time, is used only to offset the result, and it's optional, so I have the habit of deleting it. The hints for the other two (width = and samples =) are also not needed to make the expression work—they are there just to remind you what they do.

Width determines how much time (before and after the current time) is averaged to create the result. A setting of 2 samples 2 seconds means 1 second before and 1 second after the current time. The samples argument determines how many individual points within that range are actually sampled for the result; generally, the more samples, the smoother the curve. A setting of 48 means that over that 2-second width, 48 individual frame values will be sampled (appropriate for 24 fps footage).

It's also possible to smooth rotation in this manner, although I find a lighter touch (fewer samples) is often more successful. However, the best way to find out for your individual shot is by trying different settings, looking at how smooth the resulting curve (not to mention the actual motion) appears.

It's a little hard to imagine that you can smooth the motion data for the camera, causing it to go out of sync with the background, and not have them mismatch. What is actually happening, though, is that the scene motion is removed completely and then restored in a smoother state.

If expressions and arguments are gobbledygook to you, take a look at Chapter 10, then revisit this section.

The same basic approach can destabilize, rather than smooth, a camera motion. Because the expression involved requires a bit of tweaking, discussion is punted to Chapter 10.

Extend a Track

Sometimes a track point will disappear before the track is completed, either because it is obscured by a foreground object or because it has moved offscreen.

Other effects software might include a built-in option for continuing the track, but After Effects requires instead a simple expression. This works provided the tracked item travels in a more or less linear fashion, such as the taxi crossing shot in **Figure 8.27**.

Figure 8.27 The door handle of the taxi is an effective track target, but to replace the sign on top of the cab, the track must extend beyond this frame (after which the door handle exits the frame). Note that the track points are fairly evenly spaced, making this a good candidate to extend.

Following is the simple trick to extend a Position track; for a more thorough explanation of what's going on, and variations on the theme (looping incoming frames, repeating a movement pattern, or looping in *and* looping out) visit Chapter 10.

First make certain there are no unwanted extra tracking keyframes beyond where the point was still correctly tracked; this expression uses the difference between the final two keyframes to estimate what will happen next.

Reveal the property that needs extending (Position in this case), and Alt/Option-click on its stopwatch. In the text field that is revealed, replace the text (position), typing in

This technique will work in any case where the last two frames of animation reflect a delta (change) in values. Chapter 10 shows other types of available loops, as well as the ability to loop in, or to loop both in and out.

loopOut("continue"). Yes, that's right, typing; don't worry, you're not less of an artist for doing it (**Figure 8.28**).

Figure 8.28 The raspberry-colored stand-in for the replacement sign exits frame with the tracking null below it. In the Graph Editor, the dotted line shows that the expression is maintaining a steady Position change of around 2000 pixels per second.

This expression uses the *delta* (velocity and direction) of the last two frames. It creates matching linear motion (not a curve) moving at a steady rate, so it works well if those last two frames are representative of the overall rate and direction of motion.

Track for Rotoscoping

Just because it's not possible to apply a motion track to a mask point doesn't mean that you can't track a mask, and there are a number of scenarios in which it can help to do so.

One way to do it is using the techniques in the "2.5D Tracking" section above: first stabilizing the element to be masked, then animating the mask in place on a separate 3D layer, finally reapplying the overall motion via a 3D camera and the mask via a track matte.

Track mattes are the key to motion tracking mask data, because the entire layer can be attached to tracking data, while an individual mask property cannot. Create a garbage matte on a separate layer and then track it, you can precisely match its boundaries to a feature on-set, eliminating the possibility of distracting matte-chatter that can result from hand-keyframing.

Silhouette FX (www.silhouettefx.com) offers a plug-in with an integrated motion tracker for applying motion data to mask points.

Here's the basic setup:

1. Line up a solid (with or without a mask) to track (**Figures 8.29a** and **b**).

2. Track the background plate and apply the track to the solid.

3. Turn off visibility of the solid layer and draw or paste the precise mask shape to track.

4. Apply this masked solid as an alpha track matte to the layer to be masked (**Figure 8.30**).

Figures 8.29a and b This plate requires garbage mattes on all sides (a), but the precision of the front edge is essential as the shot dollies in (down the rails). The first step is just to add a solid where the front edge of the action area should be (b). (Baseball images courtesy Tim Fink Events & Media.)

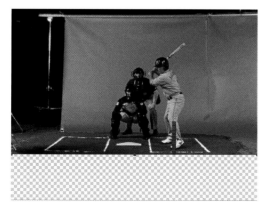

Figure 8.30 The tracking keyframes applied to the alpha matte layer can be seen moving vertically, holding it in place as the shot dollies in.

An extra boost of automation like this can even lead you to look forward to garbage matting.

Paint is much easier to track once you're comfortable with the basics of expressions. Each paint stroke contains its own transform properties, including a Position property, separate from the layer's Position property. The pickwhip can link this property directly to tracking data. (For more details, see "Track Paint and Effects" in Chapter 10.)

3D Tracks

After Effects does not include a dedicated 3D tracker, but it can import 3D tracking data created in a separate application, such as 2D3's Boujou, Pixel Farm's PF Track, or SynthEyes, from Andersson Technologies. Nor does it work with 3D mesh objects (it's the "postcards in space" model of 2D in a 3D environment), so the 3D tracking workflow operates as follows:

NOTES

After Effects can also extract camera data embedded in an RPF sequence (and typically generated in 3DS Max or Flame). Place the sequence containing the 3D camera data in a comp and choose Animation > Keyframe Assistant > RPF Camera Import.

1. Track the scene with a 3D tracking application. This generates 3D camera data, typically exportable in various 3D formats; included with these is usually an option to export a .ma file for After Effects.

   The track will ideally also generate nulls corresponding to the track points and an axis centered on the "floor," the ground plane of the shot, although you may have to specify these.

2. (Optional) Import the camera data into a 3D animation program and render 3D elements. You can also massage the 3D data for After Effects here, leaving for example only helpful nulls.

3. Import the camera data into After Effects; it imports in the form of a composition with an animated 3D camera and nulls (potentially many layers of them). Add your background plate and foreground elements; those that are 2D can be freely matched with 3D elements, which will pick up the camera movement.

Figure 8.31 shows the final result from the baseball plate; the camera follows the pitch all the way to the plate, where the batter hits it out of the park (of course). This shot is a complete mishmash of 2D and 3D elements. The ball, field, and front of the stands are computer generated, but the crowd was lifted from footage of an actual game.

Figure 8.31 True 3D tracking (done in 2D3's Boujou for this shot) is essential to this composite because the feet of the characters must be locked to the computer-generated ground, and a camera on dolly tracks wobbles and bounces. The full shot follows the ball to the plate.

Figure 8.32 shows a completely different type of shot that also began with a 3D track in Boujou. The fires that you see in the after shot are actually dozens of individual 2D fire and smoke layers, staggered and angled in 3D space as the camera flies over to give the sense of perspective. You'll find more on this shot and how it was set up in Chapter 14, "Pyrotechnics: Heat, Fire, Explosions."

Figure 8.32 Just because you're placing elements in a supposedly "2D" program such as After Effects doesn't mean you can't stagger them all over 3D space to give the illusion of depth, as with this fly-by shot. Tracking nulls from Boujou helped get the relative scale of the scene, important because the depth of the elements had to be to exact scale for the parallax illusion to work. (Final fire image courtesy ABC-TV.)

3D Tracking Data

Many people don't realize that After Effects can import Maya scenes (.ma files); but they have to be properly prepped and only include rendering cameras (with translation and lens data) and nulls. The camera data should be "baked," which is Maya parlance meaning that it should have a keyframe at every frame (search on "baking Maya camera data" in the online help for specifics on this).

3D trackers operate a bit differently than the After Effects tracker. Generally you do not begin by setting tracking points with these; instead, the software creates a swarm of hundreds of points that come and go throughout the shot, and it "solves" the camera using a subset of them.

Besides Position and Rotation, the Camera may also contain Zoom keyframes. Unless Sergio Leone has started making spaghetti westerns again, zoom shots are not the norm and any zoom animation should be checked against a camera report (or any available anecdotal data) and eliminated if bogus (it might be a push or even an unstable camera). Most 3D trackers allow you to specify that a shot was taken with a prime lens (no zoom).

Importing a Maya Scene

You import a .ma scene the same way you would any element; make sure it has the .ma extension to be recognized properly. After Effects will import either one or two compositions: one for a Maya project with a square pixel aspect ratio, and two for nonsquare (a square pixel version is nested in the nonsquare one).

Your camera may be *single-node* (in which case the camera holds all of the animation data) or *targeted*, in which case the transformation data resides in a parent node to which the camera is attached.

Depending on your tracker and your scene, you may import so many nulls with the scene that it becomes cumbersome. A composition with 500 layers, even nulls, quickly becomes unwieldy, so if possible, weed out the useless nulls, paring it down to a couple dozen of them (descriptively named) in the tracking software or 3D program. It's

TIP

Because After Effects offers no proportional 3D grids in the viewers, nulls imported with a 3D scene can be essential to scale and position elements in 3D. The scale of the scene is otherwise arbitrary.

NOTES

Instead of exporting a .ma scene, Maxon's Cinema 4D software offers its own support for After Effects integration via a plug-in available from Maxon (www.maxon.net).

TIP

Need to deal with all of those nulls in After Effects? Once you find the dozen or two that are useful to you in the scene, select those in the Timeline along with the camera and its parent null (if any). Context-click on the selected layers and choose Invert Selection to select the potentially hundreds of other unused nulls. Delete them.

usually easy to make out what the nulls correspond to in the scene if you watch them over the background plate; they tend to cluster around certain objects.

Try It Out for Yourself

If you'd like to try out a 3D tracker, look no further than the book's DVD-ROM. It includes a demo of SynthEyes, a reasonably priced 3D tracker from Andersson Technologies that has been used on feature films (**Figure 8.33**). For about the cost of a typical After Effects plug-in set, you can own your own 3D tracking software (Mac or Windows). The demo is the full version but with a time limit, and projects cannot be saved, so you must execute and export your track start to finish before quitting. The output data, however, is fully usable.

Figure 8.33 This tracking data (including nulls) began as a Maya (.ma) scene file created by SynthEyes 3D tracker. The square nulls serve as references for layer placement. This scene is available for download from www.ssontech.com if you want to try it yourself.

There are also sample files to try out before you create a scene of your own. You may have luck simply importing your shot into SynthEyes, clicking Full Automatic, and exporting the result as AfterEffects via .ma. If there's more involved in getting a good track, however, you will need

TIP

To learn more about the complex art of match moving, check out *Matchmoving: The Invisible Art of Camera Tracking* (Sybex Inc.) by Tim Dobbert, a colleague from The Orphanage.

to learn a bit more about how the software works, and it's beyond the scope of this chapter to document it. SynthEyes is the type of application that yields much better results if you carefully read the online documentation, which is available from the Help menu.

Conclusion

Despite all attempts to make it standardized and automatic, tracking remains as much art as it is science, which is probably why most large effects facilities retain a staff of match movers. Even if you've understood everything in this chapter and followed along closely, working on your own shots will open a process of trial and error.

The next chapter will delve further into the ways in which After Effects can replicate what a physical camera can do, expanding on some of the concepts touched on earlier in the "2.5D Tracking" section.

9

The Camera and Optics

A film is never really good unless the camera is an eye in the head of a poet.

—Orson Welles

The Camera and Optics

It seems as if visual effects is all about simulating the look of the real world, but that's not quite the goal; as a visual effects compositor, your actual job is to simulate the real world *as it appears through the lens of a camera.* The distinction is critical, because when photographed the world looks different—more or less real, and possibly both.

It's not too grandiose to say that cinematography is essential to compositing, because After Effects offers the opportunity to re-create and even change essential shooting decisions long after the crew has struck the set and called it a wrap. Your shot may be perfectly realistic on its own merits but it will only belong in the story if it works cinematically. Factors in After Effects that contribute to good cinematography include

- ▶ Field of view
- ▶ Depth of focus
- ▶ The shooting medium and what it tells about the storyteller
- ▶ Planar perspective and dimensionality
- ▶ Camera motion (handheld, stabilized or locked) and what it implies about point of view

These seemingly disparate points all involve understanding how the camera sees the world and how film and video record what the camera sees. All of them transcend mere aesthetics, influencing how the viewer perceives the story itself.

Cameras: Virtual and Real

We begin our exploration of virtual cinematography with the After Effects camera, which relates closely to an actual motion picture camera without actually being anything like one. Following is an examination of how 3D operates in After Effects and how the application's features—not only the camera, but also lights and shading options—correspond to real world counterparts.

See with the Camera

Toggle a layer to 3D and *voila*, its properties contain three axes instead of two—but enabling 3D without a camera is a little bit like racing a car with automatic transmission: You can't really maneuver, and before long you're bound to slam into something.

The Camera Settings dialog (**Figure 9.1**) uniquely includes a physical diagram that helps tell you what you need to know about how settings in the 3D camera affect your scene.

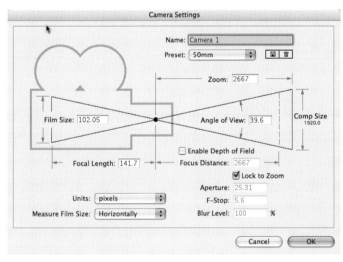

Figure 9.1 Artists love a visual UI, and the Camera Settings dialog provides one to help elucidate settings that might otherwise seem a bit abstract. The 50 mm preset is the neutral (default) setting.

Lens Settings

Although it is not labeled as such, and although After Effects displays previous camera settings by default, the true default lens preset in Camera Settings is 50 mm. This setting (**Figure 9.2**, see next page) is neither wide (as with lower values, **Figure 9.3**, see next page) nor long (as with higher values, **Figure 9.4**, see next page); and it introduces no shift in perspective.

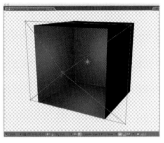  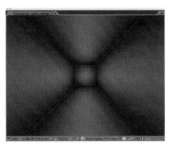

Figure 9.2 The default lens (50 mm setting). If the Z Position value is the exact inverse of the Zoom value, and all other settings are at the default, this is the view you get, and it matches the appearance of setting no After Effects camera whatsoever.

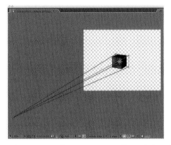 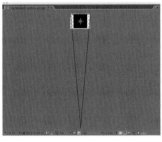 

Figure 9.3 The extreme wide or *fisheye* lens pointed inside an evenly proportioned 3D box. Note that the "long" look of the box is created by this "wide" lens, which tends to create very strange proportions at this extreme. A physical lens with anything like this angle would include extremely distorted lens curvature.

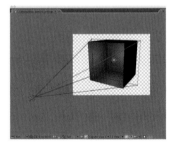 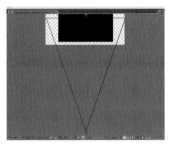 

Figure 9.4 A telephoto lens (using the 200 mm setting) pushes items together in depth space, shortening the distance between the front and back of the box dramatically.

"50 mm" is a virtually meaningless term because virtual space doesn't contain millimeters any more than it contains kilograms, parsecs, or bunny rabbits. This is the median lens length of a 35 mm SLR camera, the standard professional still image camera.

Motion picture cameras are not so standardized. The equivalent lens on a 35 mm film camera shooting Academy ratio itself has a 35 mm length. A miniDV camera, on the other hand, has a tiny neutral lens length of around 4 mm. The length corresponds directly to the size of the backplate or video pickup, the area where the image is projected inside the camera.

Lens length, then, is a somewhat arbitrary and made-up value in the virtual world of After Effects. The corresponding setting that applies universally is Angle of View, which can be calculated whether images were shot in IMAX or HDV or created in a 3D animation package.

Real Camera Settings

To understand the relationship of the After Effects camera to those of a real-world camera, look again at the Camera Settings diagram (Figure 9.1). Four numerical fields—Film Size, Focal Length, Zoom, and Angle of View—surround a common hypotenuse.

A prime (or fixed) lens would have static values for all four. A zoom lens would of course work with a fixed Film Size, but would allow Zoom and Focal Length to be adjusted, changing the Angle of View. These four settings, then, are interrelated and interdependent, as the diagram implies, and the relationship is just the same as with a real camera, which the Film Size can even help emulate. Lengthen the lens by increasing Focal Length and you decrease Angle of View.

The settings you actually use are Zoom (to animate) and Angle of View (to match real-world source).

Angle of View is the actual radius, in degrees, that fit in the view. If you're matching it, note that Camera Settings lets you specify a horizontal, vertical, or diagonal measurement in the Measure Film Size pulldown.

In After Effects, the Zoom value is the distance of the camera, in pixels, from the plane of focus. Create a camera and its Z Position is the inverse of the Zoom value, perfectly framing the contents of the comp with a Z position

NOTES

A fifth numerical field in Camera Settings, Focus Distance, is enabled by checking Enable Depth of Field; it corresponds to a camera's aperture setting, covered here separately.

of 0.0 (**Figure 9.5**). This makes for easy reference when measuring depth of field effects, and it allows you to link camera position and zoom together via expressions (for depth of field and multi-plane effects, discussed later).

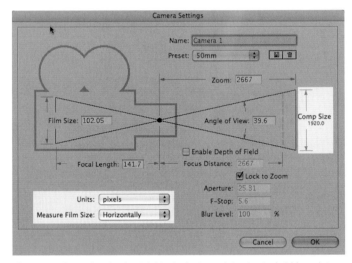

Figure 9.5 Comp Size (at the right) is the horizontal size, in pixels (although it always appears vertical in the diagram); orientation changes according to the Measure Film Size settings (left). Instead of pixels, you can measure in inches or millimeters, helpful when matching a physical camera (process described ahead).

Emulate a Real Camera

Other considerations when matching a real-world camera include

▶ **Depth of field:** This is among the most filmic and evocative additions you can make to a scene. It doesn't exist by default in After Effects the way it does with real-world optics, so you have to re-create it.

▶ **Zoom or push:** A move in or out is used for dramatic effect, but which type is it?

▶ **Motion blur and shutter angle:** These are composition (not camera) settings; introduced in Chapter 2, "The Timeline," they are further explored here.

▶ **Lens angle:** The perspective and parallax of layers in 3D space change according to the angle of the lens used to view them.

▶ **Lens distortion:** Real lenses introduce *lens distortion,* curvature most apparent with wide-angle or "fisheye" lenses. An After Effects camera has no lens, hence, no distortion, but you can re-create it (see "Lens Distortion").

▶ **Exposure:** Every viewer in After Effects now includes an Exposure control (look for the aperture icon, lower right); this (along with the effect with the same name) is mathematically similar but practically different from a physical camera. Usage of these tools is detailed in Chapter 11, "32 Bit HDR Compositing and Color Management."

▶ **Boke, halation, flares:** All sorts of interesting phenomena are generated by light interacting with the lens itself. These are subjective and almost abstract in reality, yet I think they offer a unique and beautiful aesthetic if grounded in realism.

A *camera report* is a record of the settings used when the footage was taken, usually logged by the camera assistant (or equivalent).

NOTES

The movement of the camera itself can generate motion blur (**Figures 9.6a and b**). The key is that any layers to be blurred by the motion of the camera have Motion Blur toggled on.

Figures 9.6a and b Camera movement generates motion blur (a); even on a stationary layer provided motion blur is active for the comp and layer (b). New in CS3, zooming the camera can also generate motion blur.

TIP

A potentially easier alternative to the listed steps, for those who like using expressions, is to use the following expression on the camera's Zoom property:

```
FocalLength = 35 //
➥change to your value,
➥in mm
hFilmPlane = 24.892
➥//change to your film
size, in mm (horizontal
measurement)
this_comp.width*(Focal
➥Length/hFilmPlane)
```

The Camera Report

With accurate information on the type of camera and the focal length of a shot, you know enough to match the lens of that camera with your After Effects camera.

Table 9.1 details the sizes of some typical film formats. If your camera is on the list, and you know the focal length, use these to match the camera via Camera Settings. The steps are

1. Set Measure Film Size to Horizontally. (Note that hFilmPlane below stands for "Horizontal Film Plane.")

2. Set Units to Inches.

3. Enter the number from the Horizontal column of the chart that corresponds to the source film format.

4. Set Units to Millimeters.

5. Enter the desired Focal Length.

TABLE **9.1** Typical Film Format Sizes

FORMAT	HORIZONTAL	VERTICAL
Full Aperture Camera Aperture	0.980	0.735
Scope Camera Aperture	0.864	0.732
Scope Scan	0.825	0.735
2:1 Scope Projector Aperture	0.838	0.700
Academy Camera Aperture	0.864	0.630
Academy Projector Aperture	0.825	0.602
1.66 Projector Aperture	0.825	0.497
1.85 Projector Aperture	0.825	0.446
VistaVision Aperture	0.991	1.485
VistaVision Scan	0.980	1.470
16 mm Camera Aperture	0.404	0.295
Super-16 Camera Aperture	0.493	0.292
HD Full 1.78	0.378	0.212 (Full Aperture in HD 1.78)
HD 90% 1.78	0.340	0.191 (90% Safe Area used in HD 1.78)
HD Full 1.85	0.378	0.204 (Full Aperture in HD 1.85)
HD 90% 1.85	0.340	0.184 (90% Safe Area used in HD 1.85)
HD Full 2.39	0.3775	0.158 (Full Aperture in HD 2.39)
HD 90% 2.39	0.340	0.142 (90% Safe Area used in HD 2.39)

Courtesy Stu Maschwitz/The Orphanage

Once the Angle of View matches the footage, any objects that you track in (perhaps using techniques described in Chapter 8, "Effective Motion Tracking") maintain position in the scene as the shot progresses. It's vital to get this right when the camera moves during the shot, and especially if a wide or long lens was used.

Lens Distortion

If a virtual camera is set with a wide-angle lens, as in Figure 9.2, it dramatically changes the perspective of 3D space, but it does not actually distort objects the way a real camera lens does because a digital camera uses no lens. A virtual camera can widen the view area and still scan it in a linear fashion, because all the imagery travels to a single point.

A lens curves light to project it properly across the camera backplate with physical width and height, no matter how small. To show up properly the reflected imagery must be perpendicular to the surface of the lens glass, so a wide-angle view requires not only a short lens length but also a convex lens in order to gather the full range of view.

At the extremes, this causes easily visible lens distortion; items in the scene known to contain straight lines don't appear straight at all, but bent in a curve (**Figure 9.7**). In a fisheye lens shot, it's as if the screen has been inflated like a balloon.

Included on the book's disc is a 12 minute video tutorial (courtesy fxphd.com) in which Mike Seymour shows how information including viewing angle and focus distance can be derived even if these were not recorded when the image was shot.

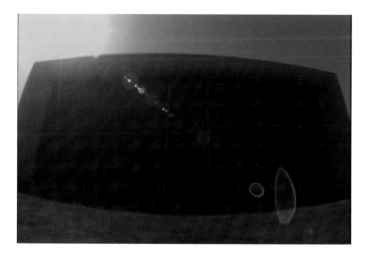

Figure 9.7 The almost psychedelic look of lens distortion at its most extreme; the lens flare itself is extremely aberrated. You can create just as wide a lens with the 3D camera, but there would be no lens distortion because there is no lens.

As you refine your eye, you may notice that many shots that aren't as extreme as a fisheye perspective contain a degree of lens distortion. Or you might find that motion tracks that are accurate on one side of the frame don't seem to apply equally well at the other side of the frame, proportions go out of whack, and things don't quite line up as they should (**Figures 9.8a** and **b**).

Figures 9.8a and b It is simply not possible to make all four corners and edges of a yellow solid line up properly with the side of a distorted building (a). Grid lines over footage of the bus clearly show distortion (b). (Building examples courtesy Stu Maschwitz; bus footage courtesy Pixel Corps.)

There's no way to introduce lens distortion directly to a 3D camera, but the Optics Compensation effect (Professional version only) is designed to add or remove it in 2D. **Figures 9.9a** and **b** shows this effect in action. Increasing the Field of View makes the affected layer more fish-eyed in appearance; to correct a shot coming in with lens distortion, check Reverse Lens Distortion and raise the Field of View (FOV) value.

Figures 9.9a and b Optics compensation takes place in a composition larger than the source; the padding gives the corners of the image space. The Beam effect can serve as a virtual plumb line (a) or it can be clear from the grid that distortion has been corrected (b).

This process is not exactly scientific, instead requiring eye-match because the Field of View settings don't correspond to measurable items in the camera report, such as the Lens Angle. Specifically

1. Having identified lens distortion in a background plate (as in Figure 9.8a), precomp the background into a new composition that is at least 20% larger than the plate to accommodate distortion.

2. Add an adjustment layer above the plate layer, and apply Optics Compensation to that layer. Check Reverse Lens Distortion and raise the Field of View (FOV) setting until all straight lines appear straight.

3. Add a Beam effect to the adjustment layer (below the Optics Compensation effect, unaffected by it). To get away from the light saber look, match Inside Color and Outside Color to some easily visible hue, then align the Starting Point and Ending Point along an apparently straight line near the edge of frame. Fine-tune the Field of View setting a little more until the line is plumb (Figures 9.9a and b).

4. Precompose all of these layers and set this new composition as a guide layer. In **Figure 9.10**, you can see that the corner pin is now successful.

Figure 9.10 Over the undistorted background plate, you can freely position, animate, and composite elements as if everything were normal. Note that the perspective is still that of a very wide-angle lens, but without the curvature.

5. To complete the shot, restore the original field of view, including distortion. First create a new comp with the original background plate (no Optics Compensation) and the precomp with the assembled foreground elements.

6. Copy Optics Compensation with the settings added in step 2 and paste it to the foreground element. Toggle Reverse Lens Distortion off. The Field of View of the background is restored, but the foreground elements match (**Figure 9.11**).

Figure 9.11 The Optics Compensation effect with Reverse Lens Distortion unchecked adds the original distortion to the foreground; features now line up properly.

Here is an original haiku (Stu Maschwitz gets the writing credit) to sum up the process:

undistort, derive
reunite distorted things
with an untouched plate

2D and 3D

The point of matching 3D lens angles (and correcting any distortion) is most often to place elements in 3D space over a 2D plate background. This is so effortlessly possible in After Effects as to seem like no big deal:

▶ A 2D background layer remains in place (usually simply filling the frame) no matter how you move the camera.

▶ 2D adjustment layers set to comp size and default position affect the whole composition, including 3D layers.

▶ 3D layers can use vital features unique to 2D compositing, such as blending modes (over 2D elements, they obey layer order, and with other 3D elements, z-space depth).

Here are special cases that require extra care:

▶ It's rarely a good idea to combine a 3D track matte and a 3D layer. A 3D layer can use a 2D layer as a track matte; it is applied just as it would be to a 2D layer. A 2D layer can use a 3D layer as a track matte; the 3D perspective of the track matte renders first and is then applied. But combine two 3D layers in this manner and the matte is first translated by the camera perspective once, then applied, and then effectively translated again as the affected layer also obeys camera perspective.

▶ Paradoxically, the only layers in After Effects that themselves can contain true 3D data are 2D layers (which may nonetheless make use of the 3D camera perspective, **Figure 9.12**).

Figure 9.12 Incredibly, particles generated by Trapcode Particular occupy true 3D space, as is evident in a perspective view. Paradoxically, the effect is applied to a 2D layer. It calculates 3D data internally using the After Effects camera as a reference, an elegant workaround for the fact that 3D layers in After Effects are always flat planes.

▶ A precomped set of 3D layers behaves like a single 2D layer unless Collapse Transformations is enabled on that layer. As described back in Chapter 4, "Optimize the Pipeline," this toggle passes through all 3D data from the precomp as if those layers lived right in the master composition.

Every one of these has potential advantages provided you understand how the image pipeline works.

TIP

Always keep in mind where the audience's attention is focused—you can employ the magician's technique, misdirection, to get away with something you shouldn't. As is detailed in the fun book *Rebel Without a Crew* (Plume, 1996), El Mariachi got completed with meager funds only because Robert Rodriguez was willing to let massive continuity errors go. He was confident that if the audience was watching for those, the story had failed.

Figure 9.13 Prominent though it may appear in this still image, the audience isn't focused on that San Francisco skyline outside the window. There's no multiplaning as the camera moves because the background skyline is a still image; no one notices because viewer attention is on the foreground character. (Image courtesy The Orphanage.)

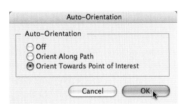

Figure 9.14 So many After Effects 3D camera tragedies could have been avoided if more users knew about this dialog box (**Ctrl+Alt+O**/ **Cmd+Option+O**). By disabling auto-orientation, you are free to move the camera anywhere without changing its direction.

Storytelling and the Camera

Locked-off shots have been used to great dramatic effect in landmark films by Welles, Hitchcock, Kubrick, and Lucas, among others, but they're the exception, not the norm, particularly in contemporary films, in which the camera point of view often can itself be a character.

In the bad old days of optical compositing, it was scarcely possible to move the camera at all. Nowadays, most directors aren't satisfied with a locked-off effects shot, yet the decision to move the camera might not happen on set, or it might have to be altered in post-production. This is no big deal; you can bend the rules, just don't break them.

Specifically, create a rough assemble with animation as early in the process of creating your shot as possible, because it will tell you a lot about what you can get away with and what needs dedicated attention. The "Sky Replacement" section in Chapter 13, "Climate and the Environment," contains an example in which a flat card stands in for a fully dimensional skyline (**Figure 9.13**). The audience should instead be focused on watching the lead character walk through the lobby, wondering what he has in his briefcase; if not, the film has more problems than can be fixed with more elaborate visual effects elements.

Camera Animation

The most common confusion about the After Effects camera stems from the fact that by default, it includes a *point of interest*, a point in 3D space at which the camera always points, for auto-orientation. The point of interest is *fully optional*, yet the setting is among the least discoverable in After Effects. To clarify

▶ Disable auto-orientation and the point of interest (making the camera a *free* camera) by context-clicking on the camera and choosing Transform > Auto-Orient (**Ctrl+Alt+O**/**Cmd+Option+O**) (**Figure 9.14**).

▶ In that same dialog, you can instead orient the camera along its path of camera motion, so that its rotation maintains tangency; in other words, it is angled the same direction as the path itself.

▶ You might want to use the point of interest but also move it and the camera together. To do this, don't attempt to match keyframes for the two properties—this is sheer madness! You can parent the camera to a null and translate that instead.

▶ Orientation works differently depending on whether auto-orientation is on (causing it to revolve around the point of interest) or not (in which case it rotates around its center, **Figure 9.15**).

▶ The auto-oriented camera always maintains an upright position; cross over the X/Y plane above the center and the camera flips. To avoid this behavior, use a free camera.

The above points come into play only with more elaborate camera animations; more modest use of the 3D camera, such as a simple camera push, raises other questions.

Push and Zoom

A camera *push* moves the camera closer to the subject; a *zoom* lengthens the lens while the camera remains stationary. **Figures 9.16a** and **b** demonstrate the difference, which is just as noticeable in After Effects as in the real world. The zoom has a more extreme effect on the foreground/background composition of the shot—often too extreme, calling too much attention to the camera itself.

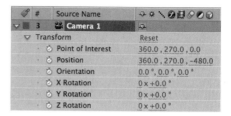

Figure 9.15 Just in case you've never taken a close look, a camera layer contains no anchor point, but includes two sets of rotation data: the Orientation (its basic angle), as well as separate X, Y, and Z Rotation values (to avoid problems with complex 3D rotations). The point of interest appears only when the default Orient Towards Point of Interest option is active (Figure 9.14).

TIP

Cycle through the camera animation tools using the **C** key to orbit, track X/Y, and track Z in the active view.

NOTES

The Y axis is upside down in After Effects 3D, just as in 2D; increasing the Y value moves a layer downward. The 0,0 point in After Effects space was placed at the upper-left corner of the frame when it was 2D only, and so it remains for consistency's sake.

Figures 9.16a and b Frame a similar shot with a long (a) and a wide (b) lens and you get an idea of the difference between a zoom and a push. A zoom merges the relative scale of objects at various depths, lowering apparent perspective.

Dramatic zooms for the most part had their heyday in 1960's-era Sergio Leone movies, while the push is a dramatic staple. The question is, to create one do you need a 3D camera, or can you simply scale 2D layers?

NOTES

The zoom may merely be out of fashion and ready to make a comeback, but it calls attention to the camera because the human vision system has no equivalent; our eyes can only push as we progress through space—they can't zoom.

NOTES

Animation > Keyframe Assistant > Exponential Scale is the old-school, pre-3D way to fake the illusion of a camera move in on a 2D layer. There is no good reason to employ this feature when you can instead animate a 3D camera.

TIP

When pushing in on multiple overlapping coplanar 3D layers, precompose before adding the camera animation and leave Collapse Transformations off. Coplanar 3D layers respect layer order, but an animated camera can easily cause rounding errors in floating point position calculation.

Scaling a 2D layer (or several parented to a null) works for a small move; however, to re-create progression through Z space the rate of scaling must increase logarithmically, which makes everything more complicated. Not only does a 3D camera move provide this type of scaling naturally, it makes it easier to add eases, stops and starts, a little bit of destabilization—whatever works.

Natural camera motion will contain keyframe eases (Chapter 2), for the human aspect. A little bit of irregularity lends the feeling of a camera operator's individual personality (**Figure 9.17**), or even dramatic interest (hesitation, caution, intrigue, a leap forward—the possibilities are many).

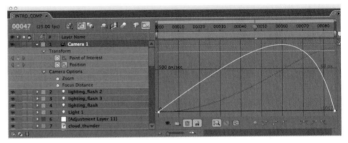

Figure 9.17 A simple camera animation can be finessed simply by applying Easy Ease (highlight keyframes and press **F9**), but why stop there? Lengthening the curve of the first keyframe gives the camera added (realistic) inertia transitioning from a static position.

A move in or out of a completely 2D shot can easily look wrong due to the lack of parallax. Likewise, tracking and panning shots, crane-ups, and other more elaborate camera moves will blow the 2.5D gag unless minute. You can, however, get away with more layering soft, translucent organic shapes, such as clouds, fog, smoke, and the like. Chapter 13 shows how, by staggering these in 3D space, you can fool the eye into seeing 3D volume.

Camera Projection

Camera projection (or *camera mapping*) typically begins with a still photo, which is then projected onto 3D objects that match the dimensions and placement of objects in the photo, and then moving the camera—typically only along the Z axis—providing the illusion that the photo is fully dimensional (right up until the camera move goes too far, revealing some area of the image that wasn't part of the photograph).

Figures 9.18a, b, and c The progression from the source image (a) through the camera move. By the final frame (c), image warping and tearing are evident, but the perspective of the image is essentially correct for the new camera position. The tearing occurs simply because as the camera moves it reveals areas of the image that don't exist in the source.

Figures 9.18a, **b**, and **c** show a camera projection that ambitiously features two parked military vehicles in the foreground. A dozen separate white solids with masks were created to form a crude 3D model, ready to receive a projected image (**Figure 9.19**). This example shows both the magic of this technique—deriving perspective shifts from a flat, still image—and the associated problems of image tearing when an area of the frame is revealed that had previously been obscured in the source photo.

The key to this effect is the setup: How is it that the one "texture" of the image (the photo) sticks to the 3D objects? The fundamental concept is actually relatively simple; getting it right is a question of managing details, and that part is fairly advanced and not for the faint of heart (which is why mention of a third-party option follows this description). The steps to projecting any still image into 3D space (an example of which, 09_cameraProjection.aep, can be found on this book's disc) are as follows:

1. Begin with an image that can be modeled as a series of planes.

2. Create a white solid for each dimensional plane in the image. Enable 3D for each, and under Material Options, change the Accepts Lights option to Off.

3. Add a camera named Projection Cam; if you know the Angle of View of your source image, add that value.

4. Add a Point light called Projector Light. Set its position to that of Projection Cam, then parent it to Projection Cam. Set Casts Shadows to On.

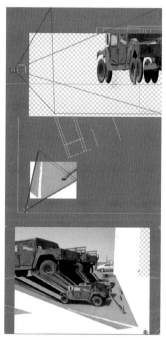

Figure 9.19 The rather complicated setup for this effect: from the top and side views you can see the planes that stand in for the vehicles and orange cone, which appears stretched along the ground plane.

5. Duplicate the source image, naming this layer Slide. Enable 3D, and in Material Options, change Casts Shadows to Only and Light Transmission to 100%.

6. Slide not located properly? Add a null object called Slide Repo; set its position to that of Projection Cam, and parent it to Projection Cam. Now parent Slide to it, and adjust its scale downward until the image is cast onto the white planes, as if projected.

7. Now comes the painful part: masking, scaling, and repositioning those white solids to build the model, ground plane, and horizon onto which the slide is projected. Toggle on the reference layer and build your model to match that, checking it with the slide every so often.

8. If planes that you know to be at perpendicular 90 degree angles don't line up, you need to adjust the Zoom value of the Projection Cam, scaling the model and slide as needed to match the new Zoom value. The example file includes an expression applied to the Scale value of the Slide layer so that the slide scales up or down to match however you adjust the Zoom of the camera, which is not necessary but is helpful.

9. Once everything is lined up, duplicate Projection Cam, and rename the duplicate (the one on the higher layer) Anim Cam. Freely move this camera to take advantage of the new dimensional reality of the scene (**Figure 9.20**).

Figure 9.20 Better than relying only on projection, which can lead to the tearing seen in Figure 9.18, is to position specific foreground layers. Here all of the people in the street are actually matted layers positioned in 3D space.

The best way to learn about this is probably to study the example file included on this book's disc; if it seems enticing rather than aggravating, feel free to give it a whirl.

Camera Blur

Camera blur is the result of objects positioned outside the camera's depth of field, whether because the lens was intentionally defocused or simply because the focal range was too shallow to capture everything sharply.

Ironically, the high-end medium of film naturally has a shallower depth of field than any video camera, and even more ironically, shallow depth of field and the aesthetic of camera blur is what you would call "cinematic" and thus largely desirable. A shallow focal range literally focuses the viewer's attention; moving areas of a shot in and out of focus, meanwhile, can create dramatic anticipation and a beautiful aesthetic.

It can be a lot of work to re-create depth of field effects in After Effects; it's better to get them in camera if possible. Nonetheless you can create specific cinematic blur effects such as a *rack focus* shot, in which the focus changes from a subject at one distance from the camera to another.

Limited focal range is a natural part of human vision, but camera lenses contribute their own unique blur characteristics that in the contemporary era are often considered aesthetically pleasing the world over. There is even a Japanese term (literally meaning "fuzzy") to describe the quality of out-of-focus light as viewed through a lens, *boke* (also *bokeh*, more phonetic but clunkier).

You can create these effects and more in After Effects. It's not automatic the way it is with the camera lens itself, and it can require patience and careful observation of nature, but if you're a compositor you have those already.

Image Planes and Rack Focus

Any time you can divide a shot into distinct planes of depth with each plane as its own layer, you can rack focus. All you need is a focal point to animate and a depth of field narrow enough to create blur everywhere but the immediate plane of focus.

Buena Software offers a set of plug-ins known as Depth Cue, which includes Camera Mapper, a plug-in that controls this process and makes it easy to clean up such tearing and stretching errors as those seen in Figure 9.18c.

A solid description of boke with links lives on the Web at http://en.wikipedia.org/wiki/Bokeh.

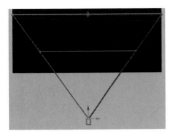

Figure 9.22 With Enable Depth of Field on, the Focus Distance is denoted by a red boundary line, easily viewed and animated in isometric views.

Narrow depth of field is created on a real camera by lowering the f-stop value, which lowers exposure as well. Not so with the After Effects 3D camera. Its Aperture and F-Stop settings (**Figure 9.21**) affect only focal depth, not exposure or motion blur. The two settings have an inverse relationship. F-Stop is the setting more commonly referenced by camera operators, and yet only Aperture appears as a property in the Timeline.

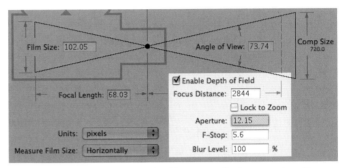

Figure 9.21 Check Enable Depth of Field in Camera Settings to activate Focus Distance (the distance in pixels of the focal point, which can be toggled to Lock to the Zoom). A low F-Stop (or high Aperture) with a Blur Level of 100% creates a shallow focal effect.

After Effects depth of field settings can be matched to a camera report, provided that it includes the f-stop setting used when the footage was shot. If so, open up the Camera Settings dialog (**Ctrl+Shift+Y/Cmd+Shift+Y**, or double-click on the Camera in the Timeline panel), check the box labeled Enable Depth of Field, and enter the value.

Figure 9.23 The final shot combines a rack focus with a gentle pull-back, using ease keyframes to animate Position and Focus Distance.

The key here is to offset at least one layer in Z space so that it falls out of focal range. Now, in the Top view, set the Focus Distance (under Options) to match the layer that will be in focus at the beginning of the shot, add a keyframe, then change the Focus Distance at another frame to match a second layer later in the shot (**Figure 9.22**).

A static focus pull doesn't look quite right; changing focus on a real camera will change the framing of the shot slightly. To sell the example shot, which starts on a view of the city and racks focus to reveal a sign in the foreground, I add a slight camera pull-back, which takes advantage of the nice shift in planes of motion from the offset layers (**Figure 9.23**).

Boke Blur

Racking focus in this manner generates camera blur that is accurate relative to the plane of focus, but it does not truly create the look of a defocused lens.

Boke connotes the phenomenon whereby points of light become discs of light (also called *circles of confusion*) that take on the character of the lens itself as they pass through the camera lens and aperture. Like lens flares (covered in Chapter 12) these are purely a phenomenon of the camera lens, not human vision; they can add beauty and suspense to a shot.

Illuminated out of focus elements in a shot are, after all, mysterious. Visual intrigue is created as the shot resolves in or out of a wash of color and light (**Figure 9.24**).

A perfect lens passes a defocused point of light to the back of the camera as a soft, spherical blur. A bright point remains bright, but is larger and softer. Ordinary blur in 8 or 16 bit per channel color mode instead merely dims the highlights (**Figures 9.25a**, **b**, and **c**).

Most camera lenses are not perfect, so instead of perfect blurred spheres, boke spheres may be brighter toward the edges than in the middle. An anamorphic lens will show squashed spheres, and as with lens flares, the shape of the aperture itself may be visible in the circles, making them hexagonal (or pentagonal, and so on, depending on the number of blades in the opening).

Figure 9.24 Even in the very first, most blurred frame of this pull-back shot, you may recognize the image content, yet its appearance is strange and compelling. With shallow depth of field, highlights in the foreground retain blur even in a focused shot.

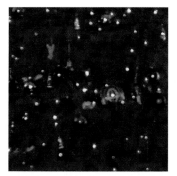

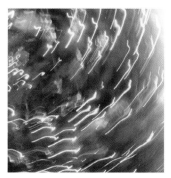

Figures 9.25a, b, and c Motion blur generated the standard way (a and b) literally pales in comparison to true motion blur on illuminated elements created by a moving camera (or objects) while the shutter is open (c).

Go for Boke

To accurately create the bloom of highlights as they are blurred requires 32 bit per channel color and source highlights that are brighter than what would be called full white in 8 or 16 bpc. This is explored and explained in Chapter 11.

The Lens Blur effect does not operate in 32 bpc—it instead mimics the behavior of bright highlights through a lens. It's more or less a direct port from Photoshop; as such, it can be slow and cumbersome in After Effects. It won't blur beyond 100 pixels, and it does not understand non-square pixels (instead creating a perfect circle every time).

Instead of 3D camera or layer data, Lens Blur can use a Depth Map Layer, using pixel values (brightness) from a specified Depth Map Channel. You can rack focus by adjusting Blur Focal Distance. Iris Shape defines polygons around the highlights, corresponding to the number of blades in the iris; these can also have a specified Iris Blade Curvature and Iris Rotation (this rotates the polygon).

The actual amount of blur is determined by Iris Radius, the bloom by Specular Threshold (all pixels above this value are highlights) and Specular Brightness, which creates the simulation of highlight bloom. These are the controls you'll tweak most (**Figure 9.26**).

The Noise controls are designed to restore noise that would be removed by the blur operation; they don't relate to the blur itself and can be ignored in favor of grain techniques described in the following section.

NOTES

The most respected third-party tool for lens blurs is Frischluft's Lenscare. The default settings are not reliable, but with adjustments and depth maps (for 3D footage), you can derive some lovely results (www.frischluft.com and on the book's DVD).

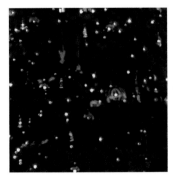 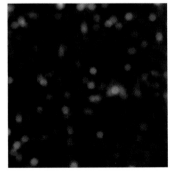

Figure 9.26 Lens Blur doesn't yield a perfect result when cranked up this high, but it does generate the disk shapes around specular highlights characteristic of Boke blur (here, set as hexagons). The result on the larger specular area of the lamp is odd (due to a low threshold of 90%), and there is no repeat edge pixel option, leading to a translucent fringe.

By no means do the settings in Lens Blur (or for that matter, third-party alternatives such as Lenscare from Frischluft) exhaust the possibilities for how defocused areas of an image might appear, especially when illuminated. Keep looking at reference and thinking of ways to re-create what you see in it (**Figure 9.27**).

The Role of Grain

Once the image passes through the lens and is recorded, it takes on another characteristic: grain. Grain is essentially high-frequency noise readily apparent in each channel of most recorded footage, although with progress in image gathering technology has come a reduction of grain. Grain can however be your friend, adding life to static imagery and camouflaging edge detail.

Grain management is an essential part of creating high-quality moving images; properly done, it is not simply switched on or off, but requires careful per-channel adjustment. There are two basic factors to consider:

▶ Size of the grain, per channel

▶ Amount of grain, or amount of contrast in the grain, per channel

The emphasis here is that these factors typically vary from channel to channel. Blue is almost universally the channel likeliest to have the most noise; happily the human eye is less sensitive to blue than red or green, but it can be bad news for blue-screen mattes.

How much grain is enough? As with color in Chapter 5, "Color Correction," the goal is typically to match what's there already. If your shot has a background plate with the proper amount of grain in it, match foreground elements to that. A fully computer-generated scene might have to be matched to surrounding shots.

Grain Management Strategies

After Effects Professional includes a suite of three tools for automated grain sampling, grain reduction, and grain generation: Add Grain, Match Grain, and Remove Grain. Add

Figure 9.27 Now that you know a little more about the phenonemon of boke and how defocused images look, study up. Does an image with shallow depth of field look more cinematic? What do you see happening in the defocused background?

NOTES

The day may come when digital cameras can deliver moving footage with no grain whatsoever. Already, all-digital movies that use no footage, such as those by Pixar, also do not use grain in the master.

NOTES

Excessive grain is often triggered by a low amount of scene light combined with a low-quality image-gathering medium, such as miniDV, whose CCD has poor light-gathering abilities.

Grain relies on your settings only, but Match Grain and Remove Grain can generate initial settings by sampling a source layer for grain patterns.

I often caution against the automated solution, but not in this case. Match Grain is not even appreciably slower with grain sampling than Add Grain, which does not sample but includes all of the same controls. Match Grain usually comes up with a good first pass at settings. In either case

1. Look for a section of your source footage with a solid color area that stays in place for 10 to 20 frames. Most clips satisfy these criteria, and those that don't tend to allow less precision anyhow.

2. Zoom to 200% to 400% on the solid color area, and create a Region of Interest around it. Set the Work Area to the 10 or 20 frames with little or no motion.

3. Add a solid small enough to occupy part of the Region of Interest. Apply a Ramp effect to the solid, and use the eyedropper tools to select the darkest and lightest pixels in the solid color area of the clip. The lack of grain detail in the foreground gradient should be clearly apparent (**Figure 9.28**).

4. Apply the Match Grain effect to the foreground solid. Choose the source footage layer in the Noise Source Layer pull-down. As soon as the effect finishes rendering a sample frame, you have a basis from which to begin fine-tuning. You can RAM Preview at this point to see how close a match you have. In most cases, you're not done yet.

Figure 9.28 Insert a small solid and add a Ramp effect, then use the eyedropper tools in Ramp to sample the brightest and darkest areas of the background. This offers a clear evaluation of a grain match once Match Grain or Add Grain is applied.

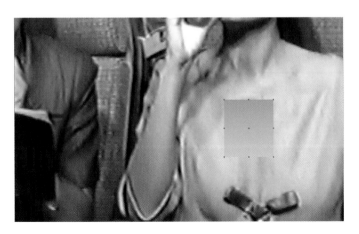

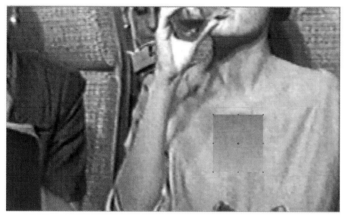

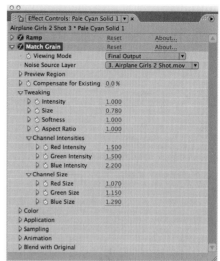

Figure 9.29 As with color matching, proper grain matching requires channel-by-channel examination. Match Grain includes the best kind of automation, enabling you easily to improve upon the initial result.

5. Twirl down the Tweaking controls for Match Grain, and then twirl down Channel Intensities and Channel Size. You can save yourself a lot of time by doing most of your work here, channel by channel.

6. Activate the red channel only in the Composition window (**Alt+1/Option+1**) and adjust the Red Intensity and Red Size values to match the foreground and background (**Figure 9.29**). Repeat this process for the green and blue channels (**Alt+2/Option+2** and **Alt+3/Option+3**). RAM Preview the result.

7. Adjust Intensity, Size, or Softness controls under Tweaking according to what you see in the RAM Preview. You may also find it necessary to reduce Saturation under Color, particularly if your source is film rather than video.

In most cases, these steps yield a workable result; the example project (09_grainMatch.aep) used for these figures is included on your disc. The effect can then be copied and pasted to any foreground layers that need grain. If the foreground layer already contains noise or grain, you may need to adjust the Compensate for Existing Noise percentage for that layer.

Use Noise as Grain

Prior to the addition of Add Grain and Match Grain to version 6.5 Professional, the typical way to generate grain was to use the Noise effect. The main advantage of the Noise effect over Match Grain is that it renders about 20x faster. However, After Effects doesn't make it easy for you to separate the effect channel by channel, and scaling it requires a separate effect (or precomping).

You can employ three solid layers, with three effects applied to each layer: Shift Channels, Noise, and Transform. You use Shift Channels to set each solid to red, green, or blue, respectively, set Blending Modes to Add, and set their Opacity very low (well below 10%, adjusting as needed). Next, set the amount of noise and scale it via the Transform effect.

If the grain is meant to affect a set of foreground layers only, hold them out from the background plate either via precomping or track mattes. If this sounds complicated, it is, which is why Match Grain is preferable unless the rendering time is really killer.

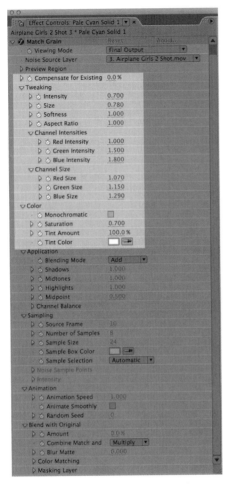

Obviously, whole categories of controls are untouched with this method (**Figure 9.30**); the Application category, for example, contains controls for how the grain is blended and how it affects shadows, midtones, and highlights individually. Typically these are overkill, as are the Sampling and Animation controls, but how far you go in matching grain before your eye is satisfied is, of course, up to you and your team. This is one more case in which slamming the result can help ascertain its effectiveness (**Figure 9.31**).

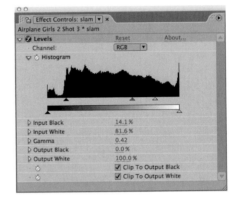

Figure 9.30 The essential controls in Match Grain contain a lot of properties, with the broadest and most used at the top: Intensity, Size, and Softness, then refining the individual Channel Intensities and Channel Size (as in Figure 9.28).

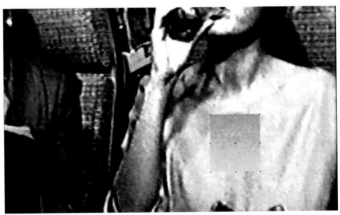

Figure 9.31 Slam the result, bringing out contrast in the grain and revealing the effectiveness of the match.

Grain Removal

Removing grain, or sharpening an image in general, is an entirely different process from adding grain. On a well-shot production, you'll rarely have a reason to reach for the Remove Grain tool.

If you do, the reason for doing so may be unique to your particular footage. In such cases, you may very well find that Remove Grain at the default settings gives you a satisfactory result. If not, check into the Fine Tuning and Unsharp Mask settings to adjust it.

Remove Grain is often best employed "behind the scenes"—not across the entire frame (**Figure 9.32**) or intermediately in combination with other effects. It is, however, a fairly sophisticated solution that can really help in seemingly hopeless situations; this book's technical editor reports having used it extensively on a feature film on which the aging lead actor needed a lot of "aesthetic" facial work done (removing wrinkles and so on).

TIP

If you're using Remove Grain to improve the likelihood of a clean blue-screen or green-screen key, apply the resulting matte back to your source footage as an alpha track matte. This offers the best of both worlds: a clean matte channel and realistic grain on the source color layer.

Figure 9.32 It may suit a still figure in a book (applied at the right side of this image), but Remove Grain on an entire shot with the default settings is rarely desirable. In full motion the grain-reduced shot looks a bit strange and retains a certain soft lumpiness.

When to Manage Grain

The most obvious candidates for grain addition are computer-generated or still image layers that lack the moving grain found in film or video footage. As soon as your shot has to match anything that came from a camera, and particularly in a large format such as HD or film, you must manage grain.

Blurred elements may also need grain addition, even if they originate as source footage. Blurry source shots contain as much grain as focused ones because the grain is an artifact of the medium recording the image, not the subject itself. Elements that have been scaled down in After Effects contain scaled-down grain, which may require restoration. Color keying can also suppress grain in the channel that has been keyed out.

NOTES

Chapter 10, "Expressions," offers a unique and highly effective strategy for removing extreme amounts of grain from a locked-off shot.

Other compositing operations will instead enhance grain. Sharpening, unless performed via Remove Grain, can strongly emphasize grain contrast in an element, typically in a not-so-desirable manner. Sharpening also brings out any nasty compression artifacts that come with footage that uses JPEG-type compression, such as miniDV video.

Lack of grain, however, is one of the big dead giveaways of a poorly composited shot. It is worth the effort to match the correct amount of grain into your shot even if the result isn't apparent as you preview it on your monitor.

Film and Video Looks

If you flipped to this section intentionally, you may be trying to do one of two things with a given shot or project:

▶ Alter the viewer's impression of how footage was shot, stylizing the footage so that a shot you took with your HDV camera looks like old Super8 film, or has a bleach bypass look. Or maybe you're trying to degrade a clean computer graphics animation so it looks like it was shot with someone's handicam.

▶ Shoot your own movie for as little as possible and maximize the production value—that is, the quality of the imagery itself.

There are so many issues connected to the second one above and beyond what you can achieve in an After Effects comp that Stu Maschwitz went and wrote a whole book about it. *The DV Rebel's Guide: An All-Digital Approach to Making Killer Action Movies on the Cheap* (Peachpit Press, 2006) is an excellent resource, not only for After Effects knowledge, but for the whole process of low-budget digital filmmaking. The first chapter lists the major factors that influence production value. Many of these, including image and sound quality, location and lighting, cannot entirely be created in After Effects, which must be why Stu's book includes a bunch of information on how to actually shoot.

The first item, however, is closer to the realm of tricks you can pull off consistently in After Effects, including the following:

▶ **Lens artifacts**—In addition to those already discussed in this chapter, such as boke and chromatic aberration, are such filmic visual staples as the vignette and the lens flare.

- **Frame rate:** Change this and you can profoundly alter the viewer's perception of footage.
- **Aspect ratio:** The format of the composition makes a huge perceptual difference as well, although it's not so simple as "wider = better."
- **Color palette:** Nothing affects the mood of a given shot like color and contrast. It's a complex subject further explored in Chapter 12.

Lens Artifacts Aren't Just Accidents

Because this chapter is all about reality as glimpsed by the camera lens, several types of lens artifacts, visual phenomena that occur only through a lens, have already appeared in this chapter, including lens distortion and lens blur (or boke).

You won't be surprised to hear that this isn't all: potentially in your palette are more phenomena of the type that professional cinematographers tended to avoid until the 1970s (when they started to be considered cool). These include lens flares, vignettes, and chromatic aberration. None of these occur with the naked eye, but remember, your target is the look of the real world as seen through the camera.

Lens Flares

Lens flares are caused by secondary reflections bouncing around between the camera elements. Because they occur within the lens, they appear superimposed over the image, even when partially occluded by objects in the foreground.

Unlike your eye, which has only one very flexible lens, camera lenses are made up of a series of inflexible lens elements; the longer the lens, the more elements within. Each element is coated to prevent reflection under normal circumstances, but with enough light flooding directly in, reflection occurs.

Artists sometimes like to get goofy and creative with lens flares; how many of us, after all, are experts in how they should look? And yet this is one more area where seemingly unsophisticated viewers can smell something fake under their noses, so certain rules apply.

Zoom lenses contain many focusing elements and tend to generate a complex-looking flare with lots of individual

CLOSE-UP

Garbage In, Garbage Out

You don't need me to tell you how difficult it is to bring a poorly shot image back from the dead, but check "The DV Rebel's Guide" for a thorough rundown of factors that go into a well-shot image, and if possible go on set to offer supervision and help eliminate flaws that will be difficult to fix in post. Among the less obvious points from the book

- When shooting digitally, keep the contrast low and overall light levels well below maximum; you are shooting the negative, not the final (**Figures 9.33a and 9.33b**).
- If using a small, light camera, mount it to something heavy to move it; that weight reads to the viewer as more expensive and more natural motion.

Figure 9.33 The low contrast source (a) of this digital image doesn't look too hot, yet because it has preserved all color, including the brightest areas of the sky, without clipping, it is possible to recover a good deal of color detail and dynamic range (b).

reflections. Prime lenses generate fewer reflections and a simpler flare.

Just as with boke, aperture blades within the lens can contribute to the appearance of flares. Their highly reflective corners often result in streaks, the number corresponding to the number of blades. The shape of the flares sometimes corresponds to the shape of the aperture (a pentagon for a five-sided aperture, a hexagon for six). Dust and scratches on the lens also reflect light.

You can create a lens flare look by hand using solids and blending modes, but most people don't have the time for this. The Lens Flare effect that ships with After Effects is a rather paltry offering and includes little in the way of customization; you're best off with Knoll Light Factory (**Figure 9.34**), which is highly customizable and derived from careful study of lens behaviors, although if you already own Tinderbox 2 from The Foundry, the T_LensFlare is still a vast improvement over the After Effects default.

Figure 9.34 Knoll Light Factory is controlled via a custom interface launched from an Options button in the Effect Controls. Presets such as this one, called "Monkey Planet," may include dozens of individually adjustable elements, listed right.

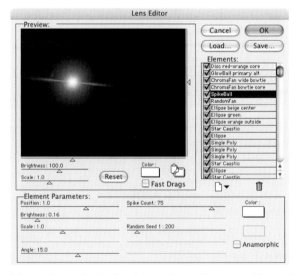

More about the behavior and application of lens flares appears in Chapter 12.

Vignettes

Vignetting is a reduction in image brightness around the edges of an image. It's generally an undesired by-product of certain lenses (particularly wide-angle fisheyes), but it is sometimes deliberately chosen because of how it helps focus attention on the center of frame. I can say with authority that several underwater shots from *Pirates of the Caribbean: At World's End* contain vignettes, because I added them myself.

It's an easy effect to create:

1   Create a black solid the size of your frame as the top layer and name it Vignette.

2   Double-click the Ellipse tool in the toolbar; an elliptical mask fills the frame.

3   Highlight the layer in the Timeline and press **F** to reveal Mask Feather.

4   Increase the Mask Feather value a lot—somewhere in the triple-digits is probably about right.

5   Lower the Opacity value (**T**) until the effect looks right; you might prefer a light vignette (10 to 15%) or something heavier (40 to 50%).

Note that the vignette is elliptical, not perfectly round, and if your project is to be seen in more than one format (see below) you'll have to decide which is the target (**Figure 9.35**). There would be no reason for a realistic vignette to appear offset.

Figure 9.35 A vignette is created with a feathered mask applied to a solid (a). If the image is reframed for display in another format, such as anamorphic, you may have to use that framing instead of the source (b).

Chromatic Aberration

Even further down the road of questionably aesthetic visual phenomena is chromatic aberration, a fringing or smearing of light that occurs when a lens cannot focus various colors on the spectrum to a single point, because of the differing wavelengths. The effect is similar to that of light passing through a prism and dispersing into a rainbow of colors.

Like vignettes, and optically related to lens flares and boke, chromatic aberration is something higher-end lenses are designed to avoid, yet it can occur even under relatively expensive and high-end shooting circumstances, particularly if there is any type of lens conversion happening.

Unlike the others, it can really look like a mistake, so it's not the kind of thing you would probably add to a clip in order to make it look cool; instead you might add it to a shot

Figure 9.36 A normal (a) and chromatically aberrated (b) image. Chromatic aberration is caused when different wavelengths of light have different focal lengths; most lenses attempt to correct for it with an added diffractive element.

CLOSE-UP

The Videotape Revolution

The debate between using 24 fps film and 29.97 fps videotape in the U.S. and other countries with NTSC has been raging since long before the digital era. It began with the advent of videotape in the 1950s, when tape was cheap and fast, if cumbersome by today's standards.

One particular experiment from this era stands out. For six episodes the producers of *The Twilight Zone* tried tape before they evidently realized it was ruining the show's mystique.

Video's higher frame rate and harder look instantly turned one of the most intriguing and ironic series of all time into something that looked more like a soap opera. To judge for yourself, rent DVDs from Season 2 that include the following videotaped episodes: "Static," "Night of the Meek," "The Lateness of the Hour," "The Whole Truth," "Twenty-Two," or "Long Distance Call."

or element to match another shot or background plate in which it appears. My recommendation in such a case?

1   Duplicate the layer twice and precompose all three.

2   Use the Shift Channels effect to leave only red, green or blue on for each layer (so you end up with one of each).

3   Set the top two layers to Add mode.

4   Scale the green channel to roughly 101% and the blue channel to roughly 102%.

5   Add a small amount of Radial Blur (set to Zoom, not the default Spin).

A before and after comparison appears in **Figure 9.36**.

Frame Rate Isn't Just Speed

One could probably write a whole book or thesis on this one topic alone, but it's no accident that film images are displayed at 24 frames per second and that newer digital formats, which could theoretically be optimized for just about any frame rate, also aim for this rate (despite how difficult it is to find a low-end camera that shoots 24p natively, with no interlacing).

The question that would generate all of the chatter is "why?" There is no logical answer, and many attempts have been made to explore alternatives. The simple truth seems to be that frame rates of 30 fps and higher feel more like direct reality, but 24 fps is just above the threshold where persistence of vision breaks down, giving it a more ephemeral and dream-like quality, just as do other cinematic conventions such as light bloom and shallow depth of field.

If you have a choice on a given project and you want it to have a cinematic look, try creating it at 24 fps and judge for yourself. After Effects is quite forgiving about letting you change frame rates mid-stream compared with most video applications; details on how the conversion actually works appeared back in Chapter 2.

If you have no choice but to work at 29.97, you still have a choice: progressive versus interlaced. It's not necessarily an error to render animation without adding interlacing; in fact, step through your favorite animated series on television and you may find that it's animated at 15 fps or less (and basically never at 59.94 fps, which is effectively what 29.97 fps interlaced means in animation terms). *South Park* doesn't count.

Format Isn't Just Display Size

As the world transitions from standard-definition to high-definition broadcast television, formats are undergoing the same transition that they made in film half a century ago. The nearly square 4:3 aspect is being replaced as standard by the wider 16:9 format, but 1.85 Academy aperture and 2.35 Cinemascope also appear as common "widescreen" formats.

A lot of artists (students, particularly) fall in love with the widescreen look for how it conjures *Star Wars* and *Lawrence of Arabia*, but if these formats aren't shown at 24 fps and don't obey other cinematic conventions outlined here, the result tends to appear a bit cheesy. So remember, it's a convention we associate with film, whether or not we know the following history.

In response to the growing popularity of television in the 1950s, Hollywood conjured up a number of different widescreen formats through experiments with anamorphic lenses and film stocks as wide as 70 mm. These systems—CinemaScope, VistaVision, Panavision, and so on—haven't completely faded away, but their presence in the modern era is mostly felt in the way that films are displayed, not how they are shot. 35 mm is once again the most popular shooting format, specifically the full-aperture version known as Super 35 mm.

Standard 35 mm film has an aspect ratio of 4:3, which is not coincidentally the same as a television. Almost all current movies are filmed in this format as if originally intended for the small screen. When shown in a theater using a widescreen aspect of 1.85:1 (also known as 16:9, the HDTV standard) or 2.35:1 (CinemaScope/Panavision), the full 4:3 negative is cropped (**Figure 9.37**). Theater patrons actually pay $10 to see less than if they waited for the movie to get broadcast full screen on cable!

The numbers "1.85" and "2.35" give the width, relative to a height of 1, so it's like saying 1.85:1 or 2.35:1. The 16:9 format, which has become popular with digital video and HD, is equivalent to a 1.77:1 ratio, slightly narrower than Academy, but wide compared to the standard television format of 4:3 (1.33: 1).

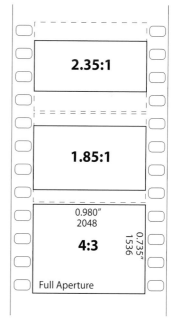

Figure 9.37 The "wider" film formats might more accurately be called "shorter" because they typically involve cropping the original 4:3 image.

Color Can Be Much More than Pretty

The influence of color decisions on the final shot, and by extension on the story being told in the shot, is an immense topic, hashed over by cinematographers and colorists the world over. Any attempt to distill this into a few pithy paragraphs would be a disservice.

Thus, if you're new to the idea of developing a color look for a film or sequence, look at references. Study other people's work for the effect of color on the mood and story in a shot, sequence, or entire film. **Figures 9.38a** and **b** show a couple of third-party tools designed specifically to give a particular look or mood to your shot.

Figure 9.38a and b Two plug-ins from Red Giant Software aim to let you add color looks like a pro. Colorista (a) is a three-way color corrector superior in fundamental ways to those found in most nonlinear editing packages including Premiere Pro. Magic Bullet Looks 3 opens up a separate user interface and can deliver looks that go beyond just color, such as a diffusion effect (b).

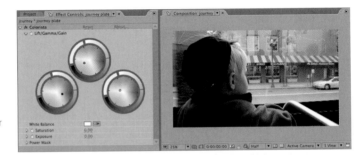

Conclusion

And really, you've just scratched the surface of what's possible. The inventive compositor can and should always look for new methods to replicate the way that the camera sees the world, going beyond realism to present what we really want to see—realism as it looks through the lens.

10

Expressions

Image courtesy of Mars Productions (www.marsprod.com). All rights reserved.

Music is math.

—Michael Sandison and Marcus Eoin
(Boards of Canada)

Expressions

Expressions are essentially about three things only:

- ▶ Links
- ▶ Patterns
- ▶ Logic

These are already in your digital artist repertoire, so why be shy about setting up the same relationships with text? Once you get over thinking that they're about something complicated and tedious like code and start thinking of them as simple solutions to common problems, the door is unlocked.

This chapter mostly offers practical real-world examples of simple expressions that can help you do things that would otherwise be difficult, tedious, or impossible. It also tries to offer pointers as to where and how you can learn to do more. Most of what is covered here amounts to one-liners, accessible to all, with practical examples of where expressions help most.

Links are the most basic thing you can do with expressions, beginning with the pickwhip. This is not a hard feature to use by itself; the real power is in learning to do simple things with those links like offsets or setting up custom controls just to help your own workflow.

Patterns sound mathematical, and it's true that you can put basic second grade math and even the high school stuff like trigonometry to use with expressions. But you don't have to go there in order to create a useful pattern; After Effects is, after all, a time- and space-based application. You can base a pattern off of time or space, or you can use properties that themselves occur in progression, such as layer index numbers.

Logic opens the door to some of the coolest stuff expressions can do. Maybe you want something to happen under a certain condition, or at a certain time, or following a set of rules. All you need to understand to get started are the basic rules for setting up a logical statement.

Values, Toggles, and Text

An expression really does one thing only: pass a data value to a property. This data value can be a

▶ Number

▶ Boolean (True/False or Yes/No)

▶ Text string (and text hardly comes into play; After Effects is mostly about numbers)

▶ Specialized value (such as a mask shape)

Essentially every piece of numerical or Boolean data that exists in your After Effects project is accessible to expressions and can be used to create animations. You can even use the text tools to pass specific text strings to your compositions.

This chapter cannot cover expressions A to Z. The goal instead is to make you familiar and comfortable with expressions that are easy to use regularly and to open the door to learning more on your own.

Values

To get started, let's try attaching some values directly to a property. One easy thing that expressions let you do is temporarily disable a property's keyframes and substitute a single value, helpful because an expression can be toggled on and off without blowing away keyframe data.

In **Figure 10.1** (see next page) an off-screen fire cause slight flickering in the foreground specular highlights; the Opacity value varies randomly between 5% and 10%. In a couple of sections I'll explain how to create this kind of randomness with expressions; for our purposes now, the animation data makes properly adjusting the layer difficult and needs to be disabled.

NOTES

The After Effects expressions language uses ECMAscript, the standardized version of what is commonly called JavaScript. After Effects makes use of many built-in JavaScript functions and objects such as mathematical operations. Many other common elements of JavaScript are too web-specific for After Effects, which also adds its own custom objects and operations.

Figure 10.1 Why is that image so dim? The keyframes creating the subtle flicker are close to 0. What's needed is a method to temporarily boost the Opacity value without changing the keyframe values.

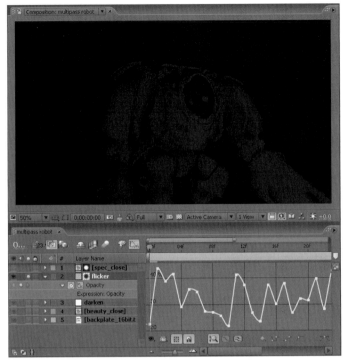

You can solo Opacity for a layer with the letter **T** and then add an expression by Alt/Option-clicking the stopwatch (there are menu and shortcut methods as well, but no one uses them). You now see:

```
transform.opacity
```

The keyframes are still fully operable because all you've done is specify the current location for the value.

Twirl layer properties up and back down again. Opacity is grouped along with the other transform properties under the twirled-down Transform. The expression is just the JavaScript equivalent of the same hierarchy, with no initial capital letters and a dot (period) separating the two layers of the hierarchy.

This is how expressions locates the source of a value. In this case, the expression leads right back to the property where it was set—and that is usually the default when you create a new expression.

Now try replacing the entire text string with a numerical value of your choice. Enter any number you like; if it falls outside of the 0 to 100 range or between whole values, After Effects simply rounds the value to the nearest number in that range. The result is shown in red to remind you that an expression is attached (**Figure 10.2**).

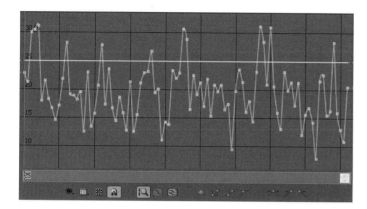

Figure 10.2 Enter a number in the expressions field to override all keyframes (jagged line) with the specified value (flat line represents value in expressions field below).

You can toggle this frozen value on and off using the button whose icon looks like an equals sign. The only real danger here is that you'll leave it active when you actually intend for it to be off.

There are two significant things to learn from this simple operation. Not only can you replace a set of keyframes without deleting them using a value of your choice, but it's also clear that all an expression needs in order to do its job is a value in a format that it understands. No matter how complicated an expression you used to create an Opacity value, the result is still a number between 0 and 100 in order for that expression to work properly.

Extra Values

Of course many useful properties in After Effects have more and other values than a single integer. It will be useful throughout this chapter to understand how to enter values into an array in After Effects.

An *array* is a property with more than one value. The most common are Anchor Point, Position, and Scale, each of which is an array of two values (on a 2D layer) or three (for 3D); 3D rotation contains arrays of three values.

CLOSE-UP

Enter the Matrix

A two-dimensional array, also known as a *matrix*, is a simple data structure; it is merely a list of values of the same type that are numbered from 0 through n. In programming numbering of an arbitrary list begins with 0 and ends with n, or number, the last value −1 in the case of 2D values, 2 for 3D values.

Each member of the list is a single channel of the array.

Add an expression for Position and you get

```
transform.position
```

but it would be just as correct to break out 2D position as

```
[position[0], position[1]]
```

or 3D position as

```
[position[0], position[1], position[2]]
```

This allows you to swap out individual values for X and Y, or X, Y and Z, respectively. Position (along with the other transforms) has subvalues, numbered beginning with zero (that's how programmers like it).

What good does that do you? You could replace all three values

```
[960, 540, 0]
```

with this static value, or you could even make one channel a static value, leaving the others to access their keyframes:

```
[position[0], 960, position[2]]
```

You can also calculate a static value to position the layer at the exact center of its composition:

```
[width/2, height/2, 0]
```

We're getting a little ahead of ourselves, however. Let's look at how to combine these individual channels of data with the ability to link them automatically.

Links and Offsets

You don't need expressions to link data in After Effects; several other valid methods exist. You can parent one layer to another, in which case all transform properties of the parent affect the child. You can precomp animations together and animate all of them as one. And there's the brute-force method of copying and pasting keyframes, which even works between two different properties if they have the same types of values (for example, an array of two numerical values).

None of these methods, however, allows for more complex relationships, such as a nonlinear relationship between two

sets of values (changing existing keyframe values by doubling or scaling them). Nor can you link in more abstract
ways, for example tying a value to an effects slider.

The key to easy linking of individual properties is the
pickwhip, a nifty tool for grabbing bits of data and turning
them effortlessly into useful bits of code (**Figure 10.3**).

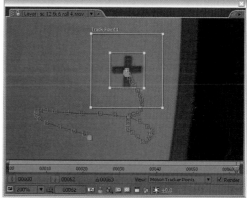

Figure 10.3 The pickwhip can reduce
or eliminate the need to hand-code
expressions.

Track Paint and Effects

Chapters 7, "Rotoscoping and Paint," and 8, "Effective
Motion Tracking," alluded to a method for combining paint
tools and the tracker. The simplest, most flexible solution
for attaching a tracker to a paint stroke is the pickwhip.

Figure 10.4 shows a motion track of a marker that needs to
be removed from a green screen background. This track
will be attached to a paint stroke that replaces the marker
with the green backing color.

Figure 10.4 The entire set moves on this shot to simulate an earthquake; the marker helps with the motion track, but then
needs to be erased.

The track doesn't have to be applied anywhere; all that's
needed is the track data itself. To view the data and remove
the marker

1. Set Track Type to Raw, create the track, and then
   use **SS** (show selected) to reveal the tracking data
   in the Timeline.

2. Add a paint stroke, making the brush big and soft
   enough that a single click wipes out the tracking

marker, leaving no visible edge around the stroke. Draw it at the first frame of the layer so that it doesn't pop on in the middle of the animation.

3   Hold the **Shift** key and press **PP** to reveal the brush in the Timeline below the tracking data, and twirl down the brush's Position property, or simply use the überkey **UU** to show all edited properties; the ones you need visible are the motion-tracked Attach Point and the brush's Position.

4   Alt/Option-click the stopwatch for the brush Position, giving you the default expression for that property.

5   Leave the text highlighted and drag the pickwhip that has just been revealed below the property up to the tracker Attach Point. You get an expression that looks something like

```
motionTracker("Tracker 1")("Track Point 1").
↪attachPoint
```

6   Preview and notice that the tracking marker is cleanly removed from start to finish.

Offset with Simple Math

Now suppose that you needed to track in a clone operation instead of a paint stroke; perhaps the tracking marker was in a place that would show up in the final shot and therefore you needed moving grain and other detail instead of the clean solid color that you get with a paint stroke.

You could create another track and offset the Attach Point, but it's simpler and more accurate to use the motion track you have and offset it. Here's how.

Create the clone just as you did the paint stroke in the above example; make your brush an appropriate size and softness. Select the area to be cloned (probably just below the marker) by Alt/Option-clicking it. A single click at the first frame of the layer should again do it. The Duration setting in the Paint panel should be at the default Constant setting to paint a series of frames, although for now we're just creating a single frame reference.

A clone stroke has a lot of properties; the two you need are the Position (under Transform) and Clone Position (under

NOTES

One major new feature in After Effects CS3 is the ability to pickwhip one mask path to another. You can't change the result in any way—for example, you can't numerically offset it—but it does make a mask an item that can be instanced and applied to multiple layers.

TIP

Adjust a brush interactively hold **Ctrl/Cmd** to drag the brush size and then release the modifier key but hold the mouse button to add the appropriate amount of softness.

Stroke Options). Notice the amount of difference between the two values; for argument's sake, let's say the latter is about 80 pixels below the former on the Y axis (meaning the value is greater by 80, because After Effects has an upside-down Y axis).

Pickwhip the Position directly as before. Do the same with the Clone Position, which for now simply has the clone in the same place as the stroke. Offsets can be done with simple math, hence the title of this section. If you remember learning early in primary about the basic math operations

```
+, -, X, ÷
```

whose equivalents in JavaScript are

```
+, -, *, /
```

you can handle this.

You can't simply add + 80 at the end of the expression—or rather, you can, but 80 will be added to the X axis (the first one, because you didn't specify). You can instead add an array: + [0, 80] is one way to affect only Y and leave the X value alone (**Figure 10.5**).

Figure 10.5 The Clone Position and Position both are pickwhipped to the tracker, but the former one is offset by 80 pixels on the Y axis.

Components and Variables

I realize that section title sounds really nerdly and could induce some eye-glazing, so I'll keep this short.

Another way to accomplish the offset on one axis is to break the array into components:

```
[motionTracker("Tracker 1")("Track Point 1").
➥attachPoint[0], motionTracker("Tracker 1")
➥("Track Point 1").attachPoint[1]]
```

and then add the 80 pixel offset to the second component

```
[motionTracker("Tracker 1")("Track Point 1").
➥attachPoint[0], motionTracker("Tracker 1")
➥("Track Point 1").attachPoint[1] +80]
```

TIP

The pickwhip doesn't have to replace an entire expression; you can use it to place one variable or component into an existing one. You can also pickwhip to one value of a property—for example, the y value only (**Figure 10.6**).

The original default expression has been used, but it has been separated into components, using subvalues, also in brackets and starting with zero, like so for a 3D array:

```
[property[0], property[1], property[3]]
```

The problem in the above case is that the default expression is so long and cumbersome. What's needed is a shorthand to stand for the long line that's repeated, motionTracker("Tracker 1")("Track Point 1").attachPoint, and that's why we have variables: to make expressions easier to write and read. Try this instead:

```
track = motionTracker("Tracker 1")("Track Point 1").
➥attachPoint
```

```
[track[0], track[1] +80]
```

I used the word "track" but it could just as easily be "p" for position or "elephant"—anything, really, that isn't already used as a keyword by JavaScript, such as "position" (which generates an error because it belongs to a defined property). The point is that the final line is now something that can be scanned and understood easily.

CLOSE-UP

Average and Center

The final example in Values (above) shows the simple way you can get a center position value for any size comp:

```
[width/2, height/2, 0]
```

Dividing by 2 gives you a value that is the average of the two added values. After Effects online help includes this example to get a position value that is exactly between two other layers:

```
(thisComp.layer(1).position +
Ð thisComp.layer(2).position)/2
```

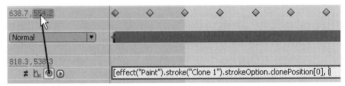

Figure 10.6 You can pickwhip to a single value instead of the entire property.

Build Controls

Expressions let you link properties to effect controls, allowing you to create custom controls in the Effect Control panel. The effects found within the Expression Controls subcategory don't do anything until you attach an expression to them. That's why they exist, to offer you a user interface for adjusting your expressions values interactively. The one you'll most often use is Slider Control; each corresponds to a different type of property (**Figure 10.7**).

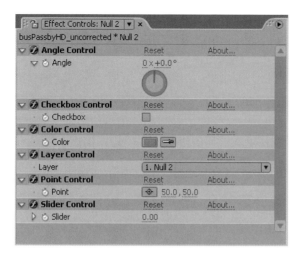

Figure 10.7 Each of these effects generates a unique type of data, but doesn't actually do anything until you link an expression to it: Angle generates radians and degrees, Checkbox is a Boolean, Color is three values between 0 and 255, Layer is a layer in the current comp, and Point is an array of two values. Only Slider generates a single floating-point number, and so it is the most used by far.

A really good already rigged example of this is found in the Animation Presets folder that you can show or hide in Effects & Presets. Try applying Presets > Transform > Separate XYX Position to any layer. An expression is applied to Position which links each of the X, Y, and Z values to slider controls in the Effect Controls. This allows you to create individual keyframes for these axes and offset the value from that of the regular Position keys.

Suppose you want a zoom control slider for a 3D camera; to try this, open the 09_rackFocus project from the previous chapter. Open the "no expressions" composition. You can't apply any effect directly to a camera, so you must apply the slider to a different layer; it hardly matters which one, because the slider will have no direct effect on the layer hosting it until an expression is linked to it.

Create a new null object called Zoom Control (editing the layer name after creating it) and apply Slider Control. Now apply an expression to the Zoom property of the camera, insert a plus sign with spaces around it after the default expression, and pickwhip to the Slider Control property. You can even pickwhip up to the Effects Controls panel instead of revealing it in the Timeline, provided you lock it first.

This expression simply adds the value of the slider to the Zoom amount. A negative slider value would effectively

TIP

You are free to change the names of layers and effects to which expressions are linked without breaking the expression; this wasn't always the case.

subtract (adding a negative number) so you could instead think of it as offsetting the value by the slider amount.

Rename Slider Control Zoomer after setting the pickwhip and behold, the connection is maintained, with the name of the control automatically changing within the expression code itself.

You can raise the slider to zoom in, but the 0 to 100 range is not sufficient for Zoom values, which can range much higher. Context-click on the property, choosing Edit Value, and change the Slider Range values (**Figure 10.8**).

Figure 10.8 You can set Slider Range values anywhere between the specified maximum and minimum values, not only for the Expression Slider but any effect.

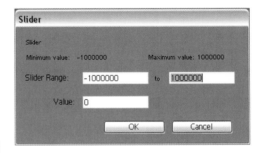

CLOSE-UP

Save Useful Expressions

If an expression uses no keyframe data, you can save an Animation Preset that contains only the expression, not the static value of the property, with Animation > Save Animation Preset.

Alternatively, you can make this slider do more within a narrower range; the Zoom values can increase logarithmically, by the square of the Zoomer value. How do you square a value? You multiply it by itself. Take the existing pickwhip path, copy it, add a * symbol directly after the original version, and then paste the copied text. Voila, the zoom control operates more like a real zoom.

Path Animation

It's standard in 3D animation programs to be able to create a path animation, whereby you draw a path and an object can be animated to follow it precisely in a nonlinear fashion, back and forth along the path, at whatever rate you choose. After Effects lacks this feature, but my pal Gary Jaeger at Core Studio figured out how to rig one up for himself and gave me permission to share it here. The key is the ValueAtTime() function, which gives you a position value given a specific time value.

To begin, make yourself a path by creating a series of position keyframes applied to a null layer called Path. Keep in mind that you can adjust their Béziers in the comp viewer when attempting to shape them precisely. Also keep in mind that if you right-click all intermediate keyframes and choose Rove Across Time, they will be evenly spaced.

Now make another null and call it Control. Apply a Slider Control and rename it U Value. Apply the following expression to the Position value for the object being animated on the path:

```
U = thisComp.layer("control").effect("U value")
➥("Slider");
```

```
thisComp.layer("path").transform.position.value_at_
➥time(U)
```

Adjust and keyframe the slider and the object travels to the appropriate time on the path.

Generate Parallax

Suppose you have a matte painting containing multiple image planes; if it's a Photoshop file, you can import it as a composition so that each layer can be offset in Z space (**Figure 10.9**). The problem is that doing so changes the appearance of the shot; as you move layers forward or backward in Z space, they must be scaled to maintain proportions.

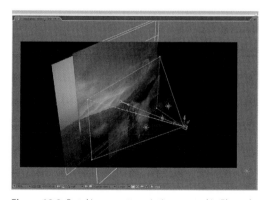 

Figure 10.9 By taking a matte painting created in Photoshop of an environment and arranging its component layers in Z space, you can create the illusion of a three-dimensional world with natural parallax when the camera is pushed in or pulled back.

Mars Productions

There's an expression I use all the time to accomplish this; it automatically scales a layer relative to the position and zoom setting of the camera. Here's how you set it up:

1. Begin with a 2D composition containing multiple layers that are meant to have depth (often a Photoshop file imported as a Composition). Enable 3D for all layers being repositioned in Z space.

2. Add a camera with the default 50 mm setting. In this exercise its name is left as the default Camera 1 for simplicity.

3. Reveal the Scale property for the 3D layers by highlighting them and pressing the **S** key.

4. For one of the layers, Option/Alt-click the Scale stopwatch to set an expression.

5. Replace the default with the following (also on the book's disc as an animation preset):

```
cam = thisComp.layer("Camera 1");
dist = length (position[2] - cam.position[2]);
s = dist / cam.zoom;
scale*s
```

This expression scales the layer proportional to its distance from the camera, and inversely proportional to the amount of camera zoom. It works with whatever scale you set for the layer to begin.

6. Reposition layers in Z space as you like; they maintain their appearance from the default camera's point of view. Now to animate the camera and see the effect of parallax, create another camera (with whatever name and settings you like, but beginning from the same default position); you can animate and zoom without affecting layer scale as you do so, which is the whole point.

It's surprising how often this comes in handy with matte paintings and various designs that require that the integrity of the 2D composition be maintained, with the addition of 3D perspective.

Patterns

It's satisfying to figure out ways to create animation patterns with expressions. Not only does it automate the process, but also they can have characteristics that would be difficult to create by hand.

There are even simple patterns that can just help you create a more elegant project. One is the ability to progress animation using time itself. The cool thing about this? By animating with time instead of with keyframes, you can use the animation in a composition of arbitrary length.

Here's a good example: Fractal Noise. It has all kinds of uses for creating smoke and fog, but by default it doesn't animate. There's an Evolution property that needs to change over time in order for that to happen.

I like to do this with a slider that can be applied right below the Fractal Noise effect. Add a Slider Control and call it Rate. Alt/Option-click the stopwatch for Evolution (in Fractal Noise) and its default expression appears in the Timeline. Replace that text with

```
time *
```

then pickwhip to Slider under Rate (you can pickwhip right up to the Effect Controls panel), giving you

```
time * effect("Rate")("Slider")
```

Adjust the Slider value to taste.

Time is evaluated in whole seconds; it does not depend on frame rate, so its rate is steady regardless no matter where it is used. Evolution occurs in degrees, so a value of 60 for Slider would have it complete a full cycle in six seconds.

Loops

Why doesn't After Effects have looping built in to the UI? I don't know, but it constitutes one of the major reasons for expressions-phobes to get hip.

In some cases, all you need to do to create a loop is to replace your source expression text with a default loop expression. These are found in the Property submenu of the Expressions menu (**Figure 10.10**).

Figure 10.10 The Expressions menu is a well-organized cheat sheet of keywords, arranged hierarchically. The Property submenu, shown here, contains several essential functions including loop.

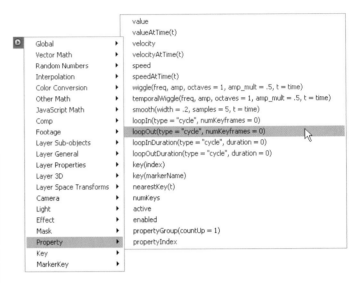

Expressions Menu and Hierarchy

The Expressions menu can be a bit overwhelming to the uninitiated—nearly two dozen submenus with several entries each. How do you find anything?

Two simple observations make this menu less daunting:

▶ Most of the entries simply point to values from After Effects to sample.

▶ The menus are organized hierarchically, from most global to most local. So at the top is the Global submenu, which has shortcuts to areas of After Effects that are available on the broadest or most global level. At the other end of the menu are Property and Key, which work on an individual property of an individual effect applied to an individual layer in an individual comp.

So don't worry, it's not as gnarly as it first appears.

The loop effects have two *arguments*, the settings found in parentheses after the command. The first one is mandatory; you must specify the type of loop you're requesting by choosing one of the three loop types, but only `"cycle"` is shown. It's a good case for a pull-down menu. The second argument, specifying how far the loop extends, is optional (and in some cases, unavailable).

The default expression works a blinking light, animated via keyframes in its Opacity property. To blink, these keyframes animate from 100% to 0% and back, then repeat. 10_loops.aep contains a light layer set to blink.

To begin, create one cycle of this animation, start to finish. You might start with a keyframe of 0%, then 100% a couple of frames later, and 0% again about a second after that.

Now set an expression for Opacity, and with the default expression still highlighted, choose

```
loopOut(type = "cycle", numKeyframes = 0)
```

Press the **Enter** key or click outside the text area. The keyframes now loop, as can be seen in the Graph Editor (**Figure 10.11**).

Figure 10.11 A simple loop expression is applied, as shown by the dotted lines. Eases into each blink in and out of the light repeat cyclically.

NOTES

For loopOut("cycle",0) to work properly, the last keyframe value must match that of the first keyframe, or the loop will be missing its first frame. This can be frustrating if you don't know the secret, and it only seems to be a problem with the "cycle" version of loopOut().

Before moving on to other looping options, check out the other arguments you can set for this expression. For example, numKeyframes specifies how many keyframes before the final one are used in the loop; set to the default of 0, it uses all keyframes. You can get rid of this argument altogether in such a case (see the sidebar, "Extraneous Verbiage"), leaving loopOut("cycle") to yield the same result. Set numKeyframes to a value of 1 and it uses the last two keyframes only.

Now, back to that missing pull-down menu. There are, in fact, four types of loops, not just one, but the other three cannot be found in the Expressions menus (they are hidden in the help documentation):

```
loopOut("cycle")
loopOut("pingpong")
loopOut("offset")
loopOut("continue")
```

Of these four, continue is the most useful by far; in fact, continue loops are among the most useful expressions period, so they get special treatment in the next section. The pingpong option is like cycle except that it alternates looping backward and forward. The offset option is similar to cycle except that, with each loop, the end frame values are added to those of the beginning frame so that the overall pattern offsets over time. Check out out 10_loops.aep for a simple illustration of these various modes.

As for the other loop types available, loopIn("cycle") provides a method to create a loop that precedes the existing keyframes, rather than following them in time. Both

CLOSE-UP

Extraneous Verbiage

How can two expressions

```
loopOut(type = "cycle",
➡ numKeyframes = 0)
loopOut("cycle")
```

bring the same result? Expressions don't do a lot of hand-holding in terms of telling you what to enter and where, but the default settings sometimes add optional keywords whose only function is to remind what the values do. In the case of this example, not only are the keywords "type =" and "numKeyframes =" optional, but the whole second argument will default to 0 if it's missing.

Now how the heck would you know this? Until you're familiar with the convention, you'd have to look it up.

`loopOutDuration()` and `loopInDuration()` enable you to specify an interval, in seconds, between loops. For example, `loopOutDuration("cycle", 2)` cycles a loop every two seconds.

Continue Loops

Although a cycle is intuitively a "loop" in the strictest sense of the word—a repeat of what came before—the continue loop is hands-down the most useful. Chapter 8 contained one use of a continue loop, to extend a motion track beyond the edges of the frame (where the tracker cannot go).

There are two basic options: `loopIn("continue")` or `loopOut("continue")`, with no second argument, because this expression can only use the vector (direction) and velocity of the animation at the first (`loopIn`) or last (`loopOut`) keyframe, and repeat it in a strictly linear fashion.

Motion Smooth and Wiggle

Chapter 8 alluded to methods for smoothing and destabilizing a camera that are preferable to the Smoother and the Wiggler, After Effects' built-in solutions that pre-date expressions. Like loops, these are easy to learn and have many uses.

If you followed the steps in Chapter 8 for using a 3D camera to motion track a scene in such a way that the track is applied only to the layer and camera, you're ready to proceed. If not, please review that section briefly if you want an idea of how the setup can be applied to a motion-tracked camera, although any camera can be destabilized (**Figure 10.12**).

To smooth some keyframes you can simply apply

`smooth()`

and to wiggle them

`wiggle(freq, amp)`

The default text is more verbose, but I'm hoping that presenting them in their minimal form makes them appear easy to begin with.

You can apply `smooth()` as is, and preview the result in the Graph Editor (**Figure 10.13**). You can of course tweak the amount of smoothing, possibly with the help the verbose parameters shown in the default expression:

`smooth(width = .2, samples = 5, t = time)`

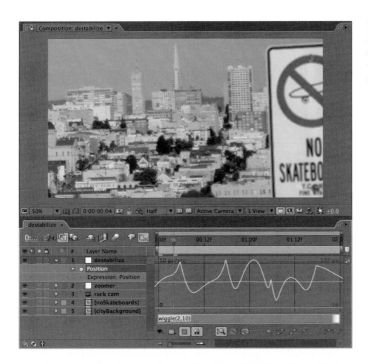

Figure 10.12 The camera in this shot is parented to a null with a `wiggle()` expression applied to its Position value to automatically destabilize the camera, making it feel handheld.

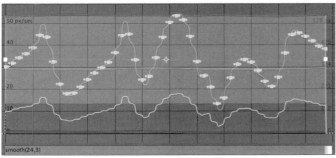

Figure 10.13 The `wiggle()` expression from the previous chapter has been converted to keyframes and then smoothed, bringing it back closer to the baseline mean.

These are the default settings; `width =`, `samples =`, and `t =` are there to offer you a clue about each argument; they don't break the expression if left in. Specifically

▶ **width** specifies the amount of time, in seconds, to either side of the current frame that is averaged into the smoothing calculation

▶ **samples** specifies how many increments to examine within that keyframe range (an odd number includes the current frame)

▶ **time** allows you to offset the smooth operation to a different time, something you'll rarely, if ever, need to do

TIP

To bake expressions data into actual keyframes, choose Animation > Keyframe Assistant > Convert Expression to Keyframes. This lets you then manipulate the resulting values as you would any keyframes in the Graph Editor.

CLOSE-UP

Wiggle versus Random

The wiggle() function adds random data to an animation channel. How does it differ from the functions in the Random Numbers submenu?

Random numbers are truly random; any number generated has no relationship to the number preceding it. They can be constrained to a particular range, and Gaussian random numbers will tend toward the center of that range (following a Gaussian distribution pattern that weights random numbers toward the median), but the effect is one of values that pop around completely randomly.

wiggle() adds an organic noise function to existing data. The randomness is therefore not quite so random: It takes existing data and deviates from it, within a set range (amplitude) and at a set number of times per second (freq). The wiggle() function, then, not only has the advantage of using animation data to determine its range, but of generating an effect that does not feel so chaotic as random data.

The wiggle expression requires two arguments by default, and has the option for as many as five. At a minimum, you must enter values for freq (frequency, the number of wiggles per second), and amplitude (the maximum amount the wiggle will change a value—in this case, the number of pixels). The full default expression reads

wiggle(freq, amp, octaves = 1, ampMult = 5, t = time)

A value below 1 is suitable for octaves, which controls how many noise samples are averaged together. A higher value for octaves doesn't mean more noise, it just means more samples, and ampMult multiplies the result—all to provide variety. For more noise, raise frequency and amplitude. Time, once again, is an offset.

To apply smooth() and wiggle() expressions to a 3D camera that has been tracked to match the background, open the example from Chapter 8, 08_tracking.aep, and re-examine the smoothCam composition.

Alternatively, to generate random numbers within a given range (rather than wiggling keyframe values), you can use the various random, Gaussian random, and noise functions found in the Random Numbers submenu (see the sidebar, "Wiggle versus Random"). Or, wiggle the temporal position of keyframes themselves (offsetting them randomly in time) with

temporalWiggle(freq, amp)

It's not the most commonly used, but you could certainly use it with the path animation example above.

Increments: Layers and Time

Some of the coolest things you can do with expressions involve increments of layer index numbers (the number of the layer to the left of the source name) or time itself. The following example makes use of both.

Time in expressions is measured in whole seconds. Frames and fields are calculated as decimal fractions of seconds. Of course, if you're ever worried about calculating this, you can use fractions instead: in 24 fps footage, frame 65 would be time = 65/24 (or 2.7083 seconds). See how easy?

You can also use `thisComp.frameDuration` to calculate time based on frames. It returns the fraction of one second that each frame lasts.

A frame's index and time are particularly useful with conditionals (below); here, they help average grain between several frames of a sequence, each on its own layer. Get ready to move beyond one-liner expressions.

Grain Average

There are cases (which don't come up all the time, but which do come up) in which the normal methods of dealing with grain—tools as powerful as the Remove Grain effect (detailed in Chapter 9, "The Camera and Optics")—just don't do the trick. The noise simply obscures too much of the source. There is an interesting alternative, one that came in handy when I was working on *The Day After Tomorrow*.

This effects plate was taken on a huge blue-screen stage: actors trudged across a snowy plain. It was meant to be snowing fairly hard in the shot, and unfortunately, it was decided to use practical snow on set. I understand that typically, as in **Figure 10.14**, this is done with little bits of plastic confetti or, the old school way, cornflakes painted white. We were already successfully adding computer-generated snow to all kinds of exterior shots. Worse, the lighting grid appeared in frame; the garbage mask to remove it left a big hole in the falling snow. I needed to get rid of the plate snow altogether and start over. Happily, it was a locked-off shot (to which I added a camera push).

TIP

Wondering what value an expression generates? You can check it by applying the Numbers effect to a solid and setting an expression for Value/Offset/Random Max. For example, try entering `thisComp.frameDuration` and you'll see the value returned by that expression.

Figure 10.14 Snow falls on a blue-screen stage.

I didn't really know how many to average (5? 20?), but I did know that if I took a series of different frames and set their Opacity correctly I could average them together to create an opaque image.

This technique removes huge flakes of snow (or any large grainy noise, including whole objects) and works as follows: on a given frame, a snowflake appears at a given place in the frame, but not in adjacent frames, so averaging them erases it.

If you composite ten frames each with an Opacity of 10%, the result is not completely opaque. Imagine holding up two pieces of paper that are 50% opaque up against a light; they would not block out the light 100%, and that is the model After Effects uses.

Without expressions, this process would be a real pain, because the number of layers needed is arbitrary, and the opacity depends on the number of layers. Each added layer would require adjusting the opacity of all of the layers. Instead, I was able to apply two expressions to one layer and simply duplicate that layer until I had enough iterations to accomplish the effect of averaging.

This same trick works with any type of noise in footage, so long as the camera is locked off. Included on this book's disc is 10_degrain.aep, which was cobbled together from a short sequence—just a few frames—shot in sequence in a downpour using a still camera. The fact that this technique basically works with such crude source should serve as an endorsement.

Drop the sequence (or noisy footage of your own) into a new composition and reveal the layer's Opacity setting. Apply an expression to Opacity and replace the default expression by typing:

```
Index*100/thisComp.numLayers
```

This expression simply says, "Multiply 100 (full opacity) by the index number of this layer, and divide this amount by the number of layers total in this composition." The keywords `thisComp` and `numLayers` are found in the expressions menus.

Next, to average together the last few frames of the composition, counting backwards for each additional layer, apply Time Remapping and add the expression

```
thisComp.duration-(index / (1/thisComp.frameDuration))
```

The duration of a composition is measured in seconds, but here the goal is to offset each layer by a single frame. By dividing `frameDuration` into 1 (or just using 24 for 24 fps, or 29.97 for 29.97, and so on), and then dividing this into `index`, the number of the layer, each successive layer in the Timeline becomes a still frame, incremented backward one frame (because the result is subtracted from the comp duration).

Now you get to use your artist's eye. Duplicate (**Ctrl+D**/**Cmd+D**) the layer until you no longer see noise being reduced in the shot; or delete excess layers if you've overshot the mark. Using all seven frames included greatly reduces the "noise" caused by the falling rain (**Figures 10.15a** and **b**).

Figures 10.15a and b In case the dramatically lower amount of rain in 10.15a isn't apparent when compared with one frame of the source (b), it should be obvious that even the passing car is removed procedurally.

Rules

Also called *If/Then statements, conditionals* are rules that open up extra possibilities by allowing you to use any value recognized by expressions as a condition for an event or a series of events to occur. The following examples allow expressions to happen under a given circumstance (at a particular time).

Triggers

Here's a simple trigger that can be set up with or without a conditional statement: A layer marker triggers a one-second dissolve, although it can be set up to trigger any transition from one keyframe value to another.

This type of trigger is handy because pressing ***** sets a marker at the current frame, even interactively while looping a RAM Preview, to begin the transition.

Add the Exposure effect to the layer. Lower the Exposure value itself until the image fades completely to black. Now set an expression for that property, and type or paste in the following:

```
if (marker.numKeys > 0){
mark = marker.key(1).time;
linear(time, mark, mark+1, 0, effect("Exposure")(3))
}
```

Here's what's happening. First, a conditional checks whether any layer markers exist. The statement is set up as

```
if (){
}
```

with the condition (that there is more than zero number of markers) in parentheses and the event that therefore occurs in brackets (and typically on separate lines to make it easier to read). No alternative to the basic if statement is offered, so when there's no marker, nothing happens.

The variable called `mark` identifies a marker (and denotes the author's vanity), the first one, `key(1)`, and specifically, the time at which that marker occurs.

The `linear(t, tMin, tMax, value1, value2)` has five required arguments that identify, in order

▶ Length of the transition (in seconds)

▶ Time transition begins

▶ Time transition ends

▶ Starting value

▶ Ending value

When current time reaches `mark` (marker 1), After Effects performs a linear transition from `0` (0%) to `1` (100%), and the transition lasts one second (until `mark + 1`, or one second past marker 1).

The Exposure setting transitions from 0, the normal image, to the setting you applied (the fade to black) before adding the expression. If you like, you can replace linear with easeOut, ease, or easeIn, each of which creates a slower transition than the previous.

Now, why go to all that trouble? It's interactive, letting you set it in real time, and can be saved and applied as an animation preset. Also, notice that you can plug in values from elsewhere for the start and end values; the linear() and ease() expressions can therefore be used to merge two animations together.

Conditionals

Setting up a set of keyframes to both loop in *and* loop out poses something of a challenge; it cannot be done without the use of a conditional statement (or a split layer). Splitting a layer is inelegant, but the conditional, on the other hand is easy to set up.

Suppose that you have an accurate track of an element's motion in the middle of its animation, but it needs to start from the beginning of the composition and extend to the end. The example of a sign attached to a passing vehicle from Chapter 8 contains just such a situation; the element is moving at just the right speed for the frames on which it's animated, and needs extending at the beginning and end (**Figure 10.16**).

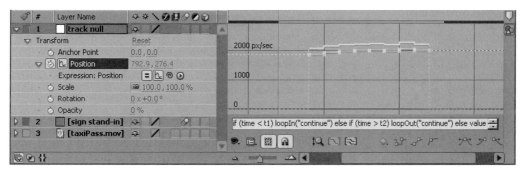

Figure 10.16 The addition of a conditional statement to the loop expression used to track the sign on top of the taxi (from Chapter 8) allows the motion to be continued both in and out, extending right off the edge of the frame in both directions.

Here is the expression to apply in such a case:

```
t1 = key(1).time;
t2 = key(numKeys).time;
if (time < t1) loopIn("continue") else if (time >
➡ t2)loopOut("continue") else value
```

There are actually several different ways you could write this expression; a different method is used in the next example. The first two lines set variables, and the third line contains the full conditional statement. Here's how it works.

The first variable corresponds to the time at which the first keyframe appears; key(1).time is how you say "the first keyframe's time" in expressions language.

Similarly, because there could be an arbitrary number of total keyframes, the final keyframe's number will be the same as the total number of keyframes, hence key(numKeys).time provides the point in time at which the expression must loop out.

Beyond the initial if statement are two more conditions, the first of which is set by else if, setting the inverse condition from the first case; "Otherwise, if we've passed the final keyframe, loop out, continuing the vector of the final two keyframes." Additional else if statements can be added as needed, and the final condition, set by else, in this case simply returns value. "Between the first and final keyframes, use the current value of each keyframe like normal."

Here's a different way to write a conditional statement, adapted from an example in After Effects online help. This one limits the expression (here for wiggle()) to occur only between the first two layer markers (**Figure 10.17**):

```
start = marker.key(1).time;
stop = marker.key(2).time;

    if ((marker.numKeys > 1) && (time > start) &&
    ➡ (time < stop)){
    wiggle(6,20);}
    else{
    value;
}
```

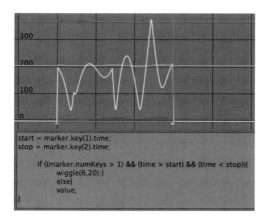

Figure 10.17 The `wiggle()` operation occurs only between the layer markers (displayed, but tiny in Graph Editor view).

Notice that there are three if statements joined by the && symbol; all three conditions must be met or the ordinary value is used instead of the `wiggle()`. If you find you have too many layer markers, you can name them and put the name in quotes instead of the index number. You can of course use any values you like for which marker number to use and the amount of wiggle.

More Information

We've only begun with what's possible using expressions. Good resources to do more are easily available, beginning with After Effects Help, which includes a dozen useful examples as well as a reference guide. I find the former more useful than the latter; most of what I've learned about expressions has been by deconstructing useful working examples, and the online help even includes examples of 2D-to-3D space transforms and other such tricky topics.

A couple of great Web sites also take up the slack:

▶ **www.motionscript.com** is the work of expressions guru Dan Ebberts. The new Expressioneer's Design Guide is full of more useful examples.

▶ **www.aenhancers.com** is a forum-based site allowing members to contribute expressions and scripts created for specific purposes, as well as areas for discussion about how they work. These sites also contain information on scripting, a feature set in After Effects that, alas, makes much of expressions look like child's play.

This book's disc also includes a couple of scripts (located in the Redefinery folder) that were created just for this book by Jeff Almasol, whose site, www.redefinery.com, contains many useful After Effects scripts. These are

▶ **rd_MergeProjects.jsx**: Suppose that you followed the advice given back in Chapters 1 and 4 and created a comp template with a custom file hierarchy for your project. The problem is that if you need to combine two such projects (by importing one into the other), you end up with two hierarchies, one nested inside the other. This script automatically merges the contents of folders in the imported project into folders with the same names in the master project.

▶ **rd_Duplink.jsx**: One very cool feature that competing programs such as Fusion 5 contain is instance objects, whereby you can duplicate an object and all properties of the duplicates (sometimes known as slave objects) update when the master is updated. This script re-creates some of this functionality; when you use it to create duplicates of a layer, it adds expressions to the types of properties that you specify (including masks, material options, and effects) linking them to the source layer, so that as you edit it, the instanced layers change.

And hold on to your hats, because the complicated stuff is by no means over. The next chapter deals with issues specific to color management, film, and a high dynamic range pipeline.

11

32 Bit HDR Compositing and Color Management

True realism consists in revealing the surprising things
which habit keeps covered and prevents us from seeing.

—Jean Cocteau (French director,
painter, playwright, and poet)

HDR Compositing and Color Management

You may already be aware that although After Effects by default matches the 8 bit per channel color limitation of your monitor, this is hardly the way to create the optimal image. Thus other modes and methods for color are available, including high bit depths, alternate color spaces and color management. Few topics in After Effects generate as much curiosity or confusion as these. Each of the features detailed here improves upon the standard digital color model you know best, but at the cost of requiring better understanding on your part.

In After Effects CS3 the process centers around Color Management, which is no longer a feature that can safely be ignored; operations essential to input and output now rely on it. The name "Color Management" would seem to imply that it is an automated process to manage colors for you, when in fact it is a complex set of tools allowing (even requiring) you to effectively manage color.

On the other hand, 32 bit High Dynamic Range (HDR) compositing is routinely ignored by artists who could benefit from it, despite that it remains uncommon for source files to contain over-range color data, which are pixel values too bright for your monitor to display.

Film can and typically does contain these over-range color values. These are typically brought into After Effects as 10 bit log Cineon or DPX files, and importing, converting, and writing this format requires a bit of special knowledge. It's an elegant and highly standardized system that has relevance even when working with the most up-to-date high-end digital cameras.

CS3 Color Management: Why Bother?

It's normal to wish Color Management would simply go away. So many of us have produced footage with After Effects for years and devised our own systems to manage color through each stage of production. We've assumed, naively perhaps, that a pixel is a pixel and as long as we control the RGB value of that pixel, we maintain control over the appearance of the image.

The problem with this way of thinking is that it's tied to the monitor. The way a given RGB pixel looks on your monitor is somewhat arbitrary—I'm typing this on a laptop, and I know that its monitor has higher contrast than my desktop monitors, one of which has a bluer cast than the other if I don't adjust them to match. Not only that, the way that color operates on your monitor is nothing like the way it works in the real world, or even in a camera. Not only is the dynamic range far more limited, but also an arbitrary gamma adjustment is required to make images look right.

Color itself is not arbitrary. Although color is a completely human system, it is the result of measurable natural phenomena. Because the qualities of a given color are measurable to a large degree, a system is evolving to measure them, and Adobe is attempting to spearhead the progress of that system with its Color Management features.

Completely Optional

The Color Management feature set in After Effects is completely optional and disabled by default. Its features become necessary in cases including, but not necessarily limited to, the following:

▶ A project relies on a color managed file (with an embedded ICC Profile). For example, a client provides an image or clip with specific managed color settings and requires that the output match.

▶ A project will benefit from a linearized 1.0 gamma working space. If that means nothing to you, read on; this is the chapter that explains it.

▶ Output will be displayed in some manner that's not directly available on your system.

▶ A project is shared and color adjusted on a variety of workstations, each with a calibrated monitor. The goal is for color corrections made on a given workstation to match once the shot moves on from that workstation.

To achieve these goals requires that some old rules be broken and new ones established.

Related and Mandatory

Other changes introduced in After Effects CS3 seem tied to Color Management but come into play even if you never enable it:

▶ A video file in a DV or other Y'CrCb (YUV) format requires (and receives) automatic color interpretation upon import into After Effects, applying settings that would previously have been up to you to add. This is done by MediaCore, a little known Adobe application that runs invisibly behind the scenes of Adobe video applications (see "Input Profile and MediaCore," below).

▶ QuickTime gamma settings in general have become something of a moving target as Apple adds its own form of color management, whose effects vary from codec to codec. As a result, there are situations in which imported and rendered QuickTimes won't look right. This is not the fault of Color Management, although you can use the feature set to correct the problems that come up (see "QuickTime," below).

▶ Linear blending (using a 1.0 gamma only for pixel-blending operations without converting all images to linear gamma) is possible without setting a linearized Project Working Space, and thus without enabling Color Management whatsoever (see the last section of this chapter).

Because these issues also affect how color is managed, they tend to get lumped in with the Color Management system when in fact they can be unique from it.

A Pixel's Journey through After Effects

Join me now as we follow color through After Effects, noting the various features that can affect its appearance or even its very identity—its RGB value. Although it's not mandatory, it's best to increase that pixel's color flexibility and accuracy, warming it up to get it ready for the trip, by raising project bit depth above 8 bpc. Here's why.

16 Bit per Channel Composites

A 16 bit per channel color was added to After Effects 5.0 for one basic reason: to eliminate color quantization, most commonly seen in the form of banding where subtle gradients and other threshold regions appear in an image. In 16 bpc mode there are 128 extra gradations between each R, G, B, and A value contained in the familiar 8 bpc mode.

Those increments are typically too fine for your eye to distinguish (or your monitor to display), but your eye easily notices banding, and when you start to make multiple adjustments to 8 bpc images, as may be required by color management features, banding is bound to appear in edge thresholds and shadows, making the image look bad.

You can raise color depth in your project by either Alt/Option-clicking on the color depth setting at the bottom of the Project panel, or via the Depth pull-down menu in File > Project Settings. The resulting performance hit typically isn't as bad as you might think.

Most digital artists prefer 8 bpc colors because we're so used to them, but switching to 16 bpc mode doesn't mean you're stuck with incomprehensible pixel values of 32768, 0, 0 for pure red or 16384, 16384, 16384 middle gray. In the panel menu of the Info panel, choose whichever numerical color representation works for you; this setting is used everywhere in the application, including the Adobe color picker (**Figure 11.1**). The following section refers to 8 bpc values in 16 bpc projects.

NOTES

Many but not all effects and plug-ins support 16 bpc color. To discern which ones do, with your project set to the target bit depth (16 bpc in this case), choose Show 16 bpc-Capable Effects Only from the Effects & Presets panel menu. Effects that are only 8 bpc aren't off-limits; you should just be careful about where you apply them—best is typically either at the beginning or the end of the image pipeline, and watch for banding.

Figure 11.1 If you hesitate to work in 16 bpc simply because you don't like the unwieldy color numbers, consider setting the Info panel to display 8 bpc while you work in 16 bpc; this change will be rippled throughout the application, including the Adobe color picker.

Monitor Calibration

Sometimes it becomes obvious that RGB values alone cannot describe pure colors; if you don't know what I'm talking about, find a still-working decade old CRT monitor and plug it in.

Assuming your monitor isn't that far out of whack, third-party color calibration hardware and software can be used to generate a profile which is then stored and set as a system preference. This monitor profile accomplishes two things:

▶ Defines a color space for compositing unique from what is properly called monitor color space

▶ Offers control over the color appearance of the composition. Each pixel has not only an RGB value but an actual precise and absolute color.

In other words, the color values and how they interrelate change, as does the method used to display them.

NOTES

Is there an external broadcast monitor attached to your system (set as an Output Device in Preferences > Video Preview)? Color Management settings do not apply to that device.

Color Management: Disabled by Default

Import a file edited in another Adobe application such as Photoshop or Lightroom and it likely contains an embedded ICC color profile. This profile can tell After Effects how the colors should be interpreted.

A file called sanityCheck.tif can be found on the book's disc; it contains data and color gradients that will be helpful later in the chapter to help understand linear color. Import this file into After Effects and choose File > Interpret Footage > Main (**Ctrl+F/Cmd+F**, or context-click instead). The familiar Interpret Footage dialog opens, with something new to CS3, a Color Management tab.

Figure 11.2 shows how this tab appears with the default settings. Assign Profile is grayed out because, as the Description text explains, color management is off and color values are not converted. You enable Color Management by assigning a Working Space.

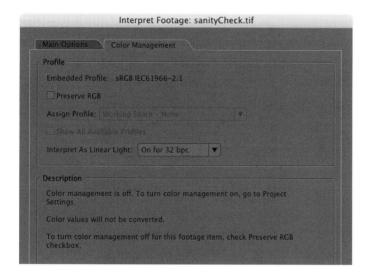

Figure 11.2 Until Color Management is enabled for the entire project, the Embedded Profile of a source image is recognized but not used to convert colors.

Project Working Space

The proper choice of a working space is the one that typically matches the "output intent," the color space corresponding to the target device. The Working Space pull-down menu containing all possible choices is located in File > Project Settings (**Ctrl+Alt+K/Cmd+Opt+K**). Those above the line are considered by Adobe to be the most likely candidates. Those below might include profiles used by such unlikely output devices as a color printer (**Figure 11.3**).

By default, Working Space is set to None (and thus Color Management is off). Choose a Working Space from the pull-down menu and Color Management is enabled, triggering the following:

▶ Assigned profiles in imported files are activated and displayed atop the Project panel when it's selected.

▶ Imported files with no assigned profile are assumed to have a profile of sRGB IEC61966-2.1, hereafter referred to as simply *sRGB*.

▶ Actual RGB values can and will change to maintain consistent color values.

Choose wisely; it's a bad idea to change working space mid-project, once you've begun adjusting color, because it will change the fundamental look of source footage and comps.

Figure 11.3 For better or worse, all of the color profiles active on the local system are listed as Working Space candidates, even such unlikely targets as the office color printer. To do a local housecleaning search for the Profiles folders on either platform—but you may need some of those to print documents!

Okay, so it's a cop-out to say "choose wisely" and not give actual advice. There's a rather large document, included on the disc and also available at www.adobe.com/design-center/aftereffects/articles/aftereffectscs3_color_mgmt.pdf, that includes a table itemizing each and every profile included in After Effects.

We can just forego that for the moment in favor of a concise summary:

▶ For HD display, HDTV (Rec. 709) is Adobe-sanctioned, but sRGB is similar and more of a reliable standard.

▶ For monitor playback, sRGB is generally most suitable.

▶ SDTV NTSC or SDTV PAL theoretically let you forego a preview broadcast monitor, although it's also possible to simulate these formats without working in them ("Display Management and Output Simulation," below).

▶ Film output is an exception, discussed later in this chapter.

To say that a profile is "reliable" is like saying that a particular brand of car is reliable: It has been taken through a series of situations and not caused problems for the user. I realize that with color management allegedly being so scientific and all, this sounds squirrelly, but it's just the reality of an infinite variety of images heading for an infinite variety of viewing environments. There's the scientifically tested reliability of the car and then there are real-world driving conditions.

Gamut describes the range of possible saturation, keeping in mind that any pixel can be described by its hue, saturation and brightness as accurately as its red, green, and blue. The range of hues accessible to human vision is rather fixed, but the amount of brightness and saturation possible is not—32 bpc HDR addresses both. The idea is to match, not outdo (and definitely not to undershoot) the gamut of the target.

Working spaces change RGB values. Open sanityCheck.tif in a viewer and move your cursor over the little bright red square; its values are 255, 0, 0. Now change the working space to ProPhoto RGB. Nothing looks different, but the values are now 179, 20, 26, meaning that with this wider gamut, color values do not need to be nearly as large in

A small yellow + sign appears in the middle of the Show Channel icon to indicate that Display Color Management is active (**Figure 11.4**).

Figure 11.4 When Use Display Color Management is active in the View menu (and after you set a Working Space) this icon changes in any viewer panel being color managed.

order to appear just as saturated, and there is headroom for far more saturation. You just need a medium capable of displaying the more saturated red in order to see it properly with this gamut. Most film stocks are capable of this, but your monitor is not.

Input Profile and MediaCore

If an 8 bpc image file has no embedded profile, sRGB is assigned (**Figure 11.5**), which is close to monitor color space. This allows the file to be color managed, to preserve its appearance even in a different color space. Toggle Preserve RGB in the Color Management tab and the appearance of that image can change with the working space—not, generally, what you want, which is why After Effects goes ahead and assigns its best guess.

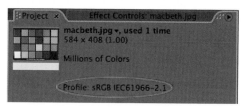

Figure 11.5 If an imported image has no color profile, After Effects assigns sRGB by default so that the file doesn't change appearance according to the working space. You are free to override this choice in the Interpret Footage dialog.

Video formats, (QuickTime being by far the most common) don't accept color profiles, but they do require color interpretation based on embedded data. After Effects CS3 uses an Adobe application called MediaCore to interpret these files automatically; it runs completely behind the scenes, invisible to you.

You know that MediaCore is handling a file when that file has Y'CbCr in the Embedded Profile info, including DV and YUV format files. In such a case the Color Management tab is completely grayed out, so there is no option to override the embedded settings.

Display Management and Output Simulation

Are we having fun yet? Output Simulation is about the most fun you can have with color management; it simulates how your comp will look on a particular device. This

NOTES

In many ways, MediaCore's automation is a good thing. After Effects 7.0 had a little checkbox at the bottom of Interpret Footage labeled "Expand ITU-R 601 Luma Levels" that obligated you to manage incoming luminance range. With MediaCore, however, you lose the ability to override the setting. Expanded values above 235 and below 16 are pushed out of range, recoverable only in 32 bpc mode.

Interpretation Rules

A file on your system named interpretation rules. txt defines how files are automatically interpreted as they are imported into After Effects. To change anything in this file, you should be something of a hacker, able to look at a line like

```
# *, *, *, "sDPX", * ~ *, *, *,
*, "ginp", *
```

and, by examining surrounding lines and comments, figure out that this line is commented out (with the # sign at the beginning) and that the next to last argument, "ginp" in quotes, assigns the Kodak 5218 film profile if the file type corresponds with the fourth argument, "sDPX"—if this makes you squirm, don't touch it, call a nerd. In this case, removing the # sign at the beginning would enable this rule so that DPX files would be assigned a Kodak 5218 profile (without it, they are assigned to the working space).

Having trouble with View > Simulate Output appearing grayed-out? Make sure a viewer window is active when you set it; it operates on a per-viewer basis.

"device" can include film projection, which actually works better than you might expect.

Figure 11.6 shows HDTV footage displayed with the sRGB working space (or, if you prefer doing it the Adobe-sanctioned way, an HDTV Rec. 709 working space). This clip is also going to be broadcast on NTSC and PAL standard definition television, and you don't have a standard def broadcast monitor to preview it.

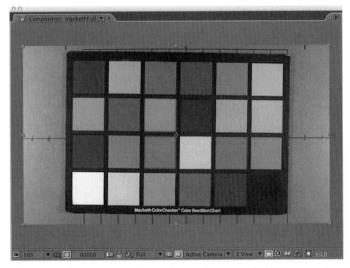

Figure 11.6 The source image is set with a working space for HDTV output (not that you can evaluate the true color in a printed figure in a book).

No problem. With the viewer selected choose View > Simulate Output > SDTV NTSC. Here's what happens:

▶ The appearance of the footage changes to match the output simulation. The viewer displays After Effects' simulation of an NTSC monitor.

▶ Unlike when you change the working space, color values do not change with output simulation.

▶ The image is actually assigned two separate color profiles in sequence: a scene-referred profile to simulate the output profile you would use for NTSC (SDTV NTSC) and a second profile that actually simulates the television monitor that would then display that rendered output (SMPTE-C). To see what these settings are, and customize them, choose View > Simulate Output > Custom to open the Custom Output Simulation dialog (**Figure 11.7a**).

This gets really fun with simulations of projected film (**Figure 11.7b**)—not only the print stock but the appearance of projection is simulated, allowing an artist to work directly on the projected look of a shot instead of waiting until it is filmed out and projected.

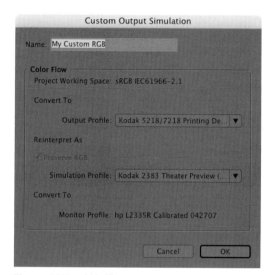

Figures 11.7a and b The two-stage conversion in Custom Output Simulation does not change the actual RGB values but, in the case of a film projection simulation, dramatically changes the look of the footage, taking much of the guesswork out of creating a file destined for a different viewing environment.

Here's a summary of what is happening to the source image in the example project:

1. The source image is interpreted on import (on the Footage Settings > Color Management tab).

2. The image is transformed to the working space; its color values will change to preserve its appearance.

3. With View > Simulate Output and any profile selected

   a. Color values are transformed to the specified Output Profile.

   b. Color appearance (but not actual values) is transformed to a specified Simulation Profile.

4. With View > Display Color Management enabled (which is required for step 3) color appearance (but not actual values) is transformed to the monitor profile (the one that lives in system settings, that you created when you calibrated your monitor, remember?)

TIP

Suppose you wish to render an output simulation (to show the filmed-out look on a video display in dailies, for example). To replicate the two-stage color conversion of output simulation, apply the Color Profile Converter effect, and match the Output Profile setting to the one listed under View > Simulate Output > Custom. Change the Intent setting to Absolute Colorimetric. Now set a second Color Profile Converter effect, and match the Input Profile to the Simulation Profile under View > Simulate Output > Custom (leaving Intent as the default Relative Colorimetric). The Output Profile in the Render Queue then should match the intended display device.

And that's all just for simulation. Let's look now at what happens when you actually try to preserve those colors in rendered output (which is, after all, the whole point, right?).

Output Profile

By default, After Effects uses Working Space as the Output Profile, and that's most often correct. Place the comp in the Render Queue and open the Output Module; on the Color Management tab you can select a different profile to apply on output. The pipeline from the last section now looks like this:

1. The source image is interpreted on import (on the Footage Settings > Color Management tab).

2. The image is transformed to the working space; its color values will change to preserve its appearance.

3. The image is transformed to the output profile specified in Output Module Settings > Color Management.

If the profile in step 3 is different from that of step 2, color values will change to preserve color appearance. If the output format supports embedded ICC profiles (presumably a still image format such as TIFF or PSD), then a profile will be embedded so that any other application with color management (presumably an Adobe application such as Photoshop or Illustrator) will continue to preserve those colors.

In the real world, of course, rendered output is probably destined to a device or format that doesn't support color management and embedded profiles. That's okay, except in the case of QuickTime, which may further change the appearance of the file, almost guaranteeing that the output won't match your composition without special handling.

QuickTime

At this writing, QuickTime has special issues of its own separate from, but related to Adobe's color management. Because Apple constantly revises QuickTime and the spec has been in some flux, the issues particular to version 7.2 of QuickTime and version 8.01 of After Effects may change with newer versions of either software.

The current problem is that Apple has begun implementing its own form of color management, one that manages only the gamma of QuickTime files by allowing it to be specifically tagged. This tag is then interpreted uniquely by each codec, so files with Photo-JPEG compression has a different gamma than files with H.264 compression. Even files with the default Animation setting, which are effectively uncompressed, display an altered gamma.

If color management is enabled, an RGB working space and output profile is a close match to the 2.2 gamma that is written to QuickTime files, so there should be little or no mismatch.

Otherwise, for QuickTime to behave as in previous versions of After Effects, toggle Match Legacy After Effects QuickTime Gamma Adjustments in Project Settings. This prevents any gamma tag from being added to a QuickTime file.

Why was the tag added in the first place? Untagged QuickTime files don't look or behave the same on Mac and Windows; the gamma changes to match the typical gamma of each platform (1.8 for Mac, 2.2 for Windows), causing problems when you render from one platform to the other using common compression formats such as Photo-JPEG or DV.

However, tagged QuickTime files rendered by After Effects 8.0.1 exhibit inconsistencies even between After Effects, QuickTime Player, and Final Cut Pro, so until the issue is solved—possibly by an update to QuickTime 7.2, or possibly by an After Effects revision—untagged QuickTimes will behave more reliably when displayed in various applications.

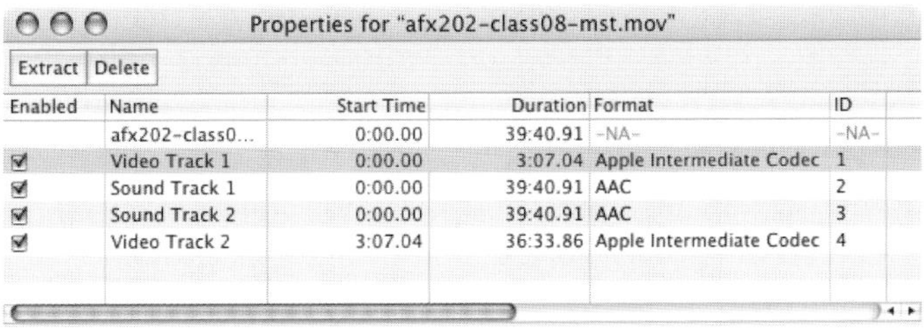

QuickTime Is Only a Container

The funny thing about QuickTime is that it isn't a format like TIFF or JPEG; instead, it's more like a container for such formats as TIFF and JPEG (specifically, the Animation and Photo-JPEG codecs, respectively). To create a QuickTime file you must choose a Compression Type, which is more like what we are used to calling a format. QuickTime stores this as a track in the movie (**Figure 11.8**).

These files contain tags to specify characteristics, such as frame rate and pixel aspect ratio, so that when they are imported into After Effects, even though you can adjust these settings manually, it knows how to handle them automatically. For the most part that is a good thing, but different applications interpret these settings differently and the gamma tag seems to yield results that are inconsistent with After Effects in some of the more popular applications that heavily use QuickTime, including Apple's own Final Cut Pro.

	Properties for "afx202-class08-mst.mov"				
Extract	Delete				
Enabled	Name	Start Time	Duration	Format	ID
	afx202-class0...	0:00.00	39:40.91	–NA–	–NA–
☑	Video Track 1	0:00.00	3:07.04	Apple Intermediate Codec	1
☑	Sound Track 1	0:00.00	39:40.91	AAC	2
☑	Sound Track 2	0:00.00	39:40.91	AAC	3
☑	Video Track 2	3:07.04	36:33.86	Apple Intermediate Codec	4

Figures 11.8 Open a QuickTime .mov file in QuickTime Player and its Properties show that it's not an image file format but is instead a container for various tracks, each with its own potentially unique format.

To Bypass Color Management

Headaches like that make many artists long for the simpler days of After Effects 7.0 and opt to avoid Color Management altogether, or to use it only selectively. To completely disable the feature and return to 7.0 behavior:

▶ In Project Settings, set Working Space to None (as it is by default).

▶ Enable Match Legacy After Effects QuickTime Gamma Adjustments.

Being more selective about how color management is applied—to take advantage of some features while leaving others disabled for clarity—is really tricky and tends to stump some pretty smart users. Here are a couple of final tips that may nonetheless help:

▶ To disable a profile for incoming footage, check Preserve RGB in Interpret Footage (Color Management tab). No attempt will be made to preserve the appearance of that clip.

▶ To change the behavior causing untagged footage to be tagged with an sRGB profile, in interpretation rules.txt find this line

    ```
    # soft rule: tag all untagged footage with an sRGB
    profile
    *, *, *, *, * ~ *, *, *, *, "sRGB", *
    ```

and add a # at the beginning of the second line to assign no profile, or change "sRGB" to a different format (options listed in the comments at the top of the file).

▶ To prevent your display profile from being factored in, disable View > Use Display Color Management and the pixels are sent straight to the display.

▶ To prevent any file from being color managed, check Preserve RGB in Output Module Settings (Color Management tab).

Note that any of the above steps is bound to lead to unintended consequences. Leaving a working space enabled and disabling specific features is tricky and potentially dangerous to your health and sanity.

Film and Dynamic Range

The previous section showed how color benefits from precision and flexibility. The precision is derived with the steps just discussed; flexibility is the result of having a wide dynamic range, because there is a far wider range of color and light levels in the physical world than can be represented on your 8 bit per channel display.

However, there is more to color flexibility than toggling 16 bpc in order to avoid banding, or even color management, and there is an analog image medium that is capable of going far beyond 16 bpc color, and even a file format capable of representing it.

Film and Cineon

Reports of film's death have been greatly exaggerated, and the latest and greatest digital capture media, such as the Red camera, can make use of much of what works with film. Here's a look at the film process and the digital files on which it relies.

After film has been shot, the negative is developed, and shots destined for digital effects work are scanned frame by frame, usually at a rate of about 1 frame per second. During this, the Telecine process, some initial color decisions are made before the frames are output as a numbered sequence of Cineon files, named after Kodak's now-defunct film compositing system. Both Cineon files and the related format, DPX, store pixels uncompressed at 10 bits per channel. Scanners are usually capable of scanning 4 K plates, and these have become more popular for visual effects usage, although many still elect to scan at half resolution, creating 2 K frames around 2048 by 1536 pixels and weighing in at almost 13 MB.

Working with Cineon Files

Because the process of shooting and scanning film is pretty expensive, almost all Cineon files ever created are the property of some Hollywood studio and unavailable to the general public. The best known free Cineon file is Kodak's original test image, affectionately referred to as Marcie

NOTES

Included on the book's disc is a Cineon sequence taken with the RED Camera, showing off that digital camera's high dynamic range and overall image quality, and provided courtesy fxphd.com. A 32 bpc project with this footage set properly to display over-range pixels is also included.

(**Figure 11.9**) and available from Kodak's Web site (www. kodak.com/US/en/motion/-support/dlad/) or the book's disc. To get a feel for working with film, drop the file called dlad_2048X1556.cin into After Effects, which imports Cineon files just fine.

Figures 11.10a, b, and c When you convert an image from log space (a) to linear (b) and then back to log (c), the bright details are lost.

Figure 11.9 For a sample of working with film source, use this image, found on the book's disc.

The first thing you'll notice about Marcie is that she looks funny, and not just because this photo dates back to the '80s. Cineon files are encoded in something called log color space. To make Marcie look more natural, open the Interpret Footage dialog, select the Color Management tab, click Cineon Settings and choose the Over Range preset (instead of the default Full Range). The log image has been converted to the monitor's color space.

It would seem natural to convert Cineon files to the monitor's color space, work normally, and then convert the end result back to log; you can reverse the Interpret Footage setting on the Color Management tab of the Output Module, but you can even preview the operation right in After Effects by applying the Cineon Converter effect and switching the Conversion Type to Linear to Log. But upon further examination of this conversion, you see a problem: With an 8 bpc (or even 16 bpc) project, the bright details in Marcie's hair don't survive the trip (**Figures 11.10a**, **b**, and **c**).

What's going on with this mystical Cineon file and its log color space that makes it so hard to deal with? And more importantly, why? Well, it turns out that the engineers at Kodak know a thing or two about film and have made no decisions lightly. But to properly answer the question, it's necessary to discuss some basic principles of photography and light.

Dynamic Range

The pictures shown in **Figure 11.11** were taken within a minute of each other from a roof on a winter morning. Anyone who has ever tried to photograph a sunrise or sunset with a digital camera should immediately recognize the problem at hand. With a standard exposure, the sky comes in beautifully, but foreground houses are nearly black. Using longer exposures you can bring the houses up, but by the time they are looking good the sky is completely blown out.

The limiting factor here is the digital camera's small dynamic range, which is the difference between the brightest and darkest things that can be captured in the same image. An outdoor scene has a wide array of brightnesses, but any device will be able to read only a slice of them. You can change exposure to capture different ranges, but the size of the slice is fixed.

Our eyes have a much larger dynamic range and our brains have a wide array of perceptual tricks, so in real life the houses and sky are both seen easily. But even eyes have limits, such as when you try to see someone behind a bright spotlight or use a laptop computer in the sun. The spotlight has not made the person behind any darker, but when eyes adjust to bright lights (as they must to avoid injury), dark things fall out of range and simply appear black.

White on a monitor just isn't very bright, which is why our studios are in dim rooms with the blinds pulled down. When you try to represent the bright sky on a dim monitor, everything else in the image has to scale down in proportion. Even when a digital camera can capture extra dynamic range, your monitor must compress it in order to display it.

NOTES

As becomes evident later in the chapter, the choice of the term "linear" as an alternative to "log" space for Cineon Converter is unfortunate, because "linear" specifically means neutral 1.0 gamma; what Cineon Converter calls "linear" is in fact gamma encoded.

Figure 11.11 Different exposures of the same camera view produce widely varying results.

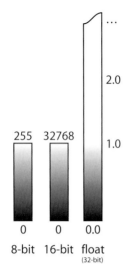

A standard 8-bit computer image uses values 0 to 255 to represent RGB pixels. If you record a value above 255—say 285 or 310—that represents a pixel beyond the monitor's dynamic range, brighter than white or overbright. Because 8-bit pixels can't actually go above 255, overbright information is stored as floating point decimals where 0.0 is black and 1.0 is white. Because floating point numbers are virtually unbounded, 0.75, 7.5, or 750.0 are all acceptable values, even though everything above 1.0 will clip to white on the monitor (**Figure 11.12**).

In recent years, techniques have emerged to create high dynamic range (HDR) images from a series of exposures—floating point files that contain all light information from a scene (**Figure 11.13**). The best-known paper on the subject was published by Malik and Debevec at SIGGRAPH '97 (www.debevec.org has details). In successive exposures, values that remain within range can be compared to describe how the camera is responding to different levels of light. That information allows a computer to connect bright areas in the scene to the darker ones and calculate accurate floating point pixel values that combine detail from each exposure.

Figure 11.12 Monitor white represents the upper limit for 8-bit and 16-bit pixels, while floating point can go beyond. Floating point also extends below absolute black, 0.0, values that are theoretical and not part of the world you see (unless you find yourself near a black hole in space).

Figure 11.13 Consider the floating point pixel values for this HDR image.

But with all the excitement surrounding HDR imaging and improvements in the dynamic range of video cameras, many forget that for decades there has been another medium available for capturing dynamic range far beyond what a computer monitor can display or a digital camera can capture.

That medium is film.

Cineon Log Space

A film negative gets its name because areas exposed to light ultimately become dark and opaque, and areas unexposed are made transparent during developing. Light makes dark. Hence, negative.

Dark is a relative term here. A white piece of paper makes a nice dark splotch on the negative, but a lightbulb darkens the film even more, and a photograph of the sun causes the negative to turn out darker still. By not completely exposing to even bright lights, the negative is able to capture the differences between bright highlights and really bright highlights. Film, the original image capture medium, has always been high dynamic range.

If you were to graph the increase in film "density" as increasing amounts of light expose it, you'd get something like **Figure 11.14**. In math, this is referred to as a logarithmic curve. I'll get back to this in a moment.

Photoshop's Merge to HDR feature allows you to create your own HDR images from a series of locked-off photos at varied exposures.

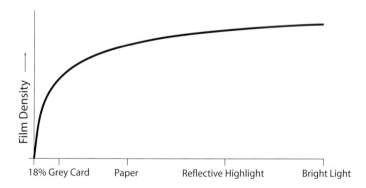

Figure 11.14 Graphing the darkening of film as increasing amounts of light expose it results in a logarithmic curve.

Digital Film

If a monitor's maximum brightness is considered to be 1.0, the brightest value film can represent is officially considered by Kodak to be 13.53 (although using the more efficient ICC color conversion, outlined later in the chapter, reveals brightness values above 70). Note this only applies to a film negative that is exposed by light in the world as opposed to a film positive, which is limited by the brightness of a projector bulb and is therefore not really considered high dynamic range. A Telecine captures the entire range of each frame and stores the frames as a sequence of 10-bit Cineon files. Those extra two bits mean that Cineon pixel values can range from 0 to 1023 instead of the 0 to 255 in 8-bit files.

Having four times as many values to work with in a Cineon file helps, but considering you have 13.53 times the range to record, care must be taken in encoding those values. The most obvious way to store all that light would simply be to evenly squeeze 0.0 to 13.53 into the 0 to 1023 range. The problem with this solution is that it would only leave 75 code values for the all-important 0.0 to 1.0 range, the same as allocated to the range 10.0 to 11.0, which you are far less interested in representing with much accuracy. Your eye can barely tell the difference between two highlights that bright—it certainly doesn't need 75 brightness variations between them.

A proper way to encode light on film would quickly fill up the usable values with the most important 0.0 to 1.0 light and then leave space left over for the rest of the negative's range. Fortunately, the film negative itself with its logarithmic response behaves just this way.

Cineon files are often said to be stored in log color space. Actually it is the negative that uses a log response curve and the file is simply storing the negative's density at each pixel. In any case, the graph in **Figure 11.15** describes how light exposes a negative and is encoded into Cineon color values according to Kodak, creators of the format.

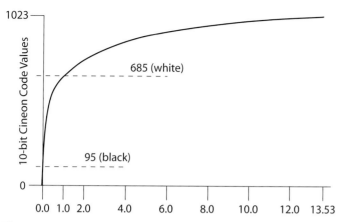

Figure 11.15 Kodak's Cineon log encoding is expressed as a logarithmic curve, with labels for the visible black and white points that correspond to 0 and 255 in normal 8-bit pixel values.

One strange feature in this graph is that black is mapped to code value 95 instead of 0. Not only does the Cineon file store whiter-than-white (overbright) values, it also has some blacker-than-black information. This is mirrored in the film lab when a negative is printed brighter than usual and the blacker-than-black information can reveal itself. Likewise, negatives can be printed darker and take advantage of overbright detail. The standard value mapped to monitor white is 685, and everything above is considered overbright.

Although the Kodak formulas are commonly used to transform log images for compositing, other methods have emerged. The idea of having light values below 0.0 is dubious at best, and many take issue with the idea that a single curve can describe all film stocks, cameras, and shooting environments. As a different approach, some visual effects facilities take care to photograph well-defined photographic charts and use the resultant film to build custom curves that differ subtly from the standard Kodak one.

As much as Cineon log is a great way to encode light captured by film, it should not be used for compositing or other image transformations. This point is so important that it just has to be emphasized again:

Encoding color spaces are not compositing color spaces.

CLOSE-UP

All About Log

You may first have heard of logarithmic curves in high school physics class, if you ever learned about the decay of radioactive isotopes.

. . . .

If a radioactive material has a half-life of one year, half of it will have decayed after that time. The next year, half of what remains will decay, leaving a quarter, and so on. To calculate how much time has elapsed based on how much material remains, a logarithmic function is used.

. . . .

Light, another type of radiation, has a similar effect on film. At the molecular level, light causes silver halide crystals to react. If film exposed for some short period of time causes half the crystals to react, repeating the exposure will cause half of the remaining to react, and so on. This is how film gets its response curve and the ability to capture even very bright light sources. No amount of exposure can be expected to affect every single crystal.

To illustrate this point, imagine you had a black pixel with Cineon value 95 next to an extremely bright pixel with Cineon's highest code value, 1023. If these two pixels were blended together (say, if the image was being blurred), the result would be 559, which is somewhere around middle gray (0.37 to be precise). But when you consider that the extremely bright pixel has a relative brightness of 13.5, that black pixel should only have been able to bring it down to 6.75, which is still overbright white! Log space's extra emphasis on darker values causes standard image processing operations to give them extra weight, leading to an overall unpleasant and inaccurate darkening of the image. So, final warning: If you're working with a log source, don't do image processing in log space!

Video Gamma Space

Because log space certainly doesn't look natural, it probably comes as no surprise that it is a bad color space to work in. But there is another encoding color space that you have been intimately familiar with for your entire computer-using life and no doubt have worked in directly: the video space of your monitor.

You may have always assumed that 8-bit monitor code value 128, halfway between black and white, makes a gray that is half as bright as white. If so, you may be shocked to hear that this is not the case. In fact, 128 is much darker—not even a quarter of white's brightness on most monitors.

NOTES

The description of gamma in video is oversimplified here somewhat because the subject is complex enough for a book of its own. An excellent one is *Charles Poynton's Digital Video and HDTV Algorithms and Interfaces* (*Morgan Kaufmann*).

A system where half the input gives you half the output is described as linear, but monitors (like many things in the real world) are nonlinear. When a system is nonlinear, you can usually describe its behavior using the gamma function, shown in **Figure 11.16** and the equation

$$\text{Output} = \text{input}^{\text{gamma}} \quad 0 <= \text{input} <= 1$$

In this function, the darkest and brightest values (0.0 and 1.0) are always fixed, and the gamma value determines how the transition between them behaves. Successive applications of gamma can be concatenated by multiplying them together. Applying gamma and then 1/gamma has the net result of doing nothing. Gamma 1.0 is linear.

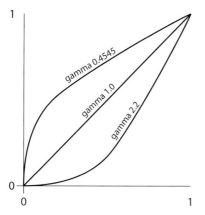

Figure 11.16 Graph of monitor gamma (2.2) with file gamma (0.4545) and linear (1.0). These are the color curves in question, with 0.4545 and 2.2 each acting as the direct inverse of the other.

Mac monitors have traditionally had a gamma of 1.8, while the gamma value for PCs is 2.2. Because the electronics in your screen are slow to react from lower levels of input voltage, a 1.0 gamma is simply too dark in either case; boosting this value compensates correctly.

The reason digital images do not appear dark, however, is that they have all been created with the inverse gamma function baked in to pre-brighten pixels before they are displayed (**Figure 11.17**). Yes, all of them.

Gamma-rama

In case all this gamma talk hasn't already blown your mind, allow me to mention two other related points.

First, you may be familiar with the standard photographic gray card, known as the 18% gray card. But why not the 50% gray card?

Second, although I've mentioned that a monitor darkens everything on it using a 2.2 gamma, you may wonder why a grayscale ramp doesn't look skewed toward darkness—50% gray on a monitor looks like 50% gray.

The answer is that your eyes are nonlinear too! They have a gamma that is just about the inverse of a monitor's, in fact. Eyes are very sensitive to small amounts of light and get less sensitive as brightness increases. The lightening in our eyeballs offsets the darkening of 50% gray by the monitor. If you were to paint a true gradient on a wall, it would look bright. Objects in the world are darker than they appear.

Getting back to the 18% card, try applying that formula to our gamma 0.4 eyes:

$$0.18^{0.4} = 0.504$$

Yep, middle gray.

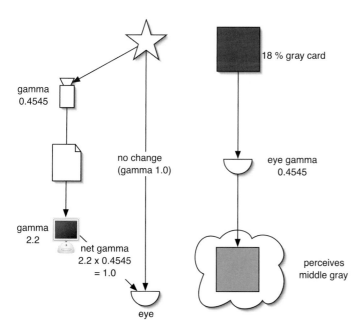

Figure 11.17 Offsetting gammas in the file and monitor result in faithful image reproduction.

Because encoding spaces are not compositing spaces, working directly with images that appear on your monitor can pose problems. Similar to log encoding, video gamma encoding allocates more values to dark pixels, so they have extra weight. Video images need converting just as log Cineon files do.

Linear Floating-Point HDR

In the real world, light behaves linearly. Turn on two lightbulbs of equivalent wattage where you previously had one and the entire scene becomes exactly twice as bright. A linear color space lets you simulate this effect simply by doubling pixel values. Because this re-creates the color space of the original scene, linear pixels are often referred to as scene-referred values, and doubling them in this manner can easily send values beyond monitor range.

The Exposure effect in After Effects converts the image to which it is applied to linear color before doing its work unless you specifically tell it not to do so by checking Bypass Linear Light Conversion. It internally applies a .4545 gamma correction to the image (1 divided by 2.2, inverting standard monitor gamma) before adjusting.

A common misconception is that if you work solely in the domain of video you have no need for floating point. But just because your input and output are restricted to the 0.0 to 1.0 range doesn't mean that overbright values above 1.0 won't figure into the images you create. The 11_sunrise. aep project included on your disc shows how they can add to your scene even when created on the fly.

The examples in **Table 11.1** show the difference between making adjustments to digital camera photos in their native video space and performing those same operations in linear space. In all cases, an unaltered photograph featuring the equivalent in-camera effect is shown for comparison.

The table's first column contains the images brightened by one stop, an increment on a camera's aperture, which controls how much light is allowed through the lens. Widening the aperture by one stop allows twice as much light to enter. An increase of three stops brightens the image by a factor of eight ($2 \times 2 \times 2$, or 2^3).

NOTES

To follow this discussion, choose Decimal in the Info panel menu. 0.0 to 1.0 values are those falling in Low Dynamic Range, or LDR—those values typically described in 8 bit as 0 to 255. Any values outside this range are HDR, 32 bpc only.

Table **11.1** Comparison of Adjustments in Native Video Space and in Linear Space

	BRIGHTEN ONE STOP	LENS DEFOCUS	MOTION BLUR
Original Image			
Filtered in Video Space			
Filtered in Linear Space			
Real-World Photo			

To double pixel values in video space is to quickly blow out bright areas in the image. Video pixels are already encoded with extra brightness and can't take much more. The curtain and computer screen lose detail in video space that is retained in linear space. The linear image is nearly indistinguishable from the actual photo for which camera exposure time was doubled (another practical way to brighten by one stop).

The second column simulates an out-of-focus scene using Fast Blur. You may be surprised to see an overall darkening with bright highlights fading into the background—at least in video space. In linear, the highlights pop much better. See how the little man in the Walk sign stays bright in linear but almost fades away in video because of the extra emphasis given to dark pixels in video space. Squint your eyes and you notice that only the video image darkens overall. Because a defocused lens doesn't cause any less light to enter it, regular 8 bpc blur does not behave like a true defocus.

The table's third column uses After Effects' built-in motion blur to simulate the streaking caused by quick panning as the photo was taken. Pay particular attention to the highlight on the lamp; notice how it leaves a long, bright streak in the linear and in-camera examples. Artificial dulling of highlights is the most obvious giveaway of nonlinear image processing.

Artists have dealt with the problems of working directly in video space for years without even knowing. A perfect example is the Screen transfer mode, which is additive in nature but whose calculations are clearly convoluted when compared with the pure Add transfer mode. Screen uses a multiply-toward-white function with the advantage of avoiding the clipping associated with Add. But Add's reputation comes from its application in bright video-space images. Screen was invented only to help people be productive when working in video space, without overbrights; Screen darkens overbrights (**Figures 11.18a**, **b**, and **c**). Real light doesn't Screen, it Adds. Add is the new Screen, Multiply is the new Hard Light, and many other blending modes fall away completely in linear floating point.

Figures 11.18a, b, and c Adding in video space blows out (a), but Screen in video looks better (b). Adding in linear is best (c).

Figures 11.19a, b, and c An HDR image is blurred without floating point (a) and with floating point (b), before being shown as low dynamic range (c). (HDR image courtesy Stu Maschwitz.)

HDR Source and Linearized Working Space

Should you in fact be fortunate enough to have 32 bit source images containing over-range values for use in your scene, there are indisputable benefits to working in 32 bit linear, even if your final output uses a plain old video format that cannot accommodate these values.

In the **Figures 11.19a**, **b**, and **c**, each of the bright Christmas tree lights is severely clipped when shown in video space, which is not a problem so long as the image is only displayed, not adjusted. Figure 11.19b is the result of following the rules by converting the image to linear before applying a synthetic motion blur. Indeed, the lights create pleasant streaks, but their brightness has disappeared. In Figure 11.19c the HDR image is blurred in 32 bit per channel mode, and the lights have a realistic impact on the image as they streak across. Even stretched out across the image, the streaks are still brighter than 1.0. Considering this printed page is not high dynamic range, this example shows that HDR floating point pixels are a crucial part of making images that simulate the real world through a camera, no matter the output medium.

The benefits of floating point aren't restricted to blurs, however; they just happen to be an easy place to see the difference most starkly. Every operation in a compositing pipeline gains extra realism from the presence of floating point pixels and linear blending.

Terminology

Linear floating-point HDR compositing uses *radiometrically linear*, or *scene-referred*, color data. For the purposes of this discussion, this is perhaps best called "linear light compositing," or "linear floating point," or just simply, "linear." The alternative mode to which you are accustomed is "gamma-encoded," or "monitor color space," or simply, "video."

Included on the disc are two similar images, sanityCheck.exr and sanityCheck.tif. The 32 bpc EXR file is linearized, but the 8 bpc TIFF file is not. Two corresponding projects are also included, one using no color profile, the other employing a linear profile. These should help illustrate the different appearances of a linear and a gamma-encoded image.

Figures 11.20a, **b**, and **c** feature an HDR image on which a simple composite is performed, once in video space and once using linear floating point. In the floating point version, the dark translucent layer acts like sunglasses on the bright window, revealing extra detail exactly as a filter on a camera lens would. The soft edges of a motion-blurred object also behave realistically as bright highlights push through. Without floating point there is no extra information to reveal, so the window looks clipped and dull and motion blur doesn't interact with the scene properly.

32 Bits per Channel

Although it is not necessary to use HDR source to take advantage of an HDR pipeline, it offers a clear glimpse of this brave new world. Open 11_treeHDR_lin.aep; it contains a comp made up of a single image in 32 bit EXR format (used to create Figures 11.19a, b, and c). With the Info panel clearly visible, move your cursor around the frame.

As your cursor crosses highlights—the lights on the tree, specular highlights on the wall and chair, and most especially, in the window—the values are seen to be well above 1.0, the maximum value you will ever see doing the same in 8 bpc or 16 bpc mode. Remember that you can quickly toggle between color spaces by Alt/Option-clicking the project color depth identifier at the bottom of the Project panel.

Any experienced digital artist would assume that there is no detail in that window—it is blown out to solid white forevermore in LDR. However, you may have noticed an extra icon and accompanying numerical value that appears

Figures 11.20a, b, and c A source image (a) is composited without floating point (b) and with floating point (c). (HDR image courtesy Stu Maschwitz.)

at the bottom of the composition panel in a 32 bpc project (**Figure 11.21**). This is the Exposure control; its icon looks like a camera aperture and it performs an analogous function—controlling the exposure (total amount of light) of a scene the way you would stop a camera up or down (by adjusting its aperture).

Figure 11.21 Exposure is an HDR preview control that appears in the Composition panel in 32 bpc mode.

Drag to the left on the numerical text and something amazing happens. Not only does the lighting in the scene decrease naturally, as if the light itself were being brought down, but at somewhere around -10.0, a gentle blue gradient appears in the window (**Figure 11.22a**).

Drag the other direction, into positive Exposure range, and the scene begins to look like an overexposed photo; the light proportions remain and the highlights bloom outward (**Figure 11.22b**).

Figures 11.22a and b At -10 Exposure (a), the room is dark other than the tree lights and detail becomes visible out the window. At +3, the effect is exactly that of a camera that was open 3 stops brighter than the unadjusted image (b).

The Exposure control in the Composition panel is a preview-only control (there is an effect by the same name that renders); scan with your cursor and Info panel values do not vary according to its setting. This control offers a quick way to check what is happening in the out-of-range areas of a composition. With a linear light image, each integer increment represents the equivalent of one photographic stop, or a doubling (or halving) of linear light value.

NOTES

Keep in mind that for each 1.0 adjustment upward or downward of Exposure you double (or halve) the light levels in the scene. Echoing the earlier discussion, a +3.0 Exposure setting sets the light levels 8x (or 2^3) brighter.

Incompatible Effects and Compander

Most effects don't, alas, support 32 bpc, although there are dozens that do. Apply a 16 bpc or (shudder) 8 bpc effect,

CLOSE-UP

Floating Point Files

As you've already seen, there is one class of files that does not need to be converted to linear space: floating point files. These files are already storing scene-referred values, complete with overbright information. Common formats supported by After Effects are Radiance (.hdr) and floating point TIFF, but the newest and best is Industrial Light + Magic's OpenEXR format. OpenEXR uses efficient 16-bit floating point pixels, can store any number of image channels, supports lossless compression, and is already supported by most 3D programs thanks to being an open source format.

If the knowledge that Industrial Light + Magic created a format to base its entire workflow around linear doesn't give it credence, it's hard to say what will.

however, and the overbrights in your 32 bpc project disappear—all clipped to 1.0. Any effect will reduce the image being piped through it to its own color space limitations. A small warning sign appears next to the effect to remind you that it does not support the current bit depth. You may even see a warning explaining the dangers of applying this effect.

Of course, this doesn't mean you need to avoid these effects to work in 32 bpc. It means you have to cheat, and After Effects includes a preset allowing you to do just that: Compress-Expand Dynamic Range (contained in Effects & Presets > Animation Presets > Image – Utilities; make certain Show Animation Presets is checked in the panel menu).

This preset actually consists of two instances of the HDR Compander effect, which was specifically designed to bring floating point values back into LDR range. The first instance is automatically renamed Compress, and the second, Expand, which is how the corresponding Modes are set. You set the Gain of Compress to whatever is the brightest overbright value you wish to preserve, up to 100. The values are then compressed into LDR range, allowing you to apply your LDR effect. The Gain (as well as Gamma) of Expand is linked via an expression to Compress, so that the values round-trip back to HDR. (**Figure 11.23**).

Figure 11.23 The Compress-Expand Dynamic Range preset round-trips HDR values in and out of LDR range; the Gain and Gamma settings of Compress are automatically passed to Expand via preset expressions. Turn off Expand and an image full of overbright values will appear much darker, the result of pushing all values downward starting at the Gain value.

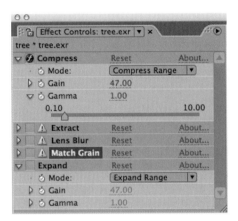

If banding appears as a result of Compress-Expand, Gamma can be adjusted to weight the compressed image more toward the region of the image (probably the shadows) where the banding occurs. You are sacrificing image fidelity in order to preserve a compressed version of the HDR pipeline.

Additionally, there are smart ways to set up a project to ensure that Compander plays the minimal possible role. As much as possible, group all of your LDR effects together, and keep them away from the layers that use blending modes, where float values are most essential. For example, apply an LDR effect via a separate adjustment layer instead of directly on a layer with a blending mode. Also, if possible, apply the LDR effects first, then boost the result into HDR range to apply any additional 32 bpc effects and blending modes.

Blend Colors Using 1.0 Gamma

After Effects CS3 adds a fantastic new option to linearize image data only when performing blending operations: the Blend Colors Using 1.0 Gamma toggle in Project Settings. This allows you to take advantage of linear blending, which makes Add and Multiply blending modes actually work properly, even in 8 bpc or 16 bpc modes.

The difference is quite simple. A linearized working space does all image processing in gamma 1.0, as follows:

```
footage --> to linear PWS ->
  Layer ->
   Mask -> Effects -> Transform ->
    Blend With Comp ->
  Comp -> from linear PWS to OM space ->
output
```

whereas linearized blending performs only the blending step, where the image is combined with the composition, in gamma 1.0:

```
footage --> to PWS ->
  Layer ->
   Mask -> Effects -> Transform -> to linear PWS ->
    Blend With Comp -> to PWS ->
  Comp -> from PWS to OM space ->
output
```

Special thanks to Dan Wilk at Adobe for detailing this out.

Because effects aren't added in linear color, blurs no longer interact correctly with overbrights (although they do composite more nicely), and you don't get the subtle benefits to Transform operations; After Effects' much maligned scaling operations are much improved in linear floating point. Also, 3D lights behave more like actual lights in a fully linearized working space.

I prefer the linear blending option when in lower bit depths and there is no need to manage over-range values; it gives me the huge benefit of more elegant composites and blending modes without forcing me to think about managing effects in linear color. Certain key effects, in particular Exposure, helpfully operate in linear gamma mode.

Output

Finally, what good is it working in linear floating point if the output bears no resemblance to what you see in the composition viewer? Just because you work in 32 bit floating point color does not mean you have to render your images that way.

Keeping in mind that each working space can be linear or not, if you work in a linearized color space and then render to a format that is typically gamma encoded (as most are), the gamma-encoded version of the working space will also be used. After Effects spells this out for you explicitly in the Description section of the Color Management tab.

To this day, the standard method to pass around footage with over-range values, particularly if it is being sent for film-out, is to use 10 bit log-encoded Cineon/DPX. This is also converted for you from 32 bpc linear, but be sure to choose the Working Space as the output profile and that in Cineon Settings, you use the Standard preset.

The great thing about Cineon/DPX with a Standard 10-bit profile is that it is a universal standard. Facilities around the world know what to do with it even if they've never encountered a file with an embedded color profile. As was detailed earlier in the chapter, it is capable of taking full advantage of the dynamic range of film, which is to this day the most dynamic display medium widely available.

Conclusion

This chapter concludes Section II, which focused on the most fundamental techniques of effects compositing. In the next and final section, you'll apply those techniques. You'll also learn about the importance of observation, as well as some specialized tips and tricks for specific effects compositing situations that re-create particular environments, settings, conditions, and natural phenomena.

SECTION III

Creative Explorations

12

Light

PLATE

LIGHT BALANCE

SHIFT CHANNELS

FINAL

Image courtesy of 4charros

There are two kinds of light: the glow that illuminates and the glare that obscures.

—James Thurber

Light

Light is the most complex phenomenon for a compositor to understand. By "understand" I mean not only scientifically but intuitively, like a painter or cinematographer.

The world of the compositor is less pure and scientific than other areas of digital production, which rely on elaborate models to simulate the way light works in the physical world. Like a painter, you observe the play of light in the three-dimensional world to re-create it two-dimensionally. Like a cinematographer, you succeed with a feeling for how lighting and color decisions affect the beauty and drama of a scene, and how the camera gathers them.

Several chapters in this book touch upon principles of the behavior of light. Chapter 5, "Color Correction," was about the bread and butter work of the compositor, matching brightness and color of a foreground and background. Chapter 9, "The Camera and Optics," was all about how the world looks through a lens. Chapter 11, "32 Bit HDR Compositing and Color Management," explored less straightforward ways in which After Effects can re-create the way color and light values behave.

This chapter is dedicated to practical situations involving light that you as a compositor must re-create. It's important to distinguish lighting conditions you can easily emulate and those that are essentially out of bounds—although, for a compositor with a good eye and patience, the seemingly "impossible" becomes a welcome challenge and a favorite war story.

Source and Direction

In many scenes, however, there is clearly more involved with light than matching brightness and contrast channel per channel. Light direction is one fundamental factor, especially where the quality of the light is *hard* (direct) rather than *soft* (diffuse).

Such a huge variety of light situations are possible in a shot, and in an infinite array of combinations, that it becomes difficult to make any broad statements stand up about lighting. This section, however, tries to pin down some general guidelines and workflows for manipulating the light situation of your scene.

Location and Quality

You may have specific information about the lighting conditions that existed when your plate footage was shot. On a set, you can easily enough identify the placement and type of each light; this information is contained to some extent in a camera report also. If the source shot was taken only with natural lighting, you only need determine the position of the sun relative to the camera (**Figure 12.1**).

Sometimes the location and direction of light is readily apparent, but not as often as you might think. Hard, direct light casts clear shadows and raises contrast, and soft, diffuse light lowers contrast and casts soft shadows (if visible at all). That much seems clear enough.

These, however, are broad stereotypes, which do not always behave as expected in the real world. Hard light aimed directly at a subject from the same direction as the camera actually flattens out detail, effectively decreasing contrast. And artificial lighting usually involves more than one light source, diffusing hard shadows (**Figure 12.2**).

Figure 12.1 Sometimes light direction and quality is plainly evident, sometimes ethereally mysterious.

Figure 12.2 Multiple lights create unpredictable overlapping light and shadow areas. (Image courtesy Pixel Corps.)

Neutralize Direction and Hotspots

When the direction or diffusion of light on a foreground element doesn't match the target background environment, that's potentially a big problem. The solution is generally to neutralize the mismatch by isolating and minimizing it, rather than actually trying to fix the discrepancy by attempting to simulate relighting the element in 2D.

Every shot in the world has unique light characteristics, but a couple of overall strategies apply. Assuming you've considered the simple solutions such as flopping the shot (where lighting is off by 180 degrees), you can

▶ Isolate and remove directional clues around the element, such as cast shadows (typically by matting or rotoscoping them out).

▶ Isolate and reduce contrast of highlights and shadows in the element itself, typically with a Levels or Curves adjustment (potentially aided by a luma matte, described below).

▶ Specifically invert the highlights and shadows with a counter-gradient.

The simple way to undo evidence of too strong a key light in a scene is to create a counter-gradient as a track matte for an adjustment layer; a Levels or Curves effect on this layer affects the image proportionally to this gradient. The Ramp effect can be set and even animated to the position of a key light hotspot (**Figure 12.3**).

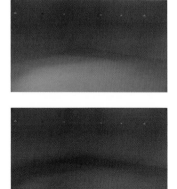
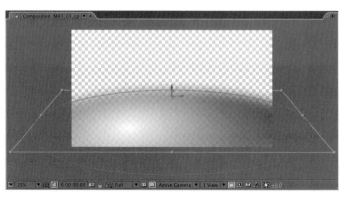

Figure 12.3 A counter-gradient is created with the Ramp effect on a solid, which in this case has been repositioned in 3D space to match the hot spot on the floor. This is then used as a track matte for an adjustment layer that lowers the brightness and contrast in the hotspot region.

A radial ramp is merely linear, which is not the correct model for light falloff. Light's intensity diminishes proportionally to its distance from the source squared, according to the *inverse square law*. An object positioned twice as far from a single light source is illuminated by one-quarter the amount of light. To mimic this with a gradient, precomp it, duplicate the radial gradient layer, and set the upper of the two layers to a Multiply blending mode (**Figures 12.4a, b,** and **c**).

Linearize Working Space

☑ Blend Colors Using 1.0 Gamma

Match Legacy After Effects QuickTime Gamma Adjustments

Figure 12.4a, b, and c A simple gradient is linear (a), but light falls off in an inverse-square proportion, which can be re-created by multiplying a second gradient with linear blending enabled (b). Remember that, as explained in the previous chapter, in After Effects CS3 you can blend with a 1.0 gamma (giving you a precise inverse-square relationship) even without a linearized working space (c).

Color Looks

Have you ever seen unadjusted source clips or behind-the-scenes footage from a movie you consider visually compelling? It's a great way to learn the bold and deliberate use of color in modern films. Look at the work prints included with a heavily color-corrected film—the magic more or less disappears.

In older films this transformation was often accomplished via physical elements such as lens filters or photochemical processes, such as the well-known bleach bypass method, but nowadays it tends to happen on such computer-driven systems as the DaVinci.

After Effects has a big advantage over a system like a DaVinci in that it is a true compositing system; the controls over image selection are much finer. The main disadvantage is that After Effects was not created solely with color timing in mind, so its principal color tools (as described in Chapter 5) are simpler and less interactive. Third-party solutions such as Colorista and Magic Bullet Looks, both from Red Giant, aim to bridge some of this gap.

Keeping in mind that your job as a compositor is to emulate the world as it looks when viewed with a camera, it can be effective to begin by emulating physical lens elements.

Use a Layer as a Lens Filter

Suppose a shot (or some portion of it) should simply be "warmer" or "cooler." With only a camera and some film, you might accomplish this transformation by adding a lens filter. It could be a solid color (blue for cooler, amber to warm things up) or a gradient (amber to white to change only the color of a sky above the horizon).

Add a colored solid and set its blending mode to Color. Choose a color that is pleasing to your eye, with brightness and saturation well above 50%. Use blue or green for a cooler look, red or yellow for a warmer one (**Figure 12.5**).

At 100%, this is the equivalent of a full-color tint of the image, which is too much. Dial Opacity down between 10% and 50%, seeking the threshold where the source colors remain discernable, filtered by the added color to set the look.

Figure 12.5 This saturated source image has four color filters applied to it as a test (you would normally choose just one to apply full frame, of course): yellow, green, blue/green, and blue. Linear blending is again enabled, so these solids applied with a Color blending mode behave a lot like lens filters of an equivalent color, but you control the opacity.

Figures 12.6a through c This Flag of Mars image (a) is made up of three fields of pure red, green, and blue. You can convert it to grayscale accurately with Tint (b), or a monochrome solid set to the blending mode Color (same result). Hue/Saturation (c) is mathematically correct but does not adjust for the perceptual differences in human color vision.

To re-create a graded filter, typically used to affect only the sky, apply the Ramp effect to the solid and change the Start Color to your tint color; an amber filter adds the look of a heavily smoggy urban day. This is best applied with an Add or Screen mode instead of Color because the default End Color, white, desaturates the lower part of the image. Sometimes, however, this might be just what you want.

Black and White

When removing color from an element entirely, there is a huge difference between using the Hue/Saturation effect and the likely alternatives. Counter-intuitively, Hue/Saturation is typically not the best choice to create a black-and-white image, because it maintains luminance proportions, and as was mentioned in a sidebar back in Chapter 6, "Color Keying," that's not how the eye sees color. **Figures 12.6a** through **c** visually illustrate the difference.

Even if converting an image to black and white is only an intermediate step, you're best off doing so either using the Tint effect at the default settings or a fully desaturated solid (black, white, or gray, it doesn't matter) with a Color blending mode. To really get the conversion right may involve adjusting or shifting color channels prior to the color-to-black-and-white conversion, as shown in the chapter opener images.

Day for Night

Stronger optical effects are even possible, such as making a daytime scene appear as if shot on a moonlit night. Known in French as *la nuit américaine* (and immortalized in Francois

NOTES

The flag of Mars is a red, green, and blue tricolor selected by the Mars Society and flown into orbit by the Space Shuttle Discovery. Seriously. It bears no apparent resemblance to the one Marvin the Martian used to claim Planet X.

TIP

Hue/Saturation is great for more subtle saturation adjustments. Use it when you're focused only on brightness and contrast (using Levels), and overall saturation is a little hot, making the element appear a little too juicy.

Truffaut's ode to filmmaking of the same name), this involves a simple trick. Shoot an exterior scene under ordinary daylight with a dark blue lens filter to compensate for the difficulty of successful low light night shoots. If there is direct sunlight, it's meant to read as moonlight.

Lighting techniques and film itself have improved since this was a common convention of films, particularly westerns, but digital cameras retain a low signal to noise ratio under low light, hence the Nightshot feature on many consumer video cameras.

Figure 12.7 shows the difference between a source image that is blue and desaturated and an actual night look; if instead you're starting with a daylight image, look at the images on the book's disc, which take the image more in that direction. Overall, remember that the eye cannot see color without light, so only areas that are perceived to be well illuminated should have a hue outside the range between deep blue and black.

Figure 12.7 An ordinary twilight shot of a house at dusk is converted to a spooky Halloween mansion. Note that the overall hue remains slightly blue, not monochrome, illuminated by its color opposite, a yellow moon. Other colors will not easily register in true low light, although this scene is much better lit than an actual moonlight shot would likely be if shot realistically. (Images courtesy Mars Productions.)

Color Timing Effects

Digital tools can of course go far beyond what is possible with lens filters. The industry standard tools rely on a *three-way color corrector*, which allows you to tint the image in three basic luminance ranges, highlights, midtones, and shadows, adjusting each separately via wheels which control hue and brightness. Premiere Pro has such an effect, which is retained if you import a project from that application despite that there is no such actual plug-in native to After Effects.

Even many Premiere Pro editors eschew this effect, however, instead using Colorista, a relatively inexpensive Red Giant plug-in (**Figure 12.8**). This effect is a lot like adding three color solids instead of one, and it lets you emulate the complex color look that is all the rage these days: blue shadows, green midtones, and orange highlights, anyone?

TIP

If you don't like the idea of adding a third-party plug-in to your workflow, there is even a free alternative wired to a Color Balance (HLS) effect included in *The DV Rebel's Guide* (Stu Maschwitz, Peachpit Press) as RebelCC.

Figure 12.8 Colorista enables a subtle (or radical) mixture of individual Lift, Gamma, and Gain (low, medium, high) color wheel controls. The result uses Output Simulation to show how these changes will look on film (covered in the previous chapter).

Source, Reflection, and Shadow

Scenes with strong prominent light sources are something of a gift to a compositor by offering a clear target. You can also make strong light choices confidently by referring to a shot that matches the target look. Either way, the message is simple: Use reference. You will be surprised how much bolder and more fascinating nature's choices are than your own, especially if you are still building your skills (and aren't we all continually doing that?).

You get the proverbial gold star for finding an unexpected surprise that works, and the play of light and shadow in the scene offers uniquely challenging and rewarding opportunities to do so. Such details can be the *kiss of love*, that something extra that nobody requested but everyone who is paying attention appreciates.

Big, bold, daring choices about light can and should become almost invisible if they are appropriate to a scene, adding to the dramatic quality of the shot instead of merely showing off what you as an artist can do.

NOTES

"Kiss of love" is a term Stu Maschwitz invented supervising *Star Wars, Episode One: The Phantom Menace* at Industrial Light + Magic. "I still use that term today," he says. "It's a great way to get an artist to think of a shot as theirs. Examples of kisses of love are reflections in things that might not strictly need it, aperture flares for lights leaving the frame (carefully matched to reference), or animating a starfighter pilot's head to turn as he banks."

You can buy a light wrap plug-in for After Effects, but this is a case where "roll your own" works just as well, if not better.

Backlighting and Light Wrap

The conditions of a backlit scene are a classic example where the compositor often does not go far enough to match what actually happens in the real world.

This technique is designed for scenes that contain back-lighting conditions and a foreground that, although it may be lit to match those conditions, lacks light wrapping around the edges (**Figure 12.9**).

Figure 12.9 The silhouetted figure has been color corrected to match the scene, but lacks any of the light wrap clearly visible around the figures seated on the beach.

Set up a light wrap effect as follows:

1. Create a new composition that contains the background and foreground layers, exactly as they are positioned and animated in the master composition. You can do this simply by duplicating the master comp and renaming it something intuitive, such as Light Wrap. If the foreground or background consists of several layers, it will probably be simpler to precompose them into two layers, one each for the foreground and background.

2. Set Silhouette Alpha blending mode for the foreground layer, punching a hole in the background (**Figure 12.10**).

Figure 12.10 Using the alpha of the layer to which it's applied, Silhouette Alpha punches a hole through that layer and all underlying layers.

3. Add an adjustment layer at the top, and apply Fast Blur.

4. In Fast Blur, check the Repeat Edge Pixels toggle on and crank up the blurriness (**Figure 12.11**).

Figure 12.11 Heavy Fast Blur causes the background image color to bleed into the area of the underlying alpha channel.

5. Duplicate the foreground layer, move the copy to the top, and set its blending mode to Stencil Alpha, leaving a halo of background color that matches the shape of the foreground (**Figure 12.12** on the next page). If the light source is not directly behind the subject, you can offset this layer to match, producing more light on the matching side.

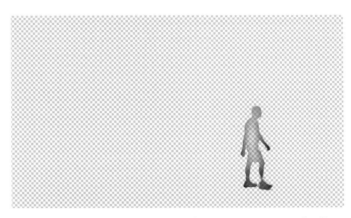

Figure 12.12 Stencil Alpha provides the inverse effect, preserving only the areas of the composition inside the alpha of the top layer to which it is applied. You have your light wrap.

6. Place the resulting comp in the master comp and adjust opacity (and optionally switch the blending mode to Add, Screen, or Lighten) until you have what you're after. You may need to go back to the Light Wrap comp to further adjust the blur (**Figure 12.13**).

Figure 12.13 The addition of light wrap causes the figure to appear as part of the scene.

When there is no fill light on the foreground subject whatsoever, most cameras are incapable of picking up as much detail in the foreground as your eye might see. In your reference photo, an unlit foreground subject might appear completely silhouetted. Because the foreground subjects are often the stars of the scene, you might have to compensate, allowing enough light and detail in the foreground that the viewer can see facial expressions and other important dramatic detail.

In other words, this might be a case where your reference conflicts with what is needed for the story. Try to strike a balance, but remember, when the story loses, nobody wins.

Flares

For our purposes a "flare" is any direct light source that appears in shot, not just a cheesy 17-element lens flare whenever the sun pokes around the moon in some science fiction television show from the early 1990s. These don't come for free in After Effects; 3D lights don't even create a visible source if placed in shot until you add the Trapcode Lux effect (included on this book's disc).

Real lens flares are never cheesy: Our eyes accept them as natural, even beautiful artifacts without necessarily understanding anything about what actually causes them (**Figures 12.14a**, **b**, and **c**).

Three-Way Blur

After Effects offers quite a few blur effects, but three are most common for general usage: Gaussian Blur, Fast Blur (which at best quality is no different but renders faster), and Box Blur, which can match the other two but offers more flexibility.

. . . .

At the default Iterations setting (1), a Box Blur can seem crude and, well, boxy, but it can approximate the look of a defocused lens without all the more complex polygons of Lens Blur; you can also hold it out to the horizontal or vertical axis to create a nice motion blur approximation (where Directional Blur is actually too smooth and Gaussian).

. . . .

Raising the Box Blur Iterations setting above 3 not only amplifies the blur but refines the blur kernel beyond anything the other two effects are capable of producing. What actually occurs is that the blur goes from a square appearance (suiting the name box blur) to a softer, rounder look. You're more likely to notice the difference working with over-range bright values in 32 bit HDR.

. . . .

Fast Blur and Box Blur also each include a Repeat Edge Pixels checkbox; enable this to avoid dark borders when blurring a full frame image. The same setting with these two effects will not, alas, produce the same amount of blur even if Box Blur is set to 3 iterations (to match Fast Blur).

Figure 12.14a, b, and c Figure 12.22a has no lens flare, when you might expect one; 12.22b has just the barest suggestion of a flare spiking out of the huge light source pouring in through the window, and 12.22c has a lens flare that is more natural but far less apparent than the flares you would get from the Lens Flare effect.

NOTES

Prior to the 1970s-era of Easy Rider and moon shots, flares were regarded as errors on the part of the cinematographer, and shots containing them were carefully noted on the camera report and retaken.

CLOSE-UP

What Causes a Lens Flare?

Unlike your eye, which has only one very flexible lens, camera lenses are typically made up of a series of inflexible lens elements. These elements are coated to prevent light reflecting off of them under normal circumstances. Extreme amounts of light, however, are reflected somewhat by each element.

Zoom lenses contain many focusing elements and tend to generate a complex-looking flare with lots of individual reflections. Prime lenses generate fewer.

Several other factors besides the lens elements also contribute to the look of a flare. Aperture blades within the lens cause highly reflective corners that often result in streaks, the number of streaks corresponding to the number of blades. The shape of the flares sometimes corresponds to the shape of the aperture (a pentagon for a five-sided aperture, a hexagon for six). Dust and scratches on the lens also reflect light.

Finally, lens flares look very different depending on whether they were shot on film or video, the excess light bleeding out in different directions and patterns.

Therefore, to get lens flares or even simple glints right (not cheesy), good reference is often key. Only a tiny percentage of your viewers may know the difference between lens flares from a 50 mm prime and a 120 mm zoom lens, yet somehow, if you get it wrong, it reads as phony to a majority of viewers. Odd.

Here are some things you should know about lens flares:

▶ They are consistent for a given lens. Their angles vary according to the position of the light, but not the shape or arrangement of the component flares.

▶ The big complex flares with lots of components are created by long zoom lenses with many internal lens elements. Wider prime lenses create simpler flares.

▶ Because they are caused within the lens, flares beyond the source appear superimposed over the image, even over objects in the foreground that partially block the source flare.

Moreover, not every bright light source that appears in frame will cause a lens flare—not even the sun. (Look again at Figure 12.14a.)

The Lens Flare effect included with After Effects is rather useless as it contains only three basic settings. Knoll Light Factory, available from Red Giant Software, is much more helpful both because the presets correspond to real lenses and because the components can be fully customized in a modular fashion. The lens flare plug-in offered by The Foundry as part of Tinderbox also makes realistic-looking flares possible, although the included defaults are not so convincing.

Reflected Light

Reflected light is a common "kiss of love" opportunity for a scene; rarely is it prominently missing, but often a surface with some degree of specularity is added to a scene which will seem more palpably real with the addition of reflected light, from a glimmer or glint to a full window reflection.

Glints are specular flares that occur when light is reflected toward the camera from shiny parts of an element in scene, such as the chrome of the taxi in **Figure 12.15**, taken from the Chapter 5 color matching example.

Figure 12.15 This sequence shows the glint that plays off the chrome areas of the taxi as it passes a spot in the frame where the sun is reflected directly into the camera lens.

There's no plug-in to create glints and no hard and fast rule about when they should appear; they are a near-pure kiss of love, although in this particular example you would expect a shiny metallic plane to cast glints just as the shiny taxi does. The glints on the taxi seem to occur just to the left of the frame's center, so you're looking for a specular hotspot on the plane that passes that point in the frame, and you get one on the tail.

By zooming in on your reference, you get the color and shape of a typical isolated glint (**Figure 12.16**). And behold, there's not much to it: a white blotch with six thin streaks coming off of it (which probably corresponds to a six-sided aperture). Looks like something you can paint rather quickly, no?

This is a perfect case in which it's best not to be a perfectionist. Close-up, the result of my quickly painted glint looks most unimpressive indeed. But place it into a fast-moving shot that was never meant to be studied frame by frame, and I've just bought myself a good dose of extra realism for a few minutes' extra work (**Figure 12.17**).

Figure 12.16 There's not a whole lot to a glint when you look at it closely, especially at video resolution.

Figure 12.17 The plane passes by, hand-painted glints added to its tail.

Light Scattering and Volume

Light scatters as it encounters particles in the air, most dramatically causing the phenomena of volumetric light or God rays. Our atmosphere does not permit light to travel directly to the camera, uninterrupted. Instead, the light ricochets off tiny particles in the air, revealing its path.

The effect can be subtle. Lights that appear in the scene, casting their beams at the camera, tend to have a glowing halo around them. If the light traveled directly to the camera, the outline of the source light would be clear. Instead, light rays hit particles on their way to the camera and head off in slightly new directions, causing a halo (**Figure 12.18**).

Figure 12.18 You're so used to seeing halos around bright lights that it just plain looks wrong to lower the exposure so that the halos virtually disappear.

Add more particles in the air (in the form of smoke, fog, or mist), and you get more of a halo, as well as the conditions under which volumetric light occurs. God rays are the result of the fact that light from an omnidirectional source, such as the sun, travels outward in a continuous arc (**Figure 12.19**).

The CC Light Rays effect is probably most helpful among those included with After Effects to re-create volumetric light effects, and even God rays. It not only boosts and causes halation around the source light, but also adds rays coming straight at camera. These rays can be made more prominent by boosting radius and intensity, but in order to create a God rays

Figure 12.19 The cathedral of light known to pious and pagan alike as God rays.

effect and not overwhelm an entire image with rays, it's usually best to make a target source and apply the effect to that. For example, you can

1. Add a solid of your preferred color.

2. Apply Fractal Noise (default settings are acceptable to begin).

3. Mask the solid around the target God rays source area. Feather it heavily.

4. Apply CC Light Rays. Place the Center at the God rays target. Boost Intensity and Radius settings until the rays are prominent.

5. For rays only (no fractal noise) set Transfer Mode to None.

6. Set a Subtract mask or Alpha Inverted track matte to create occluded areas for the rays to wrap around, as in **Figure 12.20**.

Figure 12.20 The included CC Light Rays effect is essential to creating your own volumetric light effects in After Effects. Masks or mattes can be used to occlude rays.

You can further hold out and mask out the rays as needed, even precomping and moving the source outside of frame if necessary. To make the rays animate, keyframe the Evolution property in Fractal Noise or add an expression such as `time*60` causing it to undulate over time. Different Fractal Type and Noise Type settings will also yield unique rays.

Shadows

As there is light, so must there be shadows. Unfortunately, they can be difficult to re-create in 2D because they interact with 3D space and volume, none of which 2D layers have. The behavior of shadows can be unpredictable, but luckily, your audience typically doesn't know how they should look in your scene either.

You can certainly cast a shadow from a matted layer onto a plane by positioning each of them in 3D space and properly positioning a light. Be sure that you first change Casts Shadows for the matted layer from its default Off setting to On or Only (the latter option making it possible to create a precomp containing only the shadow).

You can instead corner pin the matte to the angle at which the shadow should fall and avoid the 3D setup altogether. In either case, the problem is that the illusion breaks if the light source is more than 10 degrees off-axis from the camera. The more you light a 2D element from the side, the more it just doesn't look right (**Figure 12.21**).

There's also the possibility of cheating: if it's easy to add ground surface that would obscure a shadow (for example, grass instead of dirt), do so, and no one will even expect to see a shadow because it no longer belongs there.

Figure 12.21 Compare the fake 3D shadow with the real thing and you instantly grasp the problem with this approach. You can cast a good shadow head-on, but not at this steep an angle.

Contact Shadows

For the most part, successful shading in a 2D scene relies on scaling back expectations. There are plenty of cases where a full cast shadow would be correct and no shadow at all clearly looks wrong, but a simple contact shadow will work.

A contact shadow is a lot like a drop shadow, basically just an offset, soft, dark copy directly behind the foreground. A drop shadow, however, is good only for casting a shadow onto an imaginary wall behind a logo, whereas a contact shadow is held out to only the areas of the foreground that have contact with the ground plane.

Figure 12.22 shows a good example based on a composite from Chapter 5. The foreground can layer is duplicated and placed behind the source. A mask is drawn around the base, and it is then offset downward. A blur is applied to soften the transparency channel. That gives you the matte.

Figure 12.22 A simple contact shadow can make the difference between an object that appears to sit on a surface and an object that appears to float in space.

You might now expect to simply darken the layer down to black and lower opacity to taste, but shadows are not simply cast pools of black, they are areas of obscured light, so there is a better way. Create an Adjustment layer just below the contact shadow layer and set an Alpha track matte. Add a Levels (or if you prefer, Curves) effect and adjust brightness and gamma downward to create your shadow. Treat it like a color correction, working on separate channels if necessary; the result is typically less bland and more accurate than a simple pool of blackness.

Indirect Light

It's easy to forget the actual physics of what gives an object a certain color; it is comprised entirely of the wavelengths of light that the surface does not absorb. All of the color in our world, save that of light sources such as the sun or your computer screen, is primarily the result of reflected light.

Most surfaces in the natural world are diffuse, and they reflect light softly in all directions (**Figure 12.23**). Thus in some subtle way, adjacent physical objects can color one another, but two layers composited together completely lack these light interactions, which occasionally would be quite prominent.

Figure 12.23 The color influence of indirect light is not always so evident as here, yet this phenomenon is always in play.

Computer software is becoming better at re-creating these types of interactions. Global illumination and radiosity features have been added to 3D rendering programs over the past decade to re-create the many effects of reflected light, enhancing the realism of completely synthesized scenes. For the compositor, of course, lighting remains more art than science. The 3D artist can be more like a sculptor, letting the light play over the created work, but the compositor is more like a painter, observing and artistically interpreting the world without the benefit of realistic physics. Light that interacts directly between objects presents one more golden opportunity to make the scene feel real the way that a painter would.

Multipass 3D Compositing

Some artists, including a majority of those who work predominantly in 3D, labor under the delusion that you should finalize the look of a computer-generated element in one pass. Certainly, as it becomes more and more possible to adjust the look of a 3D model in real time (via the GPU, i.e., OpenGL) this becomes tempting.

However, it's possible to do better by dividing the render of a single element into multiple passes. This is different from rendering in layers, which while also useful for compositing is really only about separating foreground elements from the background. *Multipass rendering* is the technique of isolating individual surface qualities and creating a separate render for each. By surface qualities I mean things like specularity and wear and tear, also known as grunge. In his excellent book *Digital Lighting & Rendering, Second Edition* (Peachpit Press, 2006), Jeremy Birn calls out multiple benefits yielded by rendering a model on multiple passes, a few of which include

- ▶ **Changes** can be made with little or no re-rendering. If a shadow is too dark or a glow the wrong color, the adjustment can be made right in After Effects.

- ▶ **Integration** often requires multiple passes where the model interacts with the scene, casting a shadow on the ground or being reflected in water. If the cast shadow is simply part of a single render you lose all control over its appearance and cannot apply it as recommended in the previous section.

- ▶ **Reflections**, which often consume massive amounts of time to process, can be rendered at lower quality and blurred in After Effects.

- ▶ **Bump Maps** can be applied more selectively (held out by another pass such as a highlight or reflection pass).

- ▶ **Glows** can be created easily in 2D by simply blurring and boosting exposure of a specular pass.

- ▶ **Depth of Field** can be controlled entirely in 2D by using a Z pass as a matte for a blur adjustment layer.

- ▶ **Less render power and time** is required to render any one pass than the entire shaded model, so a lower powered computer can do more, and redoing any one element takes far less time than redoing the entire finished model.

Putting multiple passes to use is also surprisingly simple; the artistry is in all of the minute decisions about which combination of adjustments will bring the element to life. **Table 12.1** (on the next page) describes some common render passes and how they are typically used.

TABLE **12.1** Ten Typical Multipass Render Layer Types

Type	Color/ Grayscale	Typical Blending Mode	Description	Use
Diffuse	Color	Normal	Full color render; includes diffuse illumination, color correction and texture, excludes reflections, high-lights and shadows	Color basis for the element; main target for primary color
Specular	Color	Add or Screen	Isolated specular highlights	Control how highlights are rendered; can be reused to create a glow pass by simply blurring and raising exposure
Reflection	Color	Add or Screen	Self-reflections, other objects, environment	Control the prominence and color of reflections
Shadow	Grayscale	Luma Inverted Matte	Isolated translucent shadows in scene	Control appearance, color and softness of shadows; applied as a track matte to an adjust-ment layer with a Levels or Curves effect
Ambient	Color	Color	Color and texure maps without diffuse shading, specular highlights, shadows or reflections	Color reference, can be used to make the color/texture of an object more pure and visible
Occlusion	Grayscale	Luma Inverted Matte	Shadows that result from soft illumination, simulating light from an overcast sky or well-lit room	Adds natural soft shadows to an object; these can be tinted to reflect the color of reflected light
Beauty	Color	Normal	A render of all passes	Reference: this is how the object or scene would appear if rendered in a single pass
Global Illumination	Color	Add or Screen	Indirect light added to the scene by global illumination, potentially including raytraced reflections and refractions	Control intensity of indirect lighting in scene
Matte/ Mask/Alpha	Grayscale	Luma Matte	Can be used to contain multiple transparency masks for portions of the object or scene, one each on the red, green, blue and alpha channels	
Depth/Z-depth/ Depth Map	Grayscale or non-image floating point	Luma Matte	Describes the distance of surface areas from the camera	Can be used to control depth effects such as fog and lens blur, as well as light fall-off

Other passes might include: a *Fresnel* (or *Incidence*) pass showing the sheen of indirect light and applied to an adjustment layer with a Luma Matte (raise Output Black in Levels to re-create sheen); a *Grunge* or *Dirt* map, applied as a Luma Inverted Matte, allowing you to dial in areas of wear and tear with Levels on an adjustment layer; a *Light* pass for any self-illuminated details; a *Normal* pass showing the direction of surface normals for relighting purposes. Many, many more are possible—really anything you can isolate in a 3D animation program. **Figure 12.24a** through **i** show a robot set up for multipass rendering and a few of its component render layers.

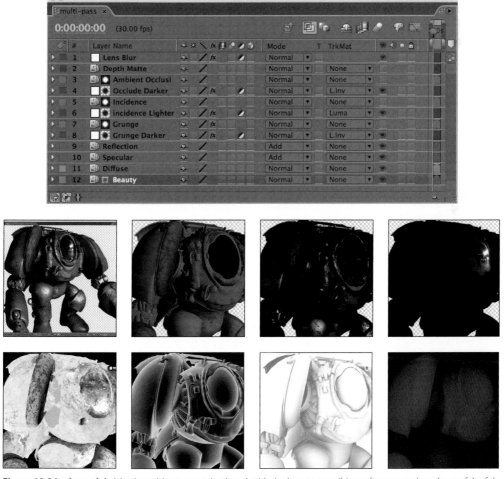

Figure 12.24a through i A basic multipass setup (a, above) with the beauty pass (b) as reference, and made up of the following color passes: diffuse (c), specular (d) and reflection (e) as well as grayscale passes applied as luma mattes to adjustment layers, each containing a Levels effect: grunge (f), incidence (g), and occlusion (h). A depth matte (i) can be applied in various ways; here it is used as reference to an adjustment layer containing a Lens Blur effect that utilizes it.

CLOSE-UP

RPF

RPF files are an Autodesk update to RLA. After Effects offers limited native support for these files (via the effects in the 3D Channel menu) but more robust support for some of the finer features of RPF such as Normal maps is only available via third-party plug-ins. Commercially available plug-ins that can translate normal maps for use in After Effects include ZBornToy (which also does amazing things with depth maps; a demo is available on this book's disc) from Frischluft and WalkerFX Channel Lighting, part of the Walker Effects collection. There is a free option for Windows only called Normality (www.minning.de/software/normality).

As mentioned in Chapter 8, After Effects can also extract camera data from RPF files (typically generated in 3DS Max or Flame); place the sequence containing the 3D camera data in a comp and choose Animation > Keyframe Assistant > RPF Camera Import.

NOTES

An EXR image can contain multiple layers, each of which can be labeled to contain specific render passes. After Effects has no ability to read these extra layers until you install the ProEXR plug-in, free from Fnordware (www.fnordware.com/ProEXR). This plug-in also allows Photoshop to read and write multilayered EXRs.

Note that none of these passes necessarily requires a transparency (alpha) channel, and at the biggest old-school effects houses it is customary not to render them, since multiple passes of edge transparency can lead to image multiplication headaches.

The general rules for multipass compositing are simple:

▶ Use the Diffuse layer as the base.

▶ Apply color layers meant to illuminate the base layer, such as specular and reflection, via Add or Screen blending modes.

▶ Apply color layers meant to darken the base layer, if any, via Multiply or Darken blending modes.

▶ Apply grayscale maps as luma mattes for adjustment layers. Apply Levels, Curves, Hue/Saturation to allow these mattes to influence the shading of the object or scene.

▶ Control the strength of any layer using that layer's Opacity.

Note that multipass renders present an excellent case to enable Blend Colors Using 1.0 Gamma in Project Settings, whether or not you assign a Working Space (and whether or not that working space is linearized).

Multipass rendering is only partially scientific and accurate; successful use of multiple passes is a highly individualized and creative sport. With the correct basic lighting setup you can use multipass renders to place a given 3D element in a variety of environments without the need for a complete re-render.

Varied environments are themselves the subject of the following chapter.

13

Climate and the Environment

Conversation about the weather is the last refuge of the unimaginative.

—Oscar Wilde

Yes, yes, let's talk about the weather.

—W. S. Gilbert, *The Pirates of Penzance*, or, *The Slave of Duty*

Climate and the Environment

Even if you're not called upon to re-create extreme climate conditions (as seems to be the case with many projects I've worked on), even a casual glance out the window demonstrates that the meteorological phenomena are always in play: a breeze blowing the trees, water and particulate in the air changing the appearance of buildings and land closest to the horizon.

This chapter offers methods to create natural elements such as particulate and wind effects, as well as to replace a sky, add mist, fog, or smoke, and various forms of precipitation. All of these are more easily captured with a camera than re-created in After Effects, but sometimes the required conditions aren't available on the day of a shoot. Mother nature is, after all, notoriously fickle, and shooting just to get a particular environment can be extraordinarily expensive.

It's rare indeed that weather conditions cooperate on location, and even rarer that a shoot can wait for perfect weather or can be set against the perfect backdrop. Transforming the appearance of a scene using natural elements is among the most satisfying things you can do as a compositor. The before and after comparison alone can be stunning, the result worthy of a blockbuster film.

Particulate Matter

Particulate matter in the air influences how objects appear at different depths. What is it? Fundamentally, it is water and other gas, dust, or visible particulate usually known as pollution. Even in an ideal, pristine, pollution-free environment there is moisture in the air—even in the driest desert, where there also might be heavier forms of particulate like dust and sand. The amount of haze in the air offers clues as to

▶ The distance to the horizon and of objects in relation to it

▶ The basic type of climate; the aridness or heaviness of the weather

▶ The time of year and the day's conditions

▶ The air's stagnancy (think Blade Runner)

▶ The sun's location (when it's not visible in shot)

The color of the particulate matter offers clues to how much pollution is present and what it is, even how it feels: dust, smog, dark smoke from a fire, and so on (**Figure 13.1**).

Figure 13.1 The same location under varied weather conditions. This type of study reveals environmental subtleties, such as how backlighting emphasizes even low levels of haze and reduces overall saturation, or how more diffuse conditions desaturate and obscure the horizon while emphasizing foreground color.

Essentially, particulate matter in the air lowers the apparent contrast of visible objects; secondarily, objects take on the color of the atmosphere around them and become slightly diffuse. This is a subtle yet omnipresent depth cue: With any particulate matter in the air at all, objects lose contrast further from camera; the apparent color can change quite a bit, and detail is softened. As a compositor, you use this to your advantage, not only to re-create reality, but to provide dramatic information.

NOTES

Particulate matter does not occur in outer space, save perhaps when the occasional cloud of interstellar dust drifts through the shot. Look at photos of the moon landscape, and you'll see that the blacks in the distance look just as dark as those in the foreground.

Match an Environment

Figure 13.2 shows how the same object at the same size can appear to be a child's toy or a large presence in the distance, with only color adjustment and composition to differentiate the two. The background has great foreground and background reference for black and white levels; although the rear plane looks icy blue against gray, it matches the look of gray objects in the distance of the image.

Figure 13.2 The difference between a toy model airplane flying close, a real airplane flying nearby, and the same plane in the distant sky, is conveyed with the use of Scale, but just as importantly, with Levels that show the influence of atmospheric haze.

The technique used here is the same as outlined in Chapter 5, "Color Correction," with the additional twist of understanding how atmospheric haze influences the color of the scene. Knowing how this works from studying a scene like this one helps you create it from scratch even without such good reference.

The plane as a foreground element seems to make life easier by containing a full range of monochrome colors. When matching a more colorful or monochrome element, you can always create a small solid and add the default Ramp effect. With such a reference element, it is simple to add the proper depth cueing with Levels, and then apply the setting to the final element (**Figure 13.3**).

Creating an Environment

Figures 13.3 Does your foreground layer lack clean black, white and gray values? Match a gradient instead, then apply the setting to the final element.

What about creating a new background from scratch, as with a matte painting or 3D rendered background? In either case there is no longer reference built into the shot, but that doesn't mean you can't still use reference if you need it; a photo containing the necessary conditions will get you started.

To re-create depth cues in a shot, you must somehow separate the shot into planes of distance. If the source imagery is computer-generated, the 3D program that created it can also generate a depth map for you to use (**Figure 13.4**). If not, you can slice the image into planes of distance, or you can make your own depth map to weight the distance of the objects in frame.

Figure 13.4 This map can be applied directly to an adjustment layer as a Luma Inverted Matte; Levels and Fast Blur effects are then used to add atmospheric haze, weighted to affect the background more than the foreground. (Image courtesy Fred Lewis/Moving Media.)

Getting reference is easy for anyone with an Internet connection these days, thanks to sites and services like flickr.com and Google image search.

There are several ways in which a depth map can be used, but the simplest is probably to apply it to an adjustment layer as a Luma (or Luma Inverted) Matte, and then add a Levels or other color correction adjustment to the adjustment layer. With the depth matte in Figure 13.4, the heaviest level adjustments for depth cueing would be applied to the furthest elements, so applying this matte as a Luma Inverted Matte and then by *flashing* the blacks (raising the Output Black level in Levels), you would instantly add the effect of atmosphere on the scene.

One good reason to use a basic 3D render of a scene as the basis for a matte painting is that the perspective and lens angle can be used not only for reference, but to generate a depth map, even if the entire scene is painted over.

Depth data may also be rendered and stored in an RPF file, as in **Figure 13.5** (which is taken from an example included on the disc as part of 13_multipass.aep). RPF files are in some ways crude, lacking even thresholding in the edges (let alone higher bit depths), but they can contain several types of 3D data, as are listed in the 3D Channel menu. This data can be used directly by a few effects to simulate 3D, including Particle Playground, which accepts RPF data as an influence map.

More extreme conditions may demand actual particles, and the phenomena that accompany them, as is explored later in this chapter.

Sky Replacement

Sky replacement is among the cheapest and easiest extensions that can be made to a shot. This opens up various possibilities to shoot faster and more cheaply. Not only do you not have to wait for ideal climate conditions, you can swap in a different sky as well as an extended physical skyline.

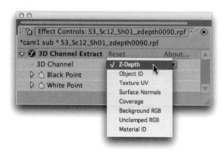

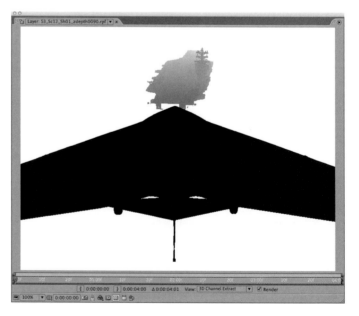

Figure 13.5 RPF images have jagged edge pixels, but a depth map does not have to be perfectly pristine. The 3D Channel Extract effect allows After Effects to work with RPF data. (Created by Fred Lewis; used with permission from Inhance Digital, Boeing, and the Navy UCAV program.)

Skies are, after all, part of the story, often a subliminal one but occasionally a starring element. An interior with a window could be anywhere, but show a recognizable skyline outside the window and locals will automatically gauge the exact neighborhood and city block of that location, along with the time of day, time of year, weather, outside temperature, and so on, possibly without ever really paying conscious attention to it.

Why spend extra production money on background conditions for a scene that could be shot cheaper elsewhere? You could spend tens (even hundreds) of thousands of dollars for that view apartment on Central Park East for a scene at golden hour (the beautiful "hour" of sunset that typically lasts about 20 minutes and is missing on an overcast day). The guerilla method would be to use your friend's apartment, light it orange, shoot all day, and add the sunset view in post. In many cases, the real story is elsewhere, and the sky is a subliminal (even if beautiful) backdrop that must serve that story (**Figures 13.6a through d**).

Figures 13.6a through d For an independent film with no budget set in San Francisco, the director had the clever idea of shooting it in a building lobby across the bay in lower-rent Oakland (a), pulling a matte from the blue sky (b), and match moving a still shot of the San Francisco skyline (from street level, c) for a result that anyone familiar with that infamous pyramid-shaped building would assume was taken in downtown San Francisco (d). (Images courtesy The Orphanage.)

The Sky Is Not (Quite) a Blue Screen

Only on the clearest, bluest days does the sky become a candidate for blue-screen keying. Look at an actual sky (there may be one nearby as you read this) or even better, study reference images, and you may notice that the blue color desaturates near the horizon, cloudless skies are not always so easy to come by, and even clear blue skies are not as saturated as they might sometimes seem.

Still, some combination of a color keyer, such as Keylight, and a hi-con luminance matte pass or a garbage matte, as needed, can remove the existing sky in your shot, leaving nice edges around the foreground. Chapter 6, "Color Keying," focuses on strategies for employing these, and Chapter 7, "Rotoscoping and Paint," describes supporting strategies when keys and garbage mattes fail.

The first step of sky replacement is to remove the existing "sky" (which may include other items at infinite distance, such as buildings and clouds) by developing a matte for it. As you do this, place the replacement sky in the background; a sky matte typically does not have to be as exacting as a blue-screen key because the replacement sky often bears a resemblance to the source (**Figure 13.7**).

Figure 13.7 A very challenging matte for several reasons, not the least of which is the uneven desaturated quality of the sky. Placing the pigeon in a radically different environment requires color and grain matching to compensate for less than stellar source.

Infinite Depth

A locked-off shot can be completed with the creation of the matte and a color match to the new sky. If, however, there is camera movement in the shot, you might assume that a 3D track is needed to properly add a new sky element.

Typically, that's overkill. Instead, consider

▶ When matching motion from the original shot, if anything in the source sky can be tracked, by all means track the source.

▶ If only your foreground can be tracked, follow the suggestions in Chapter 8, "Effective Motion Tracking," for applying a track to a 3D camera: Move the replacement sky to the distant background (via a Z Position value well into four or five digits, depending on camera settings). Scale up to compensate for the distance; this is all done by eye.

▶ A push or zoom shot (Chapter 9, "The Camera and Optics," describes the difference), may be more easily re-created using a tracked 3D camera (but look at Chapter 8 for tips on getting away with a 2D track).

The basic phenomenon to re-create is that scenery at infinite distance moves less than objects in the foreground. This is the parallax effect, which is less pronounced with a long, telephoto lens, and much more obvious with a wide angle. For the match in Figure 13.6, a still shot (no perspective) was skewed to match the correct angle and tracked in 2D; the lens angle was long enough and the shot brief enough that they got away with it. A simpler example is included on the disc in 13_skyReplace2.aep.

Fog, Smoke, and Mist

An animated layer of translucent clouds is easily enough re-created in After Effects. The basic element can be fabricated by applying the Fractal Noise effect to a solid, and then using a blending mode such as Add or Screen to layer it in with the appropriate Opacity setting. On the book's disc, 13_smokyFlyover.aep contains a simple example of layers of smoke laid out as if on a three-dimensional plane.

Fractal Noise at its default settings already looks smoky (**Figure 13.8**); switching Noise Type setting from the default, Soft Linear, to Spline, improves it. The main thing to add is motion, which I like to do with a simple expression applied to the Evolution property: time*60 (I find 60 an appropriate rate in many situations, your taste may vary). The Transform properties within Fractal Noise can be animated, causing the overall layer to move as if being blown by wind.

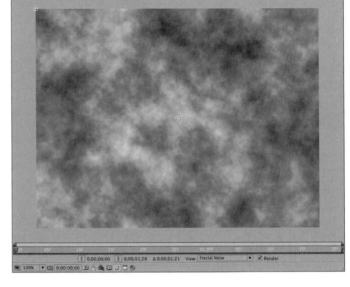

Figure 13.8 Fractal Noise (shown at the default setting, but with Noise Type set to Spline) is a decent stand-in for organic-looking fog. You can try varying the Fractal Type or Noise Type to get different looks, and you must animate the Evolution if you want any billowing of the element. Several Fractal Types are available, as seen in the pull-down menu.

NOTES

The eminently useful Fractal Noise effect, found in the Noise & Grain category, should not be confused with the far less useful (albeit pretty) Fractal effect in the Render category.

Brightness, Contrast, and Scale settings influence the apparent scale and density of the noise layer. Complexity and Sub Settings also affect apparent scale and density, but with all kinds of undesirable side effects that make the smoke look artificial. The look is greatly improved by layering at least two separate passes via a blending mode (as in the example project).

Masking and Adjusting

When covering the entire foreground evenly with smoke or mist, a more realistic look is achieved using two or three separate overlapping layers with offset positions (**Figure 13.9**). The unexpected byproduct of layering 2D particle layers in this manner is that they take on the illusion of depth and volume.

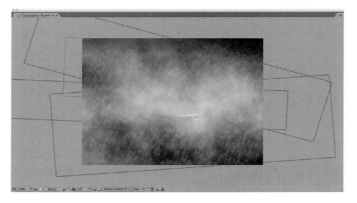

Figure 13.9 The smoke in this shot is made up of one large solid with a Fractal Noise effect that is sliced up, staggered (as seen with the layer outlines), and animated in pseudo-3D.

The eye perceives changes in parallax between the foreground and background, and automatically assumes these to be a byproduct of full three-dimensionality, yet you save the time and trouble of a 3D volumetric particle render. Of course, you're limited to instances in which particles don't interact with movement from objects in the scene; otherwise, you instantly graduate to some very tricky 3D effects.

Particle layers can be combined with the background via blending modes, or they can be applied as a Luma Matte to a colored solid (allowing you to specify the color of the particles without having a blending mode change it).

To add smoke to a generalized area of the frame, a big elliptical mask with a high feather setting (in the triple digits even for video resolution) will do the trick; if the borders of the smoke area are apparent, increase the mask feather even further (**Figure 13.10**).

NOTES

Fractal Noise texture maps can loop seamlessly (allowing reuse on shots of varying length). In Evolution Options, enable Cycle Evolution, and animate Evolution in whole revolutions (say, from $0° 2 \times 0.0°$). Set the Cycle (in Revolutions) parameter to the number of total revolutions (2). The first and last keyframes now match, and a `loopOut("cycle")` expression continues this loop infinitely.

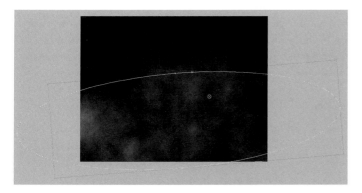

Figure 13.10 This mask of a single smoke element from the shot in Figure 13.8 has a 200-pixel feather, despite that the resolution of the shot is standard definition NTSC video (720×486). The softness of the mask helps to sell the element as smoke and works well overlaid with other, similarly feathered masked elements.

CLOSE-UP

Selling the Effect with Diffraction

There is more to adding a cloud to a realistic shot than a simple A over B comp; water elements in the air, whether in spray, mist, or clouds, not only occlude light but diffract it. This diffraction effect can be simulated by applying Compound Blur to an adjustment layer between the fog and the background and using a precomposed (or prerendered) version of the fog element as its Blur layer.

This usage of Compound Blur is is detailed further in the following chapter, where it is used to enhance the effect of smoky haze.

Moving Through the Mist

The same effect you get when you layer several instances of Fractal Noise can aid the illusion of moving forward through a misty cloud. That's done simply enough (for an example of flying through a synthetic cloud, see 13_smokyLayers. aep), but how often does your shot consist of just moving through a misty cloud? Most of the time, clouds of smoke or mist are added to an existing shot.

You can use the technique for emulating 3D tracking (see Chapter 10, "Expressions") to make the smoke hold its place in a particular area of the scene as the camera moves through (or above) it. To make this work, keep a few points in mind:

▶ Each instance of Fractal Noise should have a soft elliptical mask around it.

▶ The mask should be large enough to overlap with another masked instance, but small enough that it does not slide its position as the angle of the camera changes.

▶ A small amount of Evolution animation goes a long way, and too much will blow the gag. Let the movement of the camera create the interest of motion.

▶ Depending on the length and distance covered in the shot, be willing to create at least a half-dozen individual masked layers of Fractal Noise.

13_smokyFlyover.aep features just such an effect of moving forward through clouds. It combines the tracking of each shot carefully into place with the phenomenon of parallax, whereby overlapping layers swirl across one another in a believable manner. Mist and smoke seem to be a volume but they actually often behave more like overlapping, translucent planes—individual clouds of mist and smoke.

Billowing Smoke

Fractal Noise works fine to create and animate thin wispy smoke and mist. It will not, however, be much help if you need to fabricate thick, billowing clouds. Instead of a plug-in effect, all you need is a good still cloud element and you can animate it in After Effects. And all you need to create the element is a high-resolution reference photo—or even a bag of cotton puffs, as were used to create the images in **Figure 13.11**.

To give clouds shape and contour, open the image in Photoshop, and use the Clone Stamp tool to create a cloud with the shape you want. You can do it directly in After Effects, but this is the kind of job for which Photoshop was designed. Clone in contour layers of highlights (using Linear Dodge, Screen, or Lighten blending modes) and shadows (with Blending set to Multiply or Darken) until the cloud has the look you're after (**Figure 13.12**).

Figure 13.11 Cotton puffs can be arranged on black posterboard and photographed under daylight conditions for realistic highlights and shadows.

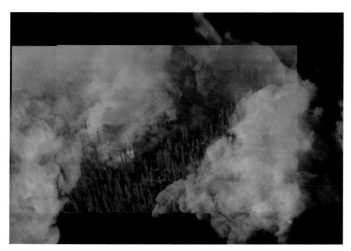

Figure 13.12 The elements from Figure 13.11 are incorporated into this matte painting, and the final shot contains a mixture of real and composited smoke.

So now you have a good-looking cloud, but it's a still. How do you put it in motion? This is where After Effects' excellent distortion tools come into play, in particular Mesh Warp and Liquify. A project containing just such a cloud animation appears on the disc as 13_smokeCloud.aep.

Mesh Warp

Mesh Warp lays a grid of Bézier handles over the frame; to animate distortion by setting a keyframe for the Distortion Mesh property at frame 0, then move the points of the grid, and realign the Bézier handles associated with each point, to bend to the vertices between points. The image to which this effect is applied follows the shape of the grid.

By default, Mesh Warp begins with a seven-by-seven grid. Before you do anything else, make sure that the size of the grid makes sense for your image; you might want to increase its size for a high-resolution project, and you can reduce the number of rows to fit the aspect ratio of your shot, for a grid of squares (**Figure 13.13**).

Figure 13.13 The Mesh Warp controls are simple, just a grid of points and vectors. You can preset the number and quality; more is not necessarily better (just more to control). Points can be multiselected and dragged, and each point contains Bézier handles for warping the adjacent vectors.

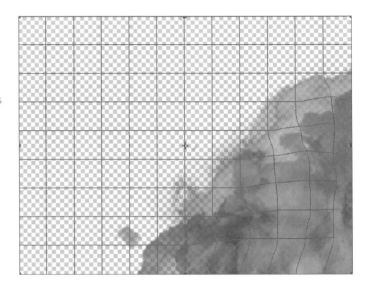

You can't typically get away with dragging a point more than about halfway toward any other point; watch carefully for artifacts of stretching and tearing as you work, and preview often. If you see stretching, realign adjacent points and handles to compensate. There is no better way to learn about this than to experiment.

I have found that the best results with Mesh Warp use minimal animation of the mesh, animating instead the element that moves underneath it.

Liquify

Mesh warp is appropriate for gross distortions of an entire element. The Liquify effect is a brush-based system for fine distortions. 13_smokeCloud.aep includes a composition that employs Liquify to swirl a cloud. Following is a brief

TIP

Mesh Warp, like many distortion tools, renders rather slowly. As you rough in the motion, feel free to work at quarter-resolution. When you've finalized your animation, you can save a lot of time by pre-rendering it (see Chapter 4, "Optimize the Pipeline").

orientation to this toolset, but as with most brush-based painterly tools, there is no substitute for trying it hands-on.

The principle behind Liquify is actually similar to that of Mesh Warp; enable View Mesh under View Options and you'll see that you're still just manipulating a grid, albeit a finer one that would be cumbersome to adjust point by point—hence the brush interface.

Of the brushes included with Liquify, the first two along the top row, Warp and Turbulence, are most often used (**Figure 13.14**). Warp has a similar effect to moving a point in Mesh Warp; it simply pushes pixels in the direction you drag the brush. Turbulence scrambles pixels in the path of the brush.

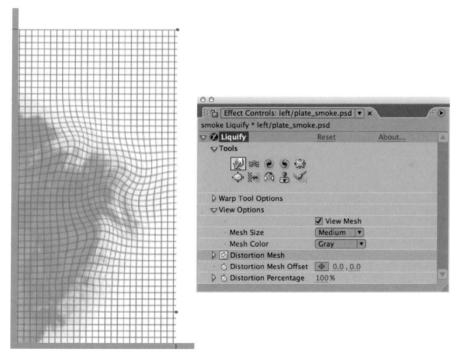

Figure 13.14 Liquify is also a mesh distortion tool, only the mesh is much finer than Mesh Warp's and it is controlled via brushes, allowing more specific distortions.

The Reconstruction brush (rightmost on the bottom row) is like a selective undo, reversing distortions at the default setting; other options for this brush are contained in the Reconstruction Mode menu (which appears only when the brush is selected).

Liquify has the advantage of allowing hold-out areas. Draw a mask around the area you want to leave untouched by Liquify brushes, but set the Mask mode to None, disabling it. Under Warp Tool Options, select the mask name in the Freeze Area Masked menu.

Liquify was a key addition to the "super cell" element (that huge swirling mass of weather) for the freezing of the New York City sequence in *The Day After Tomorrow*. Artists at The Orphanage were able to animate matte paintings of the cloud bank, broken down into over a dozen component parts to give the effect the appropriate organic complexity and dimension.

Smoke Trails and Plumes

Figure 13.15 Clearly, this effect could easily be painted with no external source whatsoever.

Many effects, including smoke trails, don't require particle generation in order to be re-created faithfully. This section is included less because the need comes up often and more to show how, with a little creativity, you can combine techniques in After Effects to create effects that you might think require a dedicated solution. Check out the reference in **Figure 13.15** and you'll notice that smoke trails are essentially just clouds.

Initial setup of such an effect is simply a matter of starting with a clean plate, painting the smoke trails in a separate still layer, and revealing them over time (presumably behind the aircraft that is creating them). The quickest and easiest way to reveal such an element over time is often by animating a mask, or you could use techniques described in Chapter 8 to apply a motion tracker to a brush.

The optional second stage of this effect would be the dissipation of the trail; depending on how much wind is present, the trail might probably drift, spread, and thin out over time. That means that in a wide shot, the back of the trail would be more dissipated than the front.

A simple method to achieve this (which could work with a distant shot, at least) would use a black-to-white gradient (created with Ramp) and Compound Blur. The gradient is white at the dissipated end of the trail and black at the source (**Figures 13.16a and b**); each point can be animated or tracked in. Compound Blur uses this gradient as its Blur Layer, creating more blur as the ramp becomes more white.

Figures 13.16a and b A gradient is created to match the start and end of the plane's trajectory, masked and precomposed (a). This is then applied via a Compound Blur to the source layer (b)—a simple example of building up your own effect with the tools at hand.

Wind

What is wind doing in this chapter? You can't see it. Nevertheless, a static environment is rarely believable if it's not the surface of the moon, and because your job is to help the viewer suspend disbelief, you may have to consider adding the influence of wind to your scene.

The fact is that most still scenes in the real world contain ambient motion of some kind. Not only objects directly in the scene, but reflected light and shadow might be changing all the time in a scene we perceive to be motionless.

As a compositor, you always look for opportunities to add to them in ways that contribute to the realism of the scene without stealing focus. Obviously, the kinds of dynamics involved with making the leaves and branches of a tree sway are mostly beyond the realm of 2D compositing, but there are often other elements that are easily articulated and animated ever so slightly. Successful examples of ambient animation should not be noticeable, and they often will not have been explicitly requested, so it's an exercise in subtlety.

Adding and Articulating Elements

To make it easier on yourself, look for elements that can be readily isolated and articulated; you should be able to mask the element out with a simple roto or a hi-con matte if it's not separated to begin with. Look for the point where the object would bend or pivot, place your anchor point there, then animate a gentle rotation. 13_ambientAnim.aep (on the disc) offers a simple animation of the arm of a street-light, held out from the background. A little warp on the clouds behind it, and this still image could convincingly be a brief moving shot (**Figure 13.17**).

Figure 13.17 The arm of the street-light is masked, its anchor point moved to the base, and a simple wiggle to the Rotation gives it ambient motion as would be caused by wind.

CLOSE-UP

Primary and Secondary

Primary animation is the gross movement of the object, the movement of the object as a whole. *Secondary animation* is the movement of individual parts of the object as a result of inertia. So, for example, a helicopter crashes to the ground: That's the primary animation. Its rotors and tail bend and shudder at impact: That's the secondary animation. For the most part, in 2D compositing, your work is isolated to primary animation.

You also have the option of acquiring and adding elements that indicate or add to the effect of wind motion. **Figure 13.18** is an element of blowing autumn leaves shot against a black background for easy removal and matting; granted, you could add an element this turbulent only to a scene that either already had signs of gusts in it or that contained only elements that would show no secondary motion from wind whatsoever.

Precipitation

You've already examined the effect of water in its gaseous form (as fog, mist, or steam); what about water in its liquid and solid states? It's rare to create elaborate water effects without relying on some even more elaborate practical or

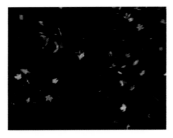

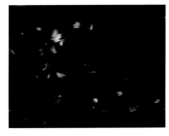

Figure 13.18 It would be very difficult to create the impression of a windstorm in a shot from scratch, but if the shot is taken in windy conditions (or using large fans on set) an element like this will enhance the impression of a blustery day. (Footage courtesy Artbeats.)

computer-generated source. I'll assume that you're trying to complete shots only in After Effects, but these techniques are equally valid even to enhance particle and water animations from a 3D animations system.

One area where After Effects' built-in features fall short is particle generation. The Particle Playground effect, which ships with the program and hasn't changed much since around version 3.0, is slow, crude, and cumbersome. I have yet to work with anyone who had the patience to coax realistic effects out of this plug-in.

If you're called upon to create rainfall or snowfall from scratch, consider the Particular plug-in from Trapcode (a demo is included on the book's disc). Not only does it outdo Particle Playground in features and ease of use, but also, if set up correctly, it allows you to refine the look interactively, instead of iteratively. There's no need to keep re-rendering.

Create Precipitation

Particular contains all the controls needed to create a great precipitation element, but it also contains a lot of controls, period. Here is a brief attempt to outline a few of the most significant ones, followed by an example of how to use a final element.

A standard particle shape can be used, or customized particles, such as an irregular snowflake shape. There are several choices of particle emitters, but one great option is to use a spotlight, making the light layer's Transform controls available to establish the position and direction of the particles in 3D space (**Figure 13.19**).

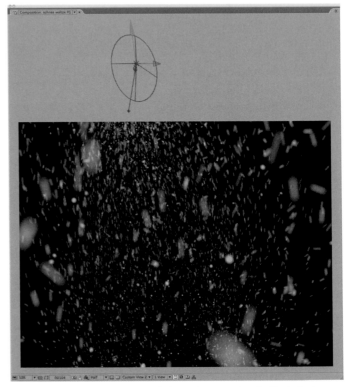

Figure 13.19 The axes belong to a light used as an emitter for Particular. It can be freely translated in 3D space.

The most important settings for precipitation are found in the Emitter and Physics categories. Emitter settings establish the amount, velocity, and direction of particles, while Physics contains controls pertaining to the environment itself: gravity, air resistance, wind, turbulence, and spin.

The Visibility category contains controls affecting the depth of your particles. You may find that, as with smoke earlier in the chapter, several planes will offer a better result than one big simulation, allowing you to control, say, the foreground separate from everything else. Particular resides on a 2D layer, but the effect is 3D-aware, so if you add a camera to the composition, the particles will behave as if seen through that camera.

Composite Precipitation

When it comes time to integrate falling rain or snow with a background plate, you can do better than a simple A over B comp; in fact, the key is to show the effect of these elements on the scene rather than showing the elements themselves.

Raindrops and snowflakes are translucent, their appearance heavily influenced by the environment. More than that, these individual bits of precipitation behave like tiny lenses that diffract light, defocusing and lowering the contrast of whatever is behind them, but also picking up the ambient light themselves. Therefore, on *The Day After Tomorrow* our crew found success with using the rain or snow element as a track matte for an adjustment layer containing a Fast Blur and a Levels effect.

To allow you to sample the results of a Particular render, included on the DVD are a foreground and background snow animation, which have been applied as follows in 13_snowfall.aep.

Blurriness is set very high (200), so that the area behind each individual raindrop or snowflake becomes a wash of color. Levels is applied with a slightly lowered (90%) Output White value, and a very high (80%) Output Black value. The precipitation is visible by its effect on the scene, lightening dark areas, darkening light ones, and adding diffusion throughout (**Figure 13.20**).

Figure 13.20 You must look closely to see the added snowfall in a still image with so many bright regions; to see it applied in motion via adjustment layers, open 13_snowfall.aep. (Source image courtesy Eric E. Yang via Creative Commons.)

Water Surface Reflection

The presence of water (outside of the shot area) is implied by the presence of its reflected light in the scene. Light from water has a compelling shape and movement, and if you've set up the scene so that the viewer knows there's a swimming pool or a lake nearby, it may even be expected.

The question is how to get the sample of the play of light, reflected off of the waves. With patient adjustments, you can use Wave World, an effect included when you register your copy of After Effects. The default settings won't do. For one thing, View must be changed to Height Map just to preview the effect, and Grid Resolution must be raised (it's set for a feeble 1990s-era computer) along with optional Pre-roll settings. Reflect Edges can be set to All. Then the trick is to set Position and Amplitude for a natural look. The compositing technique is similar to what is done with shadows (Chapter 12): Position the plane and choose a blending mode, such as Add or Vivid Light, or apply it as a Luma Matte to an adjustment layer containing Levels.

The best thing about this approach is that it works independently of the background appearance. There is no need to decide the color of the element for a given shot, and shots retain source colors, the precipitation having a similar influence on each shot in a sequence.

Conclusion

To fully mess with climatic effects may require elaborate 3D simulations, but even then, the compositing approach remains much the same. The chapter's focus has been on how elements behave in the real world, and how best to emulate that reality in After Effects. This approach should serve you well even if an element is needed—frost, say, or hail—that was not covered directly here.

The next chapter heats things up with fire, explosions, and other combustibles.

14

Pyrotechnics:
Heat, Fire, Explosions

My nature is to be on set, blowing things up.
> —Ken Ralston (winner of five Academy
> Awards for visual effects)

Pyrotechnics:
Heat, Fire, Explosions

A significant number of people first became interested in visual effects work simply because they are borderline pyromaniacs or gun nuts. You have to follow your passion in life, after all. Creating conflagration on the computer doesn't qualify for the same type of fun as blowing stuff up, but keeping these people busy either way may be better than letting them loose on society at large.

These effects have traditionally been created live on set or via practical elements such as miniatures. The craft of the on-set pyrotechnician is not obsolete by any means, but these days there are many, many cases (particularly the smaller, more common ones) in which compositing can save a lot of time and expense at the shoot, no matter the budget of the production. Blowing stuff up on set is fun, but it involves extensive setup and a not insubstantial amount of danger to the cast and crew. Second chances don't come cheap.

On the other hand, there's often no substitute for the physics of live-action mayhem. I hope it doesn't come as a disappointment to learn that not everything pyrotechnical can be accomplished start to finish in After Effects. Some effects require actual footage of physical or fabricated elements being shot at or blown up, and good reference of such events is immensely beneficial. The truth is that practical elements often rely on After Effects to look good, but the opposite, that you rely on those elements to succeed in After Effects, is equally true if not more so.

Firearms

Blanks are dangerous, and real guns deadly. To create a shot with realistic gunfire safely requires

▶ A realistic-looking gun prop in the scene

▶ Some method to mime or generate firing action on set

▶ The addition of a muzzle flash, smoke, cartridge, or shell discharge (where appropriate)

▶ The matching shot showing the result of gunfire: debris, bullet hits, even blood

After Effects can help with all of these to some extent, and some of them completely, relieving you of the need for more expensive or dangerous alternatives.

The Shoot

For the purposes of this discussion it is assumed that you begin with a plate shot of an actor re-creating the action of firing a gun, and that the gun that was used on set produces nothing: no muzzle flash, no smoke, no shell. All that's required is some miming by the actor of the recoil, or kick, which is relatively minor with small handguns, and a much bigger deal with a shotgun or fully automatic weapon.

Happily, there's no shortage of reference, as nowhere is the Second Amendment more cherished than in movies and television. Granted, most such reference is itself staged, but remember, we're going for cinematic reality here, so if it looks right to you, use it as reference.

Figure 14.1 shows something like the minimum amount that needs to be composited to create a realistic shot of a gun being fired (albeit artfully executed in this case). Depending on the gun, smoke or a spent cartridge might also be discharged. As important as the look of the frame is the timing; check your favorite reference carefully and you'll find that not much, and certainly not the flash, lingers longer than a single frame.

The actual travel of the bullet out of the barrel is not generally anything to worry about; at roughly one kilometer per second, it moves too fast to see amid all the other effects, particularly the blinding muzzle flash.

NOTES

In the period since the most recent edition of this book, the definitive text on this topic has appeared. *The DV Rebel's Guide* has been mentioned a couple of times already in this book, but its author's status in the After Effects community combined with the bullet-hole-riddled cover should be a clue that this is prime territory for Stu. Included on that book's disc are a couple of nifty After Effects tools, to create muzzle flashes and eject shells, as well as double the amount of already generous text on the subject found inside that cover.

Figure 14.1 At minimum, the firing of a gun should cause a single frame of muzzle flash and the brightening of nearby elements (including the figure holding the gun. (Image courtesy Mars Productions.)

Muzzle Flash and Smoke

The clearest indication that a gun has gone off is the flash of light around the muzzle, at the end of the barrel. This small, bright explosion of gunpowder actually lasts about $^1/_{48}$ second, short enough that when shot live it can fall between frames of film (in which case you might need to restore it in order for the action of the scene to be clear).

A flash can be painted by hand, cloned in from a practical image, or composited from stock reference. It's not too significant how you generate it, although muzzle flashes have in common with lens flares that they are specific to the device that created them. Someone in your audience is bound to know something about how the muzzle flash of your gun might look, so get reference: certain guns emit a characteristic shape such as a teardrop, cross or star (**Figure 14.2**).

Figure 14.2 The angle of the shot and the type of gun affect the muzzle flash effect. The first image is from an M16 rifle; the other is from a handgun. (Images courtesy Artbeats.)

Typically, an explosion travels in two directions from the end of the barrel: arrayed outward from the firing point and in a straight line out from the barrel. If you don't have source that makes this shape at the correct angle, it is simplest to paint it.

The key to a good muzzle flash, and to heat and light effects throughout this chapter, is to create thresholds in the matte that feel organically real. That sounds a little bit flaky, but look at all of the explosive images in this chapter; if each was instead a solid white blob with no darker thresholds, they wouldn't look hot at all. The greater the perception of shadow, the more powerful the impression of light. Very Zen.

Some guns, like rifles, may cause quite a bit of smoke, but many emit little or none at all. Obviously you're better off avoiding a situation where you need to create a lot of smoke that has to interact with agitated gunplay; a little Fractal Noise smoke at a low opacity as was introduced in the previous chapter is much simpler to create than a big gray cloud in the streaming sunlight.

Shells and Interactive Light

If the gun in your scene calls for it, that extra little bit of realism can be added with a secondary animation of a shell popping off the top of a semi-automatic. **Figure 14.3** shows how such an element looks being emitted from a real gun and shot with a high-speed shutter.

It's definitely cool to have a detailed-looking shell pop off of the gun, although the truth is that with a lower camera shutter speed, the element will become an unrecognizable blur anyhow, in which case all you need is a four-point mask of a white or brass colored solid. With animation and motion blur, the element only appears as a nearly subliminal element for two or three frames.

The bright flash of the muzzle may also cause a brief reflected flash on objects near the gun as well as the subject firing it. Chapter 12, "Light," offers the basic methodology: Softly mask a highlight area, or matte the element with its own highlights, then flash it using an adjustment layer containing a Levels effect or a colored solid with a suitable blending mode.

As a general rule, the lower the ambient light and the larger the weapon, the greater the likelihood of interactive lighting. A literal "shot in the dark" would fully illuminate the face of whomever (or whatever) fired it, just for a single frame. It's a great dramatic effect, but one that is very difficult to re-create in post. This is a rare case where firing blanks on set might be called for, unless you can fake it by dropping in a single-frame still of a bright flash on the shooter.

By contrast, or rather by reduced contrast, a daylit scene will heavily dampen the level of interactivity of the light. Instead of a white hot flash, you might more accurately have saturation of orange and yellow in the full muzzle flash element, and the interactive lighting might be minimal. This is where understanding your camera and recording medium can help you gauge the effect of a small aperture hit by a lot of light.

Hits and Squibs

Bullets that ricochet on set are known as squib hits because they typically make use of squibs, small explosives with the approximate power of a firecracker that go off during the take. Sometimes squibs are actual firecrackers.

Figure 14.3 A shell pops off of the fired handgun. It's discernable because it was shot with a very high shutter speed, but even so, it doesn't stay in frame very long, and it doesn't take much to re-create this element (or check Stu Maschwitz's *The DV Rebel's Guide* for a very cool Particle Playground-based setup to create them automatically). (Images courtesy Artbeats.)

Figure 14.4 This sequence of frames shows a second bullet hitting the cab of the truck, using two elements: the painted bullet hit and the spark element, whose source was shot on black and added via Screen mode. (Images courtesy markandmatty.com.)

It is possible to add bullet hits without using explosives on set, but frenetic gunplay will typically demand a mixture of on-set action and post-production enhancement.

Figure 14.4 shows a before-and-after addition of a bullet hit purely in After Effects. Here the bullet does not ricochet but is embedded directly into the solid metal of the truck. In such a case, all you need to do is to add the results of the damage on a separate layer at the frame where the bullet hits; you can paint this (it's a few sparks). The element can then be motion tracked to marry it solidly to the background.

At the frame of impact, and continuing a frame or two thereafter, a shooting spark and possibly a bit of smoke (if the target is combustible—not in the case of a steel vehicle) will convey the full violence of the bullets. As with the muzzle flash, this can vary from a single frame to a more fireworks-like shower of sparks tracked in over a few frames (**Figure 14.5**).

A bullet hit explosion can be created via a little miniature effects shoot, using a fire-retardant black background (a flat, black card might do it) and some firecrackers (assuming you can get them). The resulting flash, sparks, and smoke stand out against the black, allowing the element to be composited via a blending mode (such as Add or Screen), a hi-con matte (Chapter 6, "Color Keying"), or a plug-in such as Knoll UnMult. If dangerous explosives aren't your thing, even in a controlled situation, stock

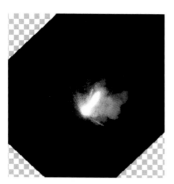
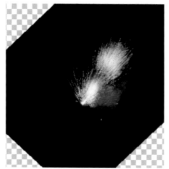

Figure 14.5 A source spark element using Add or Screen blending mode to drop out all of the black background. (Images courtesy markandmatty.com.)

footage is available. However, if debris is also part of the shot, the more that can be done practically on set, the better (**Figure 14.6**).

So to recap, a good bullet hit should include

- Smoke or sparks at the frame of impact, typically lasting between one and five frames

- The physical result of the bullet damage (if any) painted and tracked into the scene

- Debris in cases where the target is shatter-able or scatter-able

Later in this chapter, you'll see how larger explosions have much in common with bullet hits, which are essentially just miniature explosions. In both cases, a bit of practical debris can be crucial to sell the shot.

Energy Effects

Other types of blasts can of course occur in a scene. Before we move on to full explosions and fire, let's shift into the pure energy of lightning and the realm it opens up: science fiction weapons, those that appear to involve no physical matter at all.

You would think that because blasters and lightsabers and so on are more or less completely made up, they are as arbitrary a subject as, say, hamster fur simulations. However, these types of effects seem to resound deeply, and they are only one degree removed from our reality and from their real-world counterparts. There's not a huge difference between re-creating a lightning strike or compositing a lightsaber, and the more that a made-up effect is rooted in something we recognize, the better chance it has of working as an effect while seeming original and otherworldly.

The key seems to be that we know what pure photon-driven energy looks like, and so even if your shot doesn't involve a high-powered laser or a high-voltage electrical arc, those may make excellent reference as you go about creating it. Once again, the basic look is often a hot white (or bright) core surrounded by a luminescent glow or even a bit of distortion.

Figure 14.6 This debris, caused by a BB gun aimed at various breakaway objects and other debris hurled on set, would be somewhere between painful and impossible to create purely in post. (Images courtesy The Orphanage.)

Disclaimer: Although the author of this book and the guy who shot the footage used in this section are both ex-Lucas employees who worked on *Star Wars* movies (in Matt's case) and related projects (in Mark's case), this bears no relationship to the "official" method for creating a lightsaber at ILM, which will never be publicly divulged by any soul, living or otherwise.

Core and Decay

A couple of effects in the Render category of the Effects menu automatically create an element with a core and a surrounding glow. For your basic blaster or lightsaber effect, you might be tempted to reach for Beam. True, a canned effect such as this surrenders artistic control for convenience, but it lays the groundwork necessary for what this section is all about by providing an element with built-in thresholding. Not only that, but in CS3 it's now a 32 bpc effect, so the setup steps are simple.

1. Apply the Beam effect to a solid layer above the plate layer. Beam can be applied directly to the plate by checking Composite on Original, but working with the element in HDR requires that it be a separate layer.

2. Extend the length to 100% and match the Starting and Ending points to the ends of the stick.

3. Add some Thickness: 24 for Starting and 30 for Ending (the non-uniform settings lend an artificial impression of three-dimensionality with 3D Perspective checked on, as it is by default).

4. The basic element is there but it's not looking too cool. Switch the Project to 32 bpc mode and toggle Blend Colors Using 1.0 Gamma on. Because Beam is now 32 bpc you need only boost the Inside and Outside Color settings into overbright range.

5. Make sure you are using the Adobe color picker (Use System Color Picker is unchecked in Preferences > General) and click the color swatch for Inside Color. Click the R value and type *4 after the value (although the math is simple in this case), then do the same for G and B values; it's the same tone but 4 times brighter. Do the same for the Outside Color.

6. Finesse the look by manipulating the Softness and Outside Color settings in Beam and Gamma in Levels (**Figure 14.7**).

Figure 14.7 If you remain unconvinced about the power of 32 bit per channel HDR, check out how good this effect looks even though it's based on a simple (cheesy, really) Beam effect, its source colors boosted into overbright range. (Source footage courtesy markandmatty.com.)

What happens next is what gives it the cool factor, and just offhand there are several available options:

▶ Animate the saber being waved around and enable motion blur.

▶ For other types of shots: add interactive lighting where needed, such as the glow on nearby faces and passing objects.

▶ Add bullet hits, either like those discussed earlier or your own special version of energy coursing through the target.

▶ Create a unique effect, without Beam, using the basic formula: a bright (or white) core layer and a darker-colored, blurred duplicate (or several), comped together using the Add blending mode and boosted with Levels or Exposure to glow.

▶ Add distortion around the edges using techniques shown in the following section.

The same principles apply to other related effects such as lightning. After Effects includes an Advanced Lightning effect capable of generating a nice organic element, but really selling the effect has to do with adjusting the core, decay and blend to create a powerful look. Reference images are readily available and highly useful in this case (**Figure 14.8**).

TIP

With Length in Beam set to less than 100%, you can animate the beam traveling between the Starting and Ending Points using the Time setting: this is designed as a quick way to animate a blaster shot, or power-up of the saber in this case.

Figure 14.8 Actual reference images containing energy effects with realistic thresholding and interaction with the surrounding environment help you re-create the same look with seemingly ordinary After Effects effects. (Image courtesy of Kevin Miller via Creative Commons license.)

This effect is best for creating actual lightning; it's called "advanced" mostly because it doesn't automatically animate (you need to add keyframes for that). The Lightning effect doesn't create such a nice-looking initial element but it's a lot like a more organic version of Beam, with specific Start and End points and properties that can be adjusted and blended for a more subtle overall look.

Heat Distortion

Heat distortion, that strange rippling in the air that occurs when hot air is dissipated into cooler air, is another one of those effects compositors love. Like a lens flare, it's a highly visible effect that, if properly motivated and adjusted, adds instant realism.

Figures **14.9a** and **b** show the fabricated results of heat distortion in a close-up of a scene that will also incorporate fire. When your eye sees heat distortion, it understands that the environment is dynamic, even if your brain has no idea what causes the phenomenon.

What Is Actually Happening

Figures 14.9a and b Heat haze by itself can look a little odd (a) but it adds significantly to the realism of a scene containing a prominent heat source (b).

Stare into a swimming pool, and you can see displacement caused by the bending of light as it travels through the water. Rippled waves in the water cause rippled bending of light. There are cases in which our atmosphere behaves like this as well, when ripples are caused in it by the collision of warmer and cooler air, a medium that is not quite as transparent as it seems.

As you know from basic physics, hot air rises and hot particles move faster than cool ones. Air is not a perfectly clear medium but a translucent gas that can act as a lens. This "lens" is typically static and appears flat, but the application of heat causes an abrupt mixture of fast-moving hot air particles rising into cooler ambient air. This creates ripples that have the effect of displacing and distorting what is behind the moving air, just like ripples in the pool or ripples in the windows of an old house.

Because this behavior resembles a lens effect, and because the role of air isn't typically taken into account in a 3D render, it can be adequately modeled as a distortion overlaid on whatever sits behind the area of hot air.

How to Re-create It

The basic steps for re-creating heat distortion from an invisible source in After Effects are

1. Create a basic particle animation that simulates the movement and dissipation of hot air particles in the scene.

2. Make two similar but unique passes of this particle animation—one to displace the background vertically, the other to displace it horizontally—and precompose them.

3. Add an adjustment layer containing the Displacement Map effect, which should be set to use the particle animation comp to create the distortion effect, and apply it to the background.

    Particle Playground is practically ideal for this purpose because its default settings come close to generating exactly what you need, with the following minor adjustments:

    ▶ Under Cannon, move Position to the source in the frame where the heat haze originates (in this case, the bottom center as the entire layer will be repositioned and reused).

    ▶ Open up Barrel Radius from the default of 0.0 to the width, in pixels, of the source. Higher numbers lead to slower renders.

    ▶ Boost Particles Per Second to something like 200. The larger the Barrel Radius, the more particles needed.

    ▶ Under Gravity, set Force to 0.0 to prevent the default fountain effect.

    The default color and scale of the particles is fine for this video resolution example, but you might have to adjust them as well according to your shot. A larger format (in pixels) or a bigger heat source might require bigger, softer particles.

NOTES

It can be useful to generate the particles for the displacement map itself in 3D animation software, when the distortion needs to be attached to a 3D animated object, such as a jet engine or rocket exhaust. The distortion is still best created in After Effects using that map.

Figure 14.10 This displacement layer, matted against gray merely for clarity, was created with the included steps and used with the Displacement Map effect to create the effect shown in Figure 14.9.

TIP

Heat displacement often dissipates before it reaches the top of the frame. Making particles behave so that their lifespan ends before they reach the top of the frame is accurate, but painstaking. A simpler solution is to add a solid with a black-to-white gradient (created with the Ramp effect) as a luma matte to hold out the adjustment layer containing the displacement effect.

4. Now duplicate the particles layer and set the color of the duplicated layer to pure green. As you'll see below, the Displacement Map effect by default uses the red and green channels for horizontal and vertical displacement. The idea is to vary it so that the particles don't overlap by changing Direction Random Spread and Velocity Random Spread from their defaults.

5. The heat animation is almost complete; it only needs some softening. Add a moderate Fast Blur (**Figure 14.10**).

Now to put the animation to use: Drag it into the main comp, and turn off its visibility. The actual Displacement Map effect is applied either directly to the background plate or preferably to an adjustment layer sitting above all the layers that should be affected by the heat haze. Displacement Map is set by default to use the red channel for horizontal displacement and the green channel for vertical displacement; all you need to do is select the layer containing the red and green particles under the Displacement Map Layer pulldown.

Fire

Within After Effects, fire synthesis (from scratch) is way too hot to handle. If fire is at all prominent in a shot, it will require elements that come from somewhere else—most likely, shot with a camera.

Creating and Using Fire Elements

Figure 14.11 shows effects plates of fire elements. The big challenge when compositing fire is that it doesn't scale very realistically—a fireplace fire will look like it belongs in the hearth, no matter how you may attempt to scale or retime it.

Figure 14.11 Fire elements are typically shot in negative (black) space, or occasionally in a natural setting requiring more careful matting. By adjusting Input Black in Levels, you can control the amount of glow coming off the fire as it is blended via Add mode, lending the scene interactive lighting for free. (Images courtesy Artbeats.)

Fire elements are ideally shot in negative space—against a black background, or at least, at night—so that they can be composited with blending modes and a minimum of roto-scoping. Fire illuminates its surroundings—just something to keep in mind.

This, then, is a case where it can be worth investing in proper elements shot by trained pyrotechnicians (unless that sounds like no fun, but there's more involved with a good fire shoot than a camera rental and a blow torch). In many cases, stock footage companies, such as Artbeats (examples on the book's disc), anticipate your needs. The scale and intensity may be more correct than what you can easily shoot on your own unless you're pals with Mark Pauline.

All Fired Up

Blending modes and linear blending, not mattes, are the key to good looking fire composites. Given a fire element shot against black (for example, the Artbeats_RF001H_fireExcerpt.mov included on the disc and used for the depicted example), the common newbie mistake is to try to key out the black with an Extract effect, which will lead to a fight between black edges and thin fire.

A first step is to simply lay the fire layer over the background and apply Add mode. To firm up a fire (or flare, or other bright) element you can

▶ Ascertain that Blend Colors Using 1.0 Gamma is enabled in Project Settings.

▶ Apply the Knoll Unmult (this free plug-in, included on your disc makes all black areas of the image transparent).

▶ Fine-tune the result with a Levels effect, pushing in on Input White and Black (as well as color matching overall).

▶ Add an Exposure effect (with a boosted Exposure setting) to create a raging inferno.

▶ Add interactive lighting for low-lit scenes (next section).

▶ Create displacement above the open flames (as detailed in the previous section).

▶ Add an adjustment layer over the background with a Compound Blur effect, using transparency of the fire and smoke as a blur layer (**Figure 14.12**).

Figure 14.12 A subtle Compound Blur based on flame and smoke in the foreground better integrates those elements with the background.

NOTES

Compound Blur simply varies the amount of blur according to the brightness of a given pixel in the Blur Layer, up to a given maximum. It's the right thing to use not only for fire and smoke but for fog and mist; heavy particulate in the air acts like little tiny defocused lenses, causing this effect in nature.

Where there's fire there is, of course, smoke, which can at a modest level be created with a Fractal Noise effect as described in the previous chapter, bringing this shot home (**Figure 14.13**).

Figure 14.13 Finally the furniture has a motivation to jump out the window. This shot incorporates all of the techniques described in this and the previous section.

Figure 14.14 Input White and Black on the RGB and Red channels of the Levels effect allow you to accentuate or eliminate glow around the element. The better the dynamic range of the source image, the harder you can push this, so higher bit depth source can be invaluable in this case.

Light Interacts

Provided that your camera does not rotate too much, a 2D fire layer should read as sufficiently three dimensional. The key to making it interact dimensionally with a scene, particularly a relatively dark one, is often interactive light. As was stated above, fire tends to illuminate everything around it with a warm, flickering glow.

As shown in **Figure 14.14**, a fire element may include a certain amount of usable glow. Input White and Input Black in Levels control the extent to which glow is enhanced or suppressed, respectively; you can use these controls to dial it in and out.

Note, however, that this glow isn't anything particularly unique or special; you can re-create it either via a heavily blurred duplicate of the source fire or using a masked and heavily feathered orange solid, with perhaps a slight amount of wiggle added to the glow opacity to cause a bit of interactive flickering.

Dimensionality

You can pull off the illusion of fully three-dimensional fire, especially if the camera is moving around in 3D space,

Figures 14.15a, b, and c Before-and-after sequential stills of a flyover shot. Because of the angle of the aerial camera, the shot required 3D motion tracking, in this case with 2D3's Boujou. (Images courtesy ABC-TV.)

directly in After Effects. I was frankly surprised at how well this worked back when I created the shot featured in **Figures 14.15a, b**, and **c**.

As shown, the background plate is an aerial flyby of a forest. Because of the change in altitude and perspective, this shot clearly required 3D tracking (touched upon at the end of Chapter 8, "Effective Motion Tracking"). The keys to making this shot look fully dimensional were to break up the source fire elements into discrete chunks and to stagger those in 3D space so that as the plane rose above them, their relationship and parallax changed (**Figure 14.16**).

TIP

For a shot featuring a character or object that reflects firelight, there's no need to go crazy projecting fire onto the subject. In many cases, it is enough to create some flickering in the character's own luminance values, for example by wiggling the Input White value at a low frequency in Levels (Individual Controls).

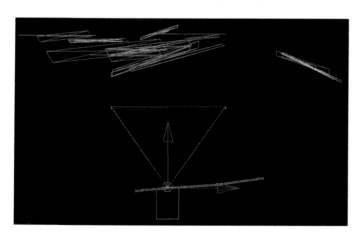

Figure 14.16 A top view of the 3D motion-tracked camera from Figure 14.15 panning past one set of fires (of which the final composition had half a dozen). The pink layers contain fire elements, the gray layers smoke.

It is easy to get away with any individual fire element being 2D in this case. Because fire changes its shape constantly, there is nothing to give away its two dimensionality. Borders of individual fire elements can freely overlap without being distracting, so it doesn't look cut out. The eye sees evidence of parallax between a couple dozen fire elements, and does not think to question that any individual one of them looks too flat. The smoke elements were handled in a similar way, organized along overlapping planes. As mentioned in the previous chapter, smoke's translucency aids the illusion that overlapping smoke layers have dimensional depth.

Explosions

The example forest fire shot also contains a large explosion in a clearing. There is not a huge fundamental difference between how you composite an explosion and how you composite fire, except that an explosion is far more likely to require a mixture of strategies. It is largely a question of what is exploding.

All explosions are caused by rapidly expanding combustible gases; implosions are caused by rapid contraction. Just by looking at an explosion, viewers can gauge its size and get an idea of what blew up, however, so you need to design the right explosion for your situation, or your result will be too cheesy even for 1980s television sci-fi. How do you do it?

Light and Chunky

Each explosion you will see is a little bit unique, but to narrow the discussion I'll organize all explosions into two basic categories. The easier one to deal with is the gaseous explosion, one made up only of gas and heat. These behave just like fire; in fact, in the shot in **Figure 14.17** the explosion is fire, a huge ball of it where something very combustible evidently went up very quickly. Maybe someone left a propane tank in the forest.

Some shots end up looking fake by using a gaseous explosion when some chunks of debris are needed. This is a prime reason that exploding miniatures are still in use, shot at high speed (or even, when possible, full-scale explosions, which can be shot at standard speed). The slower moving and bigger the amount of debris, the bigger the apparent explosion.

If your shot calls for a chunky explosion and the source lacks them, you need an alternate source. Many 3D programs these days include effective dynamics simulations; if you go that route, be sure to generate a depth map as well because each chunk will be revealed only as it emerges from the fireball. Many other concerns associated with this are beyond the scope of this discussion because they must be solved in other software.

One effect that seems to come close in After Effects is Shatter, but it's hard to recommend this unless it is specifically a pane of glass or other plane that breaks. Shatter isn't horrendous for a decade-old dynamics simulator, but its primary limitation is a huge one: It can only employ extruded flat polygons to model the chunks. A pane of glass is one of the few physical objects that would shatter into irregular but flat polygons, and Shatter contains built-in controls for specifying the size of the shards in the point of impact. Shatter was also developed prior to the introduction of 3D in After Effects; you can place your imaginary window in perspective space, but not using a camera or 3D controls.

A wide selection of pyrotechnic explosions is also available as stock footage from such companies as Artbeats. In many cases, there is no substitute for footage of a real, physical object being blown to bits (Figure 14.17).

Figure 14.17 Pyrotechnics footage is just the thing when you need a big explosion, filled with debris. (Images courtesy Artbeats.)

In a Blaze of Glory

With good reference and a willingness to take the extra step to marry your shot and effect together, you can create believable footage that would require danger or destruction if taken with a camera. Even in cases when you work on a project that had the budget to actually re-create some of the mayhem described in this chapter, you can almost always use After Effects to enhance and build upon what the camera captured. Boom.

May as well go out with a bang, after all.

Index

What's on the DVD?

Books are great for in-depth learning, but it's always good to investigate hands-on examples as well. Although this book is designed not to rely on tutorials, many of the techniques described in the text can be further explored via the dozens of projects and accompanying footage and stills included on the disc. Wherever possible, HD (1920×1080) clips from Pixel Corps, Artbeats, and fxphd are incorporated; other examples use NTSC footage and stills if that is all that's required to get the point across.

Additionally, the DVD includes demos of more than a dozen plug-ins and applications. These demos are similar to the real software for everything but output, allowing you to experiment with your own footage.

- **Duplink** and **Merge Projects** (*redefinery*): Two scripts have been created specifically for this book, available only via this disc. **Duplink** allows you to create "instance" objects of existing ones, which are linked to the source so that anything you change in it, changes in them. **Merge Projects** is for After Effects users who like to use a specific and consistent directory structure in projects; it automatically places content found in nested folders in an imported project window into folders with the same names in the master project. More information on these is included as comments in the scripts themselves (which can be opened with any text editor).

- **SynthEyes** (*Andersson Technologies*): Provides fully automatic, as well as user-controlled matchmoving for single or batchprocessed shots; a stand-alone program that exports to After Effects.

- **ZbornToy** (*Frischluft*): Enhances what you can do with RPF format files in After Effects, including relighting a 3D render that includes a normals map in After Effects.

- **Particular** (*Trapcode*): Designs 3D particle systems that simulate air resistance, gravity, and turbulence; provides real-time preview, as well as controls so you can freeze time and manipulate a camera in the scene.

- **Knoll Light Factory 2.5** (*Red Giant Software*): Includes such pre-built lighting effects as lens flares, sparkles, glows, and more; also provides individual lens components so you can create your own custom effects.

- **Primatte Keyer** (*Red Giant Software*): An alternative to Keylight. Extracts keys from any background and includes controls to handle uneven lighting, difficult shadows, light spill, and more.

- **Colorista** (*Red Giant Software*): Adds 3-way Lift/Gamma/Gain color control to After Effects, allowing you to individually style the colors of shadows, mid-tones and highlights.

- **3D Stroke** (*Trapcode*): Allows you not only to add a visible stroke to a layer's mask, but to manipulate, offset, distort and repeat that stroke shape in true 3D spaces.

- **Lux** (*Trapcode*): Simulates light reflection, using After Effects' built-in lights to create visible light that corresponds to your layers' lighting schemes.

- **Shine** (*Trapcode*): Produces a 2D light-ray effect that closely resembles volumetric light; includes controls for coloring and shimmering lights.

- **Key Correct** (*Red Giant Software*): Optimizes composites and automates color correction, blurring or feathering of edges, artifact removal, and more.

- **Magic Bullet Suite** (*Red Giant Software*): Manipulates digital video to look like film with tools for 24 p conversion, mimicking film artifacts and damage, creating film-like cross dissolves, removing DVD compression artifacts, and more.

- **Instant HD** (*Red Giant Software*): Provides higher-quality up-conversion of footage than is possible natively in After Effects.

- **Film Fix** (*Red Giant Software*): Full-featured restoration software; restores tears, removes dust and dirt, stabilizes footage transferred from film.

…art Motion Blur (*RE: Vision Effects*): Procedurally …eratesmotion blur for moving elements in a shot which …ack it (or lack enough of it); After Effects' built-in motion blur is available only on animated elements.

▶ **PV Feather** (*RE: Vision Effects*): Adds a features long missing from After Effects and available in comparable packages such as Shake: the ability to control per-vertex (or per-spline) feather of a mask.

▶ **RE: Flex** (*RE: Vision Effects*): Brings intuitive morphing and warping to After Effects.

▶ **Echospace** (*Trapcode*): Creates any number of instanced objects whose animations follow those of the master object, but can be offset in time and space.

▶ **Erodilation** and **Copy Image** (*ObviousFX*): Not demos but freeware, these plug-ins allow for quick manipulation of matte data and quick production of stills, respectively.

▶ **Sound Keys** (*Trapcode*): Generates keyframes from audio energy; enables you to select a range in an audio wave-form, then converts the frequencies into a stream of keyframes.

▶ **Starglow** (*Trapcode*): Produces an eight-pointed star-shaped glow around a source's highlights; enables you to assign each direction of the star an individual color map and streak length.

▶ Dozens of After Effects CS3 project files demonstrating techniques described in the book. These range from simple demonstrations of single concepts to completed shots.

▶ Live Action, effects and graphics footage from Artbeats: four full-length professionally shot HD clips presented exactly as they would if licensed from Artbeats, free for us according to the terms described in the End User License Agreement (EULA) in the Artbeats folder.

▶ Effects footage from Pixel Corps; nearly a dozen HD clips, predominantly blue screen and green screen shots taken with a Sony F900 HD camera; they are presented on the disk as uncompressed QuickTime files. They can be found within individual source folders for each chapter in the Examples folder.